iPad
ALL-IN-ONE

FOR

DUMMIES

A Wiley Brand

7th Edition

by Nancy Muir

FOR

DUMMIES

A Wiley Brand

iPad All-in-One For Dummies®, 7th Edition

Published by: **John Wiley & Sons, Inc.,** 111 River Street, Hoboken, NJ 07030-5774, www.wiley.com

Copyright © 2015 by John Wiley & Sons, Inc., Hoboken, New Jersey

Media and software compilation copyright © 2015 by John Wiley & Sons, Inc. All rights reserved.

Published simultaneously in Canada

For general information on our other products and services, please contact our Customer Care Department within the U.S. at 877-762-2974, outside the U.S. at 317-572-3993, or fax 317-572-4002. For technical support, please visit www.wiley.com/techsupport.

Wiley publishes in a variety of print and electronic formats and by print-on-demand. Some material included with standard print versions of this book may not be included in e-books or in print-on-demand. If this book refers to media such as a CD or DVD that is not included in the version you purchased, you may download this material at http://booksupport.wiley.com. For more information about Wiley products, visit www.wiley.com.

Library of Congress Control Number: 2014948510

ISBN 978-1-118-94441-7 (pbk); ISBN 978-1-118-94443-1 (epdf); ISBN 978-1-118-94442-4 (ePub)

Manufactured in the United States of America

10 9 8 7 6 5 4 3 2 1

Contents at a Glance

Table of Contents

Introduction

Apple turned the computing world on its ear when it introduced the iPad. This small wonder, which weighed less than a pound and a half, sold many tens of millions of units in its first few years for good reason: It's well designed and feature rich, and it opens a world of apps and media viewing in a highly portable format.

About This Book

iPad All-in-One For Dummies, 7th Edition, has one aim: to be the ultimate reference on the coolest digital device of the day. If you're reasonably computer savvy, you can use this book to get up to speed quickly the day you buy your iPad, and then you can pick up the book again anytime you feel like taking your knowledge of the iPad to the next level. Even if you've been puttering with your iPad for a while, you'll still find things between these covers that you didn't know about.

Though the iPad is relatively simple to use, a lot is packed in there, and you can get even more from it by downloading apps to do seemingly everything under the sun. This book approaches the iPad from every angle: from the basics to powerful road-warrior tools.

You can read step-by-step instructions for basic tasks, hot tips for getting the most out of iPad, and tips about apps that can take your iPad experience further.

Foolish Assumptions

To offer you a book that gives you insight into the powerful ways you can use iPad, I have to assume that you're computer and mobile-phone literate. You don't have to be an iPhone user to use this book (though iPhone has a great many similarities to iPad and shares many apps with it). You don't even have to be a Mac-oriented person — PC people do just fine with the iPad.

I also assume that you want to take your use of the iPad to the next level by getting helpful tips and advice as well as discovering several apps that are useful in expanding your iPad experience. You may use the iPad for personal pleasure or to get your work done — or both. If you travel a great deal or use the iPad to work, you'll find extra benefits in the material covered in Books III and IV.

Icons Used in This Book

Little pictures often found in the margin of technical books help you quickly find certain types of information, such as tips or warnings. Here are the icons you should look for in *iPad All-in-One For Dummies,* 7th Edition:

The Tip icon points to a tiny bit of advice about the current topic or other useful strategies for advancing your iPad experience to the next level.

The Remember icon signals either a pertinent fact that relates to the topic you're reading about (but which could also be mentioned elsewhere in the book) or a reiteration of a particularly important piece of information that's, well, worth repeating.

The Warning icon alerts you to potential pitfalls, so don't ignore it. Ignoring the Warning icon might leave you with lost data, a broken iPad, or a lost connection.

For the latest and greatest features of iPad Air 2 and iPad mini 3 , hunt for the New icon. If you own an earlier generation of iPad or iPad mini, this information can help you understand where your model might differ in its functionality. *Note:* Most features on your iPad will match this book no matter what version of iPad you have if you upgrade to the current operating system, iOS 8. However, the original iPad doesn't support iOS 8 at all, so none of the coverage in this book is relevant to that model.

The Technical Stuff icon marks iPad information that ventures beyond the basics.

Beyond the Book

This section describes where you can find the book's companion content at www.dummies.com. Here's what you can find there:

- **Cheat Sheet:** Visit www.dummies.com/cheatsheet/ipadaio to find ways to personalize various iPad and Safari browser settings and a list of free apps.

- **Dummies.com online articles:** Head to this book's Extras page located at www.dummies.com/extras/ipadaio to read about cool apps for your iPad. You'll find information about entertainment apps, apps for business power users, apps to use with iWork, and informative apps such as dictionaries and news sources.

✔ **Updates:** I provide information on changes to the iOS or iPad hardware that occur after this book's publication on my website at www.ipadmadeclear. com, so you can continue to use this book even if changes are introduced after you buy it. Please check this website periodically as Apple makes software and hardware updates to iPad now and then. You can also check for updates and corrections at www.dummies.com/extras/ipadaio.

Where to Go from Here

After you read this book's introduction, it's time to jump into all things iPad. I hope that when you turn to any chapter in this book, you'll find something you didn't know about iPad that will increase your enjoyment of your new device.

Start by checking out the basic concepts and instructions in Book I (you might be surprised at what you discover, even if you've been tinkering with your iPad for a bit) and then jump to any minibook that addresses topics you want explore next — to have fun or get work done, for example.

Wherever you dive in, you're likely to find some advice or information that will make your iPad experience even more rewarding.

The first step you should take (and this is covered in Book I, Chapter 2) is to update to the latest operating system for iPad — iOS 8, at the time this book went to press. (All steps in this book are based on iOS 8.)

Book I
Getting Started with iPad

Visit www.dummies.com for more great content online.

In this book. . .

- ✔ Discover new features in the iPad mini and fifth-generation iPad and iOS 8

- ✔ Get an overview of preinstalled apps

- ✔ Set up iPad and sync it with your computer

- ✔ Open an iCloud account and back up and share content with other devices

- ✔ Explore the iPad touchscreen and cameras

- ✔ Make settings that control how iPad works (including accessibility settings)

- ✔ Browse with Safari and its improved tabbed interface

- ✔ Set up your email account

- ✔ Learn about new features for sharing content with other people and devices

- ✔ Explore troubleshooting and maintenance advice

Chapter 1: Buying Your iPad

In This Chapter

ᐥ Finding out what's new with iPad Air 2, iPad mini 3, and iOS 8.0

ᐥ Picking the right iPad for you

ᐥ Choosing where to purchase your iPad

ᐥ Contemplating accessories for your iPad

*Y*ou've read about it and seen people using it everywhere you go. You know you can't live without your own iPad to have fun, explore the online world, read e-books, organize your photos, play games, and more.

Trust me; you've made a good decision because the iPad does redefine the computing experience in an exciting new way.

This chapter is for those of you who don't already have an iPad. Here is where you discover the different iPad models and their advantages, as well as where to buy this little gem and the accessories you can purchase to trick out your iPad.

Discovering What's New in iOS 8.0

iPad gets its features from a combination of hardware and its software operating system, with the most current operating system being iOS 8.0, though small updates appear all the time, so by the time you're reading this, you might have 8.1, 2, or 3. If you've seen an older iPad in action or own one, it might be helpful to understand what new features the iPad Air 2 and iPad mini 3 bring to the table (which are all covered in more detail throughout this book). In addition to features on previous-generation iPads through the iPad Air, the latest iPad models offer

ᐥ **Design:** iPad Air 2 is lighter (.96 lb.) and thinner (.24 inches thick) with thinner bezels for more screen area. Both iPad Air 2 and iPad mini 3 offer awesomely crisp displays with 2048 x 1536 resolution — which, trust me, makes for a very good viewing experience.

- **An improved chip:** The 64-bit A8 processor in the iPad Air 2 increases the processor and graphics speeds accomplished by the A7 chip on the previous generation iPad. The iPad mini 3 retains the A7 processor.

- **Better Wi-Fi:** Two-antennae dual-channel Wi-Fi and the use of MIMO (multiple-input, multiple output) technology allows for much faster wireless connections. In iPad Air 2, support of the latest Wi-Fi standard, 802.11 ac, ups the ante on Wi-Fi performance. Note that the iPad mini 3 doesn't support this standard.

- **M8 Motion Coprocessor:** This coprocessor on the iPad Air 2 processes game features like the gyroscope and accelerometer faster.

- **Video Recording:** Video recording features include the addition of a Slo-mo mode as well as improved stabilization and face detection.

- **Touch ID:** This security feature has been added to both iPad models. Essentially, sensors in the Home button allow you to train iPad to recognize your fingerprint and grant you access to your iPad with a finger press, as well as to use the new Apple Pay feature to buy items without having to enter your payment information every time.

- **A barometer sensor:** Only on iPad Air 2, this new sensor makes it possible for your iPad to sense air pressure and weather around you. This one's especially cool when hiking a mountain where the weather may change as you climb.

- **A "soft" SIM card:** With iPad Air 2 you get a software-based SIM card. This means that if you get an iPad that supports a 3G/4G connection through a phone carrier such as AT&T, you don't have to get a little plastic card from the service provider to hold all your account data. SIM functionality is now built into the iPad Air 2, and you can use it to connect to your account. This is great news for international travellers who can connect with another carrier without getting a physical SIM card.

Throughout this book, I point out any features that are available on only certain models of iPads, so you can use much of this book even if you own an earlier model.

Any iPad device other than the original iPad can use iOS 8.0 if you update the operating system (discussed in detail in Chapter 2 of this minibook); this book is based on version 8.0 of iOS.

This update to the operating system adds a few new features, including

- **Family Sharing:** Apple has provided a new feature called Family Sharing with iOS 8. This feature allows up to six people to partake of purchased iTunes content on their separate devices. You can also create a Family calendar that helps everybody in the family create and view upcoming family events.

- **Continuity:** This concept, enhanced in iOS 8, allows you to move from one iOS device to another to pick up where you left off using a feature called Handoff. For example, you might start to watch a TV show on your iPhone on the train but then pick up where you left off viewing the show on your iPad when you get home. You can even hand off a document or email and start where you left off on another device, as well as have text messages and phone calls ring through from your iPhone to your iPad or Mac.

- **Improved Notification Center:** Notification Center is a centralized location for reviewing things like calendar appointments, messages, and weather, With iOS 8, you can interact with notifications from the center, for example, replying to a message listed there. The new Today view lets you display your choice of notification types on both the Home and Lock screen.

- **Mail Improvements:** In iOS 8, you can access other email messages while composing a new message. You'll now be prompted to add a phone number or flight number mentioned in an email to your Calendar app. You can also flag or mark email by simply swiping across the screen to access those commands.

- **Quick Type for iPad Keyboard:** Now the iPad onscreen keyboard uses predictive technology to suggest words as you type. The keyboard also notes whether you're typing an email or message and makes suggestions based on the tone of voice each type of message calls for.

- **Improvements to the Photos App:** To help you organize your photos, in iOS 8 you can now store your photos in iCloud and download them when you want to view them via your iCloud Photo Library. Photos or videos can also be shared among up to six people's devices using Family Sharing. There are also several improved tools for editing photos in iOS 8.

- **Shazam:** Shazam is a music identifier service that has been integrated into Siri to identify songs and other media as they play around you.

- **Messaging:** The Messages app has some improvements. For example, you can name group messages by swiping down in the Details screen to access the hidden group name setting, and remove people from conversations. You can also set up a Do Not Disturb feature for certain threads so that you're not interrupted by messages on those threads, and you can record and send voice messages.

- **Siri Hands-Free:** If you are driving or otherwise occupied and want help from Siri, such as getting directions or to send a message, you can use a new feature to open Siri without touching your iPhone — as long as it is connected to a power source. With this feature enabled, all you have to do is say "Hey, Siri," and your electronic personal assistant opens, ready to hear your wish, which is, of course, Siri's command.

- **Instant Hotspot:** You've been able to use your iPhone as a hotspot in the past, essentially using your iPhone connection to get other devices online. With iOS 8, this personal hotspot is improved; nearby devices such as a computer now automatically display the iPhone as an optional network that you can join to go online.

Choosing the Right iPad for You

Though there are slight differences in thickness and weight among the different generations of the larger iPad model, if you pick up an iPad (see Figure 1-1), you're not likely to be able to tell one model from another on first glance, except that some are black and some are white or gold or silver. Newer models get gradually thinner and lighter. Still, most of their differences are primarily under the hood.

Figure 1-1: A black iPad has a classic look.

If you're in the market for a new iPad, Apple's latest offerings are iPad Air 2 and the iPad mini 3. The iPad mini is smaller, but its screen resolution matches that of the iPad Air 2. However, the iPad mini 3 lacks a few features of the iPad Air 2, including the Burst and Slo-mo features for the Camera app, the higher-end laminated display and antireflective coating, support for the latest Wi-Fi standard, and the faster A8 processor.

The larger iPad Airs have three variations:

- ✔ Case color
- ✔ Amount of built-in memory
- ✔ Method used for connecting to the Internet: Wi-Fi only, Wi-Fi or Wi-Fi and 3G/4G.

Your options in the first bullet point are silver, gold, or space gray, but if you're confused about the other two, read on; I explain these variations in more detail.

Because Apple upgrades the software and releases new versions of the hardware on a somewhat regular basis (a practice that keeps tech writers on their toes), I've avoided getting too specific on memory specifications and pricing in this chapter. However, you can go to `www.apple.com/ipad` to check out the latest details at any time.

Deciding how much memory is enough

You know that computer *memory* is a measure of how much information — for example, movies, photos, and software applications, or *apps* — you can store on a computing device. Memory can also affect your iPad's performance when handling tasks, such as streaming favorite TV shows from the World Wide Web or downloading music.

With video and audio streaming, you can enjoy a lot of content online without ever downloading the full content to your hard drive or iPad flash memory, and given that the iPad has a relatively small amount of memory in any of its models, that's not a bad idea. See Book II, Chapters 1 through 3 for more about getting your music and movies online.

Your memory options with an iPad Air 2 or iPad mini 3 are 16, 64, or 128 gigabytes (GB). You must choose the right amount of memory because you can't open the unit and add to it, as you usually can with a desktop computer. There is also no way to directly insert a flash drive (also known as a USB stick) to add backup capacity because iPad has no USB port — or CD/DVD drive, for that matter. However, Apple has thoughtfully provided *iCloud,* a service you can use to save space by backing up content to the Internet. (You can read more about that in Chapter 5 of this minibook.)

With an Apple Digital AV Adapter accessory, you can plug into the iPad to attach an HDMI-enabled display. See Book II, Chapter 3 for more about using these AV features. For example, ViewSonic offers several HDMI projectors, DVDO offers an HD Travel Kit for smartphones and tablets, and Belkin has introduced a new line of tools for HDTV streaming.

So how much memory is enough for your iPad? Here's a good rule: If you like lots of media, such as movies or TV shows, and you want to store them on your iPad (rather than experiencing or accessing this content online on sites such as Hulu or Netflix or from your Mac or PC using an app like Air Video), you might need 64GB or more. For most people who manage a reasonable number of photos, download some music, and watch heavy-duty media such as movies online, 64GB is probably sufficient. If you simply want to check email, browse the web, and write short notes to yourself, 16GB *might* be enough, but for my money, why bother?

You can't expand memory in an iPad. Apple is banking on your wanting to stream and sync content via iTunes or iCloud. Only you can decide whether that will work for you.

What's the price for more memory? For the iPad Air 2, a 16GB Wi-Fi unit (see the next section for more about Wi-Fi) costs $499; 64GB adds another $100. But doubling that to 128GB adds just $100, boosting the price to $699. If you buy an iPad mini 3, you're looking at $399, $499, or $599 for the three levels of memory it offers.

Determining whether you need Wi-Fi only or Wi-Fi and 3G/4G

Another variation on price and performance for the iPad is whether your model has Wi-Fi only or Wi-Fi and 3G/4G. Because the iPad is great for browsing online, shopping online, emailing, and so on, having an Internet connection for your device obviously is pretty essential. That's where Wi-Fi and 3G/4G come in. Both are used to connect to the Internet, and in case you need a refresher course, here's a quick summary:

- *Wi-Fi* is what you use to connect to a wireless network at home, at work, or at public locations such as your local coffee shop or an airport. This type of network uses short-range radio to connect devices to the Internet; its range is reasonably limited — so if you leave home or walk out of the coffee shop, you can't use it.

- *3G and 4G* cellphone technologies allow an iPad to connect to the Internet via a cellular network that's widespread. You use it in much the same way that you make calls from just about anywhere using your cellphone. 3G is available as of iPad 2 and all later models. As the latest cellular connection technology, it may not be available in every location. You'll still connect to the Internet when 4G service isn't available, but without the advantage of the superfast 4G technology.

You can buy an iPad with only Wi-Fi or one with both Wi-Fi and 3G (or 3G and 4G) capabilities. Getting a 3G/4G iPad costs an additional $130, but it also includes GPS so that you can get more accurate driving directions. You have to buy an iPad model for your preferred data connection provider — AT&T, Sprint, T-Mobile, or Verizon in the United States, as of this writing.

Also, to use your 3G/4G network, you have to pay AT&T, Sprint, T-Mobile, or Verizon a monthly fee. The good news is that none of these carriers requires a long-term contract, as you probably had to commit to with your cellphone and its data connection — you can pay for a connection the month you travel to Hong Kong and then get rid of it when you return home.

Features, data allowance (which relates to accessing email or downloading items from the Internet, for example), and prices vary by carrier and could change at any time, so visit each carrier's website to see what each offers. Note that if you intend to *stream* videos (watch them on your iPad from the Internet), you can eat through your data plan allowance quickly.

If you have a Wi-Fi network available and a smartphone whose data plan allows tethering over 3G/4G, you might consider just getting a Wi-Fi–only iPad model and save the rather high cost of provider data plans and the higher cost for these models if you only need 3G/4G occasionally.

Of course, AT&T, Sprint, T-Mobile, and Verizon could change their pricing and options at any time, so go to these links for more information about iPad data plans: AT&T is at www.att.com/shop/wireless/devices/ipad.jsp, Sprint's home page is http://sprint.com, T-Mobile's URL is www.T-Mobile.com, and Verizon is at www.verizonwireless.com/b2c/splash/ipad.jsp.

You can use the hotspot feature on a smartphone, which allows iPad to use your phone's 3G or 4G connection to go online if you pay for a data-use plan that supports hotspot usage with your phone service carrier. Check out the features of your phone to turn on hotspot. See Book III, Chapter 3 for more about this feature.

So how do you choose? If you want to wander around the woods or town — or take long drives with your iPad continually connected to the Internet — get 3G/4G and pay the price. But if you'll use your iPad mainly at home or using a Wi-Fi *hotspot* (a location where Wi-Fi access to the Internet is available, such as at an Internet cafe, an office, or a library), don't bother with 3G/4G. And frankly, you can now find *lots* of hotspots out there, including restaurants, hotels, airports, and more.

Because 3G/4G iPads are GPS devices, they know where you are and can act as a navigation system to get you from here to there. The Wi-Fi–only model uses a digital compass and triangulation method for locating your current position, which is less accurate; with no constant Internet connection, it won't help you to get around town. If getting accurate directions when you're on the go is one iPad feature that excites you, get 3G/4G and then see Book III, Chapter 2 for more about the Maps app.

Knowing what you need to use your iPad

Before you head off to buy your iPad, you should know what other devices, connections, and accounts you'll need to work with it optimally. At a bare minimum, you need to be able to connect to the Internet to take advantage of most of iPad's features. You can open an iCloud account (Apple's online storage and synchronization service) to store and share content online, or you can use a computer to download photos, music, or applications from non-Apple online sources such as stores or sharing sites like your local library, and then transfer them to your iPad through a process called *syncing*. You can also use a computer or iCloud to register your iPad the first time you start it, although if you have an Apple Store nearby, you can have it handle the registration for you.

Can you use iPad without owning a computer and just use public Wi-Fi hotspots to go online (or a 3G/4G connection if you have one of those models)? Yes. However, to be able to go online using a Wi-Fi–only iPad and to use many of its built-in features at home, you need to have a home Wi-Fi network available or be lucky enough to live in a town that offers town-wide Wi-Fi (or at least Wi-Fi in your neighborhood). You also need to use iCloud or sync to your computer to get updates for the iPad operating system.

For syncing with a computer, Apple's *iPad User Guide* recommends that you have

- ✔ A Mac or PC with a USB 2.0 or USB 3.0 port and one of the following operating systems:
  - Mac OS X version 10.6.8 or later
  - Windows 8, Windows 7, Windows Vista, or Windows XP Home or Professional with Service Pack 3 or later
- ✔ iTunes 11.0 or later, available at `www.itunes.com/download`
- ✔ An Apple ID and iTunes Store account
- ✔ Internet access
- ✔ An iCloud account

Apple has set up its iTunes software and the iCloud service to give you two ways to manage content for your iPad — including movies, music, or photos you've downloaded — and specify how to sync your calendar and contact information. Chapter 4 in this minibook covers those settings in more detail.

Getting Your Hands on an iPad

As of this writing, you can buy an iPad at the Apple Store and from several brick-and-mortar stores such as Best Buy, Wal-Mart, Sam's Club, and Target, and at online sites such as MacMall. You can also buy 3G/4G models, which require an account with a phone service provider, from the data providers AT&T, Sprint, T-Mobile, and Verizon, as well as from Apple.

If you get your iPad from Apple, either at one of its retail stores or through its online store, here's the difference in the buying experience.

The brick-and-mortar Apple Store advantage is that the sales staff will help you unpack your iPad and make sure it's working properly, register the device (which you have to do before you can use it), and help you learn the basics. There are also occasional workshops offered to help people learn about how to use iPads, and Apple employees are famous for being helpful to customers.

However, Apple Stores aren't on every corner, so if visiting one isn't an option (or you just prefer to go it alone), you can go to the Apple Store website (`http://store.apple.com/us/browse/home/shop_ipad/family/ipad`), as shown in Figure 1-2, and order one to be shipped to you (and even get it engraved, if you wish). Standard shipping typically is free, and if there's a problem, Apple's online-store customer service reps are very helpful — they will help you solve the problem or possibly replace your iPad.

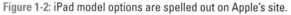

Figure 1-2: iPad model options are spelled out on Apple's site.

Considering iPad Accessories

Accessories for your iPad can make your computing life easier. You can get them from Apple or explore the broad and ever-growing world of third-party accessories.

Apple's stable of accessories

At present, Apple offers a few accessories you might want to check out when you purchase your iPad (or you can purchase them down the road), including

- **iPad Smart Case/Smart Cover:** Your iPad isn't cheap, and unlike a laptop computer, it has an exposed screen that can be damaged if you drop or scratch it. Investing in the iPad Smart Case or Smart Cover is a good idea if you intend to take your iPad out of your house — or if you have a cat or grandchildren. The iPad Smart Cover costs about $40 for polyurethane, and the Smart Case costs $70 for leather. Other cases vary in price depending on design and material.

 The official Apple iPad Smart Case has an ingenious little slot on the back. You can flip the front cover back and tuck it into the slot to make the case rest on your desk or counter at a very handy angle for viewing and typing. You can also prop up the case in a kind of U-shaped configuration to give presentations to others.

- **iPad Camera Connection Equipment:** Because there's no USB port on an iPad, you can't use a USB connection to upload photos from your digital camera or media card to your iPad. If you want to add this functionality, you can buy a MicroUSB camera connector and a MicroSD reader, each of which will set you back about $30 for the privilege.

- **Stands:** The Apple Store offers several stands, including the Incase Origami Workstation at $29.95 and the Just Mobile Upstand for iPad at $49.95. The Twelve South HoverBar Stand for iPad costs $116.95, and attaches your iPad to your computer. Twelve South BookArc is another good option at just $29.99. For a truly special handcrafted tablet stand, visit `http://www.mebskitchenwares.com/accessories.html` to buy a one-of-a-kind tablet stand made of your choice of hard woods.

- **Apple Earpods with Remote and Mic:** This device offers in-ear listening and remote control of your audio for about $29.

- **Apple Digital AV Adapter:** To make use of the HDMI technology that allows you to connect devices to output high-definition media through HDMI ports in TVs, monitors, and projectors, you can buy this adapter (see Figure 1-3) for $49.

- **AirPrint Printers:** There are printers available from HP, Canon, Brother, Lexmark, and Epson that support Apple's AirPrint feature. Prices range from $129 to $399. HandyPrint and Printopia are Macintosh apps that can make any printer shared on a network accessible to your iPad.

 It's a good idea to have a spare cable available to charge your iPad in case one gets mislaid.

Checking out what others have to offer

If you want to explore third-party accessories, there are many, and more appear all the time. Just perform a web search for *iPad accessories*. You'll find that there are suede, leather, neoprene, aluminum, and canvas cases; a variety of stands; carrying bags; screen protectors; and external batteries to supplement iPad's impressive ten-hour battery life.

Figure 1-3: Send media to other devices using this adapter.

 Want to stand out from the crowd by carrying your iPad around in a case with character? The relatively inexpensive Vintage Book case from Zazzle is a good option if you like the look of a rare book wrapped around your technology. If you're made of money, the Louis Vuitton model, a high-priced model at $795, will make you the envy of your friends. And eBags offers some nice canvas bags if your tastes, and budget, are more down to earth.

Macally's Lightning Wired keyboard is a fully extended keyboard with a number pad, which you can use with your iPad device in portrait or landscape mode. Aduro Facio offers a combination of case, stand, and keyboard all in one for only $29.99.

There are even a few clothing companies coming up with duds that can hold an iPad. (SCOTTeVEST, whose website is shown in Figure 1-4, offers a line of iPad-holding clothes. iClothing and iPad Suit are following suit — excuse the pun.

 Don't bother buying a wireless mouse to connect with your iPad via Bluetooth — the iPad recognizes your finger as its primary input device, and mice need not apply. However if you're finger-clumsy, you can also get a stylus for touch input. The Wacom Bamboo is among those that I like, but you can get less expensive ones at stores such as Amazon with several to a pack so that if you lose one, you have a spare.

Figure 1-4: Wear your iPad with style.

Chapter 2: Getting Started with iPad

In This Chapter

✔ Discovering what's in the box

✔ Getting your first look at the gadget

✔ Charging the battery

✔ Powering on your iPad and registering it

✔ Using the touchscreen

✔ Getting familiar with the split keyboard

✔ Making sure your operating system is up to date

✔ Discovering Multitasking Gestures

✔ Taking a first look at iPad's camera

✔ Understanding how to customize the Side switch

✔ Becoming familiar with the status bar

✔ Using Control Center

✔ Locking your iPad, turning it off, and unlocking it

Resolutionary
The new **iPad**

*A*fter you get your hands on an iPad, you should explore what's in the box and get an overview of the buttons and slots you'll encounter — luckily, there are very few of them.

You also need to get comfortable with the touchscreen. If you have a smartphone or computer with a touchscreen, you're ahead of the game here, but even if you do, you should take a little time to get comfortable working with using the iPad screen.

iPads (with the exception of the original iPad) have two cameras and a customizable side switch. In addition, iPad has native printing ability, all of which I introduce you to here.

Finally, after a tough day of playing with your new gadget, you need to know how to put it to sleep. I cover all these iPad basics in this chapter.

Exploring What's in the Box

When you fork over your hard-earned money for your iPad, you're left holding one box about the size of a package of copy paper. Here's what you'll find when you take off the shrink wrap and open the box:

- ✓ **iPad:** Your iPad is covered in two plastic sheets that you can take off and toss (unless you think there's a chance you'll return it, in which case you might want to keep all packaging for 14 days — Apple's return period).

- ✓ **Documentation (and I use the term loosely):** You find a small, white envelope under the iPad itself, about the size of a half-dozen index cards. Open it, and you'll find

  - *A single sheet titled iPad Info:* This pamphlet is essentially small print (that you mostly don't need to read) from folks like the FCC.

  - *A mysterious label sheet:* This contains two white Apple logo stickers. (Apple has provided these for years with its products as a form of cheap advertising when users place stickers on places like their computers or car windows.)

  - *A small card containing the actual documentation (sort of):* This displays a picture of the iPad and callouts to its buttons on one side, and the other side contains about three sentences of instructions for setting it up and info about where to go online to find out more.

- ✓ **Lightning to USB Cable:** Use this cord (see Figure 2-1) to connect the iPad to your computer, or use it with the last item in the box, which is the power adapter.

- ✓ **10W USB Power Adapter:** The power adapter (see Figure 2-1) attaches to the Lightning to USB Cable (or the Dock Connector to USB Cable) so that you can plug it into the wall and charge the battery.

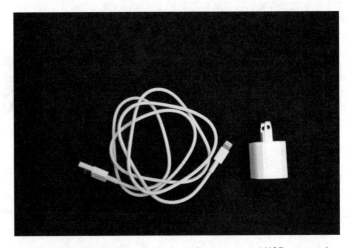

Figure 2-1: Some pretty simple gadgets for power and USB connections.

That's it. That's all there is in the box. It's kind of the typical Apple study in Zen-like simplicity.

Taking a First Look at the Gadget

The little card contained in the documentation (see the preceding section) gives you a picture of the iPad with callouts to the buttons you'll find on it. In this section, I give you a bit more information about those buttons and some other physical features of the iPad. Figure 2-2 shows you where each of these items is located.

Figure 2-2: There are probably fewer gizmos to get used to on an iPad than on the average cellphone.

Here's the rundown on what these things are and what they do:

- ✓ **(The all-important) Home button:** On the iPad, press this button to go back to the Home screen to find just about anything. The Home screen displays all your installed and preinstalled apps and gives you access to your iPad settings. No matter where you are or what you're doing, press the Home button, and you're back at home base. You can also double-press the Home button to pull up a scrollable display of apps called the App Switcher so that you can quickly move from one to another or quit apps that you don't want or need to have running. (Apple refers to this as multitasking.) If you press and hold the Home button, you open Siri, the iPad voice assistant. Finally, on recent iPad models, the Home button contains a fingerprint reader used with the Touch ID feature.

- ✓ **Sleep/Wake button:** You can use this button to power up your iPad, put it in sleep mode, wake it up, or power it down (more about this in the final section of this chapter).

- ✓ **Lightning connector:** This is where you plug in the Lightning connector at the USB end to the power adapter to charge your battery or use it without the power adapter to sync with your computer (which you find out more about in Chapter 5 of this minibook). Also use this slot for the Camera Connection Kit or to connect various AV adapter cables.

- ✓ **Cameras:** iPads (except for the original iPad) offer front- and rear-facing cameras that you can use to shoot photos or video. The rear one is on the top-right corner, and you need to be careful not to put your thumb over it when taking shots. (I have several very nice photos of my thumb already.)

- ✓ **Side switch:** In case you hadn't heard, the iPad screen rotates to match the angle you're holding it at. If you want to stick with one orientation even if you spin the iPad in circles, you can use this little switch on the iPad mini 3 to lock the screen, which is especially handy when reading an e-book. (Note that some apps can override this functionality if they require one orientation or the other.) iPad Air 2 no longer has a side switch, but you can change Rotation and Volume settings in the Control Center (swipe up from the bottom of the screen to open Control Center).

- ✓ **(Tiny, mighty) speakers:** One nice surprise when I first got my iPad Air 2 was hearing what a great little stereo sound system it has and how much sound can come from these tiny speakers. The speakers are located along one side of the iPad Air 2 and iPad mini 3.

- ✓ **Volume:** This is a volume rocker that you use like any other volume rocker: Press up for more volume and down for less. You can also use this rocker as a camera shutter button when the camera is activated.

- ✓ **Headphone jack and microphone:** If you want to listen to your music in private, you can plug a 3.5mm minijack headphone and some ⅛" headphones in here (including a set of Beats headphones sold through the

Apple Store, if you have one, which gives you sound to both ears). There's also a tiny microphone that makes it possible to speak into your iPad to deliver commands or enter content using the Siri feature. Using Siri, you can do things like make phone calls using the Internet and dictate text, or work with other apps that accept audio input.

Charging the Battery

You've heard about the awesome ten-hour battery life on your iPad, and it's all true. My iPad showed up almost fully charged from the Apple Store, but even if you got yours shipped, it should've been at least partially charged. But all batteries run down eventually (the little battery icon in the iPad Status bar tells you when you're running low), so one of your first priorities is to know how to recharge your battery. This is a pretty obvious procedure, given the few items that come with your iPad, but just in case you need help, you can follow these steps to get that battery meter up to 100 percent:

1. **Gather your iPad, Lightning to USB cable (fourth generation and later) or Dock Connector to USB Connector (earlier models), and Apple USB power adapter.**

2. **Gently plug the USB end of the Lightning to USB Cable (or the Dock Connector to USB Cable) into the USB Power Adapter.**

3. **Plug the other end of the cord (see Figure 2-3) into the Lightning Connector (or Dock Connector slot) on the iPad.**

Attach the USB connector...   Then plug this end into the iPad.

to the power adapter.

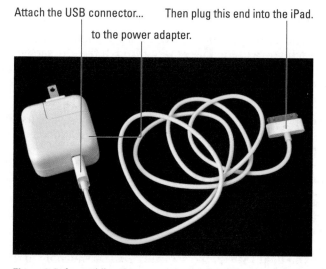

Figure 2-3: Assembling the connector cord and power adapter to charge the iPad battery.

4. **Unfold the two metal prongs on the power adapter (refer to Figure 2-3) so that they extend from it at a 90-degree angle, and plug the adapter into an electrical outlet.**

Power adapters from earlier versions of iPad or other Apple devices such as iPhone or iPod will not work with your fourth-generation iPad or later. Replacement adapters are available, however, from Apple and various third-party vendors.

Turning the iPad On and Registering It

The first time you turn on your iPad, you need to go through a sequence of setup steps. The best way to do this is to be in range of a Wi-Fi network.

When you're ready to get going with your new toy, be sure you're within range of a Wi-Fi network that you can connect with, and then hold the iPad with one hand on either side, oriented like a pad of paper. Plug the Lightning to USB Cable that came with your device into your iPad and plug the other end into a USB port on your computer, just in case you lose your battery charge during the setup process.

Now follow these steps to set up and register your iPad:

1. **Press and hold the Sleep/Wake button on the top of your iPad until the Apple logo appears.**

    In another moment, a screen appears with a cheery Hello on it.

2. **Slide your finger to the right on the screen where it says Slide to Set Up.**

3. Enter a password if you have an Apple ID, choose how other people can reach you with text messages through the Messaging app or video calls through FaceTime (choose your phone number, iCloud account, or email account), and whether to update to iCloud Drive (an online storage service).

Be sure to update to iCloud Drive on all your devices, such as iPhone, Mac, or Windows PC to make sure that your iCloud-stored documents continue to sync to them all.

4. **You next see a series of screens that involve settings such as language, country, Wi-Fi network, and use of iCloud.**

Follow the series of screens to respond to questions and make initial settings, all of which can be changed later in iPad Settings.

5. **After you deal with all the setup screens, a Welcome to iPad screen appears; tap Get Started to display the Home screen.**

You can choose to have certain items transferred to your iPad from your computer when you sync, including music, videos, downloaded apps, contacts, calendars, e-books, podcasts, and browser bookmarks. You can also transfer to your computer content that you download directly to your iPad using the iTunes and App Store apps as well as content that you gather through the Newsstand, iBooks, Podcasts, and iTunes U apps. See Book II, Chapter 1 for more about these features.

Meeting the Multi-Touch Screen

When your Home screen appears (see Figure 2-4), you'll see a pretty picture in the background and two sets of icons. One set appears in the Dock along the bottom of the screen. The *Dock* contains Messages, Mail, the Safari browser, and Music app icons by default, though you can add up to two other apps to it. The Dock appears on every Home screen. (You start with one Home screen, but adding new apps creates additional Home screens — up to 15 in all.) You can also nest apps in folders, which theoretically gives you the capability to store limitless apps on your iPad — limited, that is, only by your tablet's memory.

Figure 2-4: Icons for various apps live in the Dock or on a Home screen.

Other icons representing your installed apps appear above the Dock. (I give you an overview of the functionality of all these apps in Chapter 4 of this minibook.) Different icons appear in this area on each Home screen, but this Home screen contains most of the preinstalled apps.

This may or may not need saying, but the screen is made of glass and will smudge when you touch it and break if you throw it at the wall, and contrary to Apple's boasts, can also be scratched. So, be careful and treat it nicely.

Connecting with the touchscreen

The iPad touchscreen technology allows you to swipe your finger across the screen or tap it to provide input to the device just as you use a mouse or keyboard with your computer. You read more about using the touchscreen in the next section, but for now, go ahead and play with it for a few minutes. Just as you may have become used to with your mobile phone, you use the pads of your fingertips (not your fingernails) and do the following:

1. **Tap the Settings icon.**

   The various settings (which you read more about throughout this book) appear. (See Figure 2-5.)

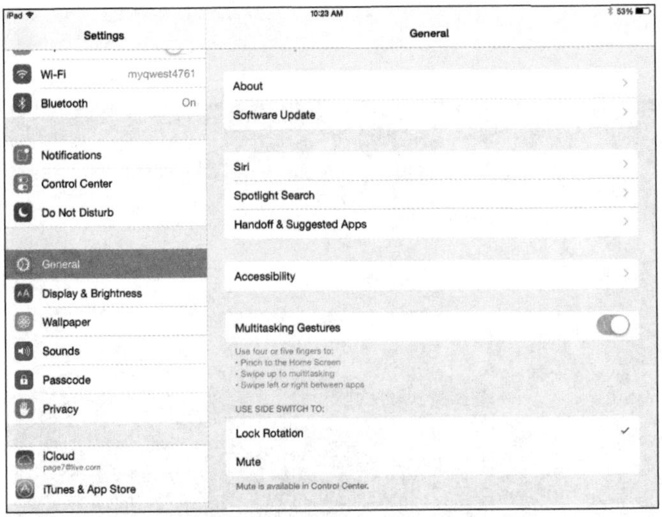

Figure 2-5: Settings is your central command for all things iPad.

2. **To return to the Home screen, press the Home button.**

3. **Swipe a finger or two from right to left on the screen.**

   Because the iPad has a few additional Home screens available (15, to be exact) that you can fill up with all the apps you'll be downloading, the screen shifts slightly to the left. (If you have more apps downloaded, filling additional Home screens, this action moves you to the next Home screen.)

With multiple Home screens in use, you get little dots at the bottom of the screen above the Dock icons, indicating which of the Home screens you're on. You can tap to the right or left of the dots to move one screen in either direction.

4. **To experience the rotating screen feature, hold the iPad firmly and turn it sideways.**

   The screen flips to a horizontal orientation. If it doesn't, check the Side switch (above the volume rocker on the side of your iPad) to make sure that it's not active. Though this Side switch can be set to mute the iPad rather than control orientation, by default it works with the orientation feature.

5. **To flip the screen back, just turn the device so that it's oriented like a pad of paper again.**

6. **Tap Music in the Dock.**

7. **Drag your finger down from the top of the screen to reveal the Notification Center (covered in Book V, Chapter 4).**

8. **Drag up from the bottom of the Home screen.**

   Notification Center disappears and the Control Center (discussed later in this chapter) is displayed.

9. **Practice multitasking by double-pressing the Home button.**

   All running apps appear in a display across the middle of the screen.

10. **Swipe to scroll through the apps, and tap one to jump to it without going back to the Home screen.**

You can customize the Home screen by changing the wallpaper and brightness. Read about making these changes in Chapter 8 of this minibook.

Goodbye, click-and-drag; hello, tap-and-swipe

If you're like me, you'll fall in love with the touchscreen interface that iPad sports. It's just so intuitive to use your finger as a pointing device — something you're probably already doing on your iPhone, laptop, or other mobile device.

You can use several methods for getting around and getting things done in iPad using its Multi-Touch screen, including

✔ **Tap once.** To open an application on the Home screen, choose a field such as a search field, select an item in a list, select an arrow to move back or forward one screen, or follow an online link, tap the item once with your finger.

✔ **Tap twice.** Use this method to enlarge or reduce the display of a web page (see Chapter 6 in this minibook for more about using the Safari web browser) or zoom in or out in the Maps app.

✔ **Pinch and expand.** As an alternative to the tap-twice method, you can pinch or expand (unpinch) two fingers (most people use their index finger and thumb) on the screen (see Figure 2-6) when you're looking at photos, maps, web pages, or email messages to quickly reduce or enlarge them, respectively.

You can use a three-finger tap to zoom your screen to be even larger, or use Multitasking Gestures to swipe with four or five fingers. (See "Exploring Multitasking Gestures," later in this chapter.) These techniques are handy if you have vision challenges.

Figure 2-6: Pinch to zoom in or out on a page.

✔ **Drag to scroll (known as *swiping*).** When you press your finger to the screen and drag to the right or left, you move from one Home screen to another. (See Figure 2-7.) Swiping to the left on the Home screen, for example, moves you to the next Home screen. Swiping up while reading an online newspaper moves you down the page, while swiping down moves you back up the page.

✔ **Flick.** To scroll more quickly on a page, quickly flick your finger on the screen in the direction you want to move.

✔ **Tap the status bar.** To move quickly to the top of a list, web page, or email message, tap the Status bar at the top of the iPad screen.

Figure 2-7: Swiping gets you around a screen quickly.

✔ **Tap and hold.** If you're in any application where selecting text is an option, such as Notes or Mail, or if you're on a web page, tapping and holding on text will select a word and bring up a contextual menu with editing tools that allow you to select, cut, copy, or paste text, and more. You can also use this tap-and-hold method to reposition the insertion point under the magnifying glass icon that appears.

Notice that when you rock your iPad backward or forward, the background moves as well. (This parallax feature was introduced in iOS 7.) You can disable this feature if it makes you seasick. Open the Settings app, tap General, tap Accessibility, and then set the Reduce Motion switch to Off.

To display the Notification Center, swipe down from the top of the screen with one finger. It lists all messages, mail, calendar events, and more in one handy spot.

If you feel like having a practice session, try the following steps from the Home screen:

1. **Tap the Safari button to display the web browser.**

    You may be asked to enter your Wi-Fi network password to access the network to go online.

2. **Tap a link to move to another page.**

3. **Double-tap the page to enlarge it; then pinch two fingers together on the screen to reduce its size.**

4. **Drag one finger around the page to scroll up or down or side to side.**

5. **Flick your finger quickly on the page to scroll more quickly.**

6. **Tap and hold your finger on text that isn't a link.**

    The word is selected, and a contextual menu appears, as shown in Figure 2-8. Its options include Define and Copy.)

7. **Release your finger.**

8. **Tap and hold your finger on a link or an image.**

    A contextual menu appears with commands that allow you to open the link or picture, open it in a new page, add it to your Reading List (see Chapter 6 in this minibook), or copy it. The menu also offers the Save Image command.

9. **Put two fingers slightly apart on the screen and then pinch them together to reduce the page.**

10. **Press the Home button to go back to the Home screen.**

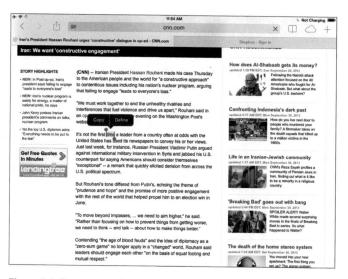

Figure 2-8: Copy text and paste it into an email or document using the Copy tool.

Displaying and using the onscreen keyboard

Part of the beauty of iPad is that it's highly portable, but that portability comes at a price: the absence of a physical keyboard. You can use a wireless or Bluetooth keyboard, but for short text entry, you don't really need either. That's where the onscreen keyboard comes into play, allowing you to enter text as you may have done on a touchscreen mobile phone.

iPad's built-in keyboard appears whenever you're in a text-entry location, such as in a Search field or when writing an email. With the debut of iOS 8, iPad makes suggestions based on the words you enter in the keyboard in the new QuickType bar above the keyboard, and can even recognize the person you're typing a message to when you're in Mail or Messages so that those suggestions are appropriate to the tone you might use with that recipient.

Follow these steps to practice using the onscreen keyboard:

1. **Tap Notes on the Home screen to open this easy-to-use notepad.**

2. **Tap the blank note or, if you've already entered notes, tap one to open it.**

   The note appears.

3. **Tap in the text of the note.**

   The onscreen keyboard appears.

4. **Type a few words using the keyboard.**

You can tap the Dictation key on the keyboard (see Figure 2-9) to activate the Dictation feature, and then speak your input. This requires that the Siri feature be turned on and an active Internet connection because the translation is done on Apple's servers.

To get the widest keyboard display possible, rotate your iPad to be in landscape (horizontal) orientation, as shown in Figure 2-9.

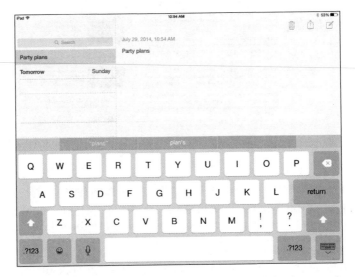

Figure 2-9: The onscreen keyboard is handiest to use in landscape orientation.

5. **If you make a mistake (and you may when you first use it), use the Delete key (the key in the top-right corner of the keyboard with a little *x* on it) to delete text to the left of the insertion point.**

6. **To create a new paragraph, press the Return key, just as you would on a computer keyboard.**

7. **To type numbers and some symbols, press one of the number keys (labeled .?123) located on either side of the spacebar (refer to Figure 2-9).**

Characters on the keyboard change. To return to the letter keyboard at any time, simply tap one of the letter keys (labeled ABC) on either side of the spacebar.

If you type a number in the number/symbol keyboard and then tap the spacebar, the keyboard automatically returns to the letter keyboard.

8. **Use the Shift keys just as you would on a regular keyboard to type uppercase letters.**

   Tapping the Shift key once causes just the next letter you type to be capitalized.

9. **Double-tap the Shift key to turn on the Caps Lock feature so that all letters you type are capitalized until you turn the feature off.**

   Tap the Shift key once to turn it off.

   You can control whether this feature is available in Settings, in the General pane's Keyboard section.

10. **To type a variation on a symbol (for example, to get alternative currency symbols when you hold down the dollar sign on the numeric keyboard), tap and hold the key until a set of alternative symbols appears (see Figure 2-10).**

    Note that displaying variations on symbols works only on some symbols.

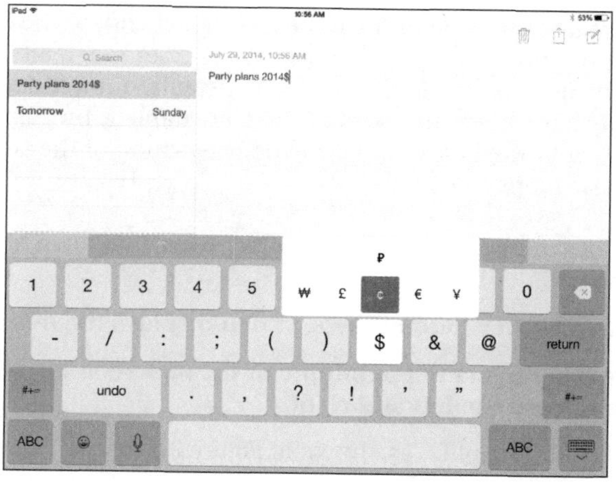

Figure 2-10: Only some symbols offer alternatives when you press and drag them.

11. **Tap the Dictation key (refer to Figure 2-9) to activate the Dictation feature, and then speak your input.**

    This works in several apps, such as Mail, Notes, and Maps. Tap the Dictation key again (or tap in the note) to turn off the Dictation feature.

12. Tap the Emoji key (a smiley face symbol to the left of the Dictation button) to display and select from a set of smiley symbols to insert in your document. Tap tabs along the bottom to display other graphic icon sets such as pictures from nature or city skylines.

13. **To hide the keyboard, press the Keyboard key in the bottom-right corner.**

14. **Tap the Home button to return to the Home screen.**

You can unlock the keyboard to move it around the screen. To do this, press and hold the Keyboard button on the keyboard and, from the pop-up menu that appears, choose Unlock. Now by pressing the Keyboard button and swiping up or down, you can move the keyboard up and down on the screen. To dock the keyboard again at the bottom of the screen, press and hold the Keyboard button and choose Dock from the pop-up menu. (For this to work, go to Settings and be sure to enable Split Keyboard in the Keyboard section of the General pane.)

To type a period and space, double-tap the spacebar. (For this to work, go to Settings and enable "." Shortcut in the Keyboard section of the General pane.)

Using the split keyboard

The *Split Keyboard* feature allows you to split the keyboard so that each side appears nearer the edge of the iPad screen. For those who are into texting with their thumbs, this feature makes it easier to reach all the keys from the sides of the device. The feature is on by default, but if it doesn't work for you, it may have been turned off. (You can enable it by going to Settings and turning on Split Keyboard in the Keyboard section of the General pane.) Follow these steps to use it:

1. **Open an application, such as Notes, where you can use the onscreen keyboard.**

2. **Tap in an entry field or page, which displays the onscreen keyboard.**

3. **Place two fingers in the middle of the onscreen keyboard and spread them toward the left and right.**

   The keyboard splits, as shown in Figure 2-11.

4. **Hold the iPad with a hand on either side and practice using your thumbs to enter text.**

5. **To reconnect the split keyboard, place two fingers on each side of the keyboard and move them together to join them again.**

When the keyboard is docked and unified at the bottom of your screen, you can also simply drag the Keyboard key upward. This both undocks and splits the keyboard. To reverse this, drag the Keyboard key downward. The split keyboard is both docked and joined into one keyboard.

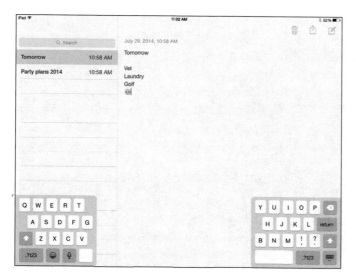

Figure 2-11: A split keyboard makes thumb entry quicker.

Flicking to search

Can't find that song you downloaded or an email from your boss? You'll be relieved to know that a search feature in iPad called *Spotlight* helps you find suggestions from the Internet, Music, iTunes, and the App Store, as well as suggestions for nearby locations, photos, music, emails, contacts, movies, and more. This search feature can be found on the screen to the left of the default Home screen.

Follow these steps to access and use Spotlight:

1. **Swipe downward near the top of any Home screen (but not from the very top or bottom of the screen).**

   The Search field appears.

2. **Tap in the Spotlight Search field.**

   The keyboard appears. (See Figure 2-12.)

3. **Begin entering a search term.**

   For example, in Figure 2-13 I typed the letter *C.* iPad might display any app, contact, music, video, or note that begins with *C.* As you continue to type a search term, the results are narrowed down to match.

4. **Tap an item in the search results to open it in the associated app or player.**

   To close the app and go back to the Search screen, tap the Home button, and then tap the left side of the Home button to display the Search screen again.

Figure 2-12: Use the familiar Search field to enter search terms.

Figure 2-13: Narrow your search by typing more letters.

5. **To enter a different search term, tap in the Search field and tap the circled X at the right end of the box or the Delete key on the keyboard to delete the current term, and then enter another.**

6. **Scroll down to the bottom of the search results and tap Search Web or Search Wikipedia to check results from those sources.**

You can use some standard search techniques to narrow your search. For example, if you want only the emails that include both Bob Smith and Jane Jones, enter *Smith, Jones* and *Bob, Jane* as your search terms. To change the search language, tap the key on the onscreen keyboard that looks like a little globe to cycle through available languages.

Updating the Operating System

This book is based on the latest version of the iPad operating system at the time, iOS 8.0. If you have an iPad (generation 4 and later can update to iOS 8.0), to make sure that you get the latest and greatest features in iPad, it's a good idea to update right now to the latest iOS (and periodically, no matter which recent model of iPad you have, to receive minor upgrades). If you've set up an iCloud account on your iPad, updates will happen automatically, or you can update over a Wi-Fi or 3G/4G connection by going to Settings and, on the General pane, tapping Software Update. Note that the original iPad model cannot run iOS 7 or later, so this book's coverage will not match its functionality in large part.

It's a good idea to have your iPad plugged into a power source before you start to download an iOS update so that the battery doesn't drain before the update is complete.

Before you perform an update to the iOS, make sure that you have updated to the latest version of iTunes on your computer. (iOS 8.0 requires iTunes 11.4 or later.) After you do, here's how to update the iOS via a connection with your computer:

1. **Plug the Lightning to USB Cable (or the Dock Connector to USB Cable) into your iPad and plug the USB end into your computer.**

    When iTunes opens on your computer, look for your iPad name in the Devices section in the Source List on the left side of the screen (see Figure 2-14).

2. **Click your iPad's name in the Devices pop-up menu and then click the Summary tab if it's not already displayed.**

3. **Read the note next to the Check for Update button to see whether your iOS is up to date; if it isn't, click the Check for Update button.**

    iTunes checks to find the latest iOS version and walks you through the updating procedure.

Your iPad has to have enough memory to download the latest iOS. If you have an iPad with smaller memory, you may actually have to remove some apps or content such as music to make room for it before the update can take place.

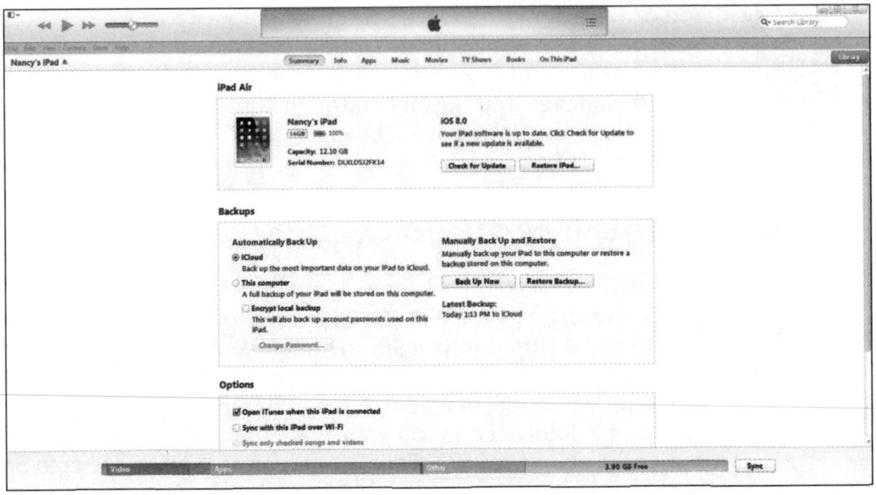

Figure 2-14: Go to the Summary tab to find out whether you need to update iOS.

A new iOS introduces new features for your iPad. If a new iOS version appears after you've bought this book, go to the companion website, www.ipadmadeclear.com, for updates on new features.

Understanding Multitasking Basics

Multitasking means that you can easily switch from one app to another without closing the first one and returning to the Home screen. This is accomplished by viewing all open apps and jumping from one to another, and quitting an app by simply swiping it upward. Follow these steps to multitask:

1. **Open an app.**
2. **Press the Home button twice.**
3. **On the App Switcher view that appears (see Figure 2-15), scroll to the left or right until you find the other open app that you want to switch to.**
4. **Tap an app to switch to it.**

Press the Home button to close the App Switcher and return to the app you were working in.

Figure 2-15: The App Switcher

Exploring Multitasking Gestures

Multitasking involves jumping from one app to another. Rather than using the Home button to open the App Switcher and then moving from one open app to another, you can use iOS's multitasking gestures. You turn on these gestures by tapping Settings on the Home screen, and then in the General pane, set the Multitasking Gestures switch to On.

Here are the three multitasking gestures:

✔ Swipe up with four or five fingers on any Home screen to reveal the App Switcher.

✔ Swipe down with four or five fingers to close the App Switcher.

✔ With an app open, swipe left or right using four or five fingers to move to the next app. (The apps are in order by what was most recently used, so swiping right opens apps from most to least recently used, whereas swiping left opens apps from least to most recently used.)

Examining Your iPad Cameras

iPad has both front- and rear-facing cameras. You can use the cameras to take still photos or shoot videos (both covered in Book II, Chapter 4). The fourth-generation iPad introduced a higher quality FaceTime front-facing camera useful for making video calls. For now, take a quick look at your cameras by tapping the Camera app icon on the Home screen. An image appears, as shown in Figure 2-16.

Switch between front and rear cameras

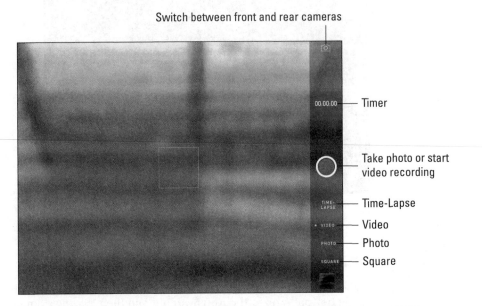

Timer

Take photo or start video recording

Time-Lapse

Video

Photo

Square

Figure 2-16: Simple tools let you start and stop a recording or switch between cameras.

The third-generation iPad introduced a super-clear Retina display and 5-megapixel rear-facing iSight camera for viewing and taking the best iPad-generated photos and video yet.

Controls located around the screen allow you to

✔ Switch between the front and rear cameras.

✔ Take a picture or start recording a video.

✔ Turn the new Time-Lapse feature on or off.

✔ Open the previously captured image or video.

When you view a photo or video, you can use several features to do things like send the image via AirDrop, post it to Facebook or Flickr, send it by email or as a tweet, print an image, use a still photo as wallpaper or assign it to a contact, or run a slideshow. See Book II, Chapters 3 and 4 for more details about using iPad cameras.

AirDrop works only with the fourth-generation (or later) iPad and original iPad mini (and later). If your iPad uses the Lightning connector (the small oval port on the bottom), it supports AirDrop.

Customizing the Side Switch

You can customize the Side switch on your iPad mini 3 (it's at the top-right side if you're holding the iPad in vertical orientation). Use these steps to set it up to either control the screen orientation or mute sound:

1. **From the Home screen, tap the Settings icon.**

2. **In the General pane, tap either the Lock Rotation or Mute option in the Use Side Switch To section to choose which feature you want the switch to control.**

3. **Tap the Home button to return to the Home screen.**

4. **Move the Side switch up or down to toggle between the settings you chose: screen rotation locked or unlocked, or sound muted or unmuted.**

If you choose to use the Side switch to mute or unmute system sound, you can use the Control Center to lock and unlock the screen rotation. This works the same way if you have set up the switch to handle screen rotation and want to mute or unmute the sound using the Control Center.

Exploring the Status Bar

Across the top of your iPad screen is the Status bar. (See Figure 2-17.) Little icons in this area can provide some useful information, such as the time, your battery charge, or the status of your wireless connection. Table 2-1 lists some of the most common items you'll find on the status bar.

Though it doesn't sport an icon, you can swipe down on the status bar to display the Notification Center. This handy feature shows you all your alerts, updates, appointments, and more in one place.

Figure 2-17: The status bar provides some handy info about your iPad.

Table 2-1		Common Status Bar Icons
Icon	*Name*	*What It Indicates*
📶	Wi-Fi	You're connected to a Wi-Fi network.
⊛	Activity	Something's in progress, such as a web page loading.
2:55 PM	Time	You guessed it: the time.
🔒↻	Screen Rotation Lock	The screen is locked and will not rotate when you turn the iPad.
▶	Play	A media element (such as a song or video) is playing.
100% ▭	Battery Life	The percentage of charge your battery has left. (It changes to a lightning bolt when the battery is charging.)

If you have GPS, 3G or 4G, and/or a connection to a virtual private network (VPN), symbols appear on the status bar when these features are activated. The GPS and 3G icons appear only with 3G/4G–enabled iPad models. If you have a 3G/4G model but no 3G/4G available, you may see an icon for EDGE. If you're out of range of 3G/4G and EDGE, you see GPRS. Essentially, iPad tries for the best connection and then jumps to a lesser connection if the best isn't available.

Using Control Center

Control Center is a one-stop screen for common features and settings such as connecting to a network, increasing screen brightness or volume, and using the Calculator or Camera. Control Center settings include

- Music playback controls
- Audio volume
- Airplane mode
- Wi-Fi connection
- Bluetooth
- Do Not Disturb
- Orientation Lock or Mute, depending on what the Side switch is set to control (the side switch is not available on the iPad Air 2, though these Control Center settings allow you to change orientation and volume settings)

✔ Opening the Clock app

✔ Using the camera

✔ AirDrop

✔ Screen brightness

To display Control Center:

1. **Swipe up from the bottom of the screen.**

2. **In the panel that appears, tap a button or slider to access or adjust a setting or app (see Figure 2-18).**

3. **Swipe down from the top of Control Center to hide it.**

Figure 2-18: Get to frequently used settings in Control Center.

Locking the iPad, Turning It Off, or Unlocking It

You've seen how simple it is to turn the power on for your iPad earlier in this chapter. Now it's time to put it to *sleep* (the iPad screen goes black, but iPad can quickly awaken again) or turn off the power to give your new toy a rest. Here are the procedures you can use:

✔ **Press the Sleep/Wake button.** iPad goes to sleep and the screen goes black. If iPad is asleep, pressing the Sleep/Wake button does its wake-up thing. If you set up a Passcode Lock in the General pane of Settings, you need to provide a passcode to wake up your iPad.

✓ **Press the Home button and then use the Slide to Unlock bar.** This wakes up iPad. Swipe the onscreen arrow on the Slide to Unlock bar to unlock the iPad.

✓ **Press and hold the Sleep/Wake button until the Slide to Power Off bar appears at the top of the screen, and then swipe the bar.** You've just turned off your iPad.

✓ **Use the Smart Cover or Smart Case accessory.** When you attach the Smart Cover and close it over your screen, iPad goes to sleep automatically; it wakes up when you pull back the cover.

iPad automatically goes into sleep mode after a few minutes of inactivity. You can change the time interval at which it sleeps by adjusting the Auto-Lock feature in Settings. (I tell you how to do that in Chapter 8 of this minibook.)

Chapter 3: Making Your iPad More Accessible

In This Chapter

*i*Pad users are all different; some face visual, motor, or hearing challenges. If you're one of these folks, you'll be glad to hear that iPad offers some handy accessibility features.

To make your screen easier to read, you can adjust the brightness or change wallpaper. You can also set up the VoiceOver feature to read onscreen elements out loud. Then there are a slew of features you can turn on or off, including Zoom, Invert Colors, Speak Selection, Large Type, and more.

If you struggle to hear your computer's sounds at times, you can do the obvious and adjust the system volume. The iPad also has settings for mono audio (useful when you're wearing headphones) and a setting to use Speak Auto-text. iPad features that help you deal with physical and motor challenges include Assistive Touch for those who have difficulty using the iPad touch screen, Switch Control for working with adaptive accessories, and the Home Click Speed and Call Audio Routing settings that allow you to adjust how quickly you have to tap the iPad screen to work with features.

Finally, the Guided Access feature provides help for those who have difficulty focusing on one task, and also provides a handy mode for showing presentations of content in settings where you don't want users to flit off to other apps, as in school or at a public kiosk.

Setting Brightness

Especially when using iPad as an e-reader, you may find that a slightly less-bright screen reduces strain on your eyes. To adjust screen brightness, follow these steps:

1. **Tap the Settings icon on the Home screen.**

2. **In Settings, tap Display & Brightness.**

3. **To control brightness manually, tap the Auto-Brightness On/Off switch (see Figure 3-1) to turn off this feature.**

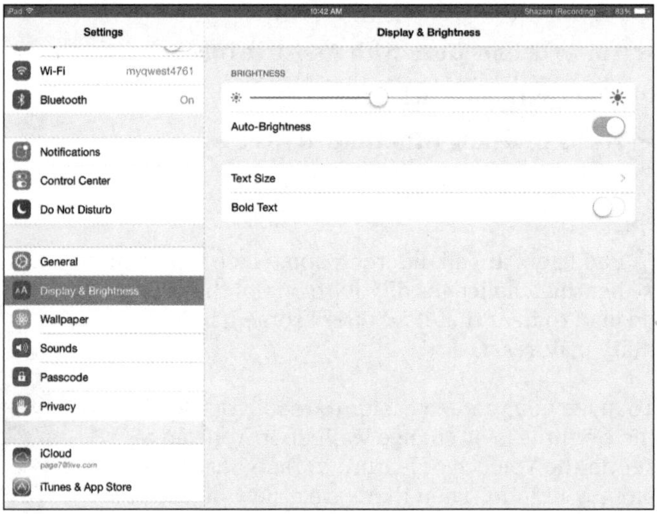

Figure 3-1: Lower brightness on your screen can also save battery life.

4. **Tap and drag the Brightness slider (refer to Figure 3-1) to the right to make the screen brighter or to the left to make it dimmer.**

5. **Press the Home button to close Settings.**

If glare from the screen is a problem for you, consider getting a *screen protector*. This thin film not only protects your screen from damage but can also reduce glare.

In the iBooks e-reader app, you can set a sepia tone for the page, which might be easier on your eyes. See Book II, Chapter 7 for more about using iBooks.

Changing the Wallpaper

The default iPad background image may be pretty, but it may not be the one that works best for you. Choosing different wallpaper may help you to see all the icons on your Home screen. Follow these steps:

1. **Start by tapping Settings on the Home screen.**

2. **In Settings, tap Wallpaper and then tap the > character to the right of Choose a New Wallpaper (see Figure 3-2).**

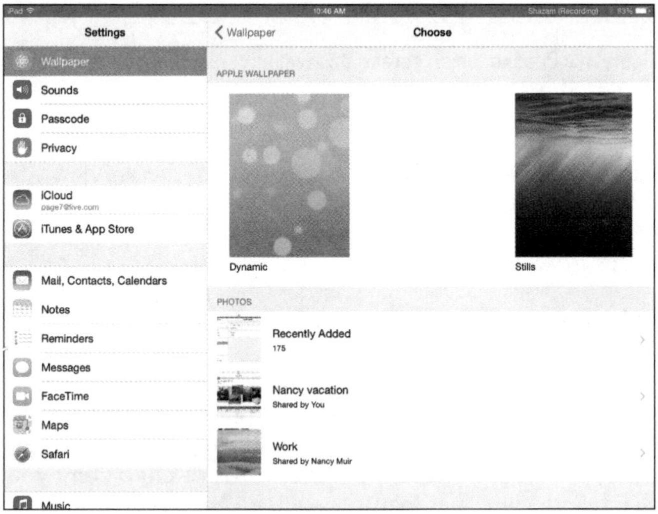

Figure 3-2: Choose from several built-in wallpapers.

3. **In the Wallpaper settings that appear, tap a wallpaper category such as Stills, as shown in Figure 3-3, to view choices; then tap a sample to select it.**

   Alternatively, on the initial wallpaper screen, tap an album in Photos to locate a picture to use as your wallpaper; then tap it.

4. **Tap Set Lock Screen, Set Home Screen, or Set Both.**

5. **Press the Home button to return to your Home screen with the new wallpaper set as the background.**

Figure 3-3: Choose which screen this wallpaper should be applied to.

If you choose a picture from your Photos gallery for wallpaper, tap the Perspective Zoom setting at the bottom of the preview screen to have the background move behind the apps on the Home page as you move the iPad around.

Setting Up VoiceOver

VoiceOver reads the names of screen elements and settings to you, but it also changes the way you provide input to the iPad. In Notes, for example, you can have VoiceOver read the name of the Notes buttons to you, and when you enter notes, it will read words or characters you've entered. It can also tell you whether features such as Auto-Correction are on. To turn on this feature, follow these steps:

1. **Tap Settings on the Home screen. Tap General and then tap Accessibility.**

2. **In the Accessibility pane shown in Figure 3-4, tap the VoiceOver button.**

3. **In the VoiceOver pane, shown in Figure 3-5, tap the VoiceOver On/Off switch to turn on this feature.**

   With VoiceOver on, you must first single-tap to select an item, such as a button, which causes VoiceOver to read the name of the button to you. Then you must double-tap the button to activate its function. (VoiceOver reminds you about this if you turn on Speak Hints, which is helpful when you first use VoiceOver, but it soon becomes annoying.)

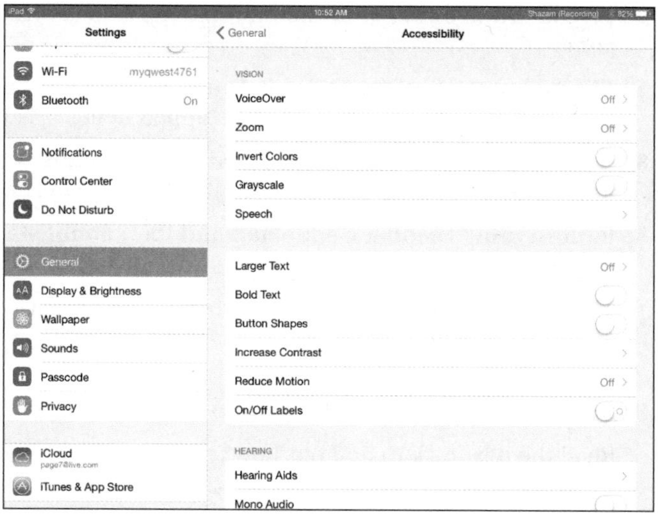

Figure 3-4: The Accessibility pane offers several helpful choices.

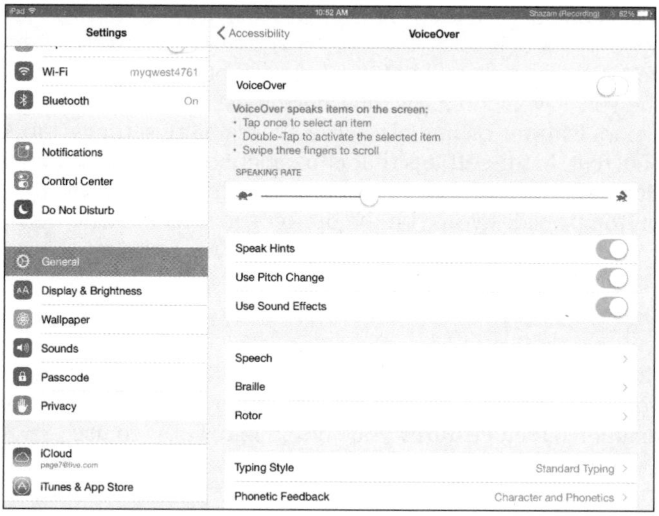

Figure 3-5: Note the Speaking Rate slider to set the speed of the VoiceOver feature.

4. **Tap the VoiceOver Practice button to select it, and then double-tap the button to open VoiceOver Practice.**

   This is the new method of tapping that VoiceOver activates.

5. **Practice using gestures such as pinching or flicking left, and VoiceOver tells you what action each gesture initiates.**

6. **Tap the Done button and then double-tap it to return to the VoiceOver pane.**

7. **Tap the Speak Hints On/Off switch, and then double-tap the same button. VoiceOver speaks the name of each tapped item.**

8. **If you want VoiceOver to read words or characters to you (for example, in the Notes app), tap and then double-tap Typing Feedback.**

9. **In the Typing Feedback pane, tap and then double-tap to select the option you prefer.**

   The Words option causes VoiceOver to read words to you, but not characters, such as the "dollar sign" ($). The Characters and Words option causes VoiceOver to read both.

10. **Press the Home button to return to the Home screen.**

    Read the next task to find out how to navigate your iPad after you've turned on VoiceOver.

You can change the language that VoiceOver speaks. In the General pane of Settings, choose Language & Region and then iPad Language and select another language. This action, however, also changes the language used for labels on apps on the Home screen and various settings and fields in iPad.

You can use the Accessibility Shortcut setting to help you more quickly turn the VoiceOver, Zoom, Switch Control, Assistive Touch, Grayscale, or Invert Colors features on and off. In the Accessibility settings, tap Accessibility Shortcut. In the settings that appear, choose what you want a triple-click of the Home button to activate. Now a triple-click with a single finger on the Home button provides you with the option you selected wherever you go in iPad.

Using VoiceOver

After VoiceOver is turned on, you need to figure out how to use it. I won't kid you — using it is awkward at first, but you'll get the hang of it! Here are the main onscreen gestures you should know how to use:

- ✔ **Tap an item to select it.** VoiceOver then speaks its name.

- ✔ **Double-tap the selected item.** This action activates the item.

- ✔ **Flick three fingers.** It takes three fingers to scroll around a page with VoiceOver turned on.

Table 3-1 provides additional gestures to help you use VoiceOver. I suggest that if you want to use this feature often, you read the VoiceOver section of the iPad's *User Guide,* which goes into a great deal of detail about the ins and outs of using VoiceOver. You'll find the *User Guide* at http://manuals.info.apple.com/MANUALS/1000/MA1565/en_US/iphone_user_guide.pdf or downloadable from the iBooks store.

Table 3-1	VoiceOver Gestures
Gesture	*Effect*
Flick right or left.	Select the next or preceding item.
Tap with two fingers.	Stop speaking the current item.
Flick two fingers up.	Read everything from the top of the screen.
Flick two fingers down.	Read everything from the current position.
Flick three fingers up or down.	Scroll one page at a time.
Flick three fingers right or left.	Go to the next or preceding page.
Tap three fingers.	Speak the scroll status (for example, line 20 of 100).
Flick four fingers up or down.	Go to the first or last element on a page.
Flick four fingers right or left.	Go to the next or preceding section (as on a web page).

If tapping with two or three fingers seems difficult for you, try tapping with one finger from one hand and one or two from the other. When double- or triple-tapping, you have to perform these gestures as quickly as you can for them to work.

Check out some of the settings for VoiceOver, including a choice for Braille, Language Rotor for making language choices, the ability to navigate images, and a setting to have iPad speak notifications.

Making Additional Vision Settings

Several Vision features are simple on/off settings, so rather than give you the steps to get to those settings repeatedly, I provide this useful bullet list of additional features that you can turn on or off after you tap Settings⇨General⇨Accessibility:

- **Zoom:** The Zoom feature enlarges the contents displayed on the iPad screen when you double-tap the screen with three fingers. The Zoom feature works almost everywhere in iPad: in Photos, on web pages, on your Home screens, in your Mail, in Music, and in Videos — give it a try!

- **Invert Colors:** The Invert Colors setting reverses colors on your screen so that white backgrounds are black and black text is white.

The Invert Colors feature works well in some places and not so well in others. For example, in the Photos application, pictures appear almost as photo negatives. Your Home screen image will likewise look a bit strange. And don't even think of playing a video with this feature turned on! However, if you need help reading text, Invert Colors can be useful in several applications.

✔ **Larger Type:** If having larger text in apps such as Contacts, Mail, and Notes would be helpful to you, you can turn on the Larger Type feature and choose the text size that works best for you.

✔ **Bold Text:** Turning on this setting will first restart your iPad (after asking you for permission to do so) and then cause text in various apps and in Settings to be bold. This is a handy setting because text in the iOS 7 redesign (also used by iOS 8) was simplified, meaning that it got thinner!

✔ **Increase Contrast:** Use this setting to set up backgrounds in some areas of iPad and apps with greater contrast, which should improve visibility.

✔ **Reduce Motion:** Tap this accessibility feature and then tap the On/Off switch to turn off the parallax effect, which causes the background of your Home screens to appear to float as you move the phone around.

✔ **Manage On/Off Labels:** If you have trouble making out colors, and so have trouble telling when an On/Off setting is On (green) and Off (white), use the On/Off Labels setting to add a circle to the right of a setting when it's off and a white vertical line to a setting when it's on (see Figure 3-6).

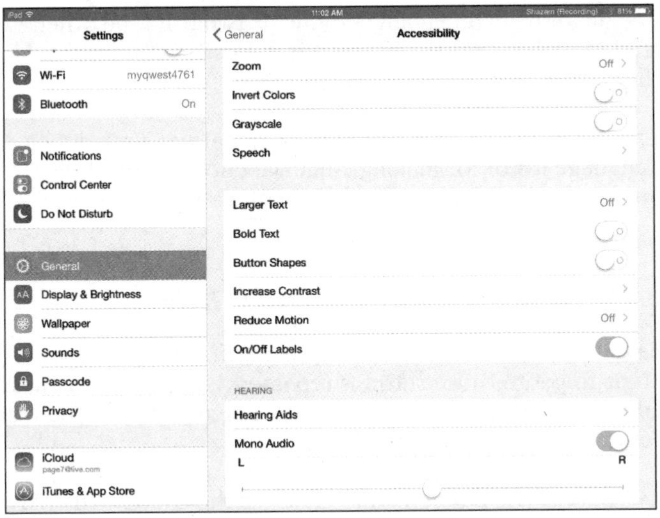

Figure 3-6: Can't see what's on and what's off? Use the Manage Labels setting.

Adjusting the Volume

Though individual apps such as Music and Video have their own volume settings, you can set your iPad system volume for your ringer (essentially alarms) and alerts as well to help you hear important alerts.

To adjust the volume, follow these steps:

1. **Tap Settings on the Home screen and then tap Sounds.**

2. **In the Sounds pane that appears (see Figure 3-7), tap and drag the Ringer and Alerts slider to the right to increase the volume of these audible attention grabbers, or to the left to lower it.**

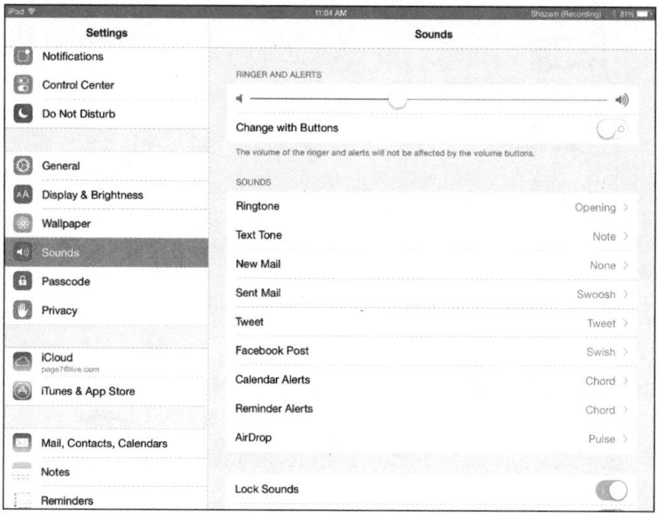

Figure 3-7: If you want to control ringer and alerts from the volume buttons, tap Change with Buttons here.

3. **Press the Home button to close Settings.**

In the Sounds pane, you can turn on or off the sounds that iPad makes when certain events occur (such as receiving new mail or Calendar alerts). These sounds are turned on by default.

Setting Up Subtitles and Captioning

Closed captioning and subtitles help folks with hearing challenges enjoy entertainment and educational content. Follow these steps to turn them on:

1. **From the Accessibility pane in Settings, tap Subtitles and Captioning.**

2. **On the following screen, shown in Figure 3-8, tap the On/Off switch to turn on Closed Captions and SDH (Subtitles for the Deaf and Hard of Hearing).**

   If you'd like, you can also tap Style and choose a text style for the captions.

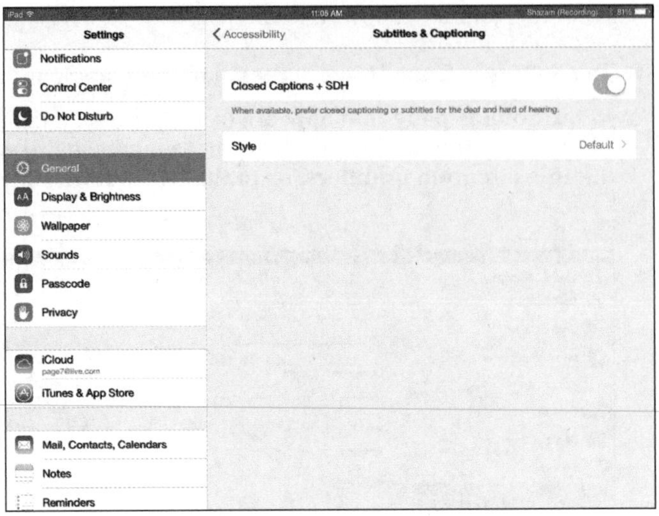

Figure 3-8: Closed-captioning is available only in certain movies.

3. **Tap the Style setting and a menu of font styles for captions and subtitles appears. Tap Default, Large Text, or Classic.**

   If you want to get your own look, tap Create New Style.

Managing Other Hearing Settings

A couple of hearing accessibility settings are simple on/off settings, including

- **Mono Audio.** Using the stereo effect in headphones or a headset breaks up sounds so that you hear a portion in one ear and a portion in the other ear, to simulate the way your ears process sounds (unless there is only one channel of sound, in which case that sound is sent to both ears). However, if you're hard of hearing or deaf in one ear, you're hearing only a portion of the sound in your hearing ear, which can be frustrating. If you have such hearing challenges and want to use iPad with a headset connected, you should turn on Mono Audio. When it's turned on, all sound is combined and distributed to both ears.

- **Have iPad Speak Auto-text.** The Speak Auto-text feature, which you access through the Speech selection under Accessibility, speaks autocorrections and auto-capitalizations (you can turn on both these features using Keyboard settings). When you enter text in an app such as Notes or Mail, the app then makes either type of change, while Speak Auto-text lets you know what change was made.

Why would you want iPad to tell you whenever an auto-correction has been made? If you have vision challenges and you know that you typed *ain't* when writing dialogue for a character in your novel, but iPad corrected it to *isn't,* you would want to know. Similarly, if your son's girlfriend's name is SUNshine (don't worry, he'll break up with her soon) and auto-capitalization corrects it (incorrectly), you need to know immediately so that you can change it back again.

Turning On and Working with AssistiveTouch

The AssistiveTouch Control panel helps those who have challenges working with buttons to provide input to iPad using the touchscreen.

To turn on AssistiveTouch, follow these steps:

1. **Tap Settings on the Home screen, and then tap General and Accessibility.**

2. **In the Accessibility pane, scroll down and tap AssistiveTouch.**

3. **In the pane that appears, tap the On/Off switch for AssistiveTouch to turn it on (see Figure 3-9).**

   A gray square (called the AssistiveTouch Control panel) then appears on the right side of the pane. This square now appears in the same location in whatever Home screen or apps you display on your iPad, though you can move it around the screen using your finger.

4. **Tap the AssistiveTouch Control panel to display options, as shown in Figure 3-10.**

Figure 3-9: Turn on the AssistiveTouch feature here.

Figure 3-10: AssistiveTouch displays a small panel that's always present.

5. **Tap Favorites or Device on the panel to see additional choices, tap Siri to activate the personal assistant feature, tap Notification Center or Control Center to display those panels, or tap Home to go directly to the Home screen.**

   After you've chosen an option, tapping the Back arrow takes you back to the main panel.

Table 3-2 shows the major options available in the AssistiveTouch Control panel and their purposes.

Table 3-2	AssistiveTouch Controls
Control	*Purpose*
Siri	Activates the Siri feature, which allows you to speak questions and make requests of your iPad.
Favorites	Displays a set of gestures with only the Pinch gesture preset; you can tap any of the other blank squares to add your own favorite gestures.
Device	You can rotate the screen, lock the screen, turn volume up or down, mute or unmute sound, or shake the iPad to undo an action using the presets in this option.
Home	Sends you to the Home screen.

In addition to using Siri, don't forget about using the Dictation key on the onscreen keyboard to speak text entries and basic keyboard commands.

Managing Home Click Speed

Sometimes if you have dexterity challenges, it's hard to double-tap or triple-tap the Home button fast enough to have an effect. Choose the Slow or Slowest setting when you tap the Home Click Speed setting to allow you a bit more time to make that second or third tap:

1. **Tap Settings➪General➪Accessibility.**

2. **Scroll down and tap Home Click Speed.**

3. **Tap the Slow or Slowest settings to change how rapidly you have to double- or triple-tap your screen to initiate an action.**

If you have certain adaptive accessories, you can use head gestures to control your iPad, highlighting features in sequence and then selecting one. Use the Switch Control feature in the Accessibility settings to turn this mode on and make settings for this feature.

Focusing Learning with Guided Access

Guided Access is a feature that you can use to limit a user's access to the iPad to a single app, and even limit access to that app to certain features. This is useful in several ways, ranging from use in a classroom to use by someone with attention deficit disorder, and even in a public setting such as a kiosk where you don't want users to be able to open other apps. To use this feature, follow these steps:

1. **Tap Settings and then tap General.**

2. **Tap Accessibility and then tap Guided Access, and on the pane that appears (see Figure 3-11), tap Guided Access to turn on the feature.**

3. **Tap Passcode Settings and then tap Set Guided Access Passcode to activate a passcode so that those using an app cannot return to the Home screen to access other apps.**

4. **In the Set Passcode pane that appears (see Figure 3-12), enter a passcode using the numeric pad. Enter the number again when prompted.**

5. **Press the Home button and tap an app to open it.**

6. **Press the Home button three times.**

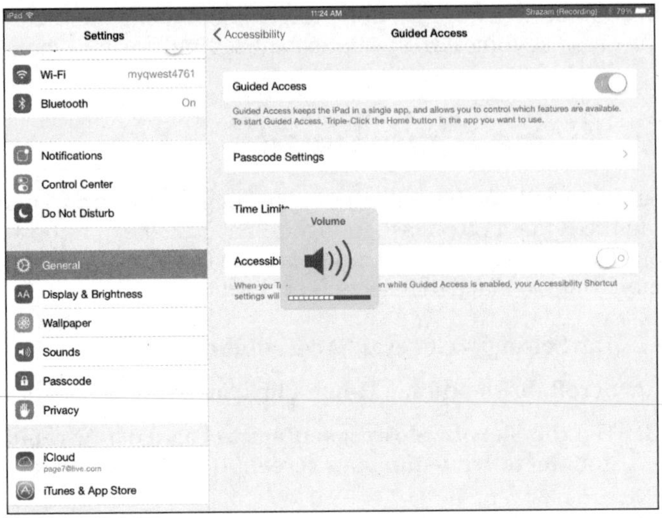

Figure 3-11: Limit accessible apps by turning on Guided Access.

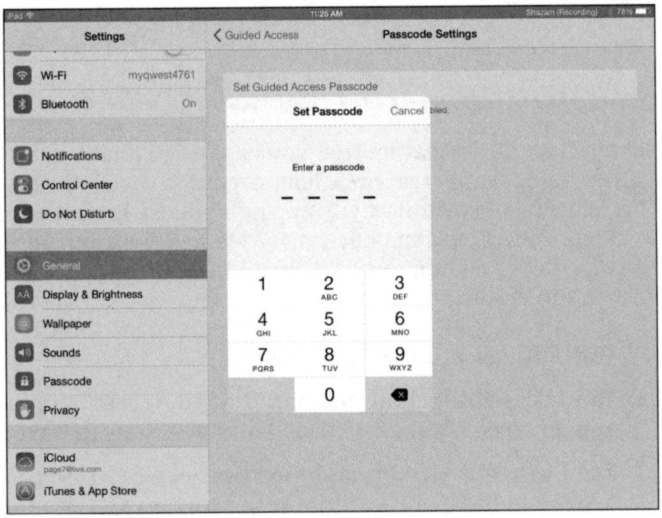

Figure 3-12: Choose a passcode you can remember.

7. **You are presented with an Option button along the bottom of the screen; tap the Option button to display options:**

   • *Sleep/Wake Button:* You can put your iPad to sleep or wake it up with a triple-tap of the Home button.

- *Volume Buttons:* You can tap to turn this Always On or Always Off. If you don't want users to be able to adjust volume using the volume toggle on the side of the iPad, for example, use this setting.

- *Motion:* Turn this setting off if you don't want users to move the iPad around — for example, to play a race car driving game.

- *Keyboards:* Use this setting to prohibit people from entering text using the keyboard when in Guided Access mode.

8. **Another setting that's displayed to the right of Options is Touch. If you don't want users to be able to use the touchscreen, turn this off.**

   You can also set a Time Limit for users to be able to work with this app.

9. **Press the Home button three times and then enter your passcode, if you set one, to return to the Home screen.**

Chapter 4: Overview of Bundled Apps

In This Chapter

- ✔ Getting the most out of the Internet with Safari, Mail, and Messages
- ✔ Using cameras and organizing and sharing your photos
- ✔ Getting organized with Calendar, Contacts, Notes, and Reminders
- ✔ Going places with Maps
- ✔ Using apps for e-reading and playing music, podcasts, and videos
- ✔ Shopping for content at iTunes and apps at the App Store
- ✔ Reading periodicals with Newsstand
- ✔ Playing around with Game Center
- ✔ Making video calls with FaceTime
- ✔ Using fun photo effects with Photo Booth

*i*Pad comes with certain functionality and applications (which you probably know as *apps,* for short) already installed. When you look at your Home screen (1 of 15 possible Home screens that you can fill with other apps without doing workarounds to add more Home screens), you'll see 15 icons for apps, plus 1 for accessing iPad Settings.

Four icons are displayed across the bottom in iPad's Dock: Messages, Mail, Safari, and Music. The other apps (Videos, Photos, Camera, Maps, Clock, Photo Booth, Calendar, Contacts, Notes, Reminders, Newsstand, iTunes Store, App Store, iBooks, Game Center, and FaceTime) are above the Dock and include apps for organizing your time and contacts, playing videos and reading periodicals, snapping pictures, gaming, shopping for content, and yet more. An Extras folder contains helpful Tips and the My Podcasts app.

The Dock icons appear on every Home screen. The others appear on the first Home screen unless you move them elsewhere. Note that you can add up to two additional apps to the Dock, if you want to have those apps available on every Home screen or replace apps in the Dock with others. With iOS 8, iBooks and Podcasts are included as bundled apps, and they appear on the second Home screen.

This chapter gives you a quick overview of what each bundled app does. You find out more about every one of them as you move through the chapters in this book.

Settings is a very important item on the Home screen you should know about: It's the central location in iPad where you can adjust all the settings for various functions, change settings for how apps (both preinstalled and the ones you add) function, and perform administrative tasks like setting up email accounts or a password. Read more about using Settings in Chapter 8 of this minibook. You can also find advice about using settings for various apps in Books II, III, and V, and information about email settings in Chapter 7 of this minibook.

Another built-in feature (but not an app on your Home screen) to check out is Siri. See Book V, Chapter 6 for more about this cool personal assistant that does everything from finding the nearest Italian restaurant to providing the latest stock quotes.

Getting Online with iPad

iPad would kind of be a very expensive calendar, address book, and music player if you couldn't go online to browse, buy things, get email, stream video and audio, and more. Two bundled apps, Safari and Mail, help to connect your iPad to many of the Internet's resources.

Going on Safari

Safari is Apple's web browser. If you've owned a Mac computer, iPhone, or iPod touch, you've already used Safari (see Figure 4-1) to navigate around the Internet, create and save bookmarks of favorite sites, and add web clips to your Home screen so that you can quickly visit favorite sites from there.

If you've been a Windows user in the past, you may also have used Safari, or you may be more familiar with browsers such as Internet Explorer, Chrome, or Firefox. If you haven't used Safari, don't worry; the browser should be pretty easy for you to get the hang of, with its familiar integrated address/ search field, tabs, navigation buttons, and bookmarks.

Using a browser on iPad is a lot of fun because of the touchscreen functionality that gives you the ability to zoom in or out on a page by flicking two fingers inward or outward. Tabbed browsing allows you to move easily among open web pages, and the All Tabs view new with iOS 8 for iPad lets you see all your open tabs as thumbnails on a single screen. You can read more about using Safari in Chapter 6 of this minibook.

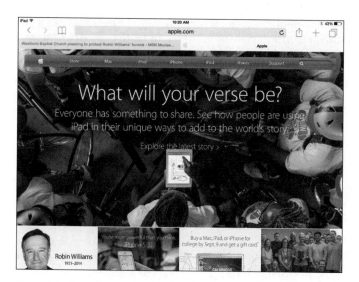

Figure 4-1: Find what you need on the web with Safari.

Be sure to check out iCloud connectivity with a feature called Handoff. If you have several Apple devices, you can use iCloud tabs to pick up where you left off searching or viewing tabs on one device on another.

You can get done much of what you want to do on your iPad by using Siri. This personal assistant, which you learn more about in Book V, Chapter 6, can help you go to a web page, create and send an email, enter an event in Reminders or Calendar, and more.

Getting Mail

iPad lets you get all your mail in one place through the Mail app — the program you use to access email accounts you set up in iPad. You can set up accounts that you have with popular email providers such as Gmail, Yahoo!, AOL, and Outlook.com. You can also access accounts through iCloud or Microsoft Exchange/Office 365. (Your work email account might use Microsoft Exchange, for example.) Almost any IMAP- or POP3-type account (the two most common mail protocols) is supported, which lets you access the email accounts you have with your Internet service provider (ISP).

After you set up an account, when you tap the Mail icon, your email will display without your having to browse to a site or sign in. Then you can use tools to move among preset mail folders, read and reply to mail, and download attached photos to the iPad. You can also use the Print feature in Mail to print your email messages to a printer that supports AirPrint. You can read more about setting up and using email accounts in Chapter 7 of this minibook.

In portrait orientation, emails are displayed full screen, and you can use a drop-down menu to view your inbox. In landscape orientation, the inbox stays put on the left side of your screen.

iPad users (except those with an original iPad or iPad 2) can use the Dictation feature to enter email addresses and messages in Mail by tapping the Dictation key on the onscreen keyboard and speaking them. See Chapter 3 in this minibook for more about the Dictation feature.

Using iMessage to connect

iPad's instant messaging app is called Messages. This app allows you to use the iMessage service to swap text messages with others in real time using a cellphone number or email address. You can forward your conversations to others as well.

You can use the Messages settings to turn on the app or allow others to get a read receipt when you've read their messages. You can also use the data in your Contacts app to make addressing messages quick and easy. New with iOS 8 comes the ability to send audio or video messages.

Shooting and Organizing Photos

All iPads (except for the original iPad) include front- and rear-facing cameras. You can use the cameras to take still photos or shoot videos (both of which are covered in Book II, Chapter 4). To review and play around with photos you snap or bring onto the iPad from another source, you have the Photos app.

Examining the iPad cameras

The third-generation and later iPads have a super-clear Retina display and rear-facing iSight camera for viewing and taking the best iPad-generated photos and video yet.

Take a quick look at your camera's features by tapping the Camera app icon on the Home screen.

You can use the controls in the Camera app to

- Switch between the front and rear cameras.
- Change from still-camera to video-camera operation by using the Camera/Video slider.
- Take a picture or start recording a video.
- Turn on a grid to help you autofocus on still photo subjects.

✔ Use square, time-lapse, or panorama settings and use filters to modify the colors and other effects on a shot.

✔ Open previously captured images or videos.

When you view a photo or video, you can use an iPad feature to send the image via a tweet or email, share it via iCloud Photo Sharing, send it to those close to you via AirDrop, post it to your Facebook or Flickr account, print images, use a still photo as wallpaper or assign it to represent a contact, or run a slideshow or edit a video. See Book II, Chapters 4 and 6 for more detail about using the iPad cameras.

Perusing your photos

Photos isn't exactly Photoshop or any other sophisticated photo-imaging program — it's just a pretty simple app for organizing and viewing photos with a few very simple editing tools including a set of filters for cool effects. Still, although it doesn't do much, its features are very easy to use.

Photos (see Figure 4-2) allows you to organize pictures in folders; email, message, or tweet photos to others or post photos to Facebook; use a photo as your iPad wallpaper; or upload someone's picture to a contact record. Photos organizes photos by year or location taken.

You can use tools to apply filters, rotate, enhance, remove red-eye, or crop photos. You can also run slideshows of your photos. You can open albums, use the pinch or expand gestures to shrink or enlarge photos, and scroll through photos with a swipe.

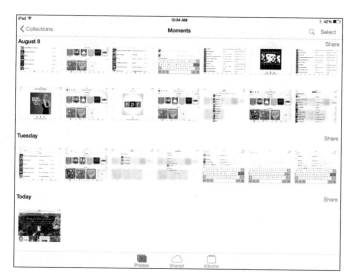

Figure 4-2: A simple but fun way to view your photos.

You can use the Photo Sharing feature to share photos among your friends. In addition, you can share photos and other content using Twitter, Flickr, iCloud Photo Sharing, or Facebook from right within several apps, including Photos.

The sexy part of Photos is the way you interact with the photos with your fingers on the touchscreen, moving from one collection to another, scrolling through collections, and expanding or shrinking photos. You can also use Photos to convert your iPad into a digital photo frame while you have it docked or charging, and you can run slideshows of your photo albums as well. If Photos sounds like fun (and it is), read more about how it works in Book II, Chapter 6.

Using Apps to Stay Organized

Scheduling your time, tracking contacts, jotting down notes — they're all a part of keeping organized in today's hectic world. iPad offers five apps to help you do just that: Calendar, Contacts, Reminders, Clock, and Notes.

 More recent iPads have native print capability, which can be useful for printing Notes documents, for example. You have to have a printer that supports AirPrint wireless printing to use this method. See Book V, Chapter 1 for more about printing.

iPads have a multitasking feature that you can turn on or off in the General pane in Settings. That means that you don't have to return to the Home screen every time you want to switch among all these great apps. As on the iPhone, multitasking is dead simple. With one app open, just press the Home button twice or place five fingers on the screen and pinch them together. A horizontal display of app icons for any open apps appears along the middle of the screen along with photos of recent contacts. Scroll to find the one you want, tap it, and it opens. To quit an app, just slide it upward. You can also use four fingers and swipe to the left or right to move through any currently running apps or apps you've used recently.

Tracking your schedule with Calendar

What would any computing device today be without a calendar feature, given our busy lives? If the calendar features on your computer and mobile phone don't already keep you on track, try iPad's Calendar. This app provides a handy onscreen daybook that you can use to set up appointments and send alerts to remind you about them. You can also sync Calendar with other calendars that you maintain online such as on Google, Yahoo!, computer-based calendars via iTunes, or iCloud.

See Chapter 5 in this minibook for more about syncing and Book V, Chapter 3 for details on using Calendar.

Keeping in touch with Contacts

Today, it's all about who you know and staying in touch. Contacts is the built-in address book feature (see Figure 4-3) for the iPad that lets you do just that. You can use Contacts to enter contact information (including photos, if you like, from your Photos app) and share contact information via Mail or Messages. You can also use a search feature to find contacts easily.

Contacts is another app that you can sync with your iPhone or computer to save you tedious reentry of information. Read more about this in Book V, Chapter 5.

TIP

Want to find your contact in the real world? Tap that person's address in Contacts, and the iPad Maps app shows you how to get there! You can also tap an address that you find in Maps and add it to Contacts.

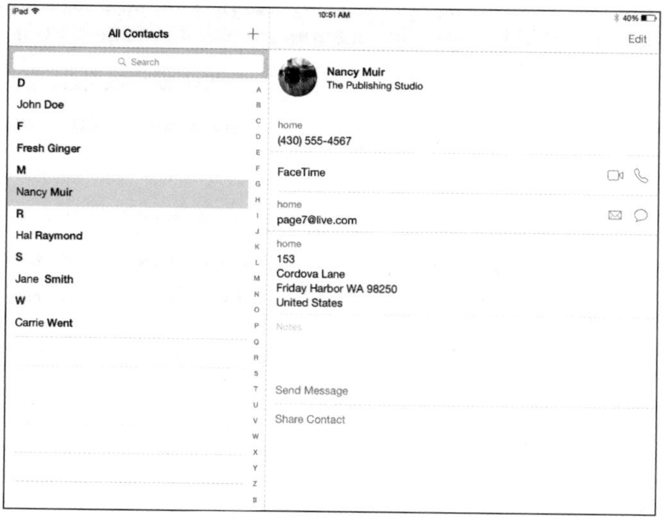

Figure 4-3: Keep the basics about all your contacts in this handy app.

Making Notes

Notes is a simple notepad app in which you can enter text or cut and paste text from a website or email. You can't do much except create and edit your notes, or email or print them — the app has no features for formatting text or inserting objects. You'll find Notes handy, though, for simple scribbles on the fly.

You'll feel right at home with the clean interface that Notes sports. The font also has a clean, sans-serif look, and the icons along the top are pretty straightforward. You can move to the previous note, email a note, trash a note, or move to the next note. You can even tap the Dictation key on the onscreen keyboard of an iPad (except for the original iPad and iPad 2) and speak your content.

If this simple note-keeper appeals to you, read more about the Notes app in Book V, Chapter 2.

You can enter info into Notes using Dictation or the onscreen keyboard. If you are a heavy note taker and dictating notes has no appeal, consider buying a compatible Bluetooth keyboard or keyboard dock for easier typing.

Keeping yourself on track with Reminders

Reminders is a handy electronic to-do list in which you can enter tasks or pull tasks from the Calendar app. You can organize reminders into custom categories and see them in a list or organized by date, which also displays a useful monthly calendar on one side of the screen.

Of course, an obvious feature of an app called Reminders is that you can set it up to remind you of an event. Location-based reminders (which work most efficiently with the always-on 3G or 4G connection on iPad 3G/4G models) prompt your iPad to remind you about an event based on your location; for example, set a reminder to buy milk when you get to a specific location, and you receive the alert when you arrive at the market. This feature uses Location Services to track your whereabouts at any point in time.

Staying on time with Clock

This app is a simple utility that is especially useful to all you world travelers. Clock allows you to display clocks from around the world side by side, so if you're in Paris, you can easily see what time it is in New York.

Clock also has a feature that lets you set alarms to keep your day on schedule. Finally, you can use timer and stopwatch features. The timer lets you do things like time the cookies you just put in the oven, and the stopwatch lets you add up the minutes of your morning jog or workout. You can even use the lap-timer feature to keep track of multiple laps in a workout, such as those runs around the track or swimming pool laps.

Going Places with Maps

The Maps app allows you to view classic maps or aerial views of addresses; get directions from one place to another by car or on foot; and check on traffic in large cities.

If you own a Wi-Fi–only iPad, a less sophisticated system than 3G/4G can identify your current location and help you find directions from there to other places. 3G/4G iPad owners enjoy a much more targeted location system using GPS, but all models can take advantage of the ability to bookmark or share locations, or add an address to Contacts.

See Book III, Chapter 2 for step-by-step procedures for using the Maps app.

Being Entertained by iPad

One of the joys of the iPad is its use as a media consumption tool. Playing music and watching videos are very entertaining uses of iPad, indeed. The bundled Music and Videos apps make playing media easy to do. In addition, by using the iBooks app, you can use your iPad as an e-reader, and the Podcasts app opens up a world of audio content.

Playing around with Music

Unless you've been living in a cave without 3G/4G or satellite TV for the last several years, you know perfectly well that the iPod has historically been the Apple-preferred player. On your iPad, the Music app is your media player with a heavy emphasis on music. You can use Music to play music, audio podcasts, or audiobooks.

One of the nicest things about Music on the iPad is the fact that the iPad comes with a very nifty sound system and stereo speakers, so listening with or without headphones will be a pleasing experience for everyone who's addicted to MP3 listening devices. You can also browse your music by a variety of criteria, such as artist, album, song, or genre.

 iOS 8 gives Siri access to the Shazam music identifier service. Sitting in a café and want to know what that song is that's playing on the music system? Just ask Siri, which checks with Shazam and offers you the chance to buy the music from the iTunes Store

Watching Videos

You can use the Videos app to play TV or movies, and it offers some useful features for controlling video playback.

The Videos app is a media player like Music, but it specializes in playing videos and offers a few more features, such as breakdowns of the various chapters in the video and information about related movies and casts for media you got from iTunes. You can move between widescreen and full-screen display, and it shines at showing high-definition content, especially with the third-generation (and later) iPad's awesome Retina display. See Book II, Chapter 3 for more on the Videos app.

Reading e-books

With iOS 8, the popular e-reader app, iBooks, comes preinstalled. Using this app, you can read books, add highlights and bookmarks to text, look up definitions, and more. You can access the iBooks Store from iBooks to buy content, or use other sources to purchase and download books.

iBooks allows you to adjust text size and background to make your book pages more readable. Also, the iPad's highly portable size makes taking your books on the road very easy. For more about downloading apps for your iPad, see Book II, Chapter 1, and to work with the iBooks's e-reader app itself, go to Book II, Chapter 7.

Listening to Podcasts

My Podcasts is another app that now comes preinstalled on your iPad in the Extras folder. My Podcasts is a gateway to a world of audio content, from popular content such as *The Daily Show* to comedy and motivational talks. Most podcasts are free, and you can download individual shows or subscribe to ones that publish on a regular basis.

Going Shopping at iTunes and the App Store

The iTunes app takes you to the iTunes Store, where you can shop'til you drop (or your iPad battery runs out of juice) for music, movies, TV shows, and audiobooks and then download them directly to your iPad. You can also preview content before you download it. See Chapter 5 in this minibook for more about how to buy apps, and www.dummies.com/extras/ipadaio for a listing of some of the very best apps out there.

Ready for more shopping? Tapping the App Store icon takes you directly to the Apple online store, where you can buy and download apps that do everything from enabling you to play games to building business presentations. At last count, more than 550,000+ apps were available for the iPad, with more being added all the time. Some were created for iPhone/iPod touch and run on the iPad; some were created especially for the iPad. And some are even free!

Check out the iTunes U app that gives you access to hundreds of great online courses from sources such as major universities. You can download iTunes U for free from the App Store.

Reading Periodicals with Newsstand

Newsstand is a handy interface for subscribing to and reading magazines, newspapers, and other periodical apps. Publications you subscribe to are laid out in neat rows on virtual shelves, and there's a handy Store button to shop for more periodicals.

Playing with Game Center

Game Center is a way to essentially browse game apps in the App Store by bestselling titles and compare your scores with your friends. Tap Game Center on your Home screen and tap one of the sets of colorful icons that appear on the Game Center screen, and you're taken to the App Store, with information about a game displayed.

From then on, it's about obtaining the game (either free or for a price through your iTunes account) and playing it. You can add friends to build your gaming social network and play and track scores for interactive games. See Chapter 5 in this minibook for more about buying apps, and Book II, Chapter 8 for more about gaming with your iPad.

Connecting with Friends on FaceTime

iPads (with the exception of the original iPad) ship with front- and rear-facing cameras, which unleash all kinds of possibilities. One of the coolest is using an app called FaceTime. The FaceTime video calling app lets you use the iPad's video cameras to talk face-to-face with someone who has an iPad (except an original iPad); Mac (running OS X 10.6.6 or later); fourth- or later-generation iPod touch; or iPhone 4 or later. (See Figure 4-4.) You can call someone via his or her iPhone cellphone number or email address.

Figure 4-4: Talk face-to-face using FaceTime.

FaceTime even works directly over a cellular connection, though you'll pay for it by eating up your data allotment.

You can also hold audio-only FaceTime sessions. This feature is handy when you don't want to drain battery power, when you want to use less bandwidth, or when you're having a bad hair day.

You'll want to start trying FaceTime with all your friends who own a compatible Apple device, so head straight to Book II, Chapter 4 to get up to speed on FaceTime features.

Exploring Fun Photo Effects with Photo Booth

The very fun Photo Booth app has been included with Mac OS X for some time, and it came to the iPad with the release of iOS 5. It lets you take photos with weird and wonderful results (see Figure 4-5). You can use the built-in effects, such as Kaleidoscope, Mirror, and Thermal Camera, along with your iPad camera, to take photos that turn out unlike any others.

Figure 4-5: Manipulate photos in a variety of ways with Photo Booth.

Chapter 5: Setting Up iTunes to Sync and Buy Apps

In This Chapter

✓ **Getting connected to the Internet**

✓ **Downloading iTunes and creating an account**

✓ **Making iPad settings in iTunes**

✓ **Syncing iPad to your computer**

✓ **Using iCloud**

✓ **Purchasing apps from the App Store**

✓ **Updating your apps**

Apple designed its iTunes desktop application as a way for you to manage settings for how your iPad syncs with your computer. Using iTunes, you can share information and content such as calendar events, pictures, music, movies, and contacts. Before you can use iTunes to sync from a PC, you have to download the software, and if you want to make purchases from the store, you need to open an iTunes account, both of which I cover in this chapter. You can also use the iCloud service to store and share content online using a Wi-Fi connection. In this chapter, I cover how to set up an iCloud account and make settings to back up and share content in the cloud.

But iTunes isn't just for syncing content. Some apps, such as Contacts and Videos, come preinstalled on your iPad. But as you know if you're an iPhone user, a world of other apps is out there, including many that are designed specifically for your iPad. After you set up iTunes, you can buy apps (or download free ones) in the App Store using your iTunes account. Some are free and some come for a price (typically from 99¢ to about $10, though a few go up to $50 or more).

In this chapter, I tell you how to connect to the Internet (you need an Internet connection to access the App Store). Then I tell you how to set iTunes and iCloud to sync your iPad with other devices and how you can acquire apps for your iPad through the App Store.

After you have an iTunes account, you can also shop iTunes for music, videos, audiobooks, and more. See Book II, Chapter 1 for more about shopping for multimedia content.

Connecting to the Internet

To browse the web, access Mail, and shop online, you first have to be connected to the Internet, so I'm putting this information right up front. How you connect to the Internet depends on which iPad model you own:

- ✔ The **Wi-Fi–only iPad** connects to the Internet, logically enough, via a Wi-Fi network. You may already have set up this type of network in your own home using your computer and some equipment from your Internet provider. You can also connect through public Wi-Fi networks *(hotspots)*. You probably have already noticed how many hotspots your town or city has: Look for Internet cafés, coffee shops, hotels, libraries, and transportation centers such as airports or bus stations. In fact, after you start looking, you'll notice lots of signs alerting you to free Wi-Fi locations — they're everywhere.

- ✔ If you own a **Wi-Fi and 3G- or Wi-Fi and 4G-enabled iPad,** you can still use a Wi-Fi connection (which is usually much faster if you have a good connection), but you can also use a paid data network through AT&T, Sprint, T-Mobile, or Verizon to connect via a cellular network just about anywhere you can get cellular phone coverage. If you have a 3G or 4G model, you don't have to do anything; with a contract for coverage, the connection is made automatically wherever cellular service is available, just as it is on your cellphone.

See Chapter 1 in this minibook for more about the capabilities of different iPad models and the costs associated with a cellular network.

When you're in range of a hotspot, a pop-up may display automatically; if it doesn't, follow these steps:

1. **Tap Settings on the Home screen.**

2. **Tap Wi-Fi.**

3. **Be sure that Wi-Fi is set to On (see Figure 5-1) and choose a network to connect to.**

   Network names should appear automatically when you're in range of networks. When you're in range of a public hotspot, if access to several nearby networks is available, you may see a message asking you to tap a network name to select it.

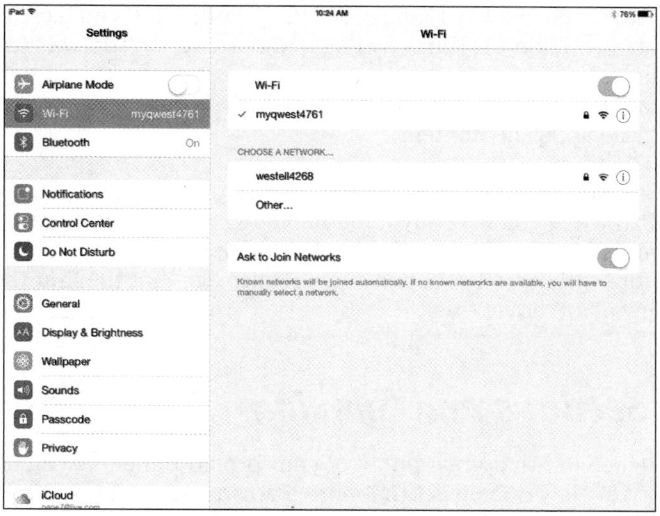

Figure 5-1: Turning on Wi-Fi.

4. **After you select a network (or if only one network is available), you may see a message asking for your password; if you do, enter the password.**

   You may need to ask the owner of the hotspot (for example, a hotel desk clerk or business owner) for this password or enter your home network password.

5. **Tap the Join button and you're connected.**

Free public Wi-Fi networks typically don't require passwords. However, it's therefore possible for someone else to track your online activities over these unsecured networks. No matter how much you might be tempted, you might want to avoid accessing financial accounts or sending unencrypted sensitive email when connected to a public hotspot.

Setting Up iTunes

Think of iTunes as Apple's version of the Mall of America. It's both one place from which you can manage your iPad settings for syncing content, and a great big online store from which you can buy content and apps for your Mac or PC, iPod touch, iPhone, and iPad. It's also the place where you can make settings for several of these devices to control how they download and share content. Even if you find some other sources of content for your iPad, it's worth having an iTunes account, if only to use the settings it provides.

Before you can use iTunes to manage your iPad, you have to download the latest version of iTunes by going to www.apple.com/itunes. You should also create an iTunes account, providing a payment method so that you can use iTunes on your computer or use the iTunes app on your iPad to purchase apps and content.

You can use an iTunes account, or an Apple ID and iCloud, to register your iPad when you first buy it before you can use it. In my case and perhaps in yours, the nice man at the Apple Store activated my iPad before I left the store with it, so I set up my own iTunes account the first time I wanted to buy a hot movie title.

Making Settings and Syncing

Remember that great photo of your promotion party you have on your hard drive? How do you get that onto iPad so you can show it off at the next family reunion? Or how about that audiobook on career success that you bought and downloaded to your laptop on your last business trip? It would sure be handy to get that sucker onto your iPad. Never fear: By making a few easy settings and syncing with your computer, you can bring all that content over in a flash.

Remember that you can also sync content using iCloud. See the section "Understanding iCloud," later in this chapter, for more about that option.

Making iPad settings using iTunes

When you plug your Lightning to USB Cable (the Dock Connector to USB Cable for third-generation iPads and earlier) into your iPad and computer and then open iTunes, a whole group of settings becomes available. These help you determine how content will sync between the two devices.

If you're using a Mac, you already have iTunes installed, but be sure that you have the latest version (at the time of this writing it's version 11.4). Open iTunes and choose Check for Updates. For Windows users, you should download the iTunes application to your computer so that you have the option of using it to *sync* (transfer) downloaded content to your iPad.

Note that you can sync wirelessly to your computer by tapping Settings on the Home screen, tapping General, and tapping iTunes Wi-Fi Sync. In the settings that appear, tap Sync Now. This works only if your computer is connected to the same Wi-Fi network.

Here's how to use the iTunes settings for your iPad:

1. **Connect your iPad to your computer using the Lightning to USB Cable.**

   Plug the Lightning end of your cable (the smaller end) into your iPad and plug the other end of the cord into a USB port on your computer.

2. **Open your iTunes software.**

   On a Mac, click the iTunes button in the Dock; on a Windows 7 computer, choose Start⇨All Programs⇨iTunes; and on a Windows 8 or 8.1 computer, simply begin to type **iTunes** from the Start screen and then click iTunes in the search results.

   iTunes opens, and your iPad is listed in the Devices section of the Source List.

3. **Click the name of your iPad in the Devices section of the Source List or the upper-right corner if the Source List isn't displayed, as shown in Figure 5-2.**

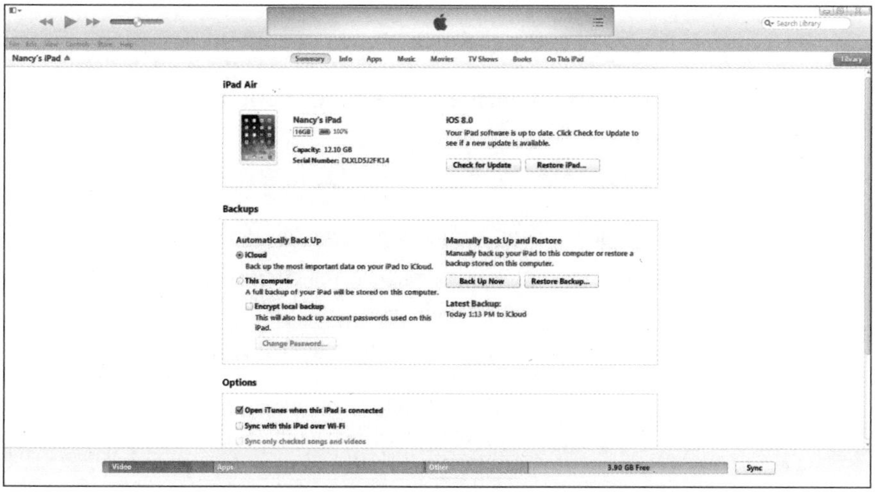

Figure 5-2: The various tabs you can use to control iPad from iTunes.

A series of tabs displays. The tabs offer information about your iPad and the settings you can use to specify which content such as music, movies, or podcasts to download and, for some content types, when to download. Figure 5-3 shows the settings on the Movies tab. The settings on the various tabs relate to the kind of content you want to download and whether you want to download it automatically when you sync or do it manually. See Table 5-1 for an overview of the settings that are available on each tab.

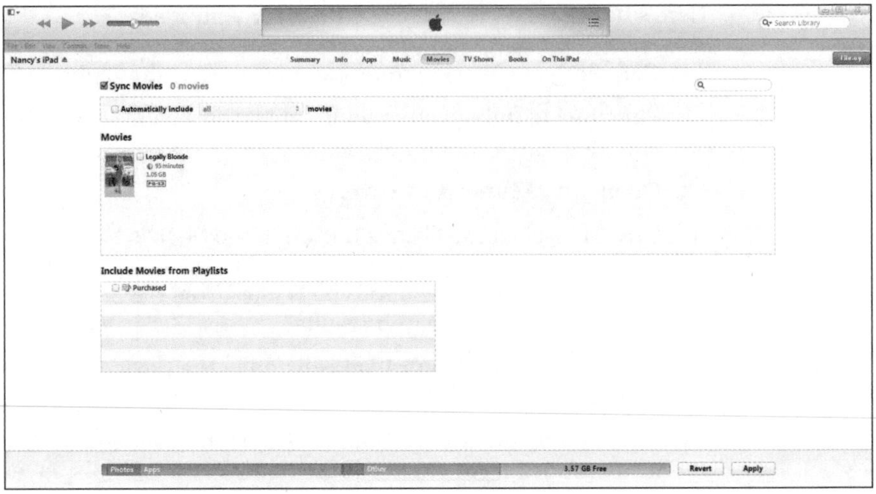

Figure 5-3: This pane includes settings to control how backups and syncing occur.

4. **Make all settings for the types of content you plan to obtain on your computer and sync to your iPad, and then click the Sync button in the bottom-right corner to sync files with the iPad.**

Table 5-1	iPad Settings in iTunes
Tab Name	*What You Can Do with These Settings*
Summary	Perform updates to iPad software and set general backup and syncing options.
Info	Specify which information to sync: Contacts, Calendars, Email accounts, Bookmarks, or Notes. Perform an advanced replacement of info on the iPad with info from the computer. Note that for users of OS X Mavericks, this tab doesn't appear, and all Info syncing must be done via iCloud.
Apps	Sync apps and data that you've downloaded to your computer to the iPad and manage the location of those apps and folders. Choose whether to automatically install new apps and organize/arrange icons, folders, and the order of Home screens.
Tones	Choose to sync selected or sync all tones.
Music	Choose which music to download to your iPad when you sync.
Movies	Specify whether to automatically download movies.
TV Shows	Choose which shows and episodes to sync automatically.
Podcasts	Choose which podcasts and episodes to sync automatically.

Tab Name	What You Can Do with These Settings
iTunes U	Sync all, a specified number of unplayed courses, or a specified number of recent items in all or selected collections.
Books	Choose to sync all or only selected audio and electronic books to your iPad.
Photos	Choose the folders or albums from which you want to download photos or albums.
On This iPad	Select content on the iPad to copy to iTunes.

Be alert to warnings when you sync your iPad and computer because, depending on your settings, you may overwrite or erase content you've downloaded when you sync. You may want to copy content that you've downloaded to your iPad directly to your iTunes library before syncing so that your computer doesn't erase what you've downloaded during the sync.

Syncing iPad to your computer

After you specify which content to download in iTunes (see the preceding section), you use the Lightning to USB Cable to connect your iPad and computer to sync info like contacts and calendar settings. Note that Wi-Fi syncing can take place when iPad is asleep and plugged into power.

With iTunes installed on your computer and an iTunes account set up, follow these steps to sync to your iPad:

1. **Plug the Lightning end (the smaller end) of your Lightning to USB Cable into your iPad.**

2. **Plug the other end of the Lightning to USB Cable into your computer.**

   iTunes opens and shows an iPad item in the Source List. (If you're displaying the Sidebar, the iPad appears there instead.)

3. **Click iPad to view its settings (see Figure 5-4), and then click the Sync button.**

   Your iPad screen should show the words *Sync in Progress;* if it doesn't, click the Sync button in the lower-right corner.

   When the syncing is complete, disconnect the cable. Any media you chose to transfer in your iTunes settings, and any new photos on your computer, have been transferred to your iPad.

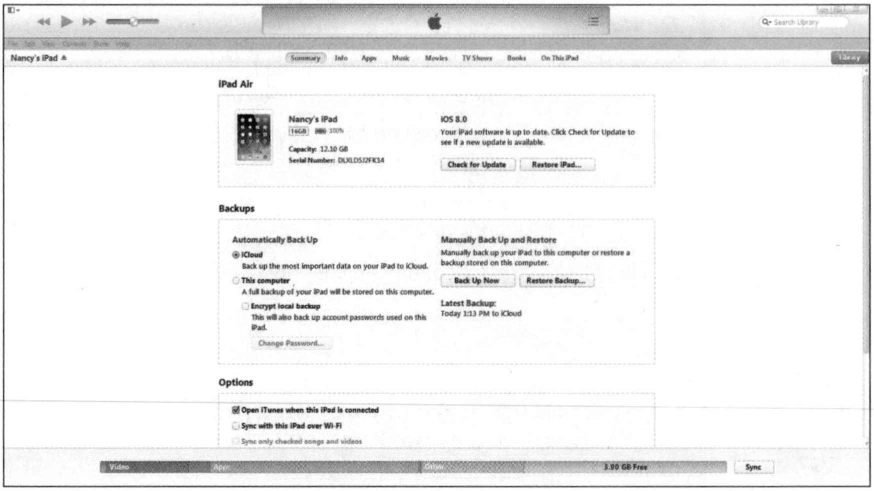

Figure 5-4: Syncing connects your computer and iPad so that you can share data.

4. **After syncing, unplug the Lightning to USB Cable from your iPad and your computer.**

Syncing wirelessly

You can also use the iTunes Wi-Fi Sync setting to allow cordless syncing if you are within range of a Wi-Fi network that has a computer connected to it with iTunes installed.

Follow these steps to make Wi-Fi syncing settings:

1. **First, with your iPad connected to your computer and with iTunes open, on the Summary tab of iTunes, click Sync with this iPad over Wi-Fi and then click Apply.**

2. **On your iPad, Tap Settings⇨General⇨iTunes Wi-Fi Sync.**

3. **In the pane shown in Figure 5-5, tap Sync Now to sync with a computer connected to the same Wi-Fi network.**

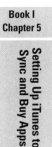

Figure 5-5: Set up your iPad to sync using the nearest Wi-Fi network.

Understanding iCloud

You have an alternative to syncing content by using iTunes. iCloud is a service that allows you to back up all your content and certain settings, such as bookmarks, to online storage. (However, note that some content, such as videos, aren't backed up, so consider an occasional backup of content to your computer or from your computer to an external storage device such as a USB stick, as well).That content and those settings are then pushed automatically to all your Apple devices through a wireless connection.

All you need to do is get an iCloud account, which is free, and then make settings on each device for which types of content you want to have pushed to each device. After you've done that, any content you create or purchase on one device — such as music, apps, books, and TV shows, as well as documents created in Apple's iWork apps, photos, and so on — can be synced among your devices automatically.

When you get an iCloud account, you get 5GB of free storage. If you want additional storage, you can buy an upgrade from one of your devices. In round numbers, 20GB is $12 a year; 200GB is $48 a year; 500 GB is $120 a year, and 1 terabyte is $240. Most people will do just fine with the free 5GB of storage. Note that items you've purchased from iTunes, which include any music such as ripped CDs that you've synced across devices using the iTunes Match service, don't count toward your data storage.

To upgrade your storage, go to iCloud in Settings, tap Storage, and then tap Buy More Storage. In the settings that appear, tap the amount you need and then tap Buy.

You can make settings for backing up your content to iCloud in the iCloud pane of Settings. You can have content backed up automatically, or you can back it up manually. See Chapter 9 in this minibook for more about this topic.

If you pay $24.99 a year for the iTunes Match service, you can sync a huge amount of audio content (up to 25,000 tracks) in your iTunes library to your devices, which may be a less expensive way to go than paying for added iCloud storage. Tap Match in iTunes or visit `www.apple.com/itunes/ itunes-match` for more information.

Getting an iCloud account

Before you can use iCloud, you need an iCloud account, which is tied to the Apple ID that you probably already have. You can turn on iCloud when first setting up your iPad or use Settings to sign up using your Apple ID. Follow these steps:

1. **When first setting up your iPad (except for an original iPad), tap Use iCloud in the sequence of screens that appears (see Figure 5-6).**

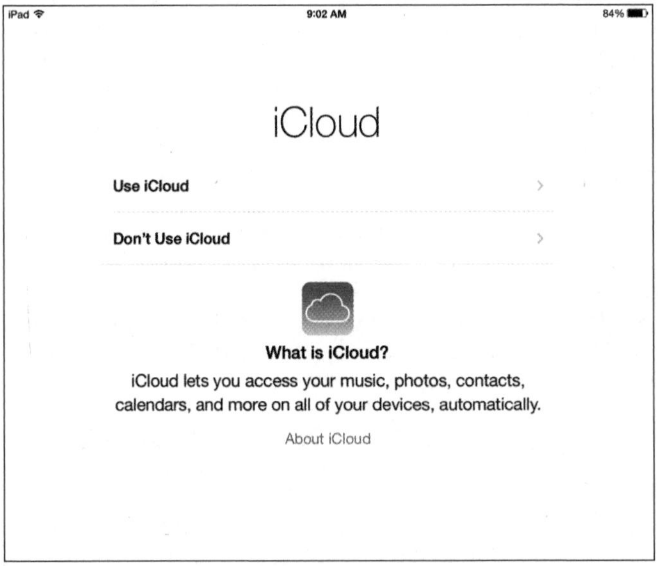

iPad 📶   9:02 AM   84% ▮

iCloud

Use iCloud   >

Don't Use iCloud   >

What is iCloud?
iCloud lets you access your music, photos, contacts, calendars, and more on all of your devices, automatically.

About iCloud

Figure 5-6: Set up iCloud while setting up your iPad.

2. **In the next screen, tap Back up to iCloud.**

   Your account is now set up based on the Apple ID you entered earlier in the setup sequence.

Here are the steps to set up iCloud backup on your iPad :

1. **Open the Settings app, tap iCloud, and then tap Backup.**

2. **In the next screen (see Figure 5-7), tap the On/Off switch to turn on iCloud Backup.**

   To perform a manual backup, tap Back Up Now.

   An alert may appear asking whether you want to allow iCloud to use the location of your iPad. Tap OK.

   Your account is now set up.

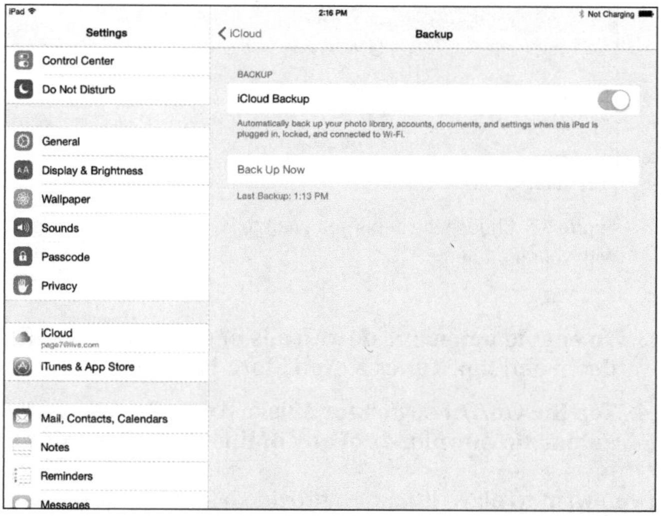

Figure 5-7: Tap the On/Off switch to turn on iCloud Backup.

Making iCloud sync settings

When you have an iCloud account up and running (see the preceding section), you have to specify which type of content should be synced with your iPad via iCloud. Note that content you purchase and download from the iTunes Store is synced among your devices automatically via iCloud. Follow these steps to specify the type of content to sync:

1. **Tap Settings and then tap iCloud.**

2. **In the iCloud settings, as shown in Figure 5-8, tap the On/Off switch for any item that's turned off that you want to turn on (or vice versa).**

You can sync Mail, Contacts, Calendars, Reminders, Safari, Notes, Photos, Passbook, Keychain (an app that stores all your passwords across all your Apple devices), Find My iPad, and iCloud Drive.

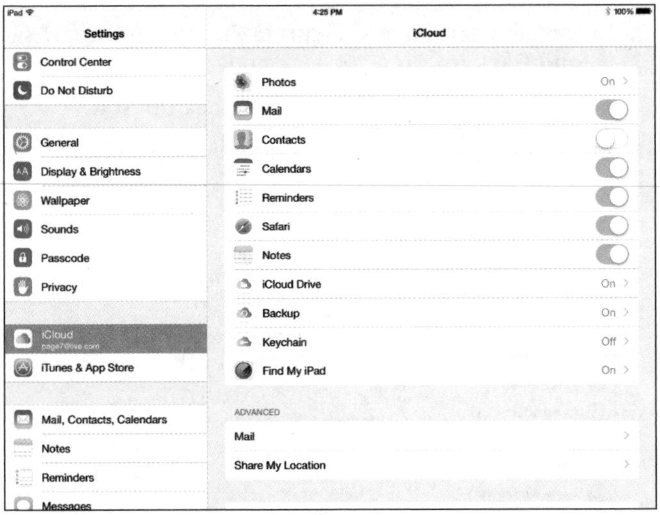

Figure 5-8: Choose the items you want to have synced over iCloud with your iPad here.

3. **To enable automatic downloads of music, apps, and books, scroll down and tap iTunes & App Store in Settings.**

4. **Tap the On/Off switch for Music, Apps, Books, or Updates to set up automatic downloads of any of this content to your iPad via iCloud.**

If you want to allow iCloud to provide a service for locating a lost or stolen iPad, tap the On/Off switch in the Find My iPad field to activate it. This service helps you locate, send a message to, or delete content from your iPad if it falls into other hands.

Buying Apps or Downloading Apps

Apps provide all kinds of functionality, from the ability to plan travel, manage finances, and find local restaurants and gas stations to hard-core business productivity and serious gaming fun. By buying and downloading apps, you can assemble a custom computing experience.

Most iPhone apps will work on your iPad, so if you own the trendy mobile phone and have favorite apps on it, you might want to use them on your iPad! Also, for more about my recommended apps, go to www.dummies.com/extras/ipadaio.

Searching the App Store

Apple isn't one to miss a profit opportunity, so naturally, one of the iPad built-in apps is the App Store. This is the apps portal that will get you to thousands of great apps for everything from games to bean counting.

If you want to get apps that aren't available in the App Store, you can join the estimated 4 million people who have done what's called *jailbreaking* to liberate their iPhones or iPads from the tyranny of getting apps solely through iTunes. Be forewarned that jailbreaking voids your iPad warranty, impedes your access to Apple updates, opens you up to the dangers of malware, and could even make it hard to download and use legitimate Apple-approved apps. A handful of jailbreaking tools cut down on the installation of malware, such as https://cydia.saurik.com/upgrading/. But again, for the average iPad user, I recommend avoiding jailbreaking.

Here's your quick introduction to using the App Store to obtain whatever apps your heart desires:

1. **Tap the App Store icon on your iPad Home screen.**

   The site shown in Figure 5-9 appears.

Figure 5-9: Viewing your purchased apps.

2. **At this point, you have several options for finding apps:**

- *Tap in the Search field,* enter a search term, and tap the Search button on the onscreen keyboard to see results.

- *Tap and swipe the screen* to scroll down to see more selections.

- *Tap the Categories button* at the top of the screen to see different categories of apps.

- *Tap the Top Charts button* at the bottom of the screen to see which free and paid apps other people are downloading most.

- Tap the Explore option to display apps in categories such as Great Free Games, Get Stuff Done, and Interactive Kids Stories. Tap a category to display apps that fit within it.

- *Tap the Popular Near Me button* at the top of the Explore view to display apps that are popular among people in or near your location. (This may or may not produce useful results, depending on where you are.)

- *Tap the Purchased button* to view apps you've already purchased, as shown in Figure 5-10. An item with a cloud symbol to the right of it means that you need to download it to use it.

- Tap the See All button in any category shown in the Featured view to view all the items in that category.

- In the Top Charts view, use the Paid, Free, and Top Grossing tabs to narrow down your search.

Figure 5-10: Viewing your purchased apps.

Getting apps from the App Store

Getting free apps or buying apps requires that you have an iTunes account, which I cover earlier in this chapter. After you have an account, you can use the saved payment information there to buy apps or download free apps. Follow these steps to get an app from the App Store:

1. **With the App Store open, tap the Search field, enter an app name (a free app that you might like to have is Netflix, for example, so I use that for these steps), and then tap the Search button on the onscreen keyboard.**

2. **Tap Netflix in the suggested search results that appear, as shown in Figure 5-11.**

Figure 5-11: Tap the app you need.

3. **In the app details, tap the price button (which in this case reads *Free*) for Netflix.**

   Note that to get a paid app, you'd tap the price button, which displays the cost of the app.

   The price button changes to read Install App (or in the case of a paid app, the button changes to read Buy App).

4. **Tap the Free (or price) button and then tap Install.**

   You may be asked to enter your iTunes password and tap the OK button to proceed. Note that an app with a cloud icon indicates one that you have already purchased but is not installed on your iPad; you can download it at no charge.

The app downloads and appears on a Home screen (probably your second Home screen if you haven't yet downloaded many apps). If you purchase an app that isn't free, at this point, your credit card is charged for the purchase price or your Store credit is reduced by the amount of purchase price.

Only preinstalled apps are located on the first iPad Home screen of your iPad by default, plus a few more such as Podcasts and iBooks on the second Home screen. Apps you download are placed on additional Home screens, and you have to scroll to view and use them. See the next section for help in finding your newly downloaded apps using multiple Home screens.

If you've opened an iCloud account, any iOS app that you purchase on your iPad can be set up to automatically be pushed to other Apple iOS devices. See earlier sections in this chapter for more about iCloud.

If you're a road warrior, you'll be glad to hear that the travel industry is all over apps to help you get around because the iPad is such a logical travel companion. Lonely Planet has released country guides for the iPad, and iPhone apps for travelers are being re-created for iPad. See Book III, Chapter 3 if you're someone who hits the road on a regular basis and wants to make the most of your iPad.

Organizing your apps

iPad can display up to 15 Home screens. By default, the first and part of the second contain preinstalled apps; other screens are created to contain any apps you download or sync to your iPad. At the bottom of any iPad Home screen (just above the Dock), dots indicate the number of Home screens, as shown in Figure 5-12.

Figure 5-12: Finding apps on the various iPad Home screens.

You can use some very nice features in iTunes to organize apps on your connected iPad, but you can also organize things right on the iPad using a few different methods.

Here's some advice on how to organize your apps:

1. **Tap the Home button to open the last displayed Home screen.**

2. **Flick your finger from right to left or tap either end of the Home screen dots to move to the next or previous Home screen.**

   Note that the dots near the bottom of the screen indicate which Home screen you're on. To move back, flick from left to right.

3. **To reorganize apps on a Home screen, press and hold any app on that page.**

   The app icons begin to jiggle, and any apps you installed will sport a Delete button (a gray circle with a black X on it (see Figure 5-13).

Figure 5-13: Move an app to another location on a Home screen.

4. **Press, hold, and drag an app icon to another location on the screen to move it.**

5. **Tap the Home button to stop all those icons from jiggling!**

To move an app from one page to another, while things are jiggling, you can press, hold, and drag an app to the left or right to move it to the next Home screen. You can also manage what app resides on what Home screen and in which folder from iTunes when you've connected iPad to iTunes via a cable or wireless sync, which may be easier for some.

You can also manage your apps from iTunes with your iPad connected using the settings on the Apps tab for that iPad. You can even reorder the Home screens there.

Press the Home button twice and you get a preview of open apps in the App Switcher. With iOS 8, you also get a row of recently used contacts with photos if the contact contains one. When you tap a contact, you then get options to call, message, or FaceTime call that person. Scroll among the apps and tap the one you want to go to. The App Switcher also allows you to swipe to move an app upward, out of this preview list, and stop it from running.

Organizing apps in folders

iPad lets you organize apps in folders so that you can find apps more easily. When you've populated a folder, you can flick it to open the folder and see all the apps in it. The process is simple. For iPad, follow these steps to get more organized:

1. **Tap and hold an app till all apps do their jiggle dance.**

2. **Drag one app on top of another app.**

   The two apps appear in a box with a placeholder name in a strip above them. (See Figure 5-14.)

Figure 5-14: Collect apps in folders to help you save Home screen space.

3. **To delete the placeholder name and change the folder name, tap in the field above the box.**

   The placeholder text is deleted, and the keyboard appears.

4. **Tap the Delete key to delete the placeholder name and then type one of your own.**

   If you change your mind and want to put the app back on the Home screen, you can easily drag it out of the folder.

5. **Tap anywhere outside the bar to save the name.**

6. **Tap the Home button to stop all that jiggling!**

   The folder appears on the Home screen where you began this process.

To get to the items stored in your folder, just double-tap it.

Deleting apps you no longer need

Not all apps are endlessly entertaining or useful. When you no longer need an app you have installed, it's time to get rid of it to save some space on your iPad. (Note, however, that you can't delete apps that were preinstalled on the iPad such as Notes, Calendar, or Photos.) If you use iCloud to push content across all Apple iOS devices, note that deleting an app on your iPad won't affect that app on other devices.

To send an app on its way, do this:

1. **Display the Home screen that contains the app you want to delete.**

2. **Press and hold the app until all apps begin to jiggle.**

3. **Tap the Delete button for the app you want to delete.**

4. **In the confirmation dialog, as shown in Figure 5-15, tap Delete to proceed with the deletion.**

5. **Tap the Rate button to rate the app or No Thanks to opt out of the survey.**

   If you have several apps to delete, you can delete them by using iTunes when your iPad is connected to your computer, making the process a bit more streamlined.

   Don't worry about wiping out several apps at one time by deleting a folder. You can't delete full folders, only individual apps within them.

Figure 5-15: Tap Cancel if you have regrets; otherwise, tap Delete to send the app on its way.

Updating apps

App developers update their apps all the time to fix problems or add new features, so you might want to check for those updates. The App Store icon on the Home screen displays the number of available updates in a red circle. Tap the App Store icon when you have some apps with updates ready.

Now you can proceed with these steps to update your apps:

1. **Tap the Updates button to access the Updates screen (see Figure 5-16) and then tap any item you want to update.**

   To update all, tap the Update All button. Note that if you have Family Sharing turned on, there will be a folder titled Family Purchases that you can tap to display apps that are shared across your family's devices. To update all of those, tap each one's Update All button.

2. **If you choose the Updates button in Step 1, in the app screen that appears, tap Update.**

   You may be asked to confirm that you want to update, or to enter your Apple ID password and then tap OK to proceed. You may also be asked to confirm that you are over a certain age or agree to terms and conditions; if so, scroll down the Terms form (reading all items as you go, of course) and at the bottom, tap Agree.

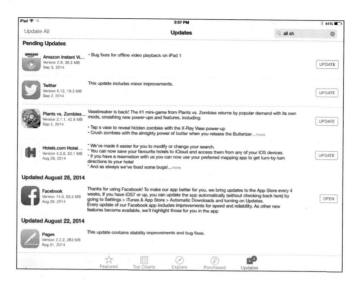

Figure 5-16: Choose what you want to update here.

You can download multiple apps at one time. If you choose more than one app to update instead of downloading them sequentially, all items are downloaded simultaneously. You can keep working in the App Store after you've initiated a download.

If you have an iCloud account and update an app on your iPad, it's also updated on any other Apple iOS devices automatically via an Internet connection. Apps updated on your other devices are also updated on your iPad if you enable automatic updates on the iPad, as explained earlier in this chapter.

Chapter 6: Browsing the Web

In This Chapter

- Discovering Safari
- Creating and using bookmarks
- Using Safari Reading List and Reader
- Saving web clips to the Home screen
- Adding an image to your Photo Library
- Emailing a link to a website
- Making private browsing and cookie settings
- Posting photos and printing from Safari
- Using iCloud tabs

Getting on the Internet with your iPad is easy using its Wi-Fi or 3G/4G capabilities. After you're online, the preinstalled browser, Safari, can take you all around the web. Safari will be familiar to you if you've used an Apple device before or the browser on your Mac or PC. On iPad, you're actually using a hybrid of the mobile version of Safari, also used on iPhone and iPod touch, and the desktop Safari.

If you've never used Safari, this chapter helps you get up to speed quickly. In this chapter, you discover how to open Safari and navigate among web pages using tabbed browsing, as well as how to use iCloud tabs to share your browsing history among devices. Along the way, you learn about All Tabs view, a version of which has been available in iPhone and now comes to the iPad. All Tabs view lets you view all your open web pages as thumbnails.

You see how to place a bookmark for a favorite site or web clip on your Home screen. You can also view your browsing history, save online images to your Photo Library, post photos to sites from within Safari, and email a hotlink to a friend. Two useful Safari features are Shared Links to see URLs posted to your Twitter timeline and iCloud Keychain, used for storing passwords and credit card information in one handy, safe place online. You explore the Safari Reader and Safari Reading List features, including the ability to save links and web pages to Reading List, and find out how to keep yourself safer while online using private browsing. I also show you the simple steps involved in printing what you find online.

Exploring Safari

If you need to know how to connect to the Internet, see Chapter 5 in this minibook. After you're connected, you're ready to browse with Safari.

If you've used Safari before, you'll notice a major difference in how it works on your iPad. It offers all the typical browser tools, but an important iPad feature is the use of gestures on the touchscreen to manipulate pages and navigate the web.

Though Safari is a fine browser, you aren't limited to it. You can download other browsers to iPad, such as Google Chrome, Atomic Web Browser, and Safe. Check out the App Store for the latest available browsers.

Try the following steps to practice using Safari:

1. **After you're connected to a network, tap the Safari icon on the Home screen.**

   Safari opens, probably displaying the Apple Home page the first time you go online. (See Figure 6-1.)

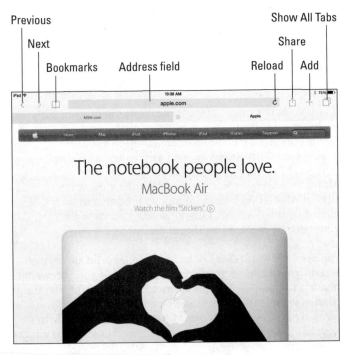

Figure 6-1: These tools will be familiar to you from almost any browser you may have used.

2. **Put two fingers together on the screen and swipe outward to enlarge the view, as shown in Figure 6-2.**

Figure 6-2: Enlarge the screen so that you can read the fine print.

3. **Double-tap the screen with a single finger to restore the default screen size.**

Using the pinch method (see Chapter 2 in this minibook) allows you to enlarge or reduce the screen to various sizes, giving you more flexibility and control than the double-tap method.

4. **Put your finger on the screen and flick upward to scroll down the page.**

5. **To return to the top of the web page, put your finger on the screen and drag downward, or tap the status bar at the top of the screen.**

When you enlarge the display, you gain more control using two fingers to drag from left to right or from top to bottom on the screen. On a reduced display, one finger works fine for making these gestures.

Navigating among web pages

I expect that you have entered URLs and used the Forward and Back buttons in a browser to navigate around the web. However, the iPad's onscreen keyboard differs slightly from a standard keyboard, and it might help you to run through how you navigate with the mobile version of Safari.

Follow these steps for a bit of navigating practice:

1. **With Safari open, tap in the Address/Search field.**

The onscreen keyboard appears, as shown in Figure 6-3.

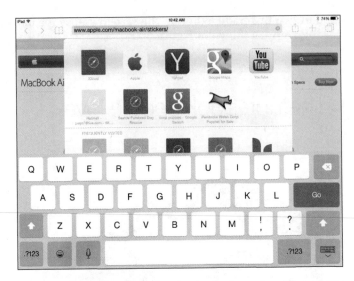

Figure 6-3: This keyboard requires you to do a few unique things to use numbers and symbols.

2. **To clear the field, press the Delete key on the keyboard. Enter a web address, using the .com key to make entry faster.**

Hold down the .com key to access options like `.edu`, `.gov`, and `.net`. If you have no website in mind, go to this book's companion site, `www.ipadmadeclear.com`.

3. **Tap the Go key on the keyboard (refer to Figure 6-3).**

The website appears.

- If, for some reason, a page doesn't display, tap the Reload icon at the end of the Address/Search field.

- If Safari is loading a web page and you change your mind about viewing the page, you can tap the Cancel icon (the *X*) that appears at the end of the Address/Search field during this process to stop loading the page.

4. **Tap the Back button to go to the last page Safari displayed.**

5. **Tap the Forward button to go forward to the page you came from when you tapped Previous.**

6. **To follow a link to another web page, tap the link with your finger.**

To view the destination web address of the link before you tap it, just touch and hold the link, and a menu appears that displays the address at the top, as shown in Figure 6-4.

Figure 6-4: You can open a link in a new page using this menu.

With iOS 8, Apple has added QuickType to support predictive text in the onscreen keyboard. This feature adds the ability for iPad to spot what you probably intend to type from text you've already entered and make a suggestion to save you time typing.

 ✔ **HandBrake:** www.handbrake.fr

 ✔ **SWF to Video Scout:** http://bytescout.com/?q=/products/enduser/swftovideoscout/swftovideoscout.html

Using tabbed browsing

Safari includes a feature called *tabbed browsing,* which allows you to have several web pages open at one time on separate tabs so that you can move easily among those sites. You may have used tabbed browsing in other popular browsers, such as the desktop version of Safari, Internet Explorer, Google Chrome, or Mozilla Firefox. This is a handy feature of Safari that's worth exploring.

To add a tab, follow these steps:

1. **With Safari open, tap the Add button (shaped like a + symbol) near the upper-right corner of the screen (refer to Figure 6-1).**

   A new tab opens with a list of your saved Favorites (see how to save Favorites later in this chapter), the Address/Search field becomes active, and the onscreen keyboard appears (see Figure 6-5).

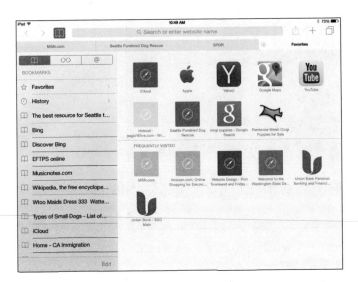

Figure 6-5: Here's where you can enter the address for the new tab you created.

2. **To add a new page (meaning that you're opening a new website), tap one of the Favorites or frequently used sites displayed (refer to Figure 6-5) or tap in the address bar that appears, enter a website address, and then tap the Go key.**

   Note that you can get to the same new page by simply tapping in the address bar from any site.

   The site opens.

3. **Switch among open sites by tapping another tab, or tap the Show All Tabs button to see all open web pages.**

   If you tap Show All Tabs, you can then tap a page to go to it or tap Done to close the All Tabs view.

4. **To close a tab, scroll to locate the tab and then tap the Close button in the upper-left corner of the tab.**

Using tabbed browsing, you can not only place a site on a tab but also place a search results screen on a tab. If you recently searched for something, those search results will be on your Recent Searches list. Also, if you're displaying a search results page when you tap the plus (+) button to add a tab, the first ten suggested sites in the results will be listed there for you to choose from.

Viewing browsing history

As you know, when you move around the web, your browser keeps a record of your browsing history. This record can be handy when you visit a site that you want to view again but whose address you've forgotten. (We've all done it.) On your iPad, you use the Bookmarks popover to get to your history.

Follow these steps to browse your browsing history:

1. **With Safari open, tap Bookmarks.**

2. **In the popover that appears, as shown in Figure 6-6, tap the Bookmarks tab.**

   Alternatively, tap and hold the Back button in Safari to quickly display a list of your browsing history.

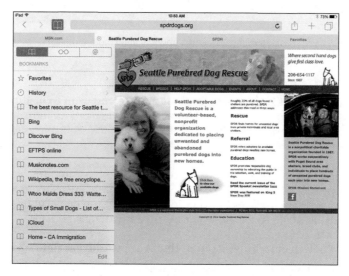

Figure 6-6: In addition to bookmarks, this menu is your gateway to your browsing history.

3. **In the Bookmarks list that appears (see Figure 6-7), tap a site to navigate to it.**

To clear the history, tap the Clear button in the bottom-right corner (see Figure 6-7). This button is useful when you don't want your spouse or children to see where you've been browsing for birthday or holiday presents!

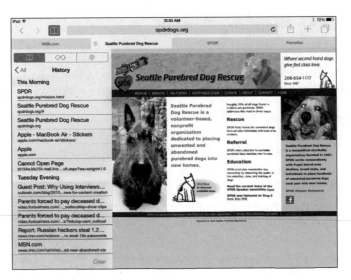

Figure 6-7: Use your finger to scroll down to view more of this list.

Searching the web

If you don't know the address of the site you want to visit (or you want to do research on a topic or find information you need online), get acquainted with Safari's Search feature on the iPad. By default, Safari uses the Google search engine.

You can use Spotlight Search on your iPad to search the web without having opened Safari first. Also, with Siri, you simply speak a request, such as "Search the web for information on dogs." You can also use the On this Page results to go to a match on the currently displayed page.

1. **With Safari open, tap in the Search/Address field. (See Figure 6-8.)**

   The onscreen keyboard appears.

2. **Tap one of the suggested sites that appears in a list or enter a search word or phrase.**

   What you enter can be a topic or a web address.

3. **In the search results that are displayed, tap a link to visit that site.**

You can change your default search engine from Google to Bing, DuckDuckGo, or Yahoo!. In Settings, tap Safari and then tap Search Engine. Tap Yahoo!, DuckDuckGo, or Bing, and your default search engine is set.

You can browse for specific items such as images, videos, or news by tapping the corresponding link at the top of the Google results screen. Also, tap the More button in this list to see additional options to narrow your results, such as searching for books or shopping sources related to the subject.

Figure 6-8: Use Search to locate a word or phrase on any site.

Adding and Using Bookmarks

Bookmarks, which you have probably used in other browsers, are a way to save sites that you visit often so that you can easily go to them again. Follow these steps to add bookmarks:

1. **With a site displayed that you want to bookmark, tap the Share button.**

2. **On the popover that appears (see Figure 6-9), tap Add Bookmark.**

3. **In the Add Bookmark dialog, as shown in Figure 6-10, edit the name of the bookmark (if you want) by tapping the name of the site and using the onscreen keyboard to edit that name.**

4. **Tap Location and choose whether to save this page to Favorites or Bookmarks.**

   Favorites is the default option, which displays this site in the Favorites list in the search suggestions.

5. **Tap the Save button.**

6. **To go to the bookmark, tap Bookmarks and then tap the History tab.**

7. **On the History list that appears (see Figure 6-11), tap the bookmarked site you want to visit.**

   If you want to save a web location to your desktop, read "Adding Web Clips to the Home Screen," later in this chapter.

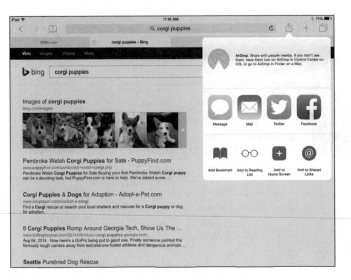

Figure 6-9: Choose to add a bookmark in this menu.

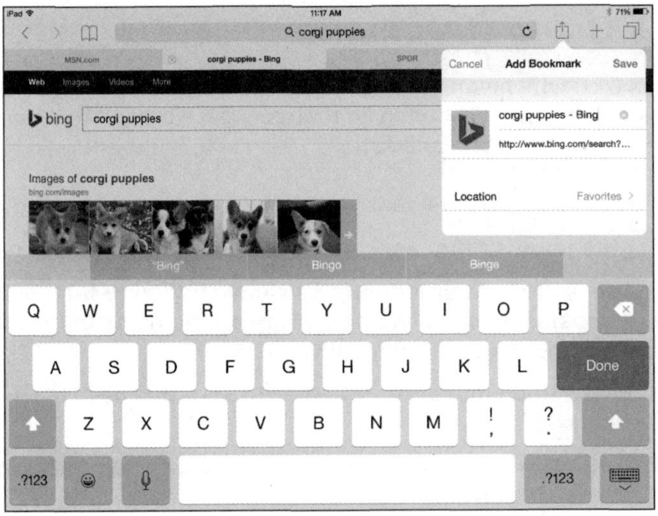

Figure 6-10: Give your bookmark a name that makes sense to you.

When you tap Bookmarks, you can tap Edit and then use the New Folder option to create folders to organize your bookmarks. First, turn on the Show Favorites Bar switch in Settings in the Safari pane. When you next add a bookmark, you can then choose, from the dialog that appears, to add the new bookmark to any folder by tapping Location.

Figure 6-11: Tap to go to a favorite bookmark.

Using Safari Reading List

Remember when you were in school and had lots of reading assignments to keep track of from all your classes? Well, after graduation, reading lists don't go away; whether you're staying up-to-date in your chosen field or just keeping up with the latest articles and information, being able to assemble a list of online reading can be a great help. The Safari Reading List provides a way to save content that you want to read at a later time so that you can easily visit it again.

You can save not only links to site pages but also the pages themselves, which allows you to read the content even when you're offline.

To use Reading List, follow these steps:

1. **With a site displayed that you want to add to your Reading List, tap the Share button.**

2. **On the menu that appears, tap Add to Reading List.**

   The site is added to your list.

3. **To view your Reading List, tap Bookmarks and then go to the Reading tab (the eyeglasses icon).**

4. **In the Reading List that appears (see Figure 6-12), tap the content you want to revisit and resume reading.**

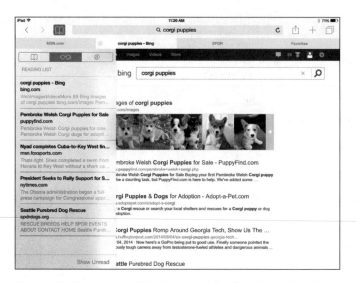

Figure 6-12: It's so easy to find where you left off reading with Safari's Reading List.

If you want to see both the Reading List material you've read and the material you haven't read, tap Show All near the bottom of the Reading List tab. To see just the material you haven't read, use the Show Unread button (refer to Figure 6-12). Be aware, however, that with websites that change content frequently, the content you placed on your Reading List may not be available at a later date.

To save an image on a web page to your Reading List, tap and hold the image until a menu appears, and then tap Add to Reading List (this is available only for some images).

To delete an item, with the Reading List displayed, swipe left or right, and the Delete button appears. Tap this button to delete the item from the Reading List.

Reading with Safari Reader

Reading content on the web isn't always user friendly. The ads, sidebars, and various distractions can take away from your reading experience. Happily, the Safari Reader feature gives you an e-reader type of experience right within your browser, removing other stories and links as well as those distracting advertisements. Not all websites support the Reader view.

1. **Tap the Reader button (see Figure 6-13) on the left side of the Search/ Address field when you're on a site where you're reading content such as an article that supports the Reader feature.**

The content appears in a reader format. (See Figure 6-14.)

Figure 6-13: The Reader button appears when the feature is available for the page you're viewing.

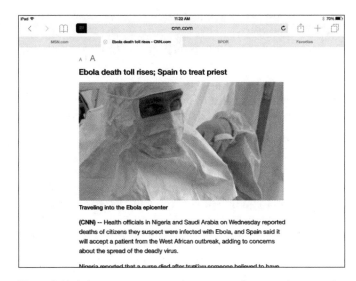

Figure 6-14: At last . . . an easy-on-the-eyes reading experience on the web!

2. **Scroll down the page.**

   The entire content is contained in this one long page.

3. When you finish reading the material, just tap the Reader button in the Search/Address field again to go back to the material's source.

If you're holding the iPad in landscape orientation, the Reader window doesn't fill the screen, and you can tap either side of the Reader window to go back to the source material.

If a video is contained in an article that you're perusing in Reader, it still appears with the standard Play button. Tap the button, and the video plays right within Reader.

When in a Reader screen, tap the small or large letter *A* at the top of the screen to adjust the font size for the article.

Adding Web Clips to the Home Screen

The Web Clips feature allows you to save a website as an icon on your Home screen so that you can go to the site at any time with one tap. You can then reorganize those icons just as you can reorganize apps icons. (See Chapter 2 in this minibook for information on organizing apps on Home screens.)

Here are the steps for adding web clips:

1. With Safari open and displaying the site you want to add, tap the Share button.

2. On the popover that appears (refer to Figure 6-9), tap Add to Home Screen.

3. In the Add to Home dialog that appears (see Figure 6-15), you can edit the name of the site to be more descriptive (if you like) by tapping the name of the site and using the onscreen keyboard to edit its name.

4. Tap the Add button.

The shortcut to the site is added to your Home screen.

You can have up to 15 Home screens on your iPad to accommodate the web clips and apps you download. You can also use folders to organize your web clips and save space on your Home screens. If you want to delete an item from your Home screen for any reason, press and hold any app on the Home screen until all items on the screen start to jiggle and Delete buttons appear on all items except preinstalled apps. Tap the Delete button on the item you want to delete, and it's gone. (To get rid of the jiggle, press the Home button.)

Figure 6-15: Give your web clip a descriptive name or use the site's URL.

Saving an Image to Your Photo Library

Have you found a photo that you like online? Maybe your BF's Facebook image or a picture of your upcoming vacation spot? You can easily save images you find online that are not protected from copying to the iPad Photos app library. Here's how:

1. **Display a web page that contains an image you want to copy.**

2. **Press and hold the image.**

   The menu in Figure 6-16 appears unless the website protects images from being copied.

3. **Tap the Save Image option (see Figure 6-16).**

   The image is saved to the Photo Library in the Photos app.

Be careful about copying images from the Internet and using them for business or promotional activities. Most images are copyrighted, and you may be violating that copyright if you use an image in (say) a brochure for your association or a flyer for your community group. Note that some search engines offer the option of browsing only for images that aren't copyrighted.

Figure 6-16: Quickly saving an online image into Photos.

Posting photos and printing from Safari

You can post photos on your iPad to sites such as eBay, Craigslist, or Facebook from within Safari. Follow these steps (to follow this example, download the Facebook for iPad app and create a Facebook account, if you haven't already):

1. **Go to Facebook and sign in.**

2. **Click an Add Photos/Video, Upload, or similar link, like the one shown in Figure 6-17.**

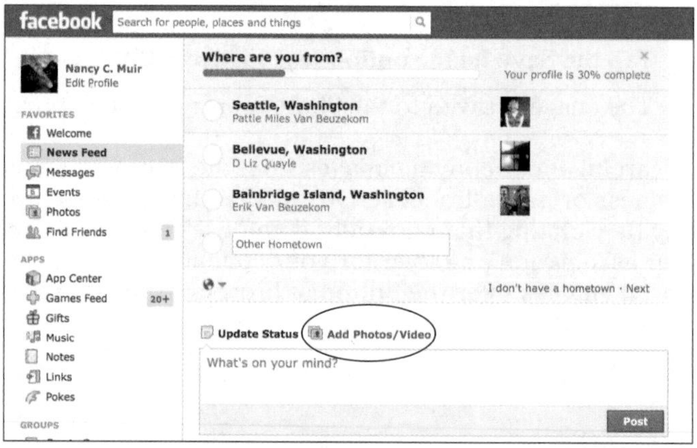

Figure 6-17: Posting photos without leaving Safari is so convenient!

3. **Tap a photo source such as Recently Added, and then tap the photo or video you want to post (see Figure 6-18).**

Figure 6-18: Find that great shot of Uncle Ernie or the Grand Canyon right here.

4. **Tap Post or Upload, depending on what the site uses, to post the photo or video.**

Sending a Link

If you find a great site that you want to share, you can do so easily by sending a link in an email; just follow these steps:

1. **With Safari open and the site you want to share displayed, tap the Share button.**

2. **On the popover that appears (refer to Figure 6-9), tap Mail.**

3. **In the message form that appears, which contains the link (see Figure 6-19), enter a recipient's email address, a subject, and your message.**

4. **Tap Send.**

   The email goes on its way.

The email is sent from the default email account that you've set up on your iPad. For more about setting up an email account, see Chapter 7 in this minibook.

Cancel	**Video - Breaking News Videos from CNN.com**	Send

To: ▓▓▓▓▓▓▓ ⊕

Cc/Bcc, From: ▓▓▓▓▓▓▓

Subject: Video - Breaking News Videos from CNN.com

http://www.cnn.com/video/standard.html?/video/bestoftv/2013/08/28/vo-mxp-topless-reporter-interviews-mayor.cnn&iref=obnetwork

Sent from my iPad

Figure 6-19: Use this simple email form to send an image and message.

When entering a user name or password in any online form, such as an email message or Search field, you can take advantage of Safari's AutoFill feature. Turn this on by going to Settings and tapping Safari. Safari can then use information from iPad's Contacts app as well as remember names and passwords that you've entered before to offer options for completing text entries as you type.

To tweet the link using your Twitter account, in Step 2 of the preceding steps, choose Tweet, enter your tweet message in the form that appears, and then tap Send. For more about using Twitter with the iPad, see Book II, Chapter 5. If you have a fourth-generation or newer iPad, you can also choose AirDrop in the same menu to share with someone in your immediate vicinity who has an AirDrop-enabled device.

A four-finger swipe from right to left on your screen gets you back to Safari from either Mail or Twitter.

Making Private Browsing and Cookie Settings

Apple has provided some privacy settings for Safari that you should consider using. Private Browsing automatically removes items from the download list, stops Safari from using AutoFill to save information used to complete your entries in the Address/Search field as you type, and erases some browsing history information. These features can keep your online activities more private. The Accept Cookies setting allows you to stop the downloading of *cookies* (small files that document your browsing history so that you can be recognized by a site the next time you go to or move within that site) to your iPad.

You can control both settings by choosing Safari in Settings. Tap to turn the Do Not Track feature on or off (see Figure 6-20). Tap the arrow next to Block Cookies and choose to never save cookies, always save cookies, or save cookies only from the current website or visited third-party and advertiser sites (the default setting).

Settings	Safari	
iCloud	GENERAL	
iTunes & App Store	Passwords & AutoFill	>
	Favorites	Favorites >
Mail, Contacts, Calendars	Open New Tabs in Background	
Notes	Show Favorites Bar	
Reminders	Show Tab Bar	
Messages	Block Pop-ups	
FaceTime	PRIVACY & SECURITY	
Maps	Do Not Track	
Safari	Block Cookies	Allow from Websites I Visit >
Music	Fraudulent Website Warning	
Videos	About Safari & Privacy...	
Photos & Camera	Clear History and Website Data	
iBooks	Advanced	>
Podcasts		

Figure 6-20: Protect your private information and activities from prying eyes with these settings.

You can also use the Clear History and the Website Data setting to clear your browsing history, saved cookies, and other data manually (refer to Figure 6-20).

Printing from Safari

If you have a wireless printer that supports the Apple AirPrint technology (most major manufacturers such as HP, Epson, Lexmark, Canon, and Brother offer at least one AirPrint model at this point), you can print web content using a wireless connection. Here's how:

1. **With Safari open and the site you want to print displayed, tap the Share button.**

2. **On the popover that appears, scroll to the right on the bottom list of buttons and then tap Print.**

3. **In the Printer Options dialog that appears (see Figure 6-21), tap Select Printer.**

4. **In the list of printers that appears, tap the name of your wireless printer.**

5. **If you need more than one copy, tap either the plus or minus button in the Copy field to adjust the number of copies to print.**

   The default is set to print one copy, so you can skip this step if you don't need more. If you have a printer capable of two-sided printing you can tap the Double-Sided switch.

6. **Tap Print to print the displayed page.**

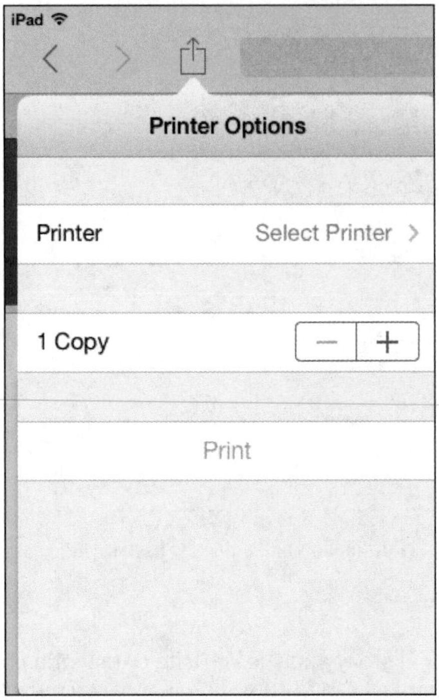

iPad 🖥

Printer Options

Printer | Select Printer >

1 Copy | − | +

Print

Figure 6-21: Print directly from your iPad if you have a compatible wireless printer.

The Mac applications Printopia and HandyPrint make any shared or network printer on your home network visible to your iPad. Printopia has more features but will cost you, whereas HandyPrint is free. A still better option is an xPrintServer because it can use AirPrint to print to all printers on your network and lets you attach a USB printer.

If you don't have an AirPrint–compatible wireless printer or don't wish to use an app to help you print wirelessly, just email a link to the web page to yourself, open the link on your computer, and print from there.

Understanding iCloud Tabs

iCloud Tabs were new with iOS 6.0. What this feature allows you to do is to access all browsing history among your different devices from any device. If you begin to research a project on your iPad before you leave home, for instance, you can then pick up where you left off as you sit in a waiting room with your iPhone.

Follow these steps to use iCloud Tabs:

1. **Check to make sure that both devices are using the same iCloud account by going to Settings⇨iCloud and checking the account name.**

2. **In Settings, tap Safari and make sure that Do Not Track is turned off; this setting allows sharing to take place among devices.**

3. **Open Safari on your iPad and click the Show All Tabs button in the upper-right corner.**

4. **Tap another device.**

   All items in your other device's browsing history are displayed (see Figure 6-22).

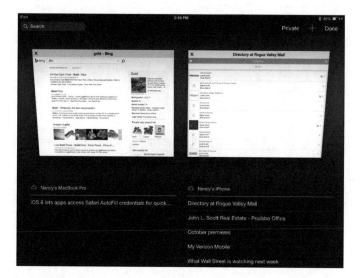

Figure 6-22: Pick up where you left off on another device using iCloud Tabs.

Chapter 7: Working with Email in Mail

In This Chapter

✓ Adding an iCloud, Gmail, Yahoo!, Outlook, or AOL account

✓ Setting up a POP3 email account

✓ Opening Mail and reading messages

✓ Formatting, searching, printing, deleting, and organizing your email

✓ Setting up a VIP list

*W*hat use would an iPad be if you couldn't stay in touch with your friends online? You can access an existing email account using the handy Mail app supplied with your iPad, or you can sign into your email account using the Safari browser. Using Mail involves adding one or more existing email accounts using iPad Settings. Then you can use Mail to write, format, retrieve, and forward messages from any email accounts you added to iPad.

Mail offers the capability to mark the messages you've read, delete messages, and organize your messages in folders, as well as use a handy Search feature. You can create a VIP list so that you are notified when that special person sends you an email.

A few new features for Mail arrived with iOS 8, including a feature that makes jumping between a draft email and other messages in your Inbox possible, as well as the ability to quickly swipe to mark an email as read or flag it for future action.

In this chapter, you find out about Mail and its various features.

If you're wondering about IM (instant messaging) and iPad, check out Book II, Chapter 5 to discover the IM app, Messages.

Adding an Account

To use the Mail app to access email on iPad, you first have to make settings for an existing email account on your iPad. You can add one or more email accounts using iPad Settings, including any email account that you've associated with an iCloud account. If you set up multiple accounts, you can then switch between accounts by tapping an account name in the upper-left corner of the displayed inbox and then tapping Accounts and choosing which account to display. Or you can use the consolidated inbox and check your mail from all active accounts on one page.

If you have an iCloud, Microsoft Exchange (mostly used for business accounts), Gmail, Yahoo!, Outlook (this includes Microsoft accounts from Live, Hotmail, and so on), or AOL account, iPad pretty much automates the setup. Here are the steps to get you going with any of these email providers:

1. **Tap Settings on the Home screen.**

2. **In Settings, tap Mail, Contacts, Calendars.**

   The settings shown in Figure 7-1 appear.

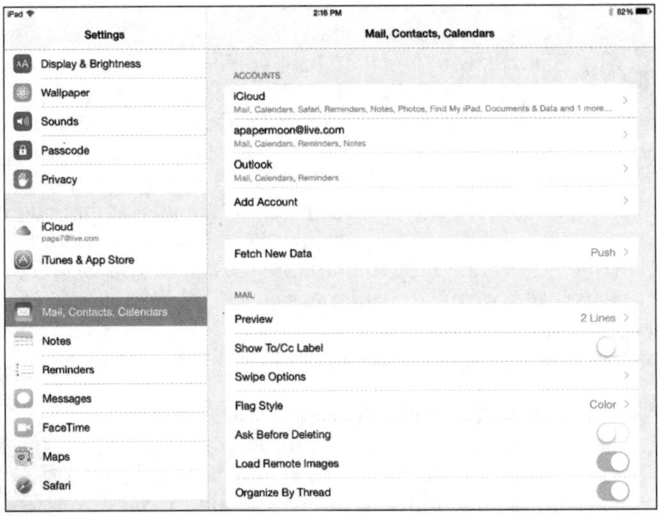

Figure 7-1: Mail settings allow you to set up multiple email accounts.

3. **Tap Add Account.**

   The options shown in Figure 7-2 appear.

4. **Tap iCloud, Exchange, Gmail, Yahoo!, AOL, or Outlook.com and then enter your account information in the form that appears (a description is optional). (See Figure 7-3.)**

5. **Tap Next.**

6. **After iPad takes a moment to verify your account information, tap any On/Off switch to have Mail, Contacts, Calendars, Notes, and/or Reminders services for that account synced with iPad.**

iCloud and Exchange support syncing all five services. Google supports all but Reminders. Other email account support is usually limited to Mail or to Mail and Notes.

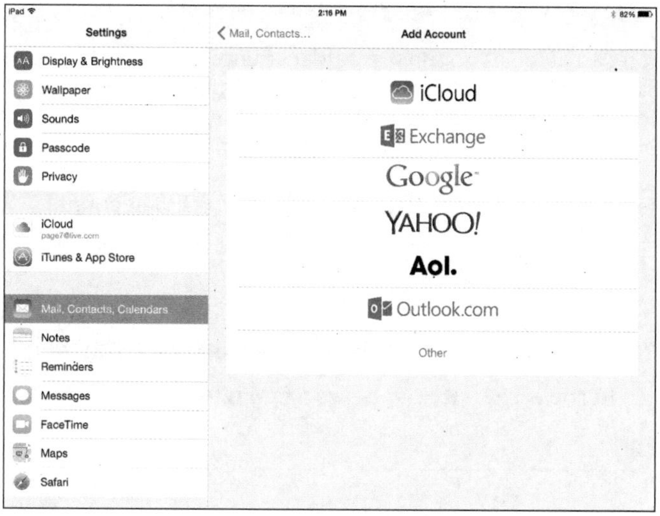

Figure 7-2: Choosing built-in email providers is a quick way to get set up, if you have an account with one.

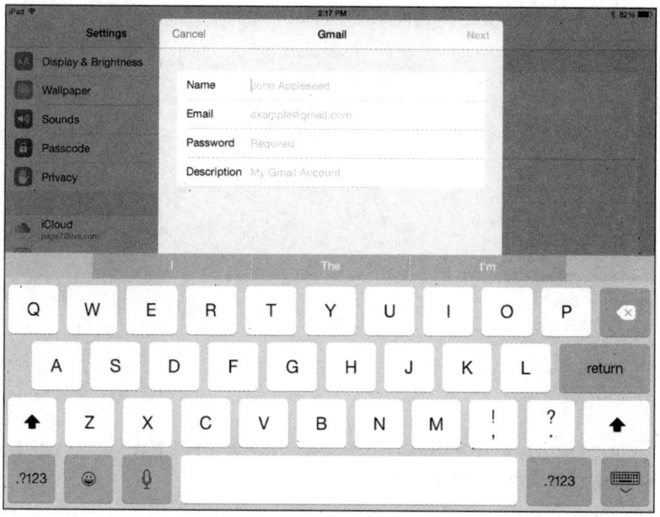

Figure 7-3: Enter your name, email address, and password, and the iPad finds your settings for you.

7. **When you're done, tap Save.**

   The account is saved, and you can now open it using Mail.

Setting Up a POP3 Email Account

You can also set up most email accounts, such as those available through EarthLink or a cable provider, by obtaining the host name from the provider. To set up an existing account with a provider other than Gmail, Yahoo!, Outlook.com, or AOL, you have to enter the account settings yourself.

Follow these steps to set up an IMAP or POP3 account:

1. **Tap Settings on the Home screen.**
2. **In Settings, tap Mail, Contacts, Calendars and then tap Add Account.**
3. **In the settings that appear (refer to Figure 7-2), tap Other.**
4. **In the screen that appears (see Figure 7-4), tap Add Mail Account.**

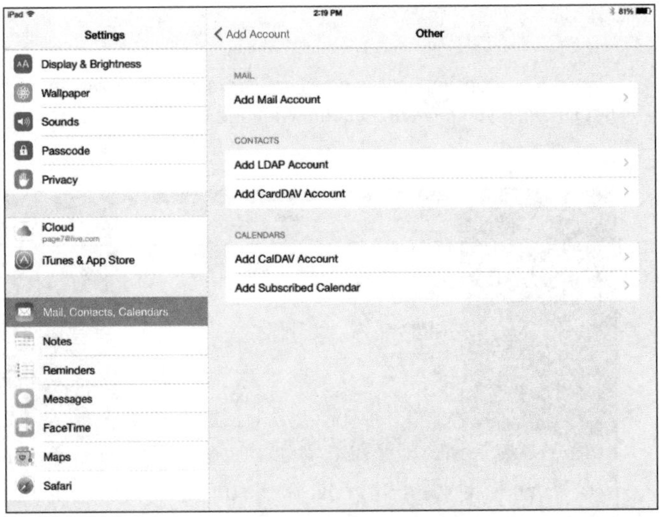

Figure 7-4: Proceed by choosing to add an email account in these settings.

5. **In the next form, enter your name and the account address, password, and description, and tap Next.**

   The iPad takes a moment to verify your account and then returns you to the Mail, Contacts, Calendars pane with your new account displayed.

Your iPad will probably add the outgoing mail server information for you, but if it doesn't, tap SMTP and enter this information.

6. Tap Done.

You can now access the account through the Mail app.

You can have more than one active account set to On for receiving email; tap the account name in Settings. When you do, you can then open different accounts to view their inboxes from within the Mail app. If you don't want a particular account's emails to be downloaded, you can turn off any active email account by opening it in Settings and tapping the On/Off switch.

If you turn on Calendars in the Mail account settings, any information you've put into your calendar in that email account is brought over into the Calendar app on your iPad and reflected in the Notification Center (discussed in more detail in Book V, Chapter 4).

Opening Mail and Reading Messages

The whole point of email is to send and receive messages. Mail offers a pretty simple interface for reading your email. It displays an open message and a pane that you can use to show inbox contents or change to a different folder. In landscape orientation, the Mailboxes/Inbox pane is always displayed, but in portrait orientation, you display it by tapping the Inbox button.

When you tap the Mail app to open it, it automatically heads out and checks for any new email. (If you use Microsoft Exchange or iCloud, you can turn on push settings to have your email host initiate a check for new messages to download them to your iPad.)

Here are some common actions in Mail:

- **To follow a link in a message,** simply tap it. Note that tapping web links opens them in Safari, and tapping address links opens the Maps app with a map to that address displayed. You can also tap phone number links to call that person, or tap flight code links to check on a flight's status in Safari.

- **To open an attachment,** tap it, and Mail presents you with a menu to select the one you want to use to open it.

- **To open a meeting invitation,** tap the meeting icon (what it looks like depends on the originating application; for example, Outlook.com uses a little calendar symbol).

iPad supports many common file types — including those that run on multiple platforms, such as PDF and text; those available on Macs, including iWork Pages and Numbers; those familiar to Windows users (though also available in Mac versions), including Microsoft Word and Excel; as well as most common graphics and audio file formats.

When your iPad gets an email, it alerts you with a little sound. If those email–received alerts are driving you nuts, you can go to Settings and, under Sounds, use the slider to lower the volume or tap the On/Off switch to turn off the chimes.

The following steps take you through the simple process of using Mail to open and read emails if you have a single email account set up on iPad:

1. **Tap the Mail app on the Home screen (see Figure 7-5), which displays the number of unread emails in your Inbox in a red circle.**

   If you have only one email account set up on your iPad, a list of messages displays (see Figure 7-6); skip to Step 3.

Figure 7-5: Without having to open Mail, you can see how many unread messages you have.

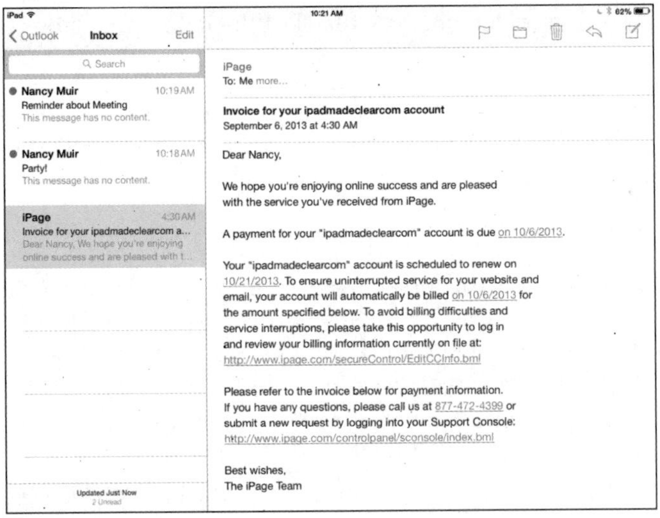

Figure 7-6: Open your inbox and view its contents.

2. **If the list doesn't display, tap the arrow with the name of the currently opened mailbox in the top-left corner (refer to Figure 7-6) to display a list of Inboxes. Tap the Inbox whose contents you want to display.**

3. **Tap a message to read it.**

The message opens, as shown in Figure 7-7.

Use gestures such as double-tapping and pinching to reduce or enlarge email.

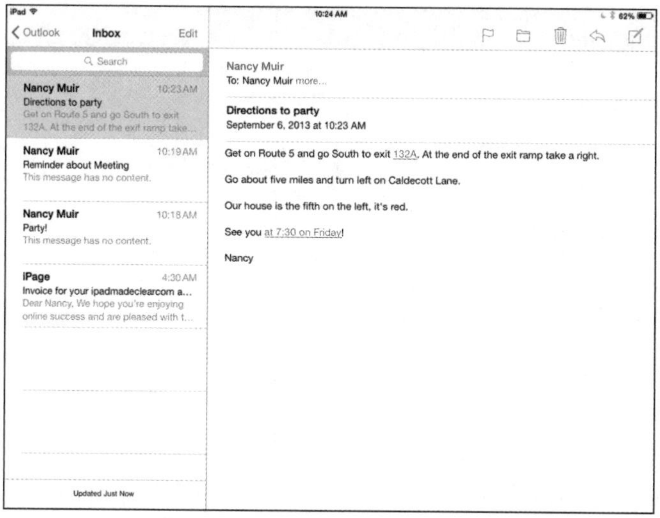

Figure 7-7: Open your email and read it.

4. **If you need to scroll to see the entire message, place your finger on the screen and flick upward to scroll down.**

You can swipe right while reading a message in portrait orientation to open the Inbox list of messages, and then swipe left to hide the list.

You can tap the Next or Previous button (top-left corner of the message in Portrait orientation) to move to the next or previous message.

If you have multiple email accounts set up, you can choose which inbox to display. From the inbox that appears when you open Mail, tap the Back button to view the list of your mailboxes (see Figure 7-8).

With several accounts set up, in addition to each account listed on the Mailboxes screen, an All Inboxes item is listed. Tapping this takes you to a consolidated Inbox containing all messages from all accounts in one place.

Email messages that you haven't read are marked with a blue circle in your inbox. After you read a message, the blue circle disappears. If you like, you can mark a read message as unread. This can help remind you to read it again later. With your messages displayed, swipe to the right on a message and then tap Mark as Unread.

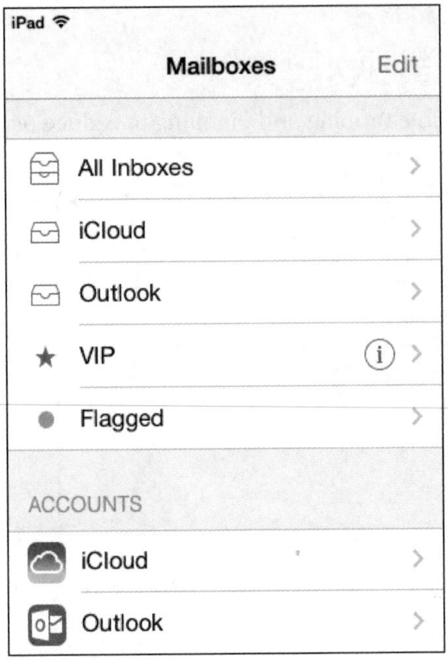

iPad 🔋

Mailboxes   Edit

📩 All Inboxes   >

📩 iCloud   >

📩 Outlook   >

★ VIP   ⓘ   >

● Flagged   >

ACCOUNTS

☁ iCloud   >

📧 Outlook   >

Figure 7-8: Mailboxes for various accounts and
the consolidated Inbox are listed here.

To escape your email now and then if you have a 3G or 4G model iPad, you
can stop retrieval of data including email by tapping Settings and then tapping Cellular and setting the Cellular Data switch to Off. Now you'll get data
on your device only if you're logged into a Wi-Fi network.

Replying to or forwarding email

Replying to or forwarding emails is pretty darn easy with iPad as well. In fact,
there's a handy button for replying or forwarding. There's also a Print command on this menu to make printing your emails to a compatible printer easy.

You can attach a photo or video to new email messages when you create
them by pressing in the message body and then tapping Insert Photo or
Video. You can also use features in apps such as Photos, Contacts, Notes,
iWork Pages, and Maps to share individual documents via email.

Here's how to use the simple Reply/Forward functions in iPad:

1. **With an email open (see the preceding section), tap the Reply button,
   as shown in Figure 7-9.**

   If you are the only recipient, there will be no Reply All option; if available,
   this option allows you to reply to the sender and all other recipients.

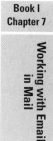

Figure 7-9: The Reply button sports a left-pointing arrow.

2. Do one of the following:

- *Tap Reply to respond to the message sender.* The reply message form shown in Figure 7-10 appears. Tap in the message body and jot down your inspired thoughts.

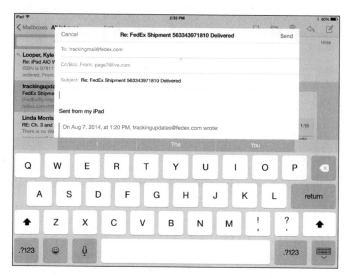

Figure 7-10: What you reply is up to you!

- *Tap Reply All to respond to the sender and all other recipients.* A message form appears with all those folks included in the To field. You can now add your response for all to see.

- *Tap Forward to send the message to somebody else.* If the email has an attachment, you can choose Include or Don't Include in the dialog that appears. The form in Figure 7-11 then appears. Enter a recipient in the To field; then tap in the message body and enter a message.

To find out how to print an email, see "Printing Emails," later in this chapter.

3. Tap Send.

The message is sent.

Figure 7-11: When you forward a message, all previous contents are included.

If you want to move an address from the To field to the Cc/Bcc field or vice versa, tap and hold the address and drag it to the other field.

Although you can choose whether to keep original attachments when *forwarding* an email, any attachments to the original email can't be included in a *reply*.

Creating and sending a new message

You're probably an old pro at creating and sending email messages, but it's worth a quick trip through the iPad's Mail feature and its approach to writing an email using the onscreen keyboard.

Note that, by default, your emails have a signature that says, "Sent from my iPad." This will definitely impress your geekiest friends, but if you want to change it to something a little more useful, just go to Settings. In the Mail section of the Mail, Contacts, Calendars settings, choose Signature. You can then enter any signature text you want. If you have multiple email accounts, Signature displays options to use the message for All Accounts or Per Account. If you choose Per Account, settings for each account appear so that you can specify unique signatures for each.

Follow these steps to create and send email:

1. **With Mail open, tap the New Message button.**

   A blank message form (see Figure 7-12) appears.

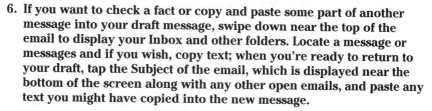

Figure 7-12: The very basic email message form.

2. **Enter a recipient's address in the To field either by typing it or by tapping the Dictation key on the iPad's onscreen keyboard (fourth-generation iPad and later) and speaking the address.**

    If you have saved addresses in Contacts, tap the plus sign (+) in an address field to choose an addressee from the Contacts list that appears.

3. **If you want to copy other people on the message, tap the Cc/Bcc field.**

   Both Cc and Bcc fields are displayed. Enter addresses in either or both. Use the Bcc field to specify recipients of blind carbon copies, which means that no other recipients are aware that that person received this reply.

4. **Enter a subject for the message in the Subject field.**

5. **Tap in the message body and type your message.**

6. **If you want to check a fact or copy and paste some part of another message into your draft message, swipe down near the top of the email to display your Inbox and other folders. Locate a message or messages and if you wish, copy text; when you're ready to return to your draft, tap the Subject of the email, which is displayed near the bottom of the screen along with any other open emails, and paste any text you might have copied into the new message.**

7. **Tap (you guessed it) Send.**

 You can also use Siri to address an email to a person for whom you've created a record in your Contacts app that includes an email address. Just press and hold the Home button and say something like "Email Joe Smith," confirm the contact, and then fill out the form that appears using either Dictation or the keyboard.

Want to shout at somebody in an email (not, of course, a practice I advocate)? You can activate Caps Lock when using the onscreen keyboard on your iPad by double-tapping either Shift key. To turn off Caps Lock, tap either Shift key once. To use this functionality, first be sure to tap Settings⇨General⇨Keyboard and enable Caps Lock.

Formatting Email

You can apply some basic formatting to email text. You can use bold, underline, and italic formats; also, you can indent text using the Quote Level feature. To use the Quote Level feature from within your emails, you need to first make sure that it's on. In Settings, tap Mail, Contacts, Calendars; next, tap Increase Quote Level and then tap the Increase Quote Level On/Off switch. This setting allows you to increase and decrease how forwarded or reply text is indented. Then follow these steps to apply formatting:

1. **Press and hold the text in a new or forwarded message and choose Select or Select All from the menu that appears to select a single word or all the words in the email.**

   Note that if you select a single word, handles appear that you can drag to add adjacent words to your selection.

2. **To apply bold, italic, or underline formatting, tap the BIU button (see Figure 7-13).**

Figure 7-13: Use BIU to add standard styles or emphasis, such as italicized book titles.

3. **In the pop-up that appears (see Figure 7-14), tap Bold, Italics, or Underline to apply the respective formatting.**

4. **To change the indent level, tap at the beginning of a line and then tap Quote Level (refer to Figure 7-13).**

5. **Tap Increase to indent the text or Decrease to move indented text farther toward the left margin.**

Figure 7-14: Choose the style that works for your message.

Searching Email

I'm sure you've never mislaid an email, but some people do it all the time. What if you want to find all messages from a certain person or that contain a certain word in the Subject field? Of course, you can enter a name or term into Spotlight Search, and results will include any emails that match the search term as well as contacts, songs, and so on. Or you can use Mail's handy Search feature to find that email. You can search To, From, and Subject fields.

Follow these steps to practice using Mail's Search feature:

1. **With Mail open, tap an account to display its Inbox.**

2. **In the Inbox, tap in the Search field.**

   The onscreen keyboard appears.

3. **Enter a search term or name, as shown in Figure 7-15.**

   Matching emails are listed in the results.

   If you have an email account set up to download messages to your device instead of accessing them from the mail server, you can use Mail to search the entire contents of the messages in that account.

To start a new search, tap the Delete key in the upper-right corner of the onscreen keyboard to delete the term, or tap the Cancel button next to the Search field.

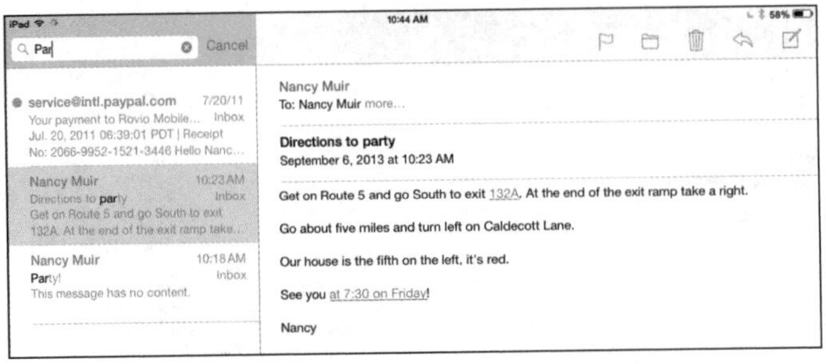

Figure 7-15: Tapping in the Search Inbox field opens the onscreen keyboard.

 You can also use the Spotlight Search feature covered in Book I, Chapter 2 to search for terms in the To, From, or Subject lines of mail messages from this search feature that searches several apps.

Mark Email as Unread or Flag for Follow-Up

With a new feature in iOS 8, you can use a simple swipe to access tools that either mark an email as unread after you've read it, which places a blue dot before the message, or flag an email, which places an orange circle before it. These methods help you to remember to reread an email that you've already read or to follow up on a message at a later time.

1. **With Mail open and an Inbox displayed, swipe to the left to display three options: More, Flag, and Trash. Note that you should swipe only about halfway across the message; swiping all the way to the left deletes the message.**

2. **Tap More.**

   On the menu shown in Figure 7-16, you're given several options, including Mark as Unread and Flag. Tapping either command applies it and returns you to your Inbox.

3. **Tap Mark as Unread.**

   Note that you can also get to the Mark as Unread command by swiping to the right on a message displayed in your Inbox.

4. **Swipe to the left on another email and then tap Flag.**

   An orange circle appears before the email.

 You can either mark an email as unread or flag it; you can't do both. Either action provides a unique visual clue indicating that you need to revisit this message before deleting it.

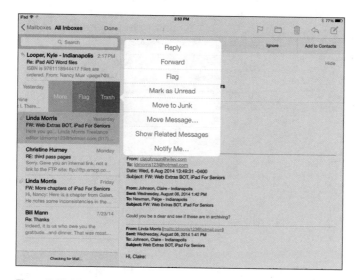

Figure 7-16: More options are offered for managing your email.

TIP

In the menu shown in Figure 7-16, you can also select Notify Me. This option causes Mail to notify you whenever somebody replies to this email thread.

Create an Event from Email Contents

Invitations sent to you in email that you accept have always been placed in the Calendar app automatically. In addition, Mail will create a Calendar event from certain information contained within an email such as a flight reservation.

To check this feature out, follow these steps:

1. **Create an email to yourself mentioning a reservation on a specific airline on a specific date and time.**

   You can also mention another type of reservation, such as for dinner, or even just a phone number.

2. **Send the message to yourself and then open Mail.**

3. **In your Inbox, open the email. Note that pertinent information is displayed in blue, underlined text.**

4. **Tap some underlined text; in the menu shown in Figure 7-17, choose Create Event.**

   A New Event form from Calendar appears.

5. **Enter additional information about the event and then tap Done.**

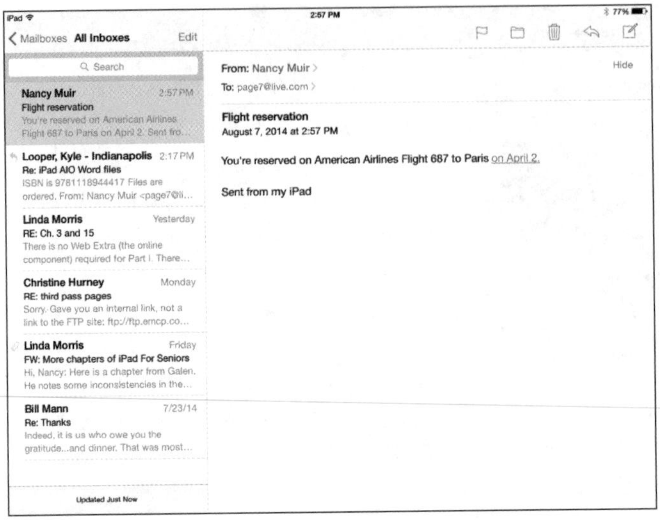

Figure 7-17: Create an event from information in your email using this menu.

Printing Emails

iPad has native printing capabilities that can be used by certain apps, including Mail. You need an AirPrint–compatible wireless printer set up to use this feature. For more about other options for printing from your iPad, see Book V, Chapter 1.

With an email message open, follow these steps to print:

1. **Tap the Reply button and then tap Print.**

2. **In the Printer Options dialog that appears (if you haven't used this feature with your printer before), tap Select Printer.**

   The iPad searches for any available printers.

3. **Tap your printer to select it.**

4. **Tap Back to return to the Printer Options dialog and use the plus or minus buttons (as necessary) in the Copies field to adjust the number of copies. If you use printer that supports two-sided printing, you can tap the Double-Sided switch to choose that option.**

5. **Tap Print.**

   Your print job is on its way to your printer.

Deleting an Email

I have friends who never delete emails, but that, frankly, drives me nuts (plus, at some point, their mailbox fills up and new emails are rejected). When you no longer want an email cluttering up your Inbox, you can delete it. When you delete an email on your iPad, it's gone from your Inbox, including the Inbox you access through your mobile phone or computer. However, for a time, you can retrieve it if your email provider offers a Trash folder for your email account and if your settings for your account with that provider don't cause emails to be deleted from their server on download.

Here's how to delete those emails you no longer want:

1. **With the Inbox displayed, tap the Edit button.**

    Circular check boxes display to the left of each message (see Figure 7-18).

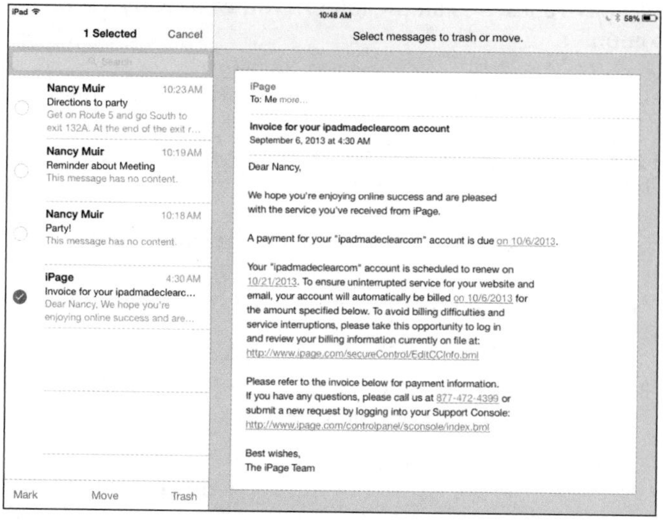

Figure 7-18: Delete several messages at one time using the Delete feature.

2. **Tap the circle next to the message you want to delete.**

    You can tap multiple items if you have several emails to delete. Messages marked for deletion show a check mark in the circular check box. (Refer to Figure 7-18.)

3. **Tap the Trash button.**

    The message(s) moves to the Trash folder.

Depending on your email provider, Mail may keep a copy of all deleted messages for a time in a Trash folder. To view deleted messages, go to the list of all mailboxes. Tap the account name in the Accounts list in the Mailboxes panel, and a list of folders appears. Tap the Trash folder, and all deleted messages display.

You can also delete an open email by tapping the Trash button in the toolbar that runs across the top of Mail or by swiping left or right on a message displayed in an Inbox and tapping the Trash button that appears.

Organizing Email

In most email accounts your ability to create folders is dependent on the email program's abilities. Some providers don't offer much support for managing messages in folders. Depending on your email provider, you may be able to move messages into any of a few predefined folders in Mail, or you may have access to all the folders you've already set up using your computer.

Assuming that you have access to folders in your email account, with the folder containing the message you want to move (for example, the Trash or Inbox if you have an Outlook.com account) displayed, tap the Edit button. Circular check boxes display to the left of each message.

Follow these steps to move any message into another folder:

1. **Tap the circle next to the message you want to move.**
2. **Tap the Move button.**
3. **In the folder list that appears (see Figure 7-19), tap the folder where you want to store the message.**

    The message is moved.

If you get a junk email, you might want to move it to the Spam or Junk Email folder. After you do, any future mail from that same sender is placed automatically in that folder.

If you have an email open, you can move it to a folder by tapping the Folder icon on the toolbar that runs along the top. The Mailboxes list displays; tap a folder to move the message.

Book I
Chapter 7

Working with Email
in Mail

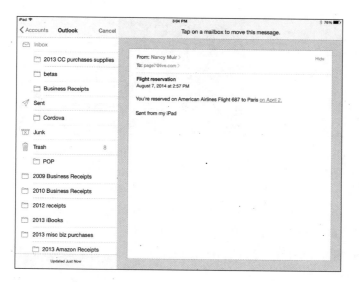

Figure 7-19: Pick a folder to move the selected message to.

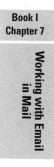

Creating a VIP List

VIP List is a way to create a list of special senders. When any of these send-ers sends you an email, it's flagged in your Inbox. You can view the VIP mail-box to just see messages from VIP contacts in one place. Also, you get a distinct notification sound when a VIP message arrives. Be sure that in Notifications settings, you have set up your Mail accounts to use Notification Center for VIP mail. Then, in the Mailboxes list of Mail, tap the Information button to the right of VIP (see Figure 7-20) and follow these steps to desig-nate a contact as a VIP:

1. **Tap Add VIP, and your Contacts list appears.**

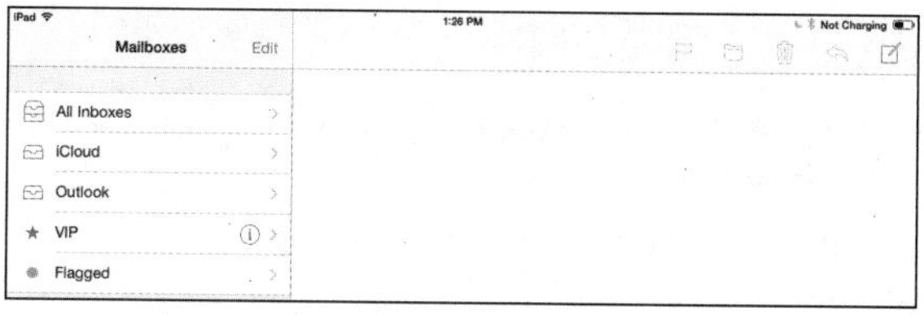

Figure 7-20: Tap here to access the VIP feature.

2. **Tap a contact to add that person to the VIP list, shown in Figure 7-21.**

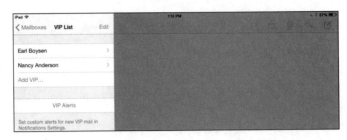

Figure 7-21: To add a VIP, that person must first be added to the Contacts app.

3. **Tap the Home button and then tap Settings.**

4. **Tap Notifications and then tap Mail.**

5. **In the settings that appear, shown in Figure 7-22, tap VIP.**

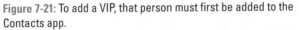

Figure 7-22: Because the VIP list displays information in Notification Center, that's the setting category you work with.

6. **Tap VIP.**

7. **Tap an alert style and choose whether a badge icon, sound, or preview should occur.**

   You can also choose to have the notification displayed on your Lock screen. (See Figure 7-23.)

8. **Tap the Home button to close Settings.**

   New mail from your VIPs now appear in Notification Center when you swipe down from the top of the screen, and depending on the settings you chose, may cause a sound to play or a badge icon to appear on your lock screen, or a blue star icon to appear to the left of these messages in your Mail inbox.

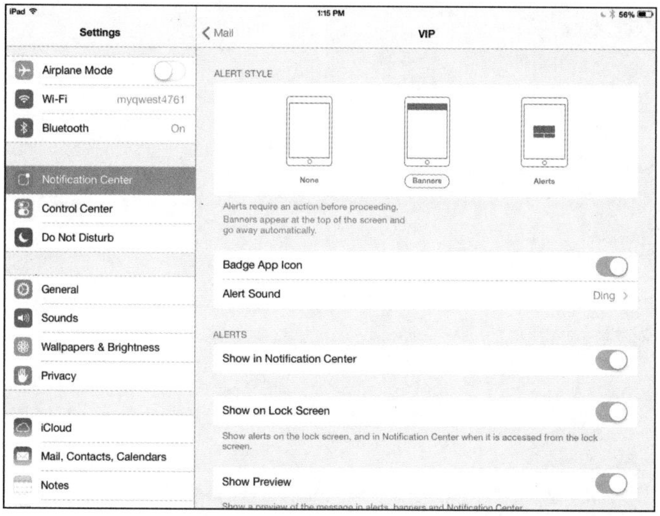

Book I
Chapter 7

Working with Email
in Mail

Figure 7-23: Choose from several options for how VIP List alerts happen.

Chapter 8: Managing iPad Settings

In This Chapter

✔ **Setting brightness and changing the wallpaper**

✔ **Controlling General settings**

✔ **Getting the sounds right**

✔ **Changing Network and Bluetooth settings**

✔ **Managing iCloud**

✔ **Getting an overview of apps settings**

The Settings app is a command center for your iPad, allowing you to adjust the functionality of features such as the screen brightness and wallpaper, sound volume, and security features. You can also set up email accounts (which I tell you about in Chapter 7 of this minibook) and control how the Calendar and Contacts apps manage their respective details. Finally, you find settings for each of the individual preinstalled apps, as well as for many apps designed for the iPad that you may have downloaded to your device.

Check out settings for the Siri personal assistant feature of iPad in Book V, Chapter 6.

In this chapter, you get some highlights of the settings you're likely to need most often and advice for how to use them.

Making Brightness and Wallpaper Settings

You might as well set up the visual side of iPad first so your interaction with the device is easy on the eyes and battery power. Two such categories in Settings help out with your display: Display & Brightness and Wallpaper.

Setting brightness

When using iPad day in and day out, you may find that a dimmer screen reduces strain on your eyes. Also, by reducing the brightness when using any app, you can save a little on your iPad's battery life.

To modify the brightness setting, follow these steps:

1. **Tap Settings on the Home screen.**

2. **In Settings, shown in Figure 8-1, tap Display & Brightness.**

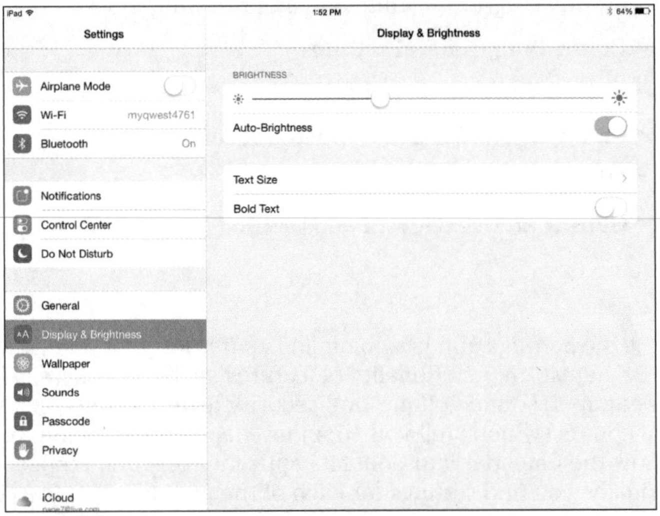

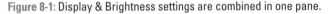

Figure 8-1: Display & Brightness settings are combined in one pane.

3. **To control brightness manually, tap the Auto-Brightness On/Off switch (refer to Figure 8-1) to turn it off.**

4. **Tap and drag the Brightness slider to the right to make the screen brighter or to the left to make it dimmer.**

5. **You can also tap the Text Size setting to choose a size of text for any apps that support the Dynamic text feature, and tap the Bold Text switch to turn on this feature that may make text easier to see.**

6. **Tap the Home button to close Settings.**

If glare from the screen is a problem for you, consider getting a screen protector. This thin film not only protects your screen from damage but also can reduce glare. These are available from a wide variety of sources (just do a web search for *iPad screen protector*) and cost about $2 each.

In the iBooks app, you can set a sepia tone for book pages, which might be easier on your eyes. See Book II, Chapter 7 for more about using iBooks.

Changing the wallpaper

Just as your desktop computer or laptop can display a pretty picture or pattern as a desktop background called a *wallpaper,* so your iPad can display an image on the Home screen and the same or another picture that displays when your iPad is locked.

The default picture may be pretty, but it may not be the background that's most appealing to you. Choosing different wallpaper may help you to see all the apps and status bar information on your Home screen, or just provide an image that appeals to your artistic sensibilities.

To change the wallpaper, do this:

1. **Tap Settings on the Home screen, and then tap Wallpaper.**

2. **In the Wallpaper settings that appear, tap Choose a New Wallpaper row.**

3. **In the pane that appears, tap either Dynamic or Stills under Apple Wallpaper to display wallpaper images.**

    Dynamic images use animation, and *stills* are static images.

    You can also use your own picture for your wallpaper. Instead of choosing Apple Wallpaper, tap a Photos collection such as Recently Added to browse your saved photos, select the picture you want to assign, and then resume with Step 5.

4. **In the Wallpaper pane (see Figure 8-2), tap a wallpaper image.**

    A preview of that wallpaper appears onscreen.

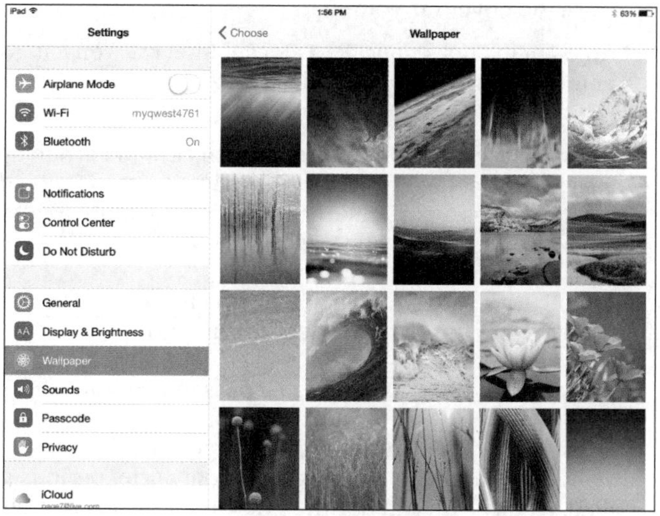

Figure 8-2: Choose from various built-in wallpapers.

5. **Tap Set Lock Screen (the screen that appears when you lock the iPad by tapping the power button), Set Home Screen (to use as the wallpaper), or Set Both.**

6. **Press the Home button.**

   You return to your Home screen where you can view the new wallpaper set as the background.

Managing General Settings

A great many of the iPad settings are tucked into the General category. These include Software Update to update the iOS, Spotlight Search, Siri, security settings such as Auto-Lock and Restrictions, and settings for things like date and time, the keyboard, and accessibility.

Here's a rundown of some of the settings you'll find tucked under General settings.

Handling security

Because you're likely to take your iPad on the road on a regular basis, it's a good idea to consider a few security features. Some save battery life and protect your data or access to certain apps.

Security settings involve three features, which you access through the General settings:

- **Lock/Unlock:** Turns off your display to save battery power when you close the cover for your iPad.

- **Auto-Lock:** Locks your iPad at a set interval. You can set the amount of time you want before your iPad goes to the Lock screen by tapping this setting.

- **Restrictions:** Allows you to restrict access to certain apps and content using a passcode (see Figure 8-3). This is useful if you don't want your kids to access a particularly adult app or simply don't want them browsing with Safari or buying things with iTunes, for example.

In addition, there are two items in the main Settings (not within General settings) that relate to security: Passcode and Privacy.

- Passcode allows you to assign a passcode to the Lock screen. You can set a passcode, turn it on or off, change the passcode, and set the time interval at which your passcode is required. This is useful if you don't want to bother with a passcode for only brief periods of locking your iPad. Finally, you can use the Erase Data setting so that multiple failed attempts to access your device results in your iPad erasing all data on it.

This could protect from prying eyes your contacts' information, for example, or map data that shows your location. Note that if Simple Passcode is turned on (the default setting), you're limited to a four-digit passcode. If you turn off the Simple Passcode setting, you can use a longer, stronger, passcode using a combination of letters and numbers.

✔ Privacy shows you which apps have requested access to your data or social accounts, and lets you enable or disable the access of an app to the various iPad features listed, such as its microphone or contacts.

WARNING!

If you forget a passcode, the only thing to do is restore iPad software, which can be a headache. The obvious advice here: Don't forget your passcode!

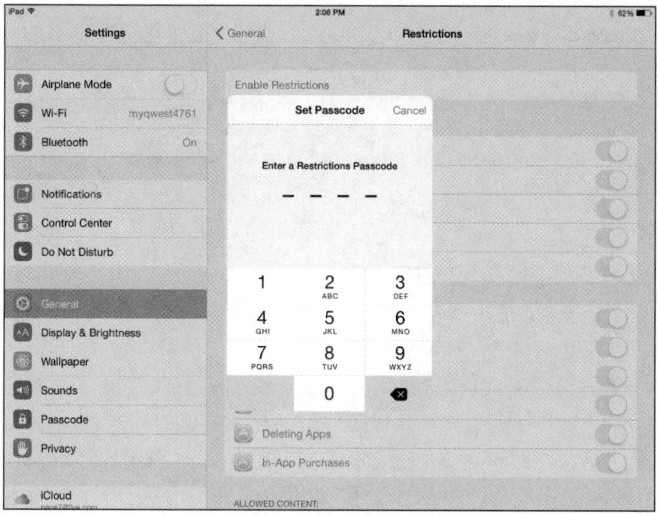

Figure 8-3: Set a password and choose the apps or content you want to restrict in this pane.

Setting the date and time

By default, your iPad is set to Cupertino time — Cupertino, California, that is, home to Apple. If you have occasion to reset the time zone or date and time, either because you live somewhere other than near Apple headquarters or you travel around with your iPad, here's how you control the time setting on your iPad:

1. **Tap Settings on the Home screen.**

2. **Tap General.**

3. **Tap Date & Time.**

   The settings shown in Figure 8-4 appear.

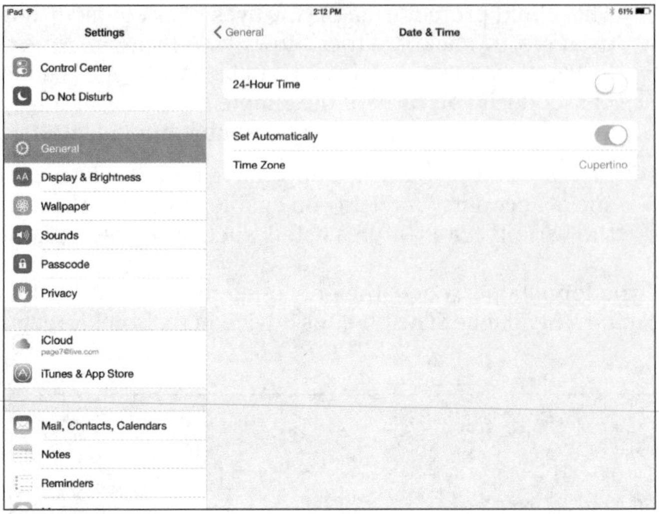

Figure 8-4: Choose the time format or time zone, or let your iPad set things up for you.

4. **Do any of the following:**

   - *Tap the Off switch to turn 24-hour time on.* This is military time, so 2 p.m. is 1400, and so on.

   - *Tap the On/Off switch for Set Automatically.* This feature sets your time and date based on your current location.

   - *Turn off the Set Automatically setting and then tap Time Zone, and a text-entry field displays along with your onscreen keyboard.* Press the Delete key to delete Cupertino, and type your location. (If you type a major city near you and in the same time zone, it comes up on a list as you type, and you can just tap to select it.)

Controlling keyboard settings

Your keyboard is one of the most important ways in which you interact with iPad, so it's helpful if you have all the onscreen keyboard settings just the way you want them. You can access these in Settings, under the Keyboard option in the General settings (see Figure 8-5), and they include the following:

- ✔ **Auto-Capitalization and Auto-Correction:** Allow iPad to help you avoid mistakes by automatically suggesting corrections to what it perceives as spelling errors, based on a built-in dictionary, or correcting capitalization mistakes you make after you finish entering a sentence.

- ✔ **Check Spelling:** If you want iPad to automatically check spelling, turning on this feature causes two things to happen: A jagged red line appears under problematic text in apps such as Notes and Mail; and as you type a word with a misspelling, a suggested correct spelling appears in a little bubble. If you also have Auto-Correction turned on, the word is corrected automatically when you finish typing it and add a space or punctuation mark (such as a period) after the word. Note that you can use the Undo key on the onscreen keyboard with numbers displayed to undo automatic changes.

✔ **Enable Caps Lock:** Activates a feature that lets you double-tap the Shift key to activate Caps Lock. Note that when Caps Lock is activated, the Shift key on the onscreen keyboard is blue, and you tap the Shift key to turn Caps Lock off. This setting is turned off by default.

✔ **"." Shortcut:** Turning this on activates a shortcut that allows you to enter a period and a space by double-tapping the spacebar.

✔ **Keyboards:** Gives you access to a choice of built-in keyboard styles such as QWERTY and AZERTY. You can also choose from dozens of language keyboard layout options, including German, Italian, Russian, Spanish, and my personal favorite, Estonian.

✔ **Split Keyboard:** Turns on a feature that allows you to break the onscreen keyboard into two pieces, one on each side of your screen, to make a more texting-like experience for those who like to type mainly with their thumbs.

✔ **Shortcuts:** Use these two settings to have iPad automatically convert common texting phrases into shortcuts — for example, you can replace omw (the shortcut) with "on my way" — or add new shortcuts to its repertoire.

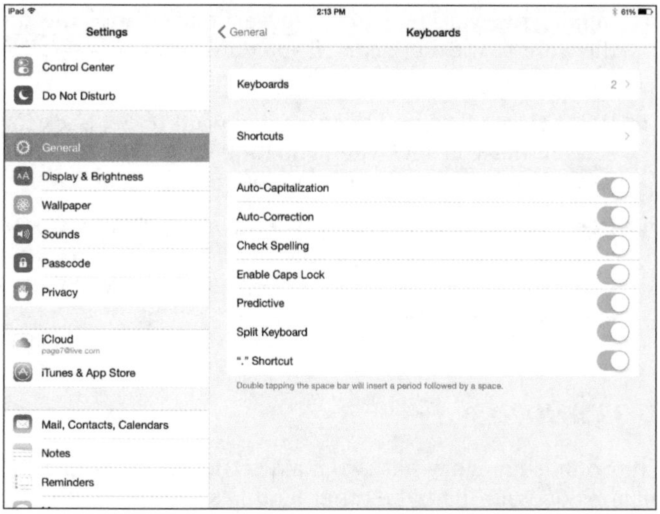

Figure 8-5: Set up your keyboard to work the way you want it to.

In addition to modifying Keyboard settings in the General category, you can tap Language & Region to access more settings. You can change the language you use for interacting with the iPad; add new keyboards; set the region format (for example, for date, time, and phone numbers); and pick which calendar to use (Gregorian, Japanese, or Buddhist).

Working with the Reset feature

If only life had a Reset button to put some things back the way they were. Well, life doesn't, but iPad does. The last item in the General settings is Reset. When you tap it, you get options for resetting the following:

- **Reset All Settings:** All the preferences and settings are reset, although information that you've added to apps such as Calendar and Contacts doesn't change at all.

- **Erase All Content and Settings:** This one both resets your settings and erases information that you've added to apps such as Calendar and Contacts. This is useful if you plan to sell your iPad (you also should turn off Find My iPad in the iCloud settings in this scenario, as otherwise the device will be locked to your Apple ID).

- **Reset Network Settings:** By choosing this, any networks you've set up are removed. iPad also turns off Wi-Fi and then turns it on again, which disconnects you from any network you're connected to. Note that the Ask to Join Networks setting stays on.

- **Reset Keyboard Dictionary:** When you turn down the iPad's suggestions of words as you type, you can add custom words to the keyboard dictionary. You do this by tapping an unrecognized word that an app has underlined; tapping the word rejects the suggestion and adds the current spelling of the word to the dictionary. If you don't want to keep all those added words, use this Reset Keyboard Dictionary option.

- **Reset Home Screen Layout:** If you want to get back to the original Home screen that you saw when you took your iPad out of its box, choose this Reset Home Screen Layout option.

- **Reset Location & Privacy:** When you use an app like Maps that checks your location, it asks you whether it's okay to do that. When you tap OK two times to let it proceed, it stops asking. If you want it to start asking again, tap this option.

Managing Sounds

The Sounds category has two main settings. One adjusts the volume level for all apps on your iPad; the other modifies whether system sounds play for events such as new email, calendar alerts, and keyboard clicks.

Adjusting the volume

Although individual applications such as Music and Videos have their own volume settings, you can set your iPad system volume as well to control the level of system sounds and sounds in apps that don't have their own volume control. This system setting is the max against which Music volume settings work; if you set volume to 80% here, for example, Music's 100% volume setting will actually be the maximum system volume, or 80%.

You can simply press the volume rocker controls on the top-right side of your iPad (when it's in portrait orientation) to increase or decrease volume. However, this doesn't change the volume of ringers and alerts unless you change one additional setting. To adjust the system volume from the Settings pane, tap Sounds. In the Sounds pane that appears (see Figure 8-6), tap and drag the slider to the right to increase the volume or to the left to lower it. Note that you can also adjust system volume in the Control Center, which you display by swiping up from the bottom of the iPad screen.

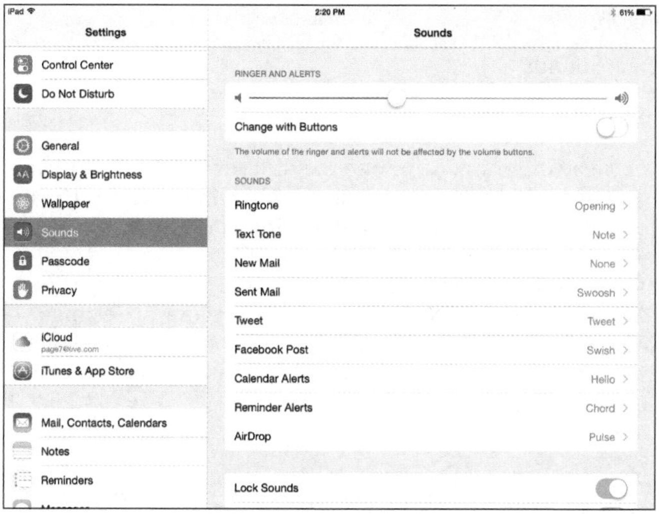

Figure 8-6: Use this familiar volume slider to adjust your system's volume.

Under General settings, make a choice from the Use Side Switch To settings to set the side switch on your iPad to mute all sounds. If you prefer to use that switch to lock screen rotation, another way to mute your iPad is to hold down the volume switch (below the Side switch on the top-right corner of the device) until the sound is effectively off. This method assumes that you have set this switch to control volume.

Turning system sounds on and off

In my experience, people are either big fans or big haters of system sounds on computers. You know, sounds like that annoying chime you hear when a new email arrives? iPad also makes sounds when certain events occur, if you want it to. You can turn on and off the following system sounds:

- ✔ Ringtone
- ✔ Text Tone
- ✔ New Mail
- ✔ Sent Mail
- ✔ Tweet
- ✔ Facebook Post
- ✔ Calendar Alerts
- ✔ Reminder Alerts
- ✔ AirDrop
- ✔ Lock Sounds
- ✔ Keyboard Clicks

To turn these off or on, or to choose different system sounds, from the Settings pane, tap Sounds and use the On/Off switch for the last two settings, or choose None or a different sound for any of the others.

You can control the Apple Push Notification Service, used to push alerts to your Apple device, via the Notifications category in Settings. This lets you control the alerts sent to you. You can turn alerts on and off, for example, which can save a bit of your battery life. You can also control alerts in a specific app's settings.

Making Network and Bluetooth Settings

You can make a few settings for your networks and Bluetooth: ones for virtual private networks (VPNs) under General settings, ones for Wi-Fi networks, and finally, settings for 3G/4G network cellular data.

You may have read in the news that your iPad and iPhone save a record of your every move. If you don't like that idea, plug your iPad or iPhone into your computer and, when iTunes opens, click your device. Then, with the Summary tab selected, click the Encrypt iPhone/iPad Backup option. Apple can find your phone if you enable Find My iPhone, but Apple can't view your backed up information in iCloud!

A *virtual private network* (VPN) allows you to set up an encrypted connection with a private network, such as one at your office, over the Internet. A VPN lets you make such a connection securely, and your iPad allows you to make settings for activating your connection through General settings.

For more about connecting to your company network remotely and configuring a VPN, see Book III, Chapter 1.

The Wi-Fi settings include simply turning Wi-Fi on or off, choosing which network to connect to, and activating a feature that joins recognized networks automatically.

I can't forget 3G and 4G. If you have a 3G or 3G/4G iPad, you can make some settings for your 3G/4G connections by tapping Settings and then tapping Cellular Data. See Book III, Chapter 1 for more about these settings.

Note that you can also use the Airplane Mode setting to turn your Wi-Fi and Bluetooth signals off when in flight and quickly turn them back on again when you're safely on *terra firma.* This setting is also available through Control Center.

Another setting that you can make in Privacy Settings to protect you when you're online is to turn Location Services on or off. Turning this on lets apps like Maps find your current physical location. If you turn this feature off and an app needs Location Services to function, it prompts you to turn it on.

Managing iCloud Settings

iCloud is Apple's online storage and sharing service. Chapter 5 of this minibook takes you through the steps involved in setting up an iCloud account, one of the things you can do using the iCloud pane in the Settings app. (See Figure 8-7.) Here are the other three main things you can control for iCloud from within Settings:

- ✔ **Turn various apps on or off for inclusion in iCloud syncs.** For example, you can set Contacts to sync contacts stored in your iCloud account. Your iCloud account can sync Mail, Contacts, Calendars, Reminders, and Notes in your iCloud account.

- ✔ **Control Storage & Backup.** This includes checking your available storage, buying additional storage, or turning iCloud Backup on or off.

- ✔ **Set Up Family Sharing.** Use this to set up an account that up to six people can use to make and share purchases using a single credit card.

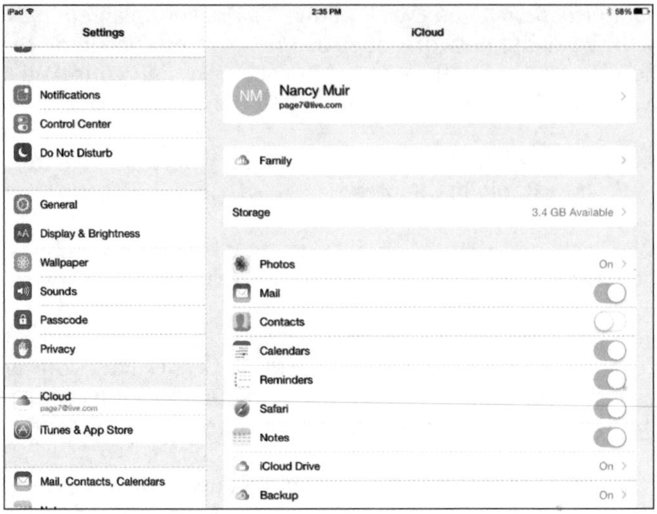

Figure 8-7: Choose which type of content to sync via iCloud here.

Settings for Individual Apps

Most bundled apps have a corresponding group of settings in the iPad. Rather than bore you by taking you through each and every one, I provide Table 8-1, which gives you an overview of most of the types of settings you can control. (Note that settings for the first three apps, Mail, Contacts, and Calendar are all included in the Mail, Contacts, and Calendars settings.) If you like to work with a particular app often, it's worth your while to explore the settings for it to see whether one might make your life with that app a bit easier.

Table 8-1	Built-In Apps Settings Overview
App	**Types of Settings**
Mail	Add Accounts, Fetch New Data Frequency, and Display Settings (how many messages to show, font size, and so on)
Contacts	Display Settings (sort order and display order)
Calendars	Turn on Alerts, Time Zone, and Default Calendar
Notes	Set Default Account for storing notes
Reminders	Sync Reminders and choose the Default List of Reminders to use when a list isn't specified
Messages	Turn On/Off, Make Send & Receive Settings, and Show/Hide Subject Field

App	Types of Settings
Music	Toggle Sounds, Volume Limit, and the Display Lyrics and Podcast Info setting; toggle iTunes Match On/Off; set up Home Sharing
Videos	Start Playing (where you left off or from the beginning), Show All Videos that have been downloaded, and Home Sharing
Photos & Camera	Photo Stream and Photo Sharing, Slideshow Settings, and Camera Grid

Also note that apps that you download, which have been designed for iPad, often appear in Settings under the Apps heading. Non-iPad apps (for example, iPhone apps) don't seem to appear. The settings vary based on the app, so go exploring and see what you find!

Chapter 9: Maintaining and Troubleshooting

In This Chapter

- ✏ **Taking care of your iPad**
- ✏ **Solving common iPad problems**
- ✏ **Finding technical support**
- ✏ **Finding a missing iPad**
- ✏ **Backing up to iCloud**

*i*Pads don't grow on trees — they cost a pretty penny. That's why you should know how to take care of your iPad and troubleshoot any problems that it might have so that you get the most out of it.

In this chapter, I provide some advice about the care and maintenance of your iPad, as well as tips about how to solve common problems, update iPad system software, and even reset your iPad should something go seriously wrong. In case you lose your iPad, I even tell you about a feature that helps you find it, activate it remotely, or even disable it if it's fallen into the wrong hands. Finally, you get information about backing up your iPad settings and content using iCloud.

Maintaining Your iPad

You have a great gadget and an investment to protect in your iPad. A few simple precautions can keep it damage-free — at least until you rush out and buy the next version.

It's wise to keep the screen clean and safe from damage, as well as maximize your battery use. The following sections tell you how.

Keeping the iPad screen clean

If you've been playing with your iPad, you know — despite Apple's claim that iPads have fingerprint-resistant screens — that iPads are fingerprint magnets. They're covered with an oil-resistant coating, but that definitely doesn't mean they're smudge-proof. One way to avoid those finger smudges is by obtaining an inexpensive stylus — just be sure it's got a soft or pliable tip and is designed for use with an iPad.

Avoid a few smudges in the first place by using a stand or dock to hold your iPad. With a stand or dock, you spend less time picking up your tablet, which cuts down on fingerprints.

Here are some tips about cleaning your iPad screen:

- **Use a dry, soft cloth.** You can get most fingerprints off with a dry, soft cloth such as the one you use to clean your eyeglasses or a cleaning tissue that's lint- and chemical-free. Or try products used to clean lenses in labs, such as Kimwipes or Kaydry, which you can get from several major retailers such as Amazon.

- **Use a slightly moistened soft cloth.** To get the surface even cleaner, very slightly moisten the cloth before you use it to clean the screen. Again, make sure that whatever cloth material you use is lint free.

- **Remove the cables.** This may go without saying, but I'll say it anyway: If you don't want a fried iPad, turn it off and unplug any cables from it before cleaning the screen with a moistened cloth.

- **Avoid moisture.** Avoid getting moisture around the edges of the screen where it can seep into the unit.

- **Never use any household cleaners on your iPad screen.** They can degrade the coating that keeps the screen from absorbing oil from your fingers.

Do *not* use premoistened lens-cleaning tissues to clean your screen. Most of these products contain alcohol, which can damage the screen's coating.

Protecting your gadget with a case

Your screen isn't the only element on the iPad that can be damaged, so consider getting a case for it so that you can carry it around the house or around town safely. Besides providing a bit of padding if you drop the device, a case makes the iPad less slippery in your hands, offering a better grip when working with it.

Several types of cases are available for iPad Air 2 and iPad mini 3, and more are showing up all the time. You can choose the Smart Cover from Apple that covers the screen, for example ($39); the Smart Case from Apple, which wraps around the iPad completely ($79 for Air 2 and $69 for iPad mini 3); or covers from other manufacturers. I've found the covers from other manufacturers to be somewhat sturdier than Apple cases. For instance, Tuff-Luv (www.tuff-luv.com) and Griffin Technology (www.griffintechnology.com) come in materials ranging from leather (see Figure 9-1) to silicone (see Figure 9-2).

Cases range in price from a few dollars to $125 or more for leather; some will cost you hundreds of dollars. Some provide a cover (see Figure 9-1), and others protect only the back and sides or, in the case of Smart Cover, only the screen. If you carry around your iPad much at all, consider a case with a screen cover to provide better protection for the screen or use a screen overlay, such as the InvisibleShield from ZAGG (www.zagg.com).

Figure 9-1: Casemaker Tuff-Luv's website, where you can find a variety of iPad cases.

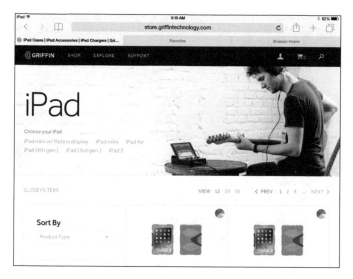

Figure 9-2: A less-expensive option is a silicone skin.

Extending your iPad's battery life

The much-touted ten-hour battery life of the iPad is a wonderful feature, but you can take some steps to extend that battery life even further. You can estimate how much battery life you have left by looking at the battery icon in the far-right end of the status bar at the top of your screen. Here are a few tips to help that little icon stay full up:

✔ **Use a wall outlet to charge.** Though it can vary depending on your computer model, generally when connected to a recent model Mac computer, iPad will slowly charge; however, some PC connections don't provide enough power to prevent battery drain. Even so, the most effective way to charge your iPad is to plug it into the wall outlet using the Lightning to USB Cable (or Dock Connector to USB Cable for pre–fourth-generation iPads) and the 10W USB Power Adapter that came with your iPad. (See Figure 9-3.)

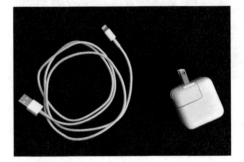

Figure 9-3: The provided cord and power adapter.

✔ **Turn off the iPad.** The fastest way to charge the iPad is to turn it off while charging it.

✔ **Consider letting your iPad totally run out of battery charge once a month** and then recharging it to prevent a memory effect that can have an effect on your lithium-ion battery life.

✔ **Avoid USB ports on keyboards.** Your battery may lose some power if you leave it connected to the USB port on a keyboard or other device.

The best way to charge your iPad is with the included cord plugged into an electrical outlet. Using your computer to charge it can take a great deal longer. There are also power strips and adapters now available that have USB ports so that you can charge several USB devices at one time.

✔ **Limit the screen's impact on the battery.** Turn off the screen when not in use because the display eats up power. Also, reduce the screen brightness in Settings to save power.

✔ **Turn off Wi-Fi.** If you're not using Wi-Fi, turn it off in Settings or in the Control Center. Constantly maintaining a Wi-Fi connection or searching for a signal can use up a bit of power.

Your iPad battery is sealed in the unit, so you can't replace it as you can with many laptops or your cellphone battery. If the battery is out of warranty, you have to fork over the money, possibly more than $100, to get a new one. If you use your iPad a great deal, consider getting the AppleCare service contract for free replacement. See the "Getting Support" section, later in this chapter, to find out where to get a replacement battery.

Apple has introduced AppleCare+. For $99, you get two years of coverage, which even covers you if you drop or spill liquids on your iPad. If your iPad has to be replaced, it costs only $50, rather than the $250 it used to cost with garden-variety AppleCare (but only for two instances). That means $149 ($99 for AppleCare+ plus $50 replacement fee) versus the $299 price Apple offered me to replace my fourth-generation iPad when it died 14 months into its life (after I was advised that Apple couldn't service it). You can also purchase it when you buy your iPad or within a month of the date of purchase. See www.apple.com/support/products/ipad.html.

Troubleshooting Your iPad

Although everyone wants to think that his or her iPad is a perfect magical machine, unburdened with the vagaries of crashing and system software bugs, that's not always the case.

Here are some common issues that can come up with your iPad, along with ways to deal with them.

Dealing with a nonresponsive iPad

If your iPad goes dead on you, it's most likely a power issue, so the first thing to do is to plug the Lightning to USB Cable (or Dock Connector to USB Cable for pre–fourth-generation iPads) into the 10W USB Power Adapter, plug the 10W USB Power Adapter into a wall outlet, plug the other end of the Lightning to USB Cable (or Dock Connector to USB Cable) into your iPad, and charge the battery.

Another thing to try — especially if you think that an app might be hanging up the iPad — is to press the Sleep/Wake button for a few seconds. Then press and hold the Home button. The app you were using should close.

You can always try the old reboot procedure, which in the case of an iPad means pressing the Sleep/Wake button on the top until the Slide to Power Off control displays. Drag the slider to the right to turn off your iPad. After a few moments, press the Sleep/Wake button to boot up the little guy again. Be sure that your battery has a decent charge because this procedure can eat up battery power.

If the situation seems drastic and none of these ideas works, try to reset your iPad. To do this, press the Sleep/Wake button and the Home button at the same time until the Apple logo appears onscreen.

Troubleshooting keyboard woes

When you're using a Bluetooth keyboard, your onscreen keyboard won't appear. The physical keyboard has, in essence, co-opted keyboard control of your device. To use your onscreen keyboard with a Bluetooth keyboard connected, you have a few options: You can turn off your connection to the Bluetooth keyboard, turn off Bluetooth in iPad's Settings or the Control Center, switch off the keyboard, or move the keyboard out of range. Your onscreen keyboard should reappear.

Are you accidentally tapping extra keys on the onscreen keyboard as you type? Wearing a wrist support can keep you from hitting extra characters with your wrists. Also, it's much easier to use the onscreen keyboard in landscape mode where it's just plain wider.

Updating software

Just as software manufacturers provide updates for your main computer, Apple occasionally updates the iPad system software to fix problems or offer enhanced features. Occasionally check for an updated version (say, every month). You can do this by opening Settings, tapping General, and then tapping Software Update.

Note that if you've chosen to back up and restore iPad via iCloud when you first set up the device or later using Settings, restoring and updating your device happens automatically. (See Chapter 5 in this minibook for more about iCloud.)

If you choose not to use iCloud, follow these steps to update the iPad system software using a connection to your computer and iTunes 11:

1. **Connect your iPad to your computer.**

2. **On your computer, open iTunes.**

3. **Click your iPad's name near the top-right corner of the screen.**

4. **Click the Summary tab, as shown in Figure 9-4.**

5. **Click the Check for Update button.**

   iTunes displays a message telling you whether a new update is available.

6. **Click the Update button to install the newest version if yours isn't up-to-date.**

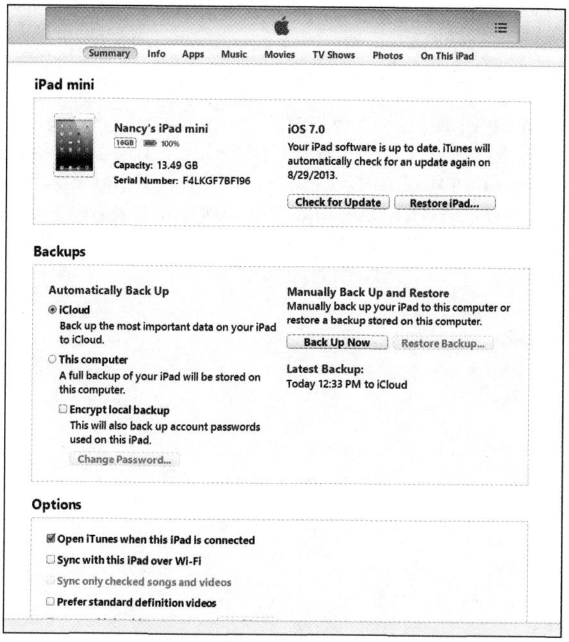

Figure 9-4: Get system updates for iPad through your iTunes account.

If you're having problems with your iPad, you can use the Update feature to try to restore the current version of the software. Follow the preceding set of steps and then click the Restore button instead of the Update button in Step 6. Typically, restoring an OS to another version does run the risk of going back to original settings, so be aware of that going in.

Restoring sound

Coincidentally, the very morning I wrote this chapter, my husband was puttering with his iPad when the sound suddenly stopped. We gave ourselves a quick course in recovering sound, so now I can share these tips with you. Make sure that

✔ **You haven't touched the volume control keys on a physical keyboard connected to your iPad via Bluetooth.** They're on the right side of the top-right side of your iPad when holding it in portrait orientation. Be sure not to touch one and inadvertently lower the sound 'til it's essentially muted.

✔ **You haven't flipped the Side switch.** If you have the Side switch set to control sound, moving the switch mutes sound on your iPad.

✔ **The speaker isn't covered up.** Make sure that you haven't covered up the speaker in a way that muffles the sound.

✔ **A headset isn't plugged in.** Sound won't play through the speaker and the headset at the same time.

✔ **The Volume Limit is set to Off.** You can set up the Volume Limit in Settings for Music to control how loudly the Music app can play (which is useful if your partner's into loud rap music). Tap Settings on the Home screen and then tap Music. In the settings that appear, tap the Volume Limit controls (see Figure 9-5) and move the slider to adjust the Volume Limit.

Settings	Music	
Privacy		
iCloud	Sound Check	◯
iTunes & App Store	EQ	Off >
	Volume Limit	Off >
Mail, Contacts, Calendars	Group By Album Artist	⬤
Notes		
Reminders	Show All Music	⬤
Messages	All music that has been downloaded or that is stored in iCloud will be shown.	
FaceTime	Genius	◯
Maps	Turning on Genius will share information about your music library anonymously with Apple. Learn More	
Safari		
	Subscribe to iTunes Match	
	Store all your music in iCloud and listen to music on iTunes Radio ad-free. Learn More	
Music		
Videos	HOME SHARING	
Photos & Camera	Apple ID: page7@live.com	
iBooks		

Figure 9-5: Volume Limit lets your iPad get only so loud.

If all else fails, reboot. That's what worked for us — just press the Sleep/Wake button until the Slide to Power Off control appears. Drag the slider to the right. After iPad turns off, press the Sleep/Wake button again until the Apple logo appears, and you may find yourself back in business, sound-wise. If you're also an iPhone user, and Siri or Voice Control stops understanding you, you'll be glad to know that this reboot trick works for them, as well!

Getting Support

As you may already know if you own another Apple device, Apple is known for its great customer support, so if you're stuck, I definitely recommend that you try them. Also, be aware that every new iPad comes with a year's coverage for repair of the hardware and 90 days of free technical support. Here are a few options that you can explore for getting help:

- ✓ **The Apple Store:** Make an appointment online or by phone and then go to your local Apple Store if one is handy to find out what the folks there might know about your problem.

- ✓ **The Apple iPad Support website:** Visit this site at `www.apple.com/ support/ipad` (see Figure 9-6) or check out the iBooks Store. Here you find online manuals, discussion forums, downloads, and the Apple Expert feature, which enables you to contact a live support person by phone.

Figure 9-6: Don't forget to check out the manuals and discussions for help.

- ✓ **The *iPad User Guide:*** You can visit `http://manuals.info.apple. com/en_us/ipad_user_guide.pdf` to view your iPad user guide. You can also download the manual and read it in most popular e-reader programs.

- ✓ **The Apple battery replacement service:** If you need repair or service for your battery, visit `www.apple.com/batteries/replacements. html`.

Note that your warranty provides free battery replacement if the battery level dips below 50 percent and won't go any higher during the first year you own it. If you purchase the AppleCare service agreement, this is extended to two years. Also note that Apple recommends that the iPad battery should be replaced only by an Apple Authorized Service Provider.

Finally, here are a few useful non-Apple discussion forums that may help provide some answers:

- **MacRumors** at `http://forums.macrumors.com/forumdisplay.php?f=137`

- **The iPad Guide** discussions at `www.theipadguide.com/forum`

- **iPad.org,** with several useful threads at `http://ipad.org/forum`

Finding a Missing iPad

You can take advantage of the Find My iPad feature to pinpoint the location of your iPad. This is a very handy feature if you forget where you left your iPad or somebody walks away with it. Find My iPad lets you not only track down the critter but also wipe off the data contained in it if you have no way to get the iPad back.

If you're using Family Sharing, your family can help each other out if someone in your family loses an iOS device. Anybody in the family can find the device and play a sound without having to sign into the missing device with its password. This works even if the ringer on the iPhone is turned off. See Book II, Chapter 1 for more about Family Sharing.

Follow these steps to set up this feature:

1. **Tap Settings on the Home screen.**

2. **Tap iCloud.**

3. **In the iCloud settings that appear, tap Find My iPad.**

4. **Tap the On switch for the Find My iPad setting (see Figure 9-7) that appears to turn the feature on if it isn't already.**

5. **Tap the Send Last Location On switch so that iPad sends your iPad's location to Apple if your battery is almost out of juice, if you'd like.**

If your iPad is ever lost or stolen, go to `www.icloud.com` on your computer and enter your ID and password. Click the Find My iPad button to display a map of its location, as shown in Figure 9-8. Click the circle representing your iPad; then click the Information button (the small *i*) in the toolbar that appears. In the dialog that appears, to erase all information from the iPad in a process called wiping, click the Erase iPad button. Remember that this action erases all content, including contacts, music, notes, and so on, for good. To lock the iPad from access by others, click the Lost Mode button.

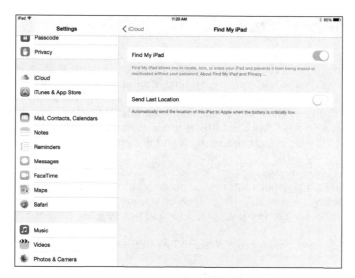

Figure 9-7: Turn the feature on or off to locate your iPad from your computer.

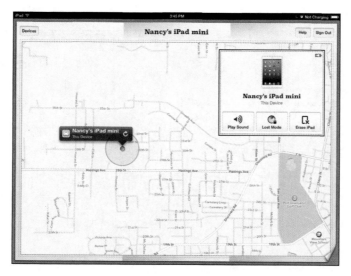

Figure 9-8: Find My iPad can pinpoint your iPad's location.

TIP

You can also tap Play a Sound to send whomever has your iPad a note saying how to return it to you — or a note that the police are on their way if it has been stolen! If you choose to play a sound, it plays for two minutes, helping you track down your iPad or anybody holding it within earshot.

Backing Up to iCloud

You used to be able to back up your iPad content only using iTunes, but with iCloud, you can back up via a Wi-Fi network to your iCloud storage. Note that whereas iTunes backs up everything, iCloud backs up only what *Apple* considers your most important content — Apple never backs up videos you get from sources other than iTunes, for example. Note that you can back up to iTunes or iCloud, but not both at the same time. However you can always sync to iTunes which copies apps and documents.

You get 5GB of storage (not including iTunes-bought music, videos, apps, and electronic books or content pushed automatically among your Apple devices by iTunes Match) for free, or you can pay for increased levels of storage (10GB for $20 per year, 20GB for $40 per year, or 50GB for $100 per year).

To perform a backup to iCloud, follow these steps:

1. **Tap Settings on the Home screen.**

   See Chapter 5 in this minibook for details on creating an iCloud account.

2. **Tap iCloud and then tap Backup (see Figure 9-9).**

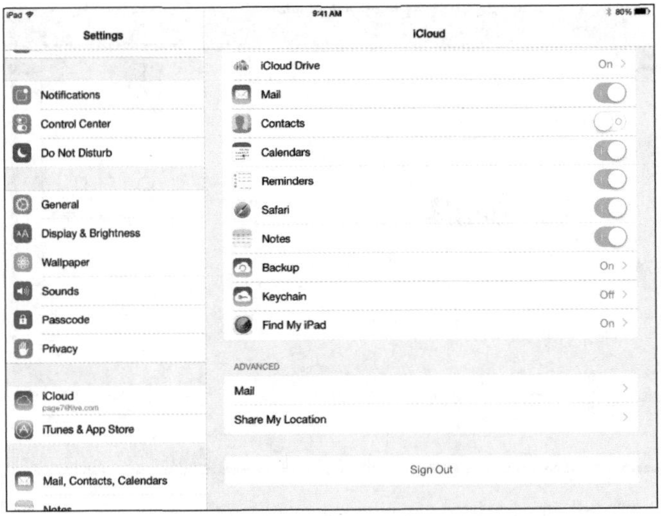

Figure 9-9: Backing up to the cloud.

3. **In the pane that appears (see Figure 9-10), tap the iCloud Backup On/ Off switch to enable automatic backups, or to perform a manual backup, tap Back Up Now.**

   A progress bar shows how your backup is moving along.

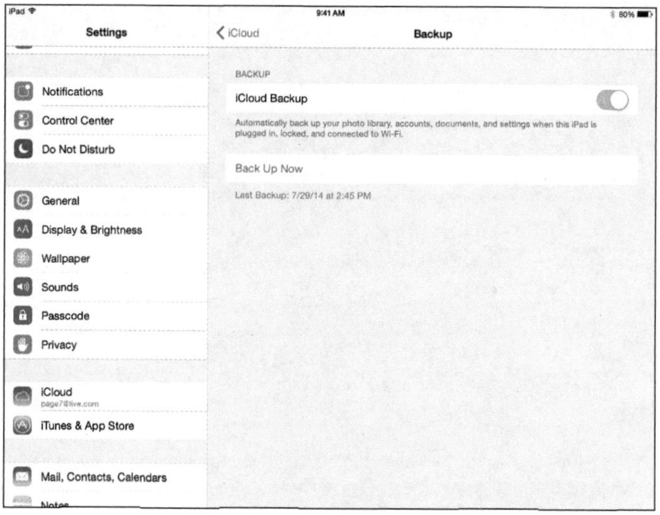

Figure 9-10: Automatic backups ensure that your data is saved.

Book II
Just for Fun

In this book. . .

- Buy and share content using the Family Sharing feature
- Find out about creating time lapse video and using smart filters on photos
- Discover how Twitter, Flickr, iCloud Sharing, and Facebook are integrated into several apps
- Use Messages to send instant messages
- Become expert at using the iBooks and other e-reader apps
- Explore Newsstand to subscribe to and read publications
- Have fun by playing games

Chapter 1: Buying Content at iTunes and Beyond

In This Chapter

- ✔ **Exploring the iTunes Store**
- ✔ **Previewing, buying, and renting media**
- ✔ **Shopping beyond iTunes**
- ✔ **Using iCloud to push purchases to all devices**
- ✔ **Setting Up Family Sharing**

*i*Pad is set up with a preinstalled iTunes Store app that makes it easy to shop for music, movies, TV shows, audiobooks, and podcasts at Apple's iTunes Store.

In this chapter, you discover how to use your iPad to find content on the iTunes Store website. That content can be downloaded directly to your iPad, or to another device and then synced to your iPad. With the new Family Sharing feature, which I cover in this chapter, as many as six people can share purchases and make purchases using the same credit card. Finally, I cover a few options for buying content from other online stores and how to download purchases automatically using iCloud.

 I cover opening an iTunes account and downloading iTunes software to your computer in Book I, Chapter 5. If you need to, handle those two tasks before digging into this chapter.

Books | Audiobooks | Podcasts | More

See A

as Songs (ack Version) ¹⁾

Live In Paris
Diana Krall

The Girl in the Other Room
Diana Krall

Qui
Dia

Exploring the iTunes Store

Whether it's your favorite shopping source or not, the iTunes Store is set up to be your most convenient source for content on your iPad at the moment. Sure, you can get content from other places, but the iTunes Store app comes preinstalled on your iPad — and Apple makes it easy to access it from various Apple devices or your PC.

$1.29

¹⁶ $0.99

Let It Snow
Diana Krall & The Clayte

Christmas Time I⁻ '
Diana Kra¹¹

So, it's time you get to know the iTunes Store: the easiest way to grab all those movies, TV shows, and music that you love for viewing and listening to on your iPad.

Visiting the iTunes Store

Using the iTunes Store from your iPad is easy with the preinstalled iTunes Store app. You just tap the iTunes Store app on the Home screen.

Now you can roam around trying different options. You have music, movies, TV shows, and audiobooks to choose from. If you begin to purchase or rent an item and you're not already signed in with your Apple ID, the dialog shown in Figure 1-1 appears, asking for your sign-in information. Enter your ID and password (you may have created one when you set up your iPad or may have already had one) and tap OK.

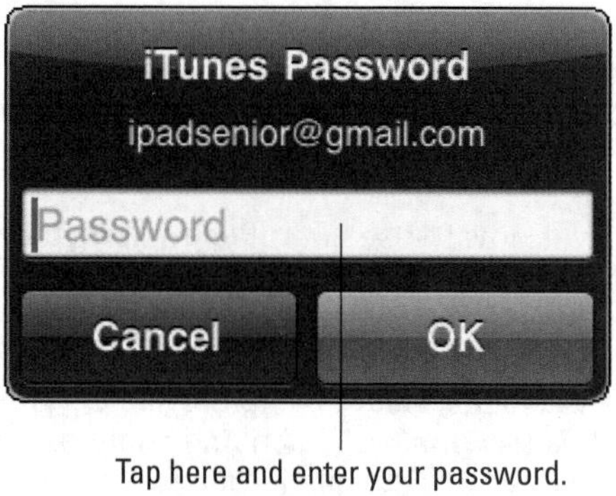

iTunes Password

ipadsenior@gmail.com

Password

Cancel   OK

Tap here and enter your password.

Figure 1-1: Log in to the iTunes Store.

Start exploring musical selections by tapping the Music button in the row of buttons at the bottom of the screen, if it's not already selected, as shown in Figure 1-2. Tap the See All link in any category of music to display more music selections.

Tap the Music button in the upper-left corner to go back to the featured Music selections; then tap the Genres button at the top left of the screen. This step displays a list of music genres that you can choose from. Tap one. Items in the genre are organized by criteria, such as New and Noteworthy Albums and iTunes Essentials. Tap any listed item to see more details about it, as shown in Figure 1-3.

The navigation techniques in these steps work essentially the same in any of the content categories (the buttons at the bottom of the screen), which include Music, Movies, Audiobooks, and TV Shows. Just tap one to explore it.

Figure 1-2: Browse selections in the iTunes Store.

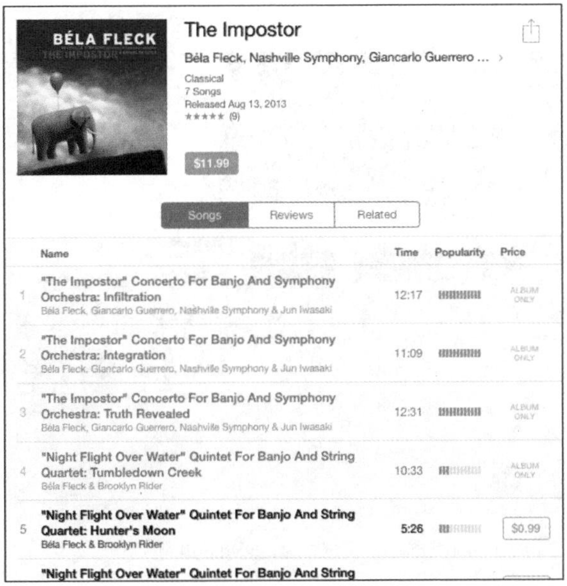

Figure 1-3: Detailed information may include the genre, release date, and song list.

If you want to use the Genius playlist feature, which recommends additional purchases based on the contents of your library, open the iTunes Store app on your iPad and tap the Genius button at the bottom of the screen. If you've made enough purchases in iTunes, song and album recommendations appear based on those purchases. You also see the content in your iTunes Match library (a fee-based music service) if you have one.

Finding a selection

You can look for a selection in the iTunes Store in several ways. You can use the Search feature, search by genres or categories, or view artists' pages. Here's how these work:

- **Search:** Tap in the Search field shown in Figure 1-4 and enter a search term, which could be a genre of music, the name of an album or song, or an artist's name, for example, using the onscreen keyboard. Tap the Search button on the keyboard or, if one of the suggestions given appeals to you, just go ahead and tap it. Search results are divided into categories such as Songs and Albums. Flick down to scroll through them and find what you need. Tap Cancel to return to the Music selections screen.

Figure 1-4: Search by composer, artist, or album title.

- **Link:** On a description page that appears when you tap a selection, you can find more offerings by people involved, such as a singer or actor, if you tap the Related tab, as shown in Figure 1-5.

Figure 1-5: If you have an artist you favor, search for him.

If you find a selection you like, tap the Share button at the top of the description page to share your discovery with a friend via Mail, Message, Twitter, or Facebook. For all sharing choices but AirDrop, a message appears with a link that your friend can click to view the selection. Enter an address in the To field and tap Send or Post. Your friend is now in the know.

Previewing music, a movie, or an audiobook

Because you've already set up an iTunes Store account (if you haven't done so yet, see Book I, Chapter 5), when you choose to buy an item, it's automatically charged to the credit card or PayPal account you have on record or against any allowance you have outstanding from an iTunes gift card.

However, you might just want to preview an item before you buy it to be sure that it's a good fit. If you like it, buying and downloading are then easy and quick.

Follow these steps to preview your content:

1. **Open the iTunes Store and locate a selection you might want to buy using any of the methods I outline in earlier sections.**

2. **Tap the item to see detailed information about it, as shown in Figure 1-6.**

3. **Sample the content:**

   • For a movie or audiobook selection, tap the Trailer button (see Figure 1-6) to play a preview.

   • For a TV show, tap an episode to get further information.

Figure 1-6: Why not preview before you buy?

- If you want to listen to a sample of a music selection, tap the track number or name of a selection with a red preview icon to the right of it, as shown in Figure 1-7. A small square appears and the track plays. Tap the square to stop the preview.

Figure 1-7: You can also preview music before you rent or buy.

If you like what you hear or see, you're ready to buy. Which brings you to the next section.

Buying a selection

Although you can find some freebies out there, and you can rent certain movies rather than buy them, you'll often have to buy the music, video, or audio that you want to enjoy. Buying involves authorizing the purchase and downloading the content to your iPad (which is done automatically after the purchasing part is complete).

Buying and downloading a movie while running your iPad on a 3G/4G network can eat up your data allocation and take a while — if such a large file can even download at all. You're better off downloading this content while connected to a Wi-Fi network. To play it safe, to disable cellular download for the iTunes Store, go to Settings⇨iTunes & App Store and turn off the Use Cellular Data switch.

When you find an item you want to buy, here's how to make your purchase:

1. **Tap the button that shows either the price (if it's a selection available for purchase; see Figure 1-8) or the word** *Free* **(if it's a selection available for free).**

   The button label changes to Buy *X,* where *X* is the particular content you're buying, such as a song or album.

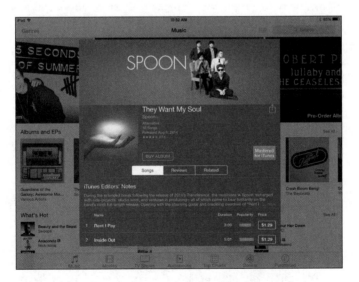

Figure 1-8: Buy the content you want using these buttons.

2. **Tap the Buy *X* button.**

   The iTunes Password dialog appears. (Refer to Figure 1-1.)

3. **Enter your password and tap OK, or if you have a credit, tap the Redeem link and enter the code provided.**

   In the confirming dialog, tap Download. The item begins downloading and is automatically charged to your credit card or against a store credit. When the download finishes, you can view the content using the Music or Videos app, depending on the type of content you bought.

If you want to buy music, you can open the description page for an album and click the album price, or buy individual songs rather than the entire album. Tap the price for a song and then proceed to purchase it.

Note the Redeem button on many iTunes Store screens. Tap this button to redeem any iTunes gift certificates you might have gotten from your generous friends, or from yourself. Your purchases are debited against your certificate balance; if the item costs more, your credit card is then charged for the remainder.

If you don't want to allow purchases from within apps (for example, Music or Videos) but rather want to allow purchases only through the iTunes Store, you can tap Settings⇨General⇨Restrictions and then tap Enable Restrictions and enter a passcode. After you set a passcode, you can tap individual apps to turn on restrictions for them, as well as for actions such as deleting apps, sharing via AirDrop, or using Siri.

Renting movies

In the case of movies, you can either rent or buy content. If you rent, which is less expensive but makes the content yours for only a short time, you have 30 days from the time you rent the item to begin to watch it. After you have begun to watch it, you have 24 hours remaining from that time to watch it as many times as you like (but only on the same device). To rent a movie, follow these steps:

1. **With the iTunes Store open, tap the Movies button.**

2. **Locate the movie you want to rent and tap to open it, as shown in Figure 1-9.**

3. **Tap the Rent button.**

   The Rent button changes to a Rent Movie button (see Figure 1-10). At this point, you may be asked to enter your Apple ID and password.

4. **Tap the Rent Movie button to confirm the rental.**

   The movie begins to download to your iPad immediately, and your account is charged the rental fee.

   After the download is complete, you can use the Videos app to watch it. (See Chapters 2 and 3 in this minibook to read about how these apps work.)

Figure 1-9: To rent, start by viewing details about the content.

Figure 1-10: If you want to watch it only once, rent and save money.

Some movies are offered in high-definition versions in addition to standard definition. These HD movies look great on that crisp, colorful iPad screen, especially if you have a third-generation (or later) iPad with Retina display. It's best to download these over a Wi-Fi connection because a 3G/4G connection could incur hefty charges.

You can also take content that you've downloaded to your computer and sync it to your iPad. See Book I, Chapter 5 for more about this process.

Shopping Anywhere Else

Many content stores have added iPad-friendly videos to their collections, so you do have alternatives to iTunes for your choice of movies or TV shows. You can also shop for music from sources other than iTunes, such as Amazon.

You can open accounts at these stores by using your computer or your iPad's Safari browser and then following a store's instructions for purchasing and downloading content. Keep in mind that costs will vary. For example, one such provider is Hulu. To get iPad-friendly content from Hulu, you have to sign up for the Hulu Plus service and pay a monthly fee (less than $10). Then, download the app directly from Hulu and start watching content.

Here are some online stores and content providers that offer iPad-compatible content:

- ✔ **TV** (www.tv.com) provides its online television and movie content to iPad.

- ✔ **Ustream** (www.ustream.tv) has a mobile app for streaming sports and entertainment programs to mobile devices.

- ✔ **ABC** (http://abc.go.com) and **CBS News** (www.cbsnews.com) stream live TV programming to the iPad.

- ✔ **Netflix** (www.netflix.com) makes movies and TV shows available that can be streamed to the iPad.

- ✔ **PBS** (www.pbs.org), the king of documentary and artsy movie programming, has several apps for iPad including Nova Elements iPad App, PBS Kids iPad app, and PBS for iPad for other programming.

- ✔ **iMP4hub** (www.imp4hub.com) is all about free MPEG-4–format movies for iPad, iPhone, and Android devices.

Additionally, if you get content onto your Mac or Windows machine, you can stream it to your iPad using Air Video ($2.99) and Air Video Server, and it will do an on-the-fly conversion. For more information, go to www.inmethod.com/air-video/index.html. Another free utility for Windows, OS X, and Linux that converts most video to an iPad-friendly format is HandBrake. Go to http://handbrake.fr for more information.

There are also apps that stream content if you pay a subscription fee or are an existing customer. Two good ones are Xfinity TV from Comcast and TWCable from Time Warner.

Enabling Autodownloads of Purchases from Other Devices

With iCloud, after you set up an iCloud account, either during the initial setup of your device or through iPad Settings, you can make a purchase or download free content on any of your Apple devices that have been set up for auto-download, and you can have those purchases automatically copied onto any or all your Apple devices. To enable this auto-download feature on iPad, follow these steps:

1. **Tap Settings on the Home screen.**

   To use iCloud, first set up an iCloud account. See Book I, Chapter 5 for detailed coverage of iCloud, including setting up your account.

2. **Tap iTunes & App Store.**

3. **In the options that appear, tap the On/Off switch to turn on any category of purchases you want to auto-download to your iPad from other Apple devices: Music, Apps, or Books (see Figure 1-11).**

At this point, Apple doesn't offer an option of auto-downloading video content using these settings, probably because video is such a memory and bandwidth hog. You can always download video directly to your iPad through the iTunes Store app or sync to your computer using iTunes to get the content or through the iTunes U app for educational content.

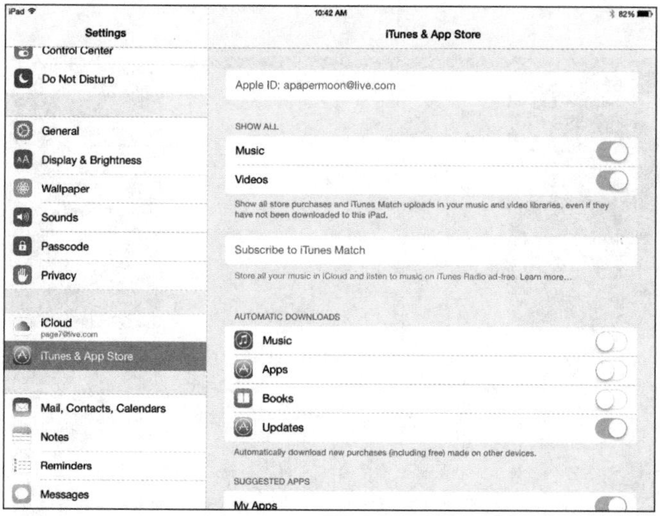

Figure 1-11: Authorize purchases from an app by turning it on here.

Setting Up Family Sharing

Family Sharing is a new feature that allows up to six people to share whatever anybody in the group has purchased from the iTunes, iBooks, and App Stores even though you don't share Apple accounts. Your family must all use one credit card to purchase items, but you can approve purchases by younger children. You can also share calendars, photos, and a family calendar (see Book V, Chapter 3 for information about Family Sharing and Calendar, and Book II, Chapter 6 for information on sharing Photos in a Family album).

Start by turning on Family Sharing:

1. **Tap Settings.**

2. **Tap iCloud and then tap Set Up Family Sharing.**

3. **Tap Get Started.**

4. **Tap Continue.**

5. **On the Share Purchases screen, tap Share Purchases from a different account to use another Apple account.**

6. **Tap Continue and check the payment method you want to use.**

7. **Tap Continue.**

8. **On the screen that appears, tap Add Family Member.**

9. **Enter the person's name (assuming that this person is listed in your contacts) or email address (see Figure 1-12).**

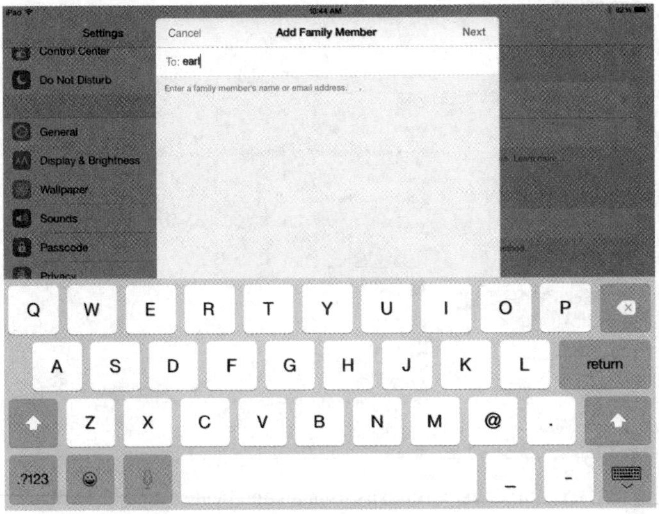

Figure 1-12: Add the family member's name or email address.

An invitation is sent to that person's email. When the invitation is accepted, the person is added to your family.

Note that the payment method for this family is displayed under Shared Payment Method in this screen. All those involved in a family have to use a single payment method for family purchases.

Chapter 2: Playing Music on Your iPad

In This Chapter

- ✔ **Viewing Music library contents**
- ✔ **Creating playlists**
- ✔ **Searching for audio**
- ✔ **Playing music and other audio**
- ✔ **Shuffling music**
- ✔ **Using AirPlay**
- ✔ **Enjoying iTunes Radio**
- ✔ **Being your own DJ with radio stations**
- ✔ **Viewing music history**

Almost everybody on Earth has heard of the iPod — that small, portable, music-playing device from Apple that's seemingly glued into the ears of many. The iPad includes an iPod-like app called Music that allows you to take advantage of the iPad's pretty amazing little sound system to play your favorite style of music or podcasts and audiobooks.

In this chapter, you can get acquainted with the Music app and its features that enable you to sort and find music and control playback from your iPad. You also get an overview of the AirPlay feature, which you can use to play music on your iPad over a home network. Finally, I introduce you to iTunes Radio.

My Stations

Songs   Albums

Looking Over Your Library of Music

In Chapter 1 of this minibook, I guide you through the process of getting content onto your iPad. After you have some audio content in the form of music, podcasts, or audiobooks, it's organized into collections, and you can find that content by categories such as artist or genre with predefined category buttons along the bottom of the Music app screen.

Viewing the library contents

You can easily view the contents of your library collections, which **you may** have synced from your computer or shared over a network, push**ed to your** device through iCloud, or downloaded directly using iPad's Wi-Fi **or Wi-Fi+** Cellular capability. (See Chapter 1 in this minibook for details.)

Take a tour of your Music library collections by following these **simple steps**:

1. **Tap the Music app, located in the Dock on the Home screen.**

   The Music library appears (see Figure 2-1).

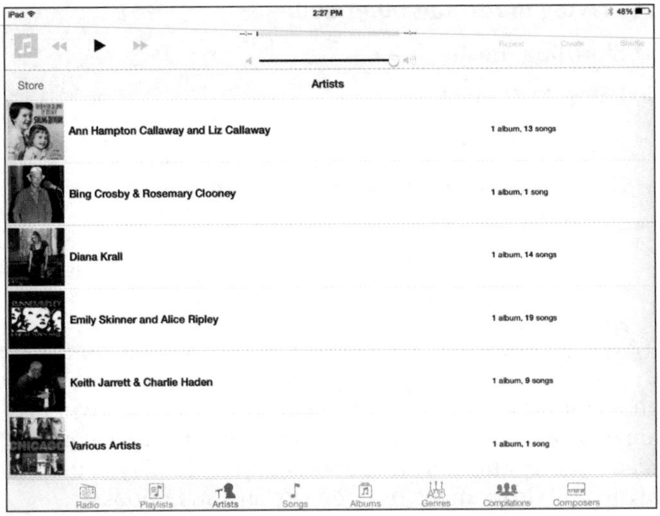

Figure 2-1: The Music library showing your music by Artists.

2. **Tap the Playlists, Artists, Songs, Albums, Genres, Compilations (such as the Best of British Rock), or Composers button at the bottom of the library to view your music according to these criteria. (Refer to Figure 2-1.)**

   The Purchased button appears only if you've already obtained content on iTunes.

3. **Tap the Radio button (see Figure 2-2) to view this feature, discussed in more detail later in this chapter.**

Figure 2-2: View stations by tapping the Radio button.

 The iTunes Store has several free items that you can download and use to play around with the features in Music, including music and podcasts. You can also sync content stored on your computer or other Apple devices to your iPad and play it using the Music app. See Book I, Chapter 5 for more about syncing.

Apple offers a service called iTunes Match (www.apple.com/itunes/ itunes-match). You pay $24.99 per year for the capability to match the music you've bought from other providers or ripped from CDs (and stored on your computer) to what's in the iTunes Store inventory. If there's a match (and there often is), that content is added to your iTunes library at 256 Kbps. If there's audio that isn't a match, it's uploaded to iCloud and synced to your iPad. Then, using iCloud, you can sync the content among all your Apple devices. The upward limit of 25,000 tracks works for most users.

 You can use the iTunes Summary tab on your computer to make a setting to sync music at 128 Kbps. Doing this saves space on your iPad if you're an avid music downloader, though the audio quality is lower. You can also make a setting for whether to download album covers in iTunes.

Creating playlists

Everybody loves *playlists.* They give you a way to compile your very own music mix to match your mood or the occasion. You can easily create your own playlists with the Music app to put tracks from various sources into collections of your choosing.

With the Music app open, follow these steps to create your own playlists:

1. **Tap the Playlists button at the bottom of the iPad screen.**

2. **Scroll up the screen and tap New Playlist in the options that are revealed.**

3. **In the dialog that appears, enter a name for the playlist and tap Save.**

4. **Tap an album such as Recently Played or Purchased, and in the list that appears (see Figure 2-3), tap the plus sign next to each item you want to include.**

   The Add symbol on selected items turn gray.

iPad 🖧		2:31 PM		◀ 🔋 100% 🔋
Store		**Songs**		Done
All That Jazz	Bebe Neuwirth & Rob Fisher	Chicago - The Musical		⊕
Allentown	Billy Joel	Greatest Hits, Vols. 1 & 2		⊕
Big Shot	Billy Joel	Greatest Hits, Vols. 1 & 2		⊕
Captain Jack	Billy Joel	Greatest Hits, Vols. 1 & 2		⊕
Divine Light	The Deer Tracks	Divine Light Remix - EP		⊕
Divine Light ([krig] Remix)	The Deer Tracks	Divine Light Remix - EP		⊕
Divine Light (Dwid Remix)	The Deer Tracks	Divine Light Remix - EP		⊕
Divine Light (Ioan Gamboa Fujur...	The Deer Tracks	Divine Light Remix - EP		⊕
Divine Light (Magnus Moody Rem...	The Deer Tracks	Divine Light Remix - EP		⊕
Divine Light (Slim Vic Club Remix)	The Deer Tracks	Divine Light Remix - EP		⊕
Don't Ask Me Why	Billy Joel	Greatest Hits, Vols. 1 & 2		⊕
♪ Songs	👥 Artists	📷 Albums	Composers	

Figure 2-3: Personalize your Music experience with custom playlists.

5. **Tap the Done button.**

6. **Tap the Playlists button.**

   Your playlist appears in the Playlists list, and you can play it by tapping the list name to reveal its songs and then tapping the Play button in the playback controls at the upper left.

You can use the Genius Playlist feature in iTunes Store to set up playlists of recommended content in your Music library. Based on items you've purchased, iTunes Store suggests other purchases that would go well with your collection. Okay, it's a way to get you to buy more music, but if you're building your music collection, it might be worth a try! Visit the iTunes site at www.apple.com/itunes for more information.

To delete a song from the playlist, swipe left to right across the name of the song you want to delete and then tap the Delete button.

Searching for audio

If you can't find what you want by going through collections or categories, you can search for an item in your Music library by using the Search feature. You can enter an artist's, audiobook author's, or composer's name or a word from the item's title in the Search field to find what you're looking for.

You can also ask Siri to play a selection or use the Spotlight Search feature from the Home screen to search for music. You can also ask Siri to identify music that's playing around you, for example in an elevator or at a club, and using the Shazam music identification service, Siri tells you the name of the tune and allows you to buy it at the iTunes Store.

With the Music app open, tap in the Search field (see Figure 2-4). The onscreen keyboard opens.

Book II
Chapter 2

Playing Music on Your iPad

![Figure 2-4 screenshot]
iPad ᚎ   2:35 PM   47%

Store   **Albums**

🔍 Search

Bing & Rosie - The Crosby-Clooney Radio Ses...	Bing Crosby & Rosemary Clooney	1 song, 3 min	
Chicagó - The Músical	Various Artists	1 song, 5 min	
Last Dance	Keith Jarrett & Charlie Haden	9 songs, 76 min	
Quiet Nights (Bonus Track Version)	Diana Krall	14 songs, 63 min	
Ripley/Skinner: Raw At Town Hall	Emily Skinner and Alice Ripley	19 songs, 84 min	
Sibling Revelry (Live)	Ann Hampton Callaway and Liz...	13 songs, 59 min	

Radio   Playlists   Artists   Songs   Albums   Genres   Compilations   Composers

Figure 2-4: Enter your search terms and see what you find!

Enter a search term in the Search field. Or tap the Dictation key (see Figure 2-5) on the onscreen keyboard of an iPad (the Dictation key is not present on the iPad 2) to speak the search term; then tap the Search button on the keyboard. Results display, narrowing the search as you type. Now just tap any item in the search results to play it.

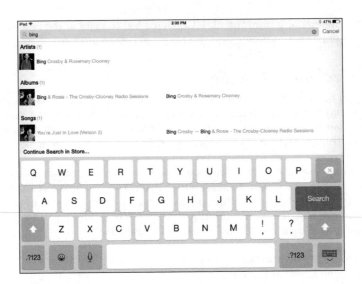

Figure 2-5: Music search results.

Playing Music and Other Audio

You have all that music and other audio content to listen to, and beyond downloading and organizing your selections, that's what Music is mainly for. You'll find the typical playback tools in the Music app, but in case you want a refresher, here's the quick rundown on how to use Music as a player.

Playing your tunes

Playing an audio file is simple, and you'll be glad to know that Music can continue to play in the background while you go about using other apps. If you're browsing in Safari, for example, with a track playing in Music, you can double-tap the Home button and a mini toolbar opens where you can control playback without leaving the browser. If your iPad is showing the Lock screen, you can also use controls displayed there to control music playback for currently playing selections.

The procedure for playing music is to basically find what you want to play, and then use the playback tools to play it. Here's how:

1. **Locate the item you want to play using the methods I describe in previous sections of this chapter.**

2. **Tap the item you want to play from the list that appears.**

   If the item is stored on iCloud, tap the iCloud symbol next to it to download it before you can play it.

The song begins playing. *Note:* If you're displaying the Songs tab, you don't have to tap an album to open a song; you need only tap a song to play it. If you're using any other tab, you have to tap items such as albums or multiple songs from one artist to find the song you want to hear.

3. **Tap Now Playing to display the album cover full screen (see Figure 2-6).**

Figure 2-6: View your album's cover as you listen.

4. **If you want to go to a specific item, such as a song in the album that's playing, tap the item you want to play from the list that appears.**

   It begins to play.

5. **Use the Previous and Next buttons that display when you tap the top of the screen (refer to Figure 2-6) to navigate the audio files.**

   The Previous button takes you back to the beginning of the item that's playing or the previous track if nothing is playing; the Next button takes you to the next item.

6. **Tap the Pause button to pause playback.**

   You can also use music controls from the Lock screen to control music that's playing.

7. **Tap and drag the line just below the album cover that indicates the current playback location on the progress bar left or right to "scrub" to another location in the song.**

8. **Don't like what's playing? Tap the Back to Library button (the < icon) in the top-left corner to return to the Playlist list, or tap the Album List button in the top-right corner to show other tracks in the album that's playing and make another selection.**

You can use Siri to play music hands free. Just press and hold the Home button, and when Siri appears, say something like "Play 'Take the A Train'" or "Play *The White Album.*"

The Home Sharing feature of iTunes allows you to share music among as many as five computers that have Home Sharing turned on (iOS devices and Apple TVs, second generation or later, don't count against that limit). To use the feature, each device has to have the same Apple ID for Home sharing. After you set up the feature via iTunes, you can retrieve music and videos from your iTunes shared library to any of the devices. For more about Home Sharing — which is discussed further in the later section, "Using AirPlay and Home Sharing" — visit this site: www.apple.com/support/homesharing.

Shuffling music

If you want to play a random selection of the music you've purchased or synced through iCloud or from your computer to your iPad, use the Shuffle feature. With the Music app open, tap the Songs or Albums button at the bottom of the screen. Next, tap the Shuffle button shown in Figure 2-7. Your content plays in random order.

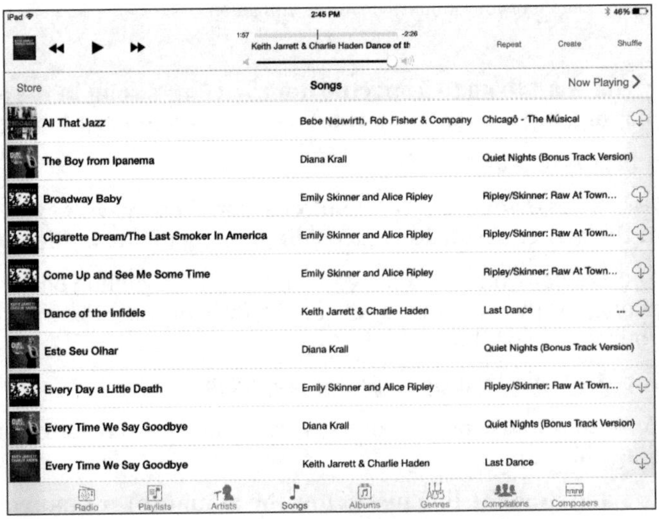

Figure 2-7: Shuffle your music for a varied musical experience.

Adjusting the volume

Music offers its own volume control that you can adjust during playback. This volume is set relative to the system volume that you control using the iPad's Settings app; if you set it to 50%, it will play at 50 percent of the system volume setting.

With Music open, tap a piece of music to play it. In the controls that appear onscreen (see Figure 2-8), press and drag the button on the Volume slider to the right for more volume or to the left for less volume. To mute your iPad's speaker at any time, press the Mute button to the right of the volume slider or, if it's set up to control volume in Settings, slide the Side switch on the side of your iPad to on.

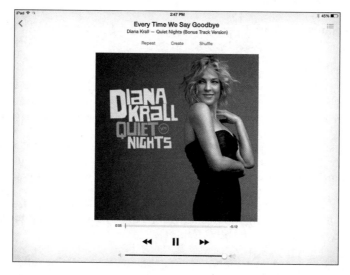

Figure 2-8: Louder or softer, just use the slider to get the effect you want.

If you have volume set at high and you're still having trouble hearing, consider getting a headset. These devices cut out extraneous noises and should improve the sound quality of what you're listening to. I recommend that you use a 3.5mm stereo headphone (a ⅛" headphone sometimes works fairly well) and insert it in the headphone jack at the top of your iPad. You can also use Apple's iPod or iPhone EarPods, which work just fine with the iPad. The iPhone EarPods include a microphone as well.

Using AirPlay and Home Sharing

AirPlay and Home Sharing are two methods of sharing music among devices.

AirPlay gives you the ability to stream audio to externally powered speakers on your wireless network as well as to home entertainment centers that include an Apple TV unit. Several speaker manufacturers have built AirPlay hardware into their systems. AirPlay streaming technology is built into the iPhone, iPod touch, and iPad, as well as being available to iTunes on Windows PCs and Macs. With AirPlay, you can send media files from one device to be played on another. You can send (say) a movie that you purchased on your iPad or a slideshow of photos to be played on your TV — and control the playback from your iPad. You can also send music to be played over speakers.

There are a few ways to do this. You can purchase an Apple TV and stream video, photos, and music to the TV, or you can purchase an AirPort Express Wi-Fi router and attach your speakers to it to play music. Finally, if you buy AirPlay–enabled wireless speakers, you can stream audio directly to them. Because this combination of equipment varies, my advice — if you're interested in using AirPlay — is to visit your nearest Apple Store or certified Apple dealer and find out which hardware combination will work best for you.

iOS 8 supports peer-to-peer AirPlay support, which means that if you can make a direct connection to AirPlay speakers or Apple TV, you can share content such as music and photos without being on the same network.

To use AirPlay with another AirPlay–enabled device on your network or in close proximity, swipe up from the bottom of your screen and tap the AirPlay button in the Control Center.

If you get a bit antsy watching a long movie, one of the beauties of AirPlay is that you can still use your iPad to check email, browse photos or the Internet, or check your calendar while the media plays.

Home Sharing is a feature of iTunes that you can use to share music and video among devices that have Home Sharing turned on. To use the feature, each device has to have the same Apple ID on your network. After it is set up via iTunes, you can stream music and videos to any of the devices, and even click and drag content between devices using iTunes on your computer. iTunes on your computer can also share its library over a network. For more about Home Sharing, visit this site: www.apple.com/support/homesharing.

Playing Music with iTunes Radio

iTunes Radio lets you access a world of radio content and even learns what kind of content you like as time passes. You can access iTunes Radio with any Apple device that has iOS 7 or later; just follow these steps:

1. **Begin by tapping the Music app on the Home screen.**

2. **Tap the Radio button at the bottom of the screen that appears.**

3. **Tap a Featured Station. (See Figure 2-9.)**

   A featured song begins to play.

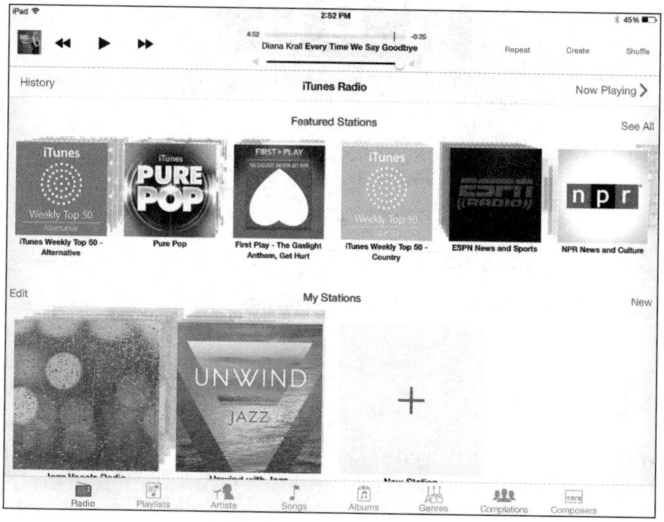

Figure 2-9: Tap a featured station to hear a featured song.

4. **Use the tools at the bottom of the screen, shown in Figure 2-10, to control playback.**

5. **Tap the Information button at the top-middle of the screen to display the options.**

6. **Choose one of the following: New Station from Artist, New Station from Song, Add to My Stations, Allow Explicit Tracks, or Share Station via AirDrop, Mail, Twitter, or Facebook.**

These choices may vary depending on the type of station you've opened; for example, they will be different on a talk radio station such as NPR. The more you use iTunes Radio, the better the program is able to build you stations that match your taste.

Figure 2-10: The usual tools for controlling playback.

Creating Stations

Are you the creative type? Do you like more than one kind of music? You'll be glad to know that you can create a radio station of your own.

1. **Tap Music in the Dock.**

2. **Tap Radio. From the iTunes Radio Home page, tap the New Station button with a bright red cross on it (see Figure 2-11).**

3. **Tap a category of music such as Classic Rock or Dance. (See Figure 2-12.)**

4. **If subcategories are then offered, tap the one you prefer and then tap the Add New button that appears to the right of the category.**

   The category is added to your stations.

Figure 2-11: Tap the red cross to create a new station.

Figure 2-12: Choose a category of music.

Viewing Your Music History

iTunes Radio offers a great way to see where you've been and where you're going, musically speaking, with its History and Wish List features. To view your music history, just follow these steps:

1. **Tap Music in the Dock.**

2. **In the screen that appears (see Figure 2-13), tap History in the top-left corner.**

Figure 2-13: Tap History to discover what you've been listening to.

3. **Tap the Played tab to see the music you've listened to (see Figure 2-14).**

4. **Tap the Wish List tab to see items you've added to your Wish List.**

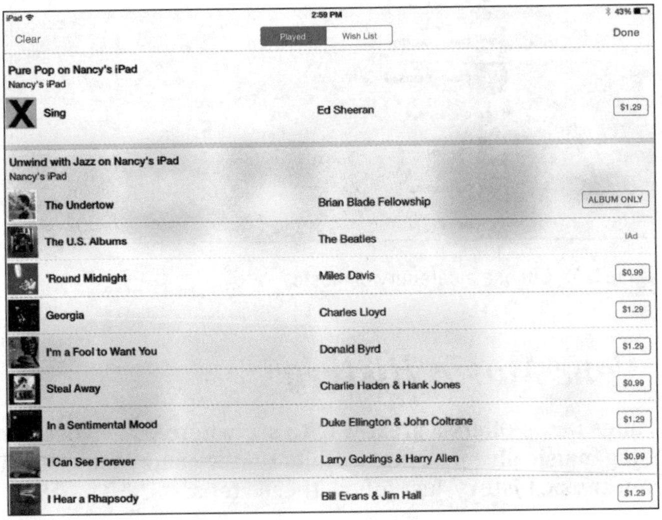

Figure 2-14: Which songs have you spent your time with?

Chapter 3: Watching Videos

In This Chapter

⮞ **Finding and playing movies, podcasts, or TV shows with Videos**

⮞ **Turning on closed-captioning**

⮞ **Going to a movie chapter**

⮞ **Deleting a video item from iPad**

⮞ **Sharing video content**

In this chapter, I cover the preinstalled app called Videos. The Videos app is a player with which you can watch downloaded movies and TV shows, as well as media you've synced from iCloud or your Mac or PC.

If you own an iPad that can run iOS 8, you can take advantage of the rear-facing iSight camera with the ability to record video in 720p HD (high definition) and video stabilization to prevent those wobbly video moments. You can also benefit from the Retina display on iPad/iPad mini to watch videos with super-high resolution, which simply means that they'll look very, very good.

If you like to view things on a bigger screen, you can use iPad's AirPlay technology and Apple TV, a device that will cost you $99, to send your iPad movies and photos to a TV that supports HDMI.

Note that iPads that can run iOS 7 or later sport two video cameras that you can use to capture your own videos. By purchasing the iMovie app (a scaled-down version of the longtime mainstay on Mac computers), you add the capability to edit those videos. You find out about both of these features in Chapter 4 of this minibook.

In this chapter, I explain all about watching, rating, deleting, and sharing video content from a variety of sources. You might want to refer to Chapter 1 in this minibook first to purchase or download one of many free TV shows or movies you can practice with.

Finding Videos

Note that you can get video content through the iTunes Store and some third-party companies that support iPad, including Netflix and ABC TV. You can also use an app such as Air Video to send content from your Mac or PC to your iPad via a wireless connection, or use the EyeTV app from your Mac to send live TV or recordings. Some of the content you find online is free, and some shows or movies will cost you a few bucks.

You can also view videos you stream from a Home Sharing–enabled iTunes library over a home network, which can really save space on your iPad because the content can be stored on another device (such as a hard drive attached to your Mac or PC). Turn on Home Sharing in the Video category of Settings on your iPad.

This chapter focuses mainly on the bundled Videos app, but you should also note that more and more online content providers are making it possible to view videos on their sites. For example, you can go to Flickr and use its HTML5 player for video playback. Also, using Family Sharing, you have access to videos purchased by anybody in your Family Sharing group.

See Chapter 1 in this minibook for more about buying or renting movies or TV shows using the iTunes Store and setting up a Family Sharing account. For information about shooting your own videos, see Chapter 4 in this minibook.

Playing Movies or TV Shows

Did you realize that your iPad is a miniature home entertainment center? The built-in Videos app can play TV shows and movies.

Also, note that you can stream video content from your iPad to play on your TV. Buy an app such as Samsung TV Media Player, and you can fling video content playing on your iPad to your Samsung Smart TV.

When you first open the Videos app, you may see relatively blank screens with a note that you don't own any videos and a link to the iTunes Store. After you purchase TV shows and movies or rent movies, you see tabs for the different kinds of content you own. Use the steps in Chapter 1 of this minibook to download video content to your iPad. After you download content, use these steps to work with Video's familiar playback tools to play it:

1. **Tap the Videos app on the Home screen to open the application.**

2. **On a screen like the one shown in Figure 3-1, tap the appropriate category at the top of the screen (Movies, Rentals, or TV Shows, depending on the content you've downloaded).**

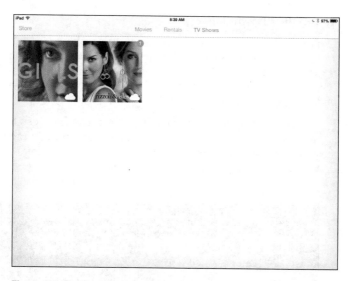

Figure 3-1: Choose the type of content you want to view.

3. **Tap an item to open it.**

   A description appears, as shown in Figure 3-2. TV Shows includes the Episodes, Details, and Related tabs; Movies contains the Details, Chapters, and Related tabs.

Figure 3-2: You can get information about the media on this opening screen.

4. **Tap the Play button.**

   For TV Shows, tap the Episodes tab to display episodes with a play button for each; for Movies, the Play button appears no matter which tab is selected. Tap the Play button, and the movie or TV show begins playing. (If you see a small cloud button instead of a Play button, tap it to download the content from iCloud.)

   The progress of the playback displays in the Progress bar, showing how many minutes you've viewed and how many remain (see Figure 3-3). If you don't see this bar, tap the screen once to display it briefly, along with a set of playback tools at the bottom of the screen.

Figure 3-3: Use the standard playback controls to play your content.

5. **With the playback tools displayed, take any of these actions:**

   - *Tap the Pause button to pause playback.*

   - *Tap either Go to Previous Chapter or Go to Next Chapter to move to a different location in the video playback if the video supports chapters.*

   - *Tap the circular button on the Volume slider and drag it left or right to decrease or increase the volume, respectively.*

   - *Tap the circular button on the Progress bar to move to another spot in the video.*

6. **To stop the video and return to the information screen, tap the Done button to the left of the Progress bar.**

Watching non-iTunes videos

Are you limited to iTunes video content on your iPad or viewing all your downloaded content on the smaller screen? Not at all. You can connect iPad to your television, so you can watch videos on the more vision-friendly larger screen. To do this, you have to buy the Digital AV Adapter at the Apple Store. The Apple Digital AV Adapter is a $39.95 accessory; the Apple TV costs $99. You also need any other appropriate cables for your TV to complete the connection. (Or you can use AirPlay via an Apple TV.)

Note that iPad supports only the following video formats: H.264 video up to 1080p, 30 frames per second; MPEG-4 video, up to 2.5 Mbps, 640 by 480 pixels, 30 frames per second; and Motion JPEG (M-JPEG), up to 35 Mbps, 1280 by 720 pixels, 30 frames per second. You can use conversion software such as Mac AVI to iPad Video Converter to be able to convert,

edit, and play AVI movies on your iPad. You can also stream with Air Video Live Conversion or use the free HandBrake app to convert to an iPad-friendly format.

In addition, you can rip Blu-ray video disc content to an iPad-compatible format and then transfer the content by syncing to your computer using iTunes. You can use the Blu-ray Ripper for Mac here: www.aunsoft.com/blu-ray-ripper-mac. You can use the free Windows Aiseesoft Blu-ray to iPad Ripper at www.aiseesoft.com/blu-ray-ripper.html to handle the transfer.

Finally, check out the Air Video app from InMethod. Using this app, you can stream content to your iPad, convert content, or save content to iTunes, which you can then sync to your iPad.

**Book II
Chapter 3**

Watching Videos

You can set up widescreen viewing options in the Videos section of Settings. For more about using Settings, see Book I, Chapter 8.

Note that if you've watched a video and stopped it partway through, the next time you open the video in iPad, it opens, by default, at the last location that you were viewing. To start a video from the beginning, just as with most players, you simply tap and drag the circular button on the Progress bar all the way to the left. You can also change the default setting from starting where you left off to starting from the beginning in iPad's Settings app under Video.

Turning on Closed-Captioning

If you have hearing challenges or are a fan of foreign flicks, you'll be glad to know that iPad offers support for closed-captioning and subtitles. This feature requires that you have content that supports closed-captioning (not all shows or movies do) and that you go to Settings to turn on the feature. Look for the CC logo on media that you download to use this feature; be aware that video you record using the iPad video camera won't have this capability.

Turn on the feature in Settings by following these steps:

1. **Tap Settings on the Home screen.**

2. **On the screen that appears, tap General⇨Accessibility and then tap Subtitles & Captioning.**

3. **In the menu that displays on the right side of the screen (see Figure 3-4), tap the Closed Captions & SDH On/Off switch to turn on the feature.**

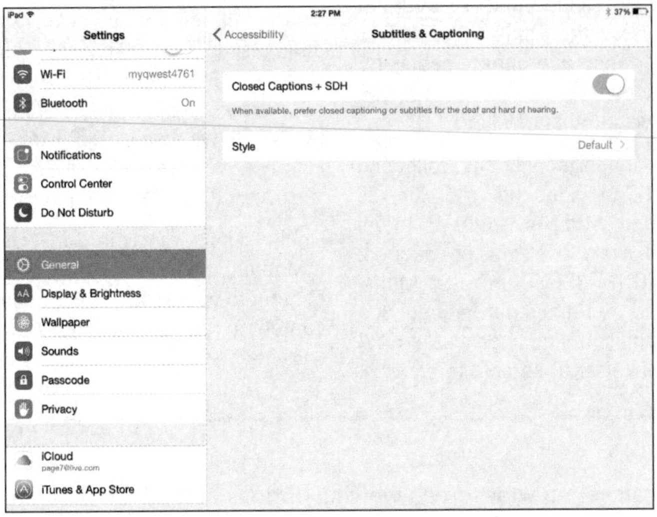

Figure 3-4: Go to Settings on your Home screen to access video settings.

Now when you play a movie with closed-captioning support, you can click the Audio and Subtitles button to the right of the playback controls to manage these features.

Going to a Movie Chapter

You know that movies you view on a DVD or online are usually divided into *chapters,* so you can jump from one part to another quickly. Jumping to another chapter using the Videos app is a pretty simple procedure. Follow these steps:

1. **Tap Videos on the Home screen.**

2. **Tap the Movies tab if it isn't already displayed.**

3. **Tap the title of the movie you want to watch.**

   Information about the movie displays.

4. **Tap the Chapters tab.**

   A list of chapters displays, as shown in Figure 3-5.

5. **Tap a chapter to play it.**

Figure 3-5: Click a chapter in this list to go to it.

You can also use the playback tools to go back one chapter or forward one chapter. For more information, see the "Playing Movies or TV Shows" section, earlier in this chapter.

Deleting Video Content

Media files can, as you know, take up lots of space in a computing device. Even if you bought the iPad model with the largest amount of memory, its memory can fill up fast. When you've bought content from the iTunes Store, you can always download it again, so if you're not planning on watching an item again soon, deleting it from your iPad and freeing up some space is a good idea. Or, sync with iTunes on a computer again to get the content back on your iPad. If you want to delete content that you didn't purchase from the iTunes Store, be sure to back it up to your computer first; otherwise, you can't get at it again when it's gone from your iPad.

Note that if you rent content and delete it after watching it, you can't get it back without paying for it again.

To delete items that aren't stored in iCloud (items stored in iCloud have a little cloud next to them), tap Videos on the Home screen. Locate the item you want to delete on the Movies, TV Shows, or Rentals tab and then press and hold the item; a Delete button appears. Tap the Delete button, and the item is deleted. (To delete multiple items, tap the Edit key instead at this point.)

If you buy a video using iTunes Store, you'll find it saved in iCloud. You can tap the iCloud button to download the video.

Sharing Your Favorite Videos

You can share your opinion about a video using Mail, Twitter, or Facebook:

1. **Tap the Videos app on the Home screen to open it and then tap the Store button. Find a video you want to share and tap it.**

2. **In the information screen shown in Figure 3-6, tap the Share button (a box with an arrow at the top of it, at the top of the screen).**

Figure 3-6: Choose a method of sharing.

3. **Tap Mail, Twitter, or Facebook to use one of these methods of sharing your enthusiasm for the item.**

4. **In the corresponding form, enter a recipient in the To field if required and then add to the message (see Figure 3-7), if you like.**

   If you chose to post to your Facebook page, enter your message in the Facebook form.

Figure 3-7: Enter your message and then send it.

5. **Tap the appropriate Send (or Post) button to send your recommendation by your preferred method.**

When you're viewing information about a video in the iTunes Store, you can tap the Related tab to find information about other movies or TV shows watched by those who watched this one.

Chapter 4: Getting the Most Out of iPad Cameras and FaceTime

In This Chapter

⤙ **Looking good in photos**

⤙ **Exploring Photo Booth**

⤙ **Taking videos**

⤙ **Making video calls with FaceTime**

*W*ith its gorgeous Retina screen (from third-generation iPads on), iPad is a natural for viewing photos and videos. It supports most common photo formats, such as JPEG, TIFF, and PNG. You can shoot your photos and videos by using the built-in cameras in iPad with preprogrammed square or panorama modes, and edit your images using filters that are new with the Camera app that comes with iOS 7. Additionally, you can sync photos from your computer, iPhone, or digital camera, and save images you find online or receive by email to your iPad.

If you have the third-generation or later iPad, you have a built-in iSight camera for your rear-facing camera. This improvement on previous iPad cameras is a 5-megapixel beauty with an illumination sensor that adjusts for whatever lighting is available. Face detection balances focus across as many as ten faces in your pictures. The video camera option offers 1080p HD (high-definition video) with video stabilization that makes up for some shaking as you hold the device to take videos.

When you have photos to play with, the Photos app lets you organize photos from the Camera Roll and view photos in albums, one by one, or in a slideshow. A new feature lets you view photos by the year they were taken, with images divided into collections by the location or time you took them. You can also AirDrop, email, message, post to Facebook, or tweet a photo to a friend, or print it. And if you like to play around with photo effects, you'll enjoy the photo-editing features as well as the preinstalled app, Photo Booth.

If video is more up your alley, in this chapter, you also discover how to use the video cameras in iPad. For those who want to share videos of themselves and their surroundings with others, I cover using the video cameras along with FaceTime to make video calls.

Working with Photos

iPads (except for the original iPad) come with cameras — two, to be exact. These cameras allow you to capture video and photos. And because one camera is front-facing and the other is rear-facing, you can switch between them to capture images of yourself holding the iPad or images of what you're looking at.

On an iPad, the front-facing camera captures high-definition video at 720p; the rear-facing camera captures high-definition video at 1080p.

When you capture photos, they appear in the Photos app's Camera Roll, where you can view them, email them, and so on. (See Chapter 6 in this mini-book for more about using the Photos app.) The Photo Streams feature lets you share groups of photos with people using iCloud on an iOS 6 device or later, or on a Mac computer with the Mountain Lion OS or later installed, or on a PC via iCloud. (See Book V, Chapter 1 for more about sharing files using iCloud.)

The cameras in the iPad are just begging to be used, so get started!

Taking pictures with the iPad camera

When you use an iPad camera, you can switch it between a standard camera and a video camera, and choose whether to use the front or rear camera. To work with the standard camera to take pictures, follow these steps:

1. **Tap the Camera app icon on the Home screen to open the app.**

   If the orange-highlighted word in the row of words below the Capture button (see Figure 4-1) is Video, slide up to set Photo (the still camera) as the active setting rather than video.

2. **Set the Square option using the same slider control below the Capture button.**

   This setting lets you create square images like those you see on the popular Instagram site.

Figure 4-1: The Camera app.

3. **Move the camera around until you find a pleasing image, and then you can do a couple of things at this point to help you take your photo:**

   - Tap the area of the grid where you want the camera to autofocus.

   - Pinch the screen to display a zoom control; drag the circle in the zoom bar to the right or left to zoom in or out on the image. Note that zooming doesn't change resolution and so can degrade the image.

4. **Tap the Capture button at the right side of the screen.**

   You've just taken a picture, and it's stored automatically in the Photos app Camera Roll.

5. **Tap the icon in the top-right corner to switch between the front camera and rear camera.**

   You can now take pictures of yourself.

6. **Tap the Capture button, hold and release it to take another picture.**

   Alternately, you can use the volume rocker as a shutter release. Remember to smile!

7. **To view the last photo taken, swipe to the left or tap the thumbnail of the latest image in the bottom-right corner of the screen (visible in Figure 4-2).**

   The Photos app opens and displays the photo.

Figure 4-2: The latest photo you took appears as a thumbnail.

8. **Tap Done.**

   You return to the Camera app.

9. **Tap the Home button to close the Camera app and return to the Home screen.**

Printing photos

If you have a printer that's compatible with Apple AirPrint technology, you can print photos. As of this writing, most major manufacturers offer printers that have this capability, and you can bet that Apple's working with other manufacturers to provide more compatible choices. However, if you don't want to spring for one of these models, you can also use apps such as Printopia and HandyPrint to provide this functionality to other printers on your network.

If you don't have access to this kind of wireless printer, when you plug iPad into your computer, you can sync both devices via iTunes.

To print a photo, do this:

1. **With Photos open, maximize the photo you want to print.**

2. **Tap the Share icon and then tap Print.**

   The Printer Options dialog appears. (See Figure 4-3.)

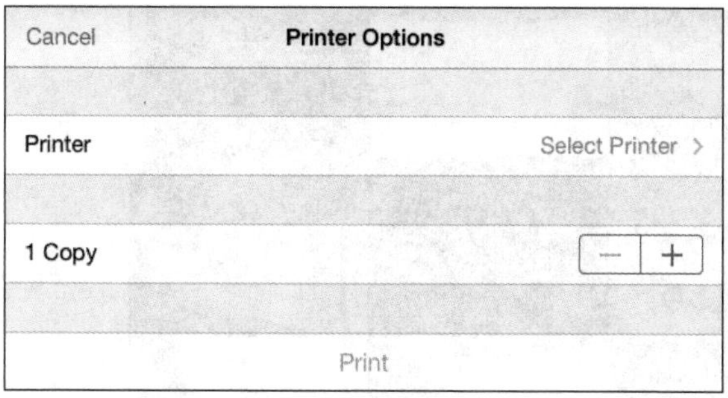

Cancel	**Printer Options**	
Printer		Select Printer >
1 Copy		— +
	Print	

Figure 4-3: The Printer Options dialog.

3. **Tap Select Printer.**

   iPad searches for a compatible wireless printer.

4. **Tap the plus or minus signs in the Copy field to set the number of copies to print.**

5. **Tap the Print button.**

   Your photo goes on its way to your printer.

Playing around with Photo Booth

Photo Booth is a photo-manipulation app that goes hand in hand with the still camera built into the iPad (except for the original iPad) hardware. You can use this app to capture photos using various fun effects, such as Kaleidoscope and X-Ray. You can then copy or email photos from within Photo Booth.

Note that photos you take with Photo Booth open automatically and are saved to your Photos app's Camera Roll.

Here's how to take photos using Photo Booth effects:

1. **Tap the Photo Booth icon on the Home screen.**

   The different possible effects that can be used in the current view of the camera appear. (See Figure 4-4.)

2. **Tap an effect.**

3. **Tap the Capture button.**

   An image using that effect is captured. (See Figure 4-5.)

   To return to the various effects, tap the Effects button in the bottom-left corner of the screen.

Figure 4-4: Effects from mild to wild.

Figure 4-5: My front hallway, with the Light Tunnel effect applied.

The image appears along with a filmstrip of all the images you've captured using Photo Booth.

4. **If you want to delete a photo, tap the Share icon, tap a photo, tap the Trash button that appears, and then tap Delete Photo.**

5. **Press the Home button.**

   You return to the Home screen, and your photos are available in the Camera Roll folder of the Photos app.

Capturing Your Own Videos with the Built-in Cameras

In iPads, two video cameras that can capture video from either the front or rear of the device make it possible for you to take videos that you can then share with others.

To record a video, follow these steps:

1. **Tap the Camera app on the Home screen.**

   The Camera app opens.

2. **Tap and slide the line of words below the red Record button so that Video becomes the orange selection.**

   This step switches from the still camera to the video camera (as shown in Figure 4-6).

Figure 4-6: It takes one tap to move between camera and video.

3. **If you want to switch between the front and rear cameras, tap the icon near the top-right corner of the screen (refer to Figure 4-6).**

4. **Tap the red Record button (refer to Figure 4-6) to begin recording the video.**

   The Record button turns into a red square when the camera is recording, as shown in Figure 4-7.

Figure 4-7: Use the Record button to begin and end shooting a video.

5. **To stop recording, tap the Record button again.**

   A thumbnail link to your new video displays in the bottom-left corner of the screen.

6. **Tap the video to play it, share it, or delete it.**

   In the future, you can find and play the video in your gallery when you open the Photos app.

Before you start recording, make sure you know where the camera lens is (in the top-center portion of the device on the front and top-right side of the back when holding iPad in a portrait orientation) — while holding the iPad and panning, you can easily put your fingers directly over the lens!

Getting Face to Face with FaceTime

FaceTime is an excellent video-calling app that's available on the iPhone 4 and later and is now available on iPads (except for the original iPad). The app lets you call people who have FaceTime on their iOS 5 or later devices using a phone number or an email address. You and your friend or family member can see each other as you talk, which makes for a much more personal calling experience.

In iOS 7, the ability to make audio-only FaceTime calls has been added. The audio quality beats a phone call by quite a bit, and the audio-only calls don't require quite so robust a connection or use as much data bandwidth as a video FaceTime call does.

You can also show the person on the other end of the call your surroundings by using the rear iPad camera and panning around you. The possibilities are limitless: Show your husband the toy you're thinking of buying your son for his birthday, let your girlfriend see your new car while she's busy at work, or share your artwork or trip to the wine country with friends.

You can use your Apple ID and email address to access FaceTime, so after you install it, it works pretty much out of the box. See Book I, Chapter 5 for more about getting an Apple ID.

If you're having trouble using FaceTime, make sure the feature is turned on. Tap Settings on the Home screen and then tap FaceTime. Tap the On/Off switch to turn it on, if necessary. You can also select the email and phone account that can be used to make phone calls to you on this Settings page.

Who can use FaceTime

Here's a quick rundown of what device and what iOS you need for using FaceTime's various features:

- ✓ FaceTime is available on all iPads except the original iPad.
- ✓ You can call people who have iPhone 4 or later, iPad 2 or later, fourth-generation iPod touch, or a Mac (running OS X 10.6.6 or later).
- ✓ You can use a phone number to connect with iPhone 4 or later.
- ✓ You can connect using an email address with a Mac, iPod touch, or iPad.

Making a FaceTime call

You can make and receive calls with FaceTime using a phone number (iPhone 4/4s/5/5s/5c) or an email account (iPad 2 or later, iPod touch fourth-generation or later, or a Mac running OS X 10.6.6 or later), and show the person on the other end what's going on around you.

If you have a Wi-Fi–only iPad and use FaceTime over a Wi-Fi network, that limits the places from which you can make or receive video calls to your home wireless network or a public hotspot. On the other hand, you avoid costly data usage over a 3G or 4G network with this setup even if you own a 3G/4G iPad model.

You have to use the appropriate method for placing a FaceTime call, depending on the kind of device the person you're calling has. If you're calling an iPhone 4 or later user, use a phone number the first time you call, and thereafter, you can use the phone number or email address; if you're calling an iPad 2 or later, an iPod touch, or a FaceTime for Mac user, you have to make the call using that person's email address.

You can't adjust audio volume from within the app or record a video call. Nevertheless, on the positive side, though its features are limited, this app is very straightforward to use.

Follow these steps to use FaceTime:

1. **Connect to a Wi-Fi or cellular (with iOS 6 or later) network.**

   See Book I, Chapter 5 for details on connecting.

2. **If you know that the person you're calling has FaceTime on an iPhone 4 or later, an iPad 2 or later, or a Mac, add the person to your iPad Contacts.**

   See Book V, Chapter 5 for how to do this if that person isn't already in Contacts.

3. **Tap the FaceTime app icon on the Home screen.**

   The first time you use the app, you may be asked to select the phone number and email account you want to use for FaceTime calls and then to click Next. The FaceTime screen appears.

4. **Tap the Contacts button in the bottom-right corner of the screen.**

5. **Scroll to locate and tap a contact's name.**

   The contact's information displays (as shown in Figure 4-8).

   You can also place a FaceTime call using Siri. Just say something like "Make a FaceTime call to Joey" and confirm Joey's contact information, and the call is placed.

Figure 4-8: Information displayed in Contacts.

6. **Tap the contact's stored phone number or email address and then tap the Call button (shaped like a phone handset).**

   You've just placed a FaceTime call!

When you call somebody using an email address, the person must be signed in to his Apple ID account and have verified that the address can be used for FaceTime calls. iPad 2 or later and iPod touch (fourth-generation and later) users can make this setting by tapping Settings and then FaceTime; FaceTime for Mac users make this setting by choosing FaceTime➪Preferences.

When the person accepts the call, you see the person's image and a small, draggable box containing your image (referred to as a Picture in Picture, or PiP). (See Figure 4-9.)

You can also simply go to the Contacts app, find a contact, tap the FaceTime icon in that person's record, and then tap her phone number or email address in the pop-up menu that appears to make a FaceTime call.

Figure 4-9: A FaceTime call in progress.

 To view recent calls, tap the Recents button (refer to Step 4). Tap a recent call to call the person back.

Accepting or ending a FaceTime call

If you're on the receiving end of a FaceTime call, accepting the call is about as easy as it gets. When the call comes in, follow these steps:

1. **Tap the Answer button to take the call or tap the Decline button to reject it. (See Figure 4-10.)**

   If you want to decline the call and get a reminder to call back later, tap the Reminder button. You can choose to get a reminder in an hour or when you leave your current location. If you'd rather not answer but send a message to the caller, such as "Can't talk right now" or "Call me later," tap the Message button. If you do accept the call, chat away with your friend and tap the FaceTime button if you want to view video images.

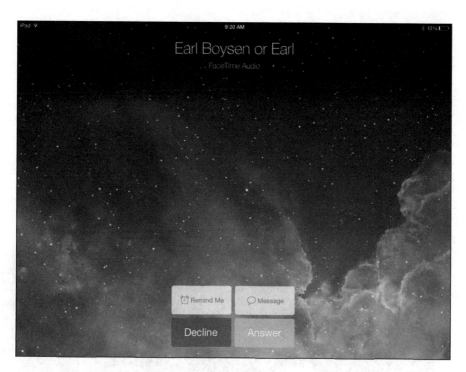

Figure 4-10: You're it; accept or decline the call.

2. **When you're done talking, tap the End button (shown in Figure 4-11).**

   The call ends.

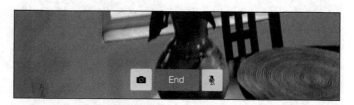

Figure 4-11: Ending a FaceTime call.

To mute sound during a call, tap the Mute button, which looks like a microphone with a line through it. Tap the button again to unmute your iPad or iPhone.

To add a caller to your Favorites list, with FaceTime open, tap the Favorites button (marked with a star icon), and then tap the plus sign and select the person's name from the contact list to add the person to Favorites. You can then locate the person to make a call to her by tapping Favorites and choosing that person from a short list rather than scrolling through all your contacts.

Switching views

When you're on a FaceTime call, you might want to use iPad's built-in camera to show the person you're talking to what's going on around you. Tap the Switch Camera button (refer to Figure 4-11) to switch from the front-facing camera that's displaying your image to the rear-facing camera that captures whatever you're looking at (shown in Figure 4-12).

Figure 4-12: Show your friend what's in front of you.

Tap the Switch Camera button again. You switch back to the front camera, displaying your image.

Chapter 5: Getting Social with Twitter, Facebook, and iMessage

In This Chapter

🖝 Using Twitter or Facebook on iPad

🖝 Creating an iMessage account

🖝 Using iMessage to address, create, read, and send messages

🖝 Deleting a conversation

🖝 Sending audio, video, and maps

*U*nless you've spent the last few years working in Antarctica without a radio, you know that Twitter is a social networking service referred to as a *microblog* because it involves only short posted messages. Twitter support is incorporated into the iPad's iOS, so you can tweet people from within the Safari, Photos, Camera, Maps, and other apps.

The Facebook app can also be activated through Settings. Facebook, the most popular social networking site, is integrated into iPad. You can also post messages and items such as photos to your Facebook page right from within several apps.

Messages is an app used for instant messaging (IM). IM involves sending a text message to somebody's iPhone, iPod touch, iPad, or Mac (using any phone number or email address that the person has registered to her iCloud account) to carry on an instant conversation. With iOS 8 comes a few new features for Messages, including the capability to opt out of certain conversations, leave group conversations, and share your current location.

In this chapter, I introduce you to ways in which iPad makes use of Twitter, Facebook, and instant messaging to let you stay connected to the world.

Experiencing Twitter and Facebook on iPad

Twitter and Facebook are the darlings of the social networking world. Twitter, as a microblog, allows you to post only short messages (up to 140 characters) called tweets. Facebook is much more robust, allowing lengthy postings as well as photographs, videos, and various gifting schemes to woo Facebook friends. The use of each is integrated into iPad, typically via the Share feature in apps. When you tap the Share button, you can tap the Twitter or Facebook button to share the selected content via those services, if you have installed their apps and enabled them in Settings (see Figure 5-1).

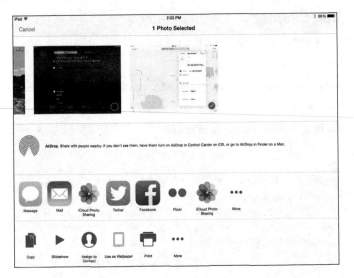

Figure 5-1: Use app-sharing features to tweet or post to Facebook.

Connecting your iPad to Facebook and Twitter

Facebook and Twitter are integrated into the sharing feature of iPad. When you're in an app such as Maps and you tap the Share button, you can post an item, such as a map, to Twitter or Facebook. This integration is described in the next task.

Before you use these integrated features, however, you have to have an account on those systems, install the Twitter and/or Facebook app, and enter information about your accounts. Follow these steps to do this with Facebook:

1. **Tap Settings and then tap Facebook.**

2. **In the settings that appear (see Figure 5-2), tap the Install button to install the app.**

3. **When prompted, enter your Apple ID and password.**

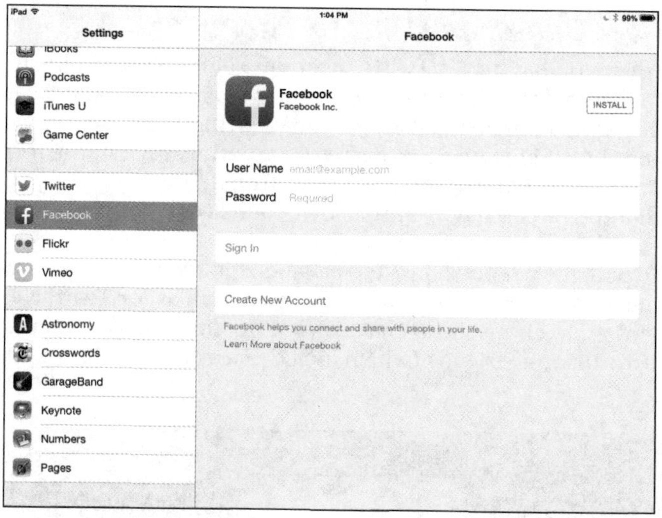

Figure 5-2: Tap the Install button, and the Facebook app appears on one of your many Home screens.

4. **Enter your Facebook username and password and then tap Sign In.**

5. **On the confirming screen, tap the Sign In button.**

Note that signing into Facebook downloads all Facebook friends to your Contacts app and downloads any Facebook events to your Calendar app on iPad. You can turn off individual apps that use your Facebook account one by one in the main Facebook settings.

Twitter is a social networking service that involves posting very short messages (*tweets;* limited to 140 characters; an attachment such as a photo may limit this character count further) online so that your friends can see what you're up to. The ability to tweet is integrated into several apps. You can post tweets using the Share button within Safari, Photos, Camera, and Maps. First, go to Settings and tap Twitter. Then tap the Install button and add your account information.

Many readers already have a Twitter account and are hooked on tweeting. If you've never tweeted, you can go to www.twitter.com to sign up with the service; then activate Twitter in Settings and use the Twitter for iPad app to manage your Twitter account. After you have an account, you can post tweets, have people follow your tweets, and follow the tweets that other people post.

Tweeting or posting to Facebook

When you have your Twitter account set up, you can be in a compatible app such as Safari, Photos, Camera, and Maps, and choose Twitter in the screen that appears when you tap the Share button. You see a Tweet form like the one shown in Figure 5-3. Just write your message in the form and then tap Send. Note that a number in the bottom-left corner lets you know how many characters you have left to use in your tweet.

To post to Facebook, just tap Facebook in the Share menu (refer to Figure 5-2), and follow pretty much the same procedure as for Twitter, except that you are allowed to choose who can see your posting: the general public, your friends, just you, or all friends (which includes friends of your friends).

Figure 5-3: Tweeting is a simple menu choice in several apps.

See Book I, Chapter 6 or Chapters 3 and 6 in this minibook for more about tweeting in the Safari or Photos apps.

When you're filling in the tweet or Facebook posting, you can tap Location and then tap Enable in the dialog that appears to turn on Location Services, which allows Twitter to ascertain your location and share it with others. Be cautious about using this feature; if many people follow you on Twitter, they can use your location to track your movements and know where you live, where you go to school, where you socialize, and so on. This information can be used to commit a variety of online and offline crimes.

Setting Up an iMessage Account

iMessage is a messaging service that is available through the preinstalled Messages app that allows you to send and receive instant messages (IMs) to and from others using an Apple iOS device (and on your Mac, if you have OS X Mountain Lion or later).

Instant messaging differs from email or posting to Facebook in an important way. Whereas you might email somebody and wait days or weeks before that person responds, or you might post a comment to your Facebook timeline that could sit a while before anybody views it, instant messaging communication happens almost immediately. You send an IM, and it appears on somebody's Mac, iPhone, iPod touch, or iPad right away; if the person wants to participate in a live conversation, that conversation begins immediately, allowing a back-and-forth dialogue in real time.

To set up iMessage, follow these steps:

1. **Tap Settings on the Home screen.**

2. **Tap Messages.**

   The settings shown in Figure 5-4 display.

3. **If iMessage isn't set to On, tap the On/Off switch (shown in Figure 5-4) to turn it on.**

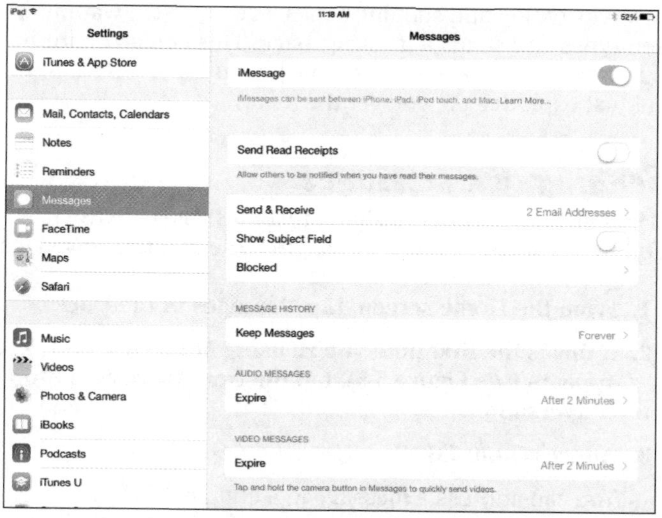

Figure 5-4: Turn on iMessage in Settings.

4. **Check the Send & Receive setting to be sure that the email account associated with your iPad is correct.**

   This should be set up automatically based on your Apple ID.

5. **To allow a notice to be sent to a sender to indicate that you've read a message, tap the On/Off switch for Send Read Receipts.**

   You can also choose to show a subject field in your messages.

6. **If you want to include a subject field in messages, tap the On/Off switch for the Show Subject Field option.**

7. **Tap the Home button to close Settings.**

 Messages adds your iPhone's number (if you have an iPhone using the same iCloud account) automatically as a location to which people can message you. Your iCloud email addresses are also added automatically. To add other email accounts for Messages to use, tap the Send & Receive button, tap Add Another Email, and then follow the directions to add another email account. To delete an account, tap the information button to the right of it, tap Remove This Email, and then confirm the deletion.

Using Messages to Create and Send Text, Audio, and Video Messages

Now you're ready to use iMessage. This is a remarkably simple process that involves typing and sending a message and then waiting while the other person types and sends a message back. This can go on for hours, so prepare a quick exit message ahead of time, just in case. (I have to walk my dog, the cat just exploded . . . you get the idea.)

Sending text messages

If you just have words to share, text messages are the tried-and-true method. Follow these steps to use Messages to send a text-based instant message:

1. **From the Home screen, tap Messages in the Dock.**

2. **If this is the first time you're using Messages, on the screen that appears (see Figure 5-5), tap the New Message button to begin a conversation.**

3. **Address your IM.**

   You can address a message in a couple of ways:

   • Begin to type a name, email address, or phone number in the To field, or tap the iPad's Dictation key (not present on the iPad 2) on the onscreen keyboard and speak the address, and a list of matching contacts appears.

• Tap the plus icon to the right of the address field, and the All Contacts list displays, as shown in Figure 5-6.

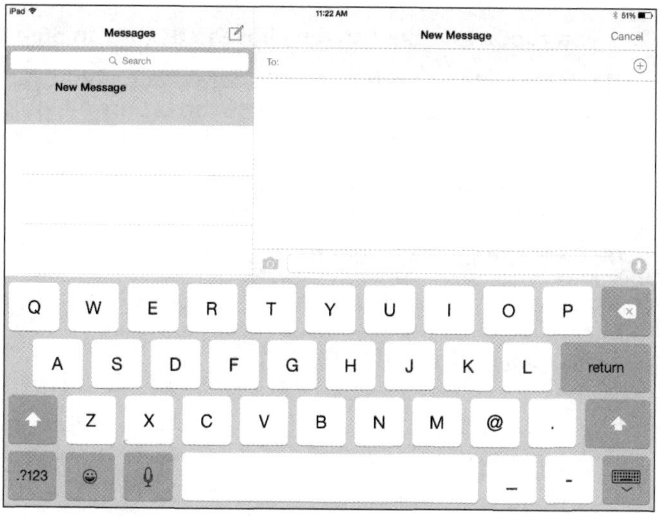

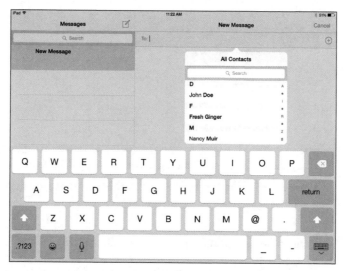

Figure 5-5: Get the conversation going here.

Figure 5-6: You can choose somebody to message from your Contacts list.

You can send messages only to people who have an iCloud account that includes an email address or phone number.

You can also use Siri (not present in iPad 1 or 2) to send a message by simply pressing and holding the Home button, speaking your command, and then selecting the correct contact and method of messaging (phone or email).

4. **Tap a contact on the list you chose to display in Step 3.**

   If the contact has both an email address and phone number stored, the Info dialog appears, allowing you to tap one or the other, according to which method you want to use for addressing the message.

5. **To create a message, simply tap in the message field near the bottom of the screen and type or dictate your message.**

6. **To send the message, tap the Send button.**

   When your recipient(s) responds, you see the conversation displayed on the right side of the screen, as shown in Figure 5-7. Tap in the message field again to respond to the last comment.

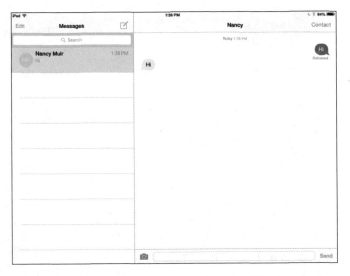

Figure 5-7: Follow the conversation as you and your friend text back and forth.

Here are some additional tips for using Messages:

- **Talking with multiple people:** You can address a message to more than one person by simply choosing more recipients in Step 4 in the preceding list.

- **Canceling a message:** If you begin a conversation and change your mind before sending your message, tap the Cancel button near the top right of the screen.

✔ **Viewing a conversation:** Your conversations are listed in the left pane of the Messages app. Tap one, and the various comments in it display, along with a note of the date and time of each comment.

Sending and receiving audio messages

With iOS 8, when you're creating a message, you can also create an audio message. With Messages open:

1. **Tap the New Message button in the top-right corner of the left pane.**

2. **Enter an addressee's name, email address, or phone number in the To field.**

3. **Tap and hold the Microphone button (the microphone symbol to the right of the message entry field; see Figure 5-8).**

4. **Speak your message or record a sound or music near you.**

5. **Tap the Send button (an upward-pointing arrow at the top of the recording circle). The message appears as an audio track in the recipient's Messages inbox. To play the track, she just holds the phone up to her ear or taps the Play button.**

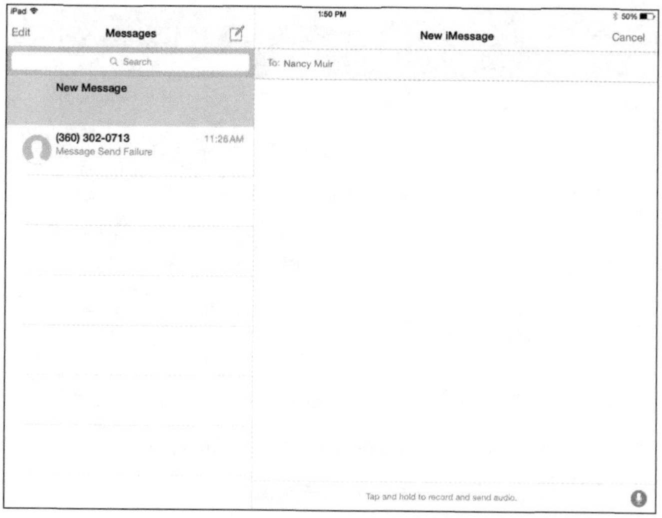

Figure 5-8: Tap the Microphone button.

Sending a photo or video

When you're creating a message, you can also create a short video message, which can be a fun way to share your surroundings as well as your ideas. With Messages open:

1. Tap the New Message button in the top-right corner.

2. Tap the camera icon on the left of the message entry field; then, in the popover that appears (see Figure 5-9), tap Photo Library and select a photo.

   You are returned to the message.

3. If you prefer to capture a photo or video, with the choices in Figure 5-9 displayed, tap Take Photo or Video and then tap the Capture button to take a photo.

   Alternatively, you can move the slider at the bottom right to select Video. Move the phone around to take a video and tap the red Stop button when you've recorded what you want to record. Tap the Use Photo or Use Video button. Your photo or video is attached to your message.

4. To send multiple photos or videos, repeat Step 3 for each one.

5. Tap Send to send your message and attachments.

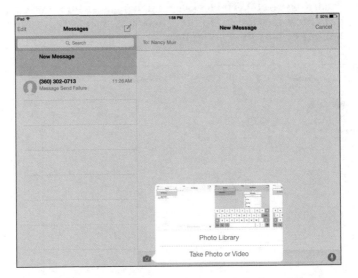

Figure 5-9: Use a photo you've already captured or take a photo or video now to send.

Sending a map of your location

When sending a message, you can also send a map showing your current location by following these steps:

1. Tap a message that you've received and then tap Details.

2. **Tap Send My Current Location (see Figure 5-10), and a map will be inserted as a message attachment. If asked, tap Allow Messages to Access Your Location.**

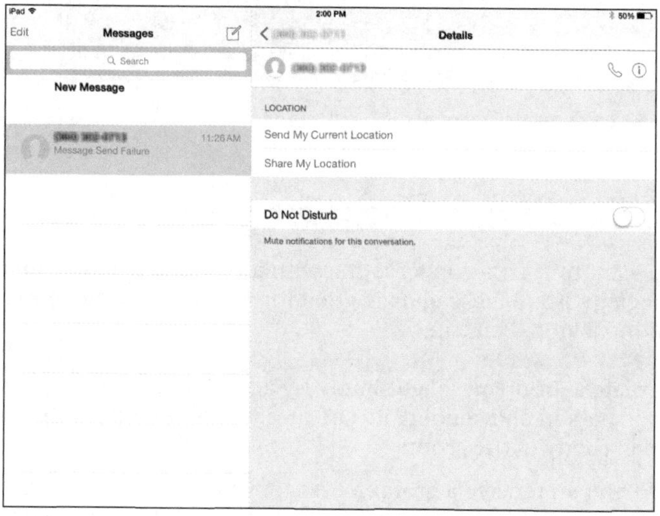

Figure 5-10: Choose to send your location to provide a map to the message recipient.

You can also share your location in the middle of a conversation rather than send a map attachment with your message. In the screen shown in Figure 5-10, tap Share My Location and then tap Share for One Hour, Share Until End of Day, or Share Indefinitely. A map showing your location will appear above your conversation until you stop sharing.

Clearing a Conversation

When you're done chatting, you might want to clear a conversation to remove the clutter before you start a new one.

To clear a conversation, follow these steps:

1. **With Messages open, swipe to the right on the message you want to delete.**

2. **Tap the Delete button next to any item you want to clear and then tap Delete. (See Figure 5-11.)**

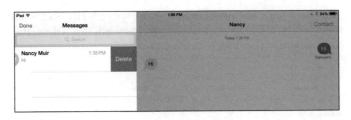

Figure 5-11: Get rid of yesterday's IM with a tap.

Understanding Group Messaging

If you want to start a conversation with a group of people, you can use group messaging. Group messaging is great for keeping several people in the conversational loop. You can

✔ Create a group message simply by addressing a message to more than one person and sending it. The message and replies to it are delivered to everybody in the group.

✔ When you receive a group message, you can manage your participation in the conversation by tapping the Details button. To temporarily mute notifications of responses to a conversation, set the Do Not Disturb switch to Off. Set Do Not Disturb back On to again receive contributions to the conversation. Tap Leave This Conversation to permanently exit the conversation.

Chapter 6: Playing with the Photos App

In This Chapter

- ✔ Importing photos from iPhone or a digital camera
- ✔ Viewing an album or individual photos
- ✔ Editing photos
- ✔ Organizing photos
- ✔ Sharing and deleting photos
- ✔ Running a slideshow
- ✔ Working in iCloud Photo Library

With its gorgeous screen, iPad is a natural for taking and viewing photos. It supports most common photo formats, such as JPEG, TIFF, and PNG. With an iPad, you can shoot your own photos using the built-in cameras (see Chapter 4 in this minibook for more about using them) with preprogrammed square or panorama modes, and edit your images using smart adjustment filters. You can also sync your photos from iCloud or your computer, iPhone, or digital camera using the iCloud Photo Library. You can save images that you find online to your iPad or receive them by Mail or Messages to your iPad.

 turn on Wi-Fi and Bluetooth to share with people via

After you have photos to play with, the Photos app lets you organize photos from the Camera Roll, viewing them in albums, one by one, or in a slideshow, and you can view photos by the year they were taken, with images divided into collections by the location or time you took them. You can also AirDrop, email, message, post to Facebook, or tweet a photo; print it; or use your expensive gadget as an electronic picture frame. Finally, this chapter discusses the Photo Stream feature, which you can use to share groups of photos with people using iCloud on a Mac or iOS device.

Getting Photos into iPad

Before you can play around with photos, you have to take some with the iPad camera, covered in Chapter 4 in this minibook, or get them onto your iPad from another source. You have a few different ways to get photos from elsewhere. You can buy an accessory to import them from your camera or iPhone; save a photo that you find on the web or receive as an email, message, or tweet attachment; have somebody send you a photo via AirDrop from another nearby device; or sync to iCloud or your computer to download photos you've saved there. The whole syncing process is discussed in Book I, Chapter 5. The two other methods are explained here.

Screenshots you take of your iPad screen are also saved to the Camera Roll album. To take a screenshot, display what you want to shoot, press and hold the Home button, tap the Sleep/Wake button, and then release. You'll find your screenshot in the Photos Camera Roll album.

Importing photos from a digital camera

Your iPad camera and a computer aren't the only sources of photos. You can import photos from a digital camera and photos or videos from your iPhone/iPod touch if you buy the Lightening to USB Camera Adapter from Apple, which will set you back about $29, and the SD Card Reader to import image files from an SD card, also available at $29. You can also take advantage of the iOS 8 iCloud Photo Library, which stores images taken on any of your iOS devices.

You can find information in Book I, Chapter 5 about syncing iCloud content or your computer with your iPad to port over photos. You can also find out how to take and use photos from the iPad's built-in camera in Chapter 4 of this minibook.

Follow these steps to import photos, after you have the adapters described earlier in this section in hand:

1. **Start the import process by putting your iPad to sleep using the switch on the top right.**

2. **Insert the Lightening to USB Camera Connector into the Dock Connector slot of your iPad.**

3. **Connect the USB end of the cord that came with your digital camera or iPhone into the Camera Connector.**

4. **Connect the other end of the cord that came with your camera into that device.**

5. **Wake your iPad.**

   The Photos app opens and displays the photos on the digital camera.

6. **Tap Import All on your iPad.**

   If you want to import only selected photos, tap individual photos and then tap Import. Finally, tap Import rather than Import All.

   The photos are saved to the Last Import album.

7. **Disconnect the cord and the adapter.**

   You're done!

You can also import photos stored on an *SD (secure digital)* memory card often used by digital cameras as a storage medium. Simply put the iPad to sleep, connect the SD Card Reader to the iPad, insert the SD card containing the photos, and then follow Steps 5 through 7 in the preceding list.

Remember that with AirDrop you can quickly send photos directly from your iPhone 5 or later to your iPad (fourth-generation or later, or mini), as long as the devices are within about 12 feet of each other, as well as to mid-2012 or newer Macs running OS X Yosemite.

Saving photos from the web

The web offers a wealth of images that you can download to your Photo Library on the iPad. The built-in Safari browser makes it simple to save any image you come across to your iPad. (Of course, you should be careful not to violate copyrights when using pictures you've grabbed online.)

Several search engines have advanced search features that allow you to search for only nonlicensed images, meaning, at least theoretically, that you don't have to pay for the images. But it's always a good idea to get written permission to use an image, especially if you intend to use it to make money (as with a company brochure or online course).

Follow these steps to save images from the web:

1. **Open Safari and navigate to the web page containing the image you want.**

2. **Press and hold the image.**

   A popover appears, as shown in Figure 6-1.

3. **Tap Save Image.**

   The image is saved to your Camera Roll album in the Photos app.

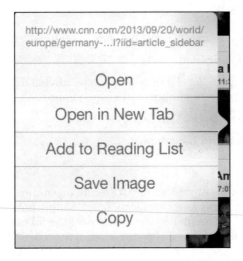

http://www.cnn.com/2013/09/20/world/
europe/germany-...l?iid=article_sidebar

Open

Open in New Tab

Add to Reading List

Save Image

Copy

Figure 6-1: Use this menu to save an image to your iPad.

For more about how to use Safari to navigate to or search for web content, see Book I, Chapter 6.

A number of sites protect their photos from being copied by applying an invisible overlay. This blank overlay image ensures that you don't actually get the image you're tapping. Even if a site doesn't take these precautions, be sure that you don't save images from the web and use them in ways that violate the rights of the person or entity that owns them.

Looking at Photos

Pictures were made to be looked at, so knowing how to view the albums and individual photos that you manage to get into your iPad is a way to tap into the key strength of the Photos app. In this section, you get some tips for taking your viewing experience to the max.

If you want to do more than look at photos, check out a few of these photo-editing apps that were designed to work with iPad: Adobe Photoshop Touch, Photogene for iPad from Mobile Pond, PhotoForge for iPad from GhostBird Software, and the free PhotoPad by ZAGG. All are available through the App Store.

Viewing an album

The Photos app organizes your pictures into albums using such criteria as the folder on your computer from which you synced the photos or photos captured using the iPad camera (which are stored in the Recently Added album). You may also have albums for images that you synced from devices such as your iPhone or digital camera, and collections of your photos by year or location.

To view your albums, start by tapping the Photos app on the Home screen. Tap the Albums tab shown in Figure 6-2. Now you can tap an album, and the photos in it display.

Figure 6-2: Switch between individual photos, photos stored on iCloud, and albums using these tabs.

If you're on a Windows PC, check out two products for managing and syncing photos to iPad: Lightroom from Adobe (www.adobe.com) or Adobe's Photoshop Elements (version 8 or later). You can also create picture subfolders in Windows Explorer or the Photo folder hierarchy on a Mac, and when you sync, each subfolder becomes an album on your iPad.

Viewing individual photos

After you figure out what album your images are in, you have several fun ways to interact with individual photos. The iPad touchscreen is the key to this very tactile experience.

Tap the Photos app on the Home screen and then tap the Photos tab at the bottom of the screen (shown in Figure 6-3). Your photos are displayed by criteria, such as the time taken or location.

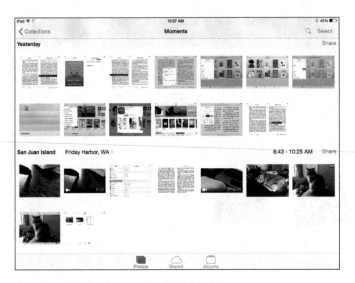

Figure 6-3: Viewing thumbnails of individual photos.

Now try these techniques:

- **Full-screen view:** To view a photo, tap the photo's thumbnail. You can also pinch your fingers together on the photo and then spread your fingers apart. The picture enlarges.

- **Browsing an album:** Tap to display an album and then flick your finger to the left or right to scroll through the individual photos in that album.

- **Multiple photos:** To reduce the display size of an individual photo and return to the multipicture view, place two fingers on the photo and then pinch them together. You can also tap the Back button (the < icon) in the top-left corner (which may display different words depending on where you are in a collection of photos) to view the next highest level of photo collection.

- **Twirling:** Place two fingers on a photo and spin them to the left or right. This maneuver, known as *grab and spin,* twirls the photo on the screen and returns you to the folder view (and it's lots of fun to do).

Do you like to associate a face with a name? Doing so can help you keep your clients or other contacts straight. You can place a photo on a person's information page in the Contacts app on your iPad. For more about how to do this, see Book V, Chapter 5.

Editing Photos

The Photos app also lets you do some simple editing of your photos, and with iOS 8, you have several new editing tools to work with, including smart adjustment filters and smart composition tools. Editing features allow you to rotate images, enhance image quality, get rid of that pesky red-eye effect, or crop to exactly the area of the image that you want to display. You can also work with the newly available filters to apply effects to your images.

Follow these steps to edit photos:

1. **Tap the Photos app on the Home screen to open it.**

2. **Using methods previously described in this chapter, locate a photo that you want to edit.**

3. **Tap Edit.**

   The Edit Photo screen, shown in Figure 6-4 with Filters displayed, appears.

Figure 6-4: Photos provides some simple but useful tools to edit photos.

4. **At this point, you can take a few possible actions:**

- *Enhance:* Tap Enchance to turn it on or off. Enhance improves the overall "crispness" of the figure with one tap.

- *Crop:* To crop the photo to a portion of its original area, tap the Crop button. You can then tap any corner of the image and drag inward or outward to remove areas of the photo. Tap Crop and then Save to apply your changes.

- *Filters:* Apply any of nine filters such as Fade, Mono, or Noir to change the feel of your image. These effects adjust the brightness of your image or apply a black-and-white tone to your color photos. Tap the Filters button in the middle of the tools at the bottom of the screen and scroll to view available filters. Tap one and then tap Apply to apply the effect to your image.

- *Smart Adjustments:* Tap Light, Color, or B&W to access a slew of tools that you can use to tweak contrast, color intensity, shadows, and more.

- *Red Eye:* Adjusts those dreaded red-eye effects that are caused by reflections of flash in eyes in some photos that include faces.

In each of the editing features, you see Cancel, Undo, and Revert to Original buttons. If you don't like the changes you made, use these to stop making changes or undo the changes you've already made. Choosing Cancel will end the editing session, and Revert to Original leaves you in Editing mode.

Organizing Photos

You can organize photos in albums so that you can locate them more easily in the future. To do this, follow these steps:

1. **Display an album such as Recently Added.**

2. **Tap the Select button in the top-right corner and then tap individual photos to select them.**

   Small check marks appear on the selected photos (see Figure 6-5).

3. **Tap the Add To button and then tap Add to Album (which appears only if you've previously created albums) or New Album.**

4. **Tap an existing album or enter a name for a new album (depending on your previous selection) and tap Save.**

   If you created a new album, it appears in the Album screen with the other albums.

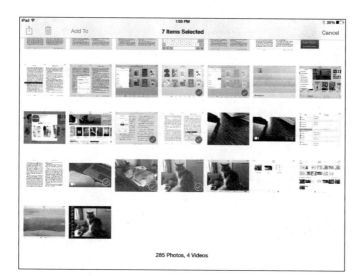

Figure 6-5: Select the photos you want to work with here.

You can also tap the Share or Delete button when you've selected photos in Step 2 of this task. This allows you to share or delete multiple photos at a time.

Accessing Photos by Years and Location

You can view your photos in logical categories such as Years and Moments. These so-called smart groupings let you, for example, view all photos taken this year or all the photos from your summer vacation. Follow these steps to view your photos by date or by a location where they were taken:

1. **Tap Photos on the Home screen to open it.**

2. **Tap Photos at the bottom of the screen.**

   The display of photos by date appears. (See Figure 6-6.)

3. **Tap the Collections button in the top-left corner and you see collections of photos by date range or location (see Figure 6-7).**

4. **Tap Years in the top-left corner and you see all your photos grouped by year taken.**

5. **Tap Collections in the top-right corner to display photos by location.**

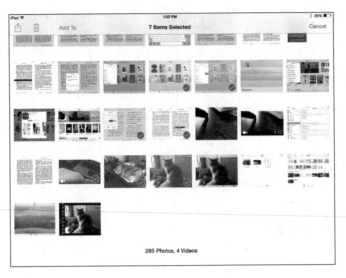

Figure 6-6: Peruse you entire year of photos from this view.

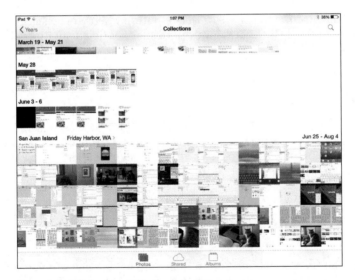

Figure 6-7: Drill down to find photos by date taken.

To go back to larger groupings, such as from a moment in a collection to the larger collection to the entire last year, just keep tapping the Back button at the top-left of the screen (which will be named after the next collection up in the grouping hierarchy, such as Collections or Years).

Sharing Photos

Part of the fun of taking photos is sharing those images with others. It's easy to share photos stored on your iPad by posting them to Facebook, tweeting, sending via iMessage, posting to a Flickr account, sharing via iCloud Photo Sharing, or sending them as email attachments. You have to go to Facebook or Twitter using a browser and set up an account before you can use this feature. Follow these steps to share photos:

1. **Tap the Photos app icon on the Home screen.**

2. **Tap the Photos or Album tab and locate the photo you want to share.**

3. **Tap the photo to select it and then tap the Share button (which looks like a box with an arrow jumping out of it).**

   The menu shown in Figure 6-8 appears.

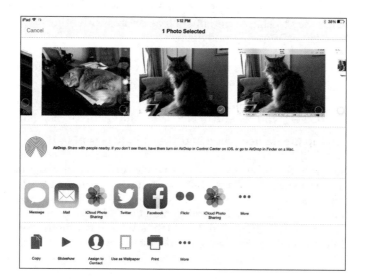

Figure 6-8: The Sharing menu offers different options.

4. **Tap additional photos across the top to share if you wish; then tap the Message, Mail, iCloud Photo Sharing, Twitter, Facebook, or Flickr option.**

5. **In the message form that appears, make any modifications that apply in the To, Cc/Bcc, or Subject fields for email, or enter your Facebook posting or tweet text.**

6. **Tap the Send or Post button, depending on which sharing method you chose.**

   The message and photo are sent to any recipients or are posted.

You can also tap AirDrop in Step 4 above and then tap a nearby AirDrop–enabled device to share the photo with that device instantly. See the next task for more about this feature.

You can also copy and paste a photo into documents, such as those created in the Pages word-processor app. To do this, press and hold a photo in Photos until the Copy command appears. Tap Copy and then, in the destination app, press and hold the screen and tap Paste.

Sharing a Photo Using AirDrop

AirDrop provides a way for those with fourth-generation iPad, iPad mini, and later iPads to share content such as photos with others who are nearby who have an AirDrop–enabled device:

1. **Follow the steps in the previous task to locate a photo you want to share and then tap the Share button.**

   If an AirDrop–enabled device is in your immediate vicinity (within 10 feet), you see the device listed at the top of the Share popover.

2. **Tap the device name and your photo is sent to it.**

Note that the other device has to have AirDrop enabled and be a compatible Mac or iOS device. To enable an iOS device, you open the Control Center (swipe up from the bottom of any screen) and tap the AirDrop button in the bottom center of the Control Center. On a Mac, open a Finder window or tab and then click AirDrop in the Sidebar. Whichever method you use, choose Contacts Only or Everyone to specify who you can interact with via AirDrop.

Sharing Photos Using Photo Stream

Photo Stream allows you to automatically send copies of any new photos to any of your iCloud devices and to share photo streams with others when you're connect to a Wi-Fi network. You can also subscribe to another person's photo stream if he or she shares it with you. First you should set up Photo Stream. Follow these steps to share your photos using Photo Stream:

1. **Tap Settings⇨Photos & Camera. Tap the On switch for My Photo Stream to share among your devices; tap Photo Sharing to share with others.**

2. **To share a photo stream with somebody else, return to the Home screen, tap Photos, and then tap Shared at the bottom of the screen. If you don't see tiles for the shared streams, tap Sharing at the upper left to get them.**

3. **Tap the Add button (the + symbol in the top-left corner) or the New Shared Album tile to create a new shared Photo Stream album.**

4. **In the form that appears (see Figure 6-9), enter a name for the shared album and tap Next.**

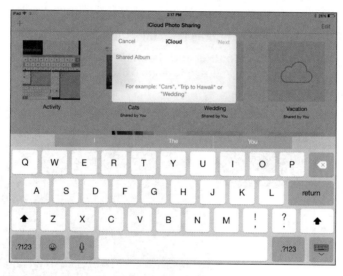

Figure 6-9: Fill out this form to post your photo.

5. **Enter the recipients' names (if they're in Contacts) or email addresses and then tap Create.**

   Your contacts receive an email message with a link that allows them to join your Photo Stream.

6. **Tap the new Photo Sharing folder that you just created and then tap the Add tile (with a plus sign on it). Tap individual photos to include and then tap Done.**

7. **Enter a message, if you like, and then tap Post.**

To add people to a shared Photo Stream that you created, tap the shared album to open it and then tap People in the upper right of the screen. Tap Invite people in the popover that appears, to share the Photo Stream with more people. To uninvite someone from the Photo Stream, tap that person's name and scroll down to the bottom of the popover; tap Remove Subscriber.

Running a Slideshow

You can run a slideshow of your images in Photos and even play music and choose transition effects for the show. This is a great way to give a presentation to a client on your easy-to-carry iPad or show your friends a slideshow of your latest travel adventure.

To use the slideshow feature, follow these steps:

1. **Tap the Photos app on the Home screen.**

2. **Tap the Photos tab and then tap Select.**

3. **Tap a series of photos in a collection.**

4. **Tap the Share button and then tap Slideshow to see the Slideshow Options dialog, shown in Figure 6-10.**

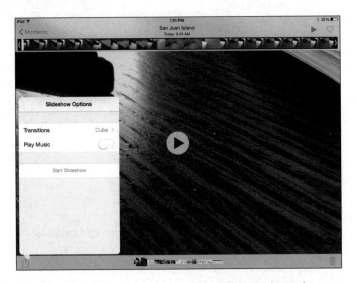

Figure 6-10: Use this dialog to add transition effects and start the slideshow.

5. **If you want to play music along with the slideshow, tap the On/Off switch in the Play Music field.**

6. **To choose music to play along with the slideshow, tap Music and, in the list that appears, tap any selection from your Music library.**

7. **In the Slideshow Options dialog, tap the transition effect that you want to use for your slideshow (refer to Figure 6-10).**

8. **Tap Back and then tap the Start Slideshow button.**

   The slideshow begins.

To run a slideshow that includes only the photos contained in a particular album, tap the Album tab in Step 2, tap an album to open it, and then tap the Slideshow button in the top-right corner to make settings and run a slideshow.

Deleting Photos

You might find that it's time to get rid of some of those old photos of the family reunion or the last project you worked on. If a photo wasn't transferred from your computer but instead was downloaded or captured as a screenshot on the iPad, you can delete it using this procedure:

1. **Tap the Photos app on the Home screen.**

2. **Tap the Albums or Photos tab; if you tap the Album tab, then tap an album to open it.**

3. **Tap Select and then tap either an individual photo or multiple photos.**

4. **Tap the Trash button, as shown in Figure 6-11.**

5. **Tap the Delete Photo button that appears to finish the deletion.**

Figure 6-11: If you don't need it anymore, delete it!

Working in iCloud Photo Library

iCloud Photo Library automatically backs up all your photos and videos to the cloud from all your devices that use the same iCloud account.

To turn on the iCloud Photo Library feature and view shared photos, follow these steps:

1. **In Settings, tap Photos & Camera, and then tap the On switch for iCloud Photo Library to post all your photos to this library in the cloud.**

2. **Tap Home and then tap the Photos app to open it.**

3. **Tap Shared at the bottom to view all photos and videos stored in the iCloud Library.**

With all these photos available to you, you'll need to be able to search your library for the one you want. From the Photos tab, tap the Search button at the top of the screen. A list of so-called "smart" suggestions appears. Tap one of these suggestions or enter the date or time of the photo, a location, or an album name such as "Vacation" in the Search field to locate the photo.

Chapter 7: Using Your iPad as an E-reader

In This Chapter

✔ Discovering how iPad differs from other e-readers

✔ Finding and buying books at iBooks

✔ Navigating a book

✔ Working with bookmarks, highlights, and the dictionary

✔ Organizing books in collections

✔ Experiencing periodicals with Newsstand

Apple has touted the iPad as a great e-reader, so though it isn't a traditional dedicated e-reader device like the Amazon Kindle Paperwhite, you won't want to miss out on this cool functionality.

Apple's preinstalled iBooks app is what turns your iPad into an e-reader. *iBooks is* an application that enables you to buy and download books from Apple's iBooks Store and other e-book sources, as well as to read PDF files. You can also use several other free e-reader apps, for example Kindle or Stanza, to download books to your iPad from a variety of online sources, such as Amazon and Google, so you can read to your heart's content.

Another preinstalled app, Newsstand, has a similar look and feel to iBooks, but its focus is on subscribing to and reading magazines, newspapers, and other periodicals.

In this chapter, you discover the options available for reading material, and I tell you how to buy books and subscribe to periodicals. You also find out how to navigate a book or periodical and adjust the brightness and type, as well as how to search books and organize your iBooks and Newsstand libraries.

Discovering How the iPad Differs from Other E-readers

An *e-reader* is any electronic device that enables you to download and read books, magazines, PDF files, or newspapers, as well as documents such as manuals or reports. Some e-readers use E Ink technology to create a paper-like reading experience. These devices, such as Kindle Paperwhite, are portable and typically dedicated only to reading electronic content.

The iPad is a bit different: As you know, it isn't used for only reading books, and it allows you to download other e-reader apps such as Kindle in addition to the preinstalled iBooks app. Also, the iPad doesn't offer the paper-like reading experience — you read from a computer screen (though you can adjust the brightness of the screen and change its background color).

When you buy a book or magazine online (or get one of many free publications), it downloads to your iPad in a few seconds using your Wi-Fi or 3G/4G connection. After you have your e-reader app and some content, iPad offers several navigation tools to move around an electronic book, all of which you explore in this chapter.

iBooks contains tools for reading and interacting with book content. The development of books with interactive content has so far been targeted primarily at the textbook market, and you can even create and publish your own interactive textbooks using a Mac app called iBooks Author.

Finding and Buying E-books

Before you can read books or other publications, you have to get your iPad's hands on them (so to speak). This involv0es downloading e-reader software and then using it or online stores to buy publications. I start by introducing you to iBooks, the e-reader that came preinstalled on your iPad.

You can also buy content on your computer and sync your purchases to your iPad using iTunes or iCloud. See Book I, Chapter 5 for more about this topic.

Finding books at the iBooks Store

You can shop using Apple's iBooks Store by tapping the iBooks app on the Home screen to open it.

If you become addicted to iBooks, consider placing it in the iPad Dock for quick access from any Home screen. To do this, tap and hold the app till all apps jiggle, and then tap and drag the iBooks app to the Dock. Press the Home button, and the jiggling stops.

The iBooks Library opens (see Figure 7-1). The first time you use it, you see a bookshelf with no books on it. (If you don't see the bookshelf, tap the My

Books button to go there. Note that any PDF documents you download don't appear on this bookshelf; you have to tap the PDF Collection to view them (more about Collections later).

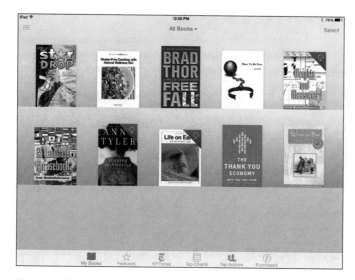

Figure 7-1: Your virtual iBooks bookshelf.

Tap the Featured button at the bottom of the screen. In the iBooks Store, shown in Figure 7-2, featured titles are shown by default. These consist of several rows of books in categories such as Hot This Week and Popular on iBooks.

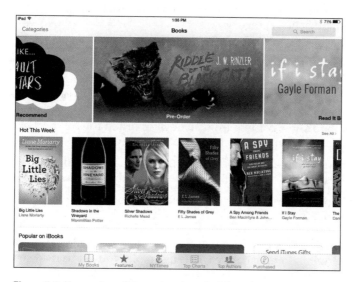

Figure 7-2: Use various links and tools to find the content you want.

Try any of the following methods to find a book:

✔ Tap the Search field at the top right of the screen and type a search word or phrase using the onscreen keyboard.

✔ Tap the Categories button at the upper left of the screen and scroll down to browse links to popular categories of books, as shown in Figure 7-3.

Figure 7-3: Find your publication using Categories.

✔ Tap See All on the right side above different categories of books to view all titles in a category.

✔ Tap the appropriate button at the bottom of the screen to view categories: *The New York Times* bestsellers list; books listed on Top Charts; and Top Authors.

✔ Tap Purchased at the bottom of the screen to see any books you've bought on devices signed in with the same Apple ID. You can tap the All tab to show content from all devices or tap the Not on This iPad tab to see only content purchased on other devices.

Scroll to the bottom of many screens to access Quick Links, which include shortcuts to Best of the Month, Free Books, and Award Winners.

✔ Tap a suggested selection or featured book to display more information about it.

To avoid buyer's remorse, you can sometimes download free samples before you buy. If the publisher provides a sample, you get to read several pages of the book to see whether it appeals to you, and it doesn't cost you a dime! Look for the Get Sample button when you view details about a book to get your free preview.

Exploring other e-readers

Though iBooks can handle content from many ePub sources, such as Google and Project Gutenberg, you may prefer to explore the tools offered by other e-readers. Your iPad is capable of using other e-reader apps to display book content from other bookstores, so you can get books from sources other than iBooks Store. To do so, first download another e-reader application such as Kindle from Amazon or the Barnes & Noble Nook from the iPad App Store. (See Book I, Chapter 5 for how to download apps.) You can also download a non-vendor-specific app such as Bluefire Reader, which handles ePub and PDF format, as well as most formats that public libraries use. Then use that application's features to search for, purchase, and download content.

Book II
Chapter 7

The Kindle e-reader application is shown in Figure 7-4. After downloading the free app from the App Store, you just open the app, go to the Amazon Kindle Store and enter the email address associated with your Amazon account and password. Any content you have already bought from Amazon for the Kindle is archived online and can be downloaded using your Kindle app on your iPad for you to read anytime you like. Use features such as changing the background to a sepia tone or changing the font to enhance your reading experience. Tap the Device tab to see titles stored on your iPad. To delete a book from this e-reader, just press the title with your finger, and the Remove from Device button appears.

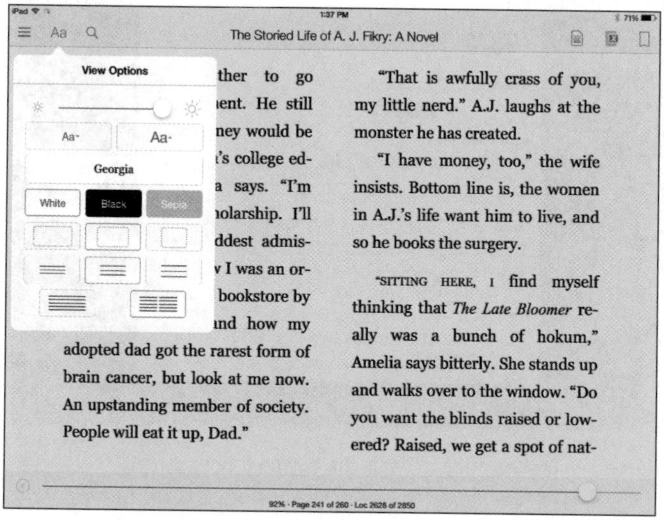

Figure 7-4: Kindle was one of the first free e-reader apps for iPad.

You can also get content from a variety of other sources: Project Gutenberg (www.gutenberg.org), Google, some publishers like Baen (www.baen.com), and so on. Get the content using your computer if you want and then just add it to Books in iTunes and sync to your iPad.

You can also sync books you've downloaded to your computer to your iPad by syncing to the computer and your iTunes account. Using this method, you can find lots of free books from various sources online, as long as they're in the ePub or PDF format, and drag them into your iTunes Books Library; then simply sync them to your iPad. If you have a Mac you can just drag the books directly into your connected iPad. See Book I, Chapter 5 for more about syncing. You can also download books from the web and use an online file-sharing site such as Dropbox to make them available to iBooks via an Internet connection, or right-click a title and select Open In to send a book to your iPad.

Buying iBooks

If you have set up an account with iTunes, you can buy books at the iBooks Store easily using the iBooks app. (See Book I, Chapter 5 for more about iTunes.) To buy a book, follow these steps:

1. **When you find a book in the iBooks Store that you want to buy, tap it, and then tap its price button, as shown in Figure 7-5.**

Figure 7-5: Tap the price to begin the buying process.

The button changes to a Buy Book button, as shown in Figure 7-6. (If the book is free, these buttons are labeled Free and Get Book, respectively.)

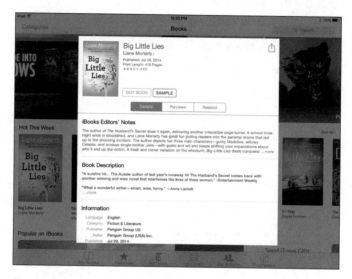

Figure 7-6: Tap the Buy Book button to buy the book.

2. **Tap the Buy Book (or Get Book) button.**

   If you haven't already signed in, the iTunes Password dialog appears.

3. **Enter your password and tap OK.**

   The book appears on your bookshelf, and the cost is charged to whichever payment method you specified when you opened your iTunes account — or the cost is deducted from your store credit, if you have a balance.

If you have signed in, your purchase is accepted immediately. No returns are allowed, so tap carefully!

With Family Sharing, as many as six people can make purchases for iOS devices, including e-books, using the same credit card. See Book II, Chapter 1 for more about setting up Family Sharing.

Experiencing E-reading

After you have an e-book in iBooks, put on some music, settle back in a comfortable chair, and read it. Luckily, reading an e-book is just as easy as (or perhaps easier than) reading a paperback. The next section shows how to do it.

Navigating an e-book

Here are the simple steps involved in making your way around an e-book using the iBooks e-reader:

1. **Tap iBooks, and if your Library (the bookshelf) isn't already displayed, tap the My Books button.**

2. **Tap an e-book to open it.**

   The book opens, as shown in Figure 7-7. Note that if the book is stored online, which you can discern by the cloud and down-arrow icon in its top-right corner, downloading it to your iPad may take a few moments. (If you hold your iPad in portrait orientation, it shows one page; if it's in landscape orientation, it shows two by default.)

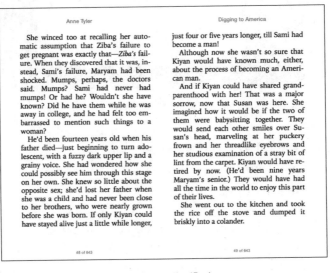

Figure 7-7: Landscape orientation on the iPad.

3. **Take any of these actions to navigate the book:**

   CONTENTS

   - *To go to the book's Table of Contents:* Tap the Table of Contents button near the top-left corner of the page (it looks like a little bulleted list) to go to the book's Table of Contents (see Figure 7-8) and then tap the name of a chapter to go to that chapter.

   - *To turn to the next page:* Tap your finger anywhere on the right edge of a page.

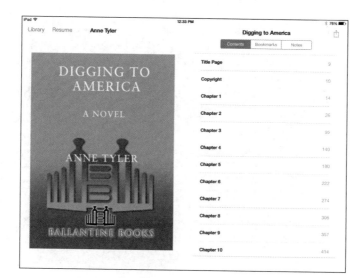

Figure 7-8: Use this virtual Table of Contents to go where you like in your e-book.

- *To turn to the preceding page:* Tap your finger anywhere on the left edge of a page.

- *To move to another page in the book:* Tap and drag the slider at the bottom of the page to the right or left.

To return to the Library to view another book at any time, tap the Library button. If the button isn't visible, tap anywhere on the page, and the tools appear.

Adjusting brightness

iPad doesn't offer a simulated page surface as some dedicated e-readers such as most Kindle e-readers do, so it's important that you make the reading experience as comfortable on your eyes as possible by adjusting the brightness.

iBooks offers an adjustable brightness setting that you can use to make your book pages comfortable for you to read. Follow these steps to make an adjustment:

1. **With a book open, tap the Display button, which is represented by a capital and lowercase A, as shown in Figure 7-9.**

   A dialog containing the iBooks Brightness slider and other settings appears.

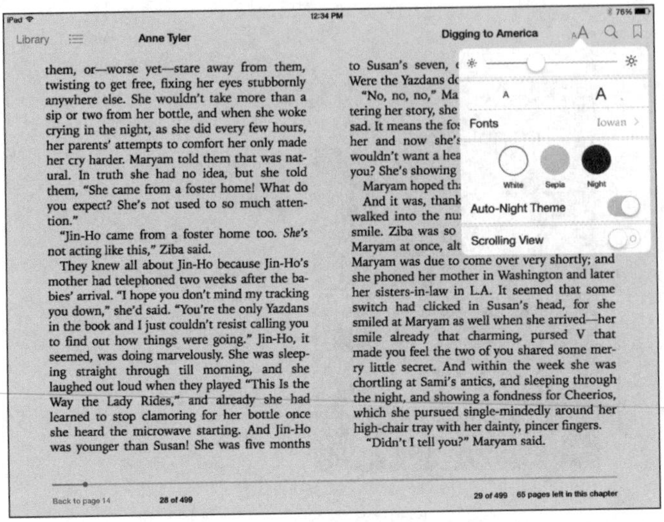

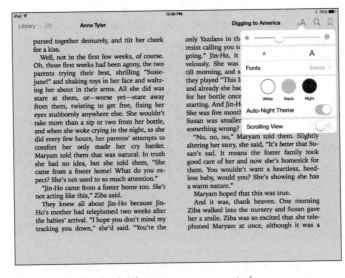

Figure 7-9: The Fonts button gives you access to a wealth of settings.

2. Tap and drag the slider (see Figure 7-10) to the right to make the screen brighter or to the left to dim it.

Figure 7-10: Adjusting brightness can ease eyestrain.

3. Tap anywhere in the book to close the Display dialog.

Experiment with the brightness that works for you. It's commonly thought that bright white computer screens are hard on the eyes, so setting the brightness to halfway (default) or below or choosing a sepia background is probably a good idea. Changing background color is covered in the next task.

Changing the page background and font size and type

If the type on your screen is a bit small for your taste, you can change to a larger font size or choose a different font for readability. Follow these steps:

1. With a book open, tap the Display button.

It sports a small letter *a* and a large capital *A*, as shown in Figure 7-11.

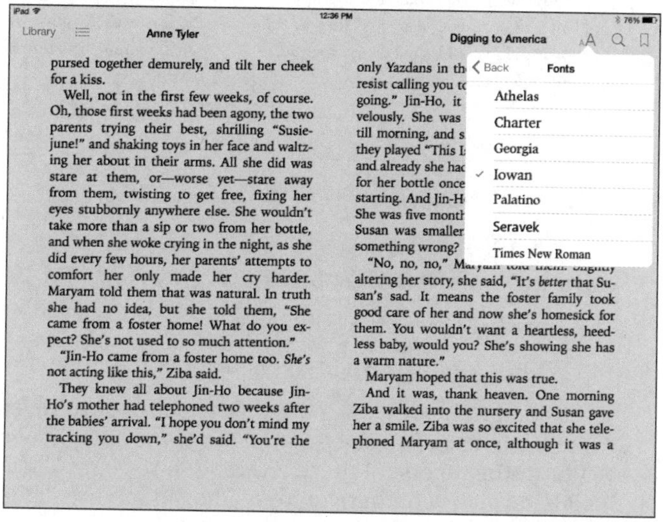

Figure 7-11: Need larger type? Set that up here.

2. In the Display dialog that appears, tap the small letter *a* button on the left to use smaller text, or tap the button labeled with the capital *A* on the right to use larger text.

3. Tap the Fonts button.

The list of fonts, as shown in Figure 7-12, appears. This list may vary slightly if Apple adds more or you're using a language other than English on your iPad.

Glancing skyward, Sanchez was the first to pick up Dean as he descended toward the ship. "Last package inbound."

Harvath and Kass looked up.

It took a moment to make him out. With their dark parachutes, blackened faces, and dark tactical clothing, they were intentionally difficult to spot.

"He's coming in too fast," said Kass. "Slow up, Wiggy. Slow up."

Harvath could see that Dean was fighting the same battle he had on his jump. It was very hard to gauge both the wind and the speed of the ship.

"He's going to drill right through the deck!" Sanchez exclaimed.

Because they didn't put their earpieces in until after they landed, there was no way the men on the ship could warn their teammate.

While Kass kept repeating *slow up*, Harvath

said a silent prayer.

Then, they all

only came in too f

zone entirely.

No one knew

not, but if he was

Breaking ranks, Ka

The aft portion

the tanker's superstructure was composed of the open-air deck where Harvath, Sanchez, and Kass had landed, as well as an additional, extremely narrow deck one level down that jutted out at the very rear of the ship.

Coming in as hot as he had, Dean had needed to buy time to slow down—even if only milliseconds. Realizing this, he had made a judgment call and chose to land on the lower deck. What he hadn't counted on was slamming into one of the ship's mooring winches.

< Back   Fonts

✓ Original

Athelas

Charter

Georgia

Iowan

Palatino

16 of 47

17 of 47   27 pages left in this chapter

Figure 7-12: Though limited, a selection of fonts is available in iBooks.

4. Tap a font name to select it.

The font changes on the book page.

5. Tap White, Sepia, or Night to choose the theme you want to display.

If you want to have a sepia tint on the pages or to reverse black and white, which can be easier on the eyes, you can change from the default White setting to one of these. Turning Auto-Night Theme to On lets your iPad determine whether you're reading in dimmer light and adjust to the Night theme accordingly.

6. Tap outside the Display dialog to return to your book.

Some fonts appear a bit larger on your screen than others because of their design. If you want the largest font, use Iowan.

If you're reading a PDF file, you're reading a picture of a document rather than an electronic book, so be aware that you can't modify the page's appearance using the Display dialog.

Searching in your book

You may want to find a certain sentence or reference in your book. To search for a word or phrase, follow these steps:

1. **With a book displayed, tap the Search button shown in Figure 7-13.**

   The onscreen keyboard appears.

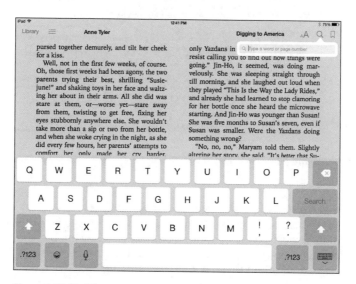

Figure 7-13: Find the content you need using the iBooks Search feature.

2. **Enter a search term or tap the Dictation key and speak the search term; then tap the Search key on the keyboard.**

   iBooks searches for any matching entries.

3. **Use your finger to scroll down the entries (see Figure 7-14), and tap one to go to that spot in the book.**

   You can use either the Search Google or Search Wikipedia button at the bottom of the Search popover if you want to search for information about the search term online.

TIP

You can also search for other instances of a particular word while in the book pages by pressing on and holding the word and then tapping Search on the list that appears.

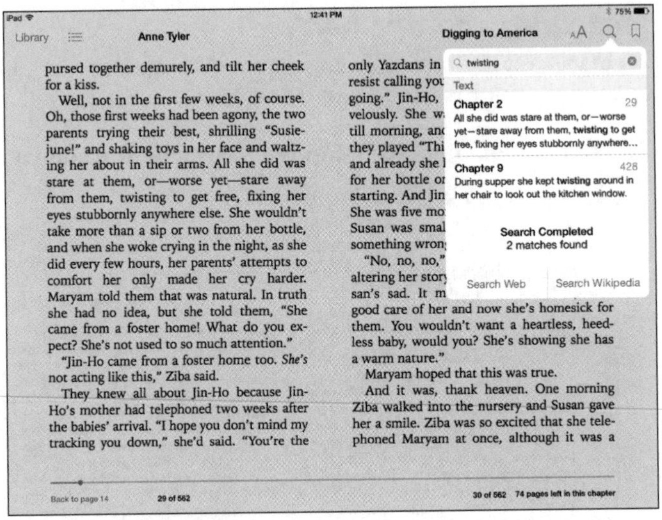

Figure 7-14: Find a spot in your e-book.

Using bookmarks and highlights

Bookmarks and highlights in your e-books are like favorites that you may be familiar with saving in your web browser: They enable you to revisit a favorite page or refresh your memory about a character or plot point. Note that iBooks can retain these bookmarks and highlights across iDevices and Macs.

To add and use bookmarks and highlights, follow these steps:

1. **With a book open to a page you want to bookmark, tap the Bookmark button (the red ribbon) in the upper-right corner, as shown in Figure 7-15.**

   A colored bookmark is placed on the right-hand page.

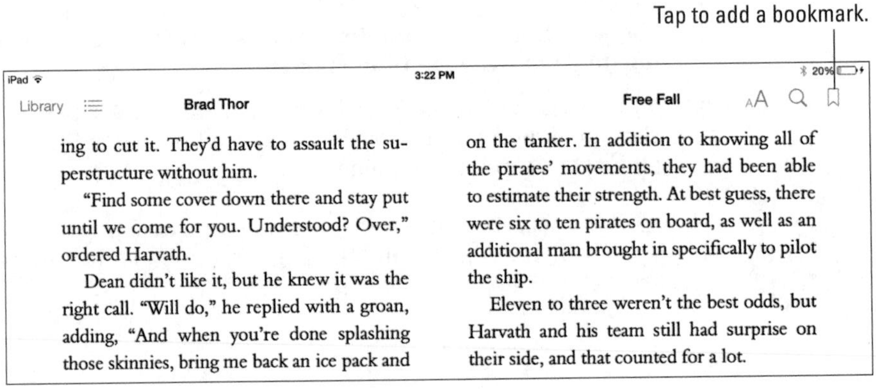

Tap to add a bookmark.

Figure 7-15: Assign a bookmark to a page.

2. To highlight a word or phrase, press on the text.

The contextual menu shown in Figure 7-16 appears.

3. Tap the Highlight button.

A colored highlight is placed on the word.

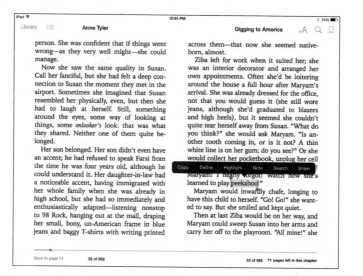

Figure 7-16: Use these tools to perform a variety of actions.

4. To change the color of the highlight on a word, remove the highlight, or add a note, tap the highlighted word and then tap Highlight.

The toolbar shown in Figure 7-17 appears. Note that a shortcut for removing a bookmark is to simply tap the Bookmark button in the top-right corner of the page.

5. Tap one of these items:

- *Colors:* Tap the color button and then tap any colored circle to change the highlight color.

- *Remove Highlight:* Tapping the white circle with a red line through it removes the highlight.

- *Note:* Tap the Note icon to add a note to the item.

- *Share:* Tap this button to choose from sharing the highlighted text via Messages, Mail, Twitter, or Facebook.

- *More Toolbar Options:* You can tap the button at the right end of the toolbar to access Copy, Define, and Search tools.

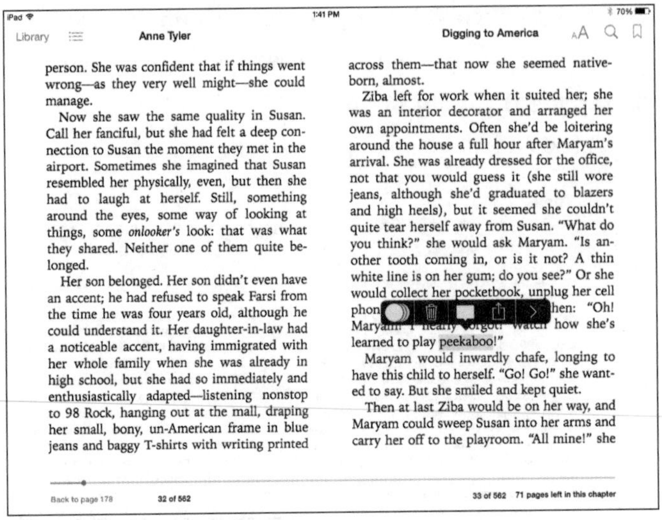

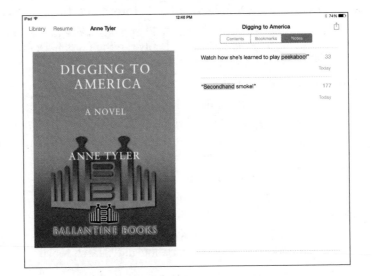

Figure 7-17: Choose the highlight color from this menu.

6. **Tap outside the highlighted word to close the menu.**

7. **To go to a list of bookmarks and notes, tap the Table of Contents button on a book page.**

8. **In the Table of Contents, tap the Bookmarks or Notes tab.**

   As shown in Figure 7-18, all contents, bookmarks, or notes (including highlights) display on their respective tabs.

Figure 7-18: Tap the highlight or bookmark you want to display in this list.

CONTENTS

9. **Tap a bookmark or note in one of these lists to go to that location in the book.**

TIP iPad automatically bookmarks the page where you left off reading in a book, so you don't have to do it manually. A feature called Continuity allows you to pick up where you left off on one iOS device, such as the iPad, on another, such as your iPhone.

Checking Words in the Dictionary

I know that some people just skip over words they don't understand when reading, but being a writer, I like to know what every word means. If you do, too, you'll appreciate the iPad's built-in dictionary. As you read a book, if you come across unfamiliar words, don't skip over them — take the opportunity to learn a word! The built-in dictionary in iBooks even recognizes many proper names, such as historical figures and geographic locations.

Follow these steps to look up a word in the dictionary:

1. **With a book open, press your finger on a word and hold it until the menu shown in Figure 7-19 appears.**

Book II Chapter 7

Using Your iPad as an E-reader

iPad 📶   12:49 PM   ⚡ 74% 🔋

Library ☰   Anne Tyler   Digging to America   aA Q 🔖

have one of her own, he had felt compelled to go along with her plan. He had hidden his doubts from everyone but his mother; to her he had poured them out, stopping by her house several times a week as furtively as if she were the Other Woman and sitting in her kitchen, letting his cup of tea grow cold, clamping his hands between his knees and talking on and on while Maryam listened non-committally. "I know Ziba believes that we'll be rescuing someone," he said. "Some child who never had a chance, some disadvantaged orphan. But it's not as simple as she thinks, changing a life for the better! It's so easy to [Copy] [Define] [Highlight] [Note] [Search] [Share] it seems to me. Easy to bomb a building to smithereens but hard to build one; easy to damage a child but hard to fix one who has problems. I don't think Ziba knows this. I think she just imagines we'll swoop up some lucky baby and give it a perfect life."

He waited for his mother to contradict him (he *wanted* her to contradict him), but she didn't. She took a sip of her tea and set down

her cup. He said, "And it's not as if children come with return guarantees. You can't sim-ply hand them back if they don't work out."

"You can't hand a birth child back either," his mother said.

"But it's less likely you would want to. A birth child is blood-related; you recognize cer-tain traits and so you tolerate them better."

"Or worse," his mother said. "Traits in yourself that you've always disliked. That happens too, on occasion."

It did? He decided not to pursue this. He stood up and circled the kitchen, fists thrust deep in his pockets, and when his back was toward her he said, "Also, um, I worry that this child will feel out of place. He or she will always look so unmistakably foreign to other people, so Korean or Chinese. You know?"

He turned back to find his mother regard-ing him with what seemed to be amusement, but she said nothing.

"I realize that sounds very superficial," he told her.

She waved a hand dismissively and took an-

Back to page 176   178 of 562   179 of 562   21 pages left in this chapter

Figure 7-19: Check a selected word in the built-in dictionary.

2. **Tap the Define button.**

A definition popover appears, as shown in Figure 7-20.

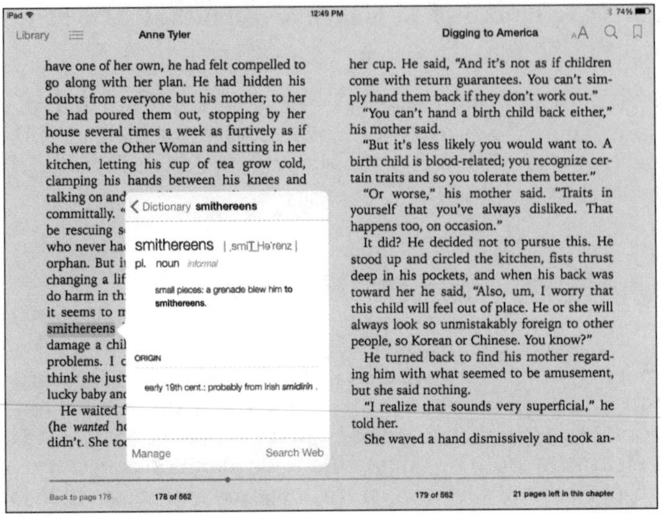

Figure 7-20: Quickly find definitions for words by using the dictionary.

3. **Tap the definition and scroll down, if necessary, to view more.**

4. **When you finish reviewing the definition, tap anywhere on the page.**

The definition disappears.

TIP

You can also tap the Search Web button to look for information about a word from web sources, and tap the Manage button to choose which dictionary your definitions come from.

Organizing Your Library

iBooks lets you create collections of books to help you organize them by your own logic, such as Tearjerkers, Work-Related, and Great Recipes. You can place a book in only one collection, however. To create a collection from the Library bookshelf:

1. **Tap Select.**

2. **Now tap one or more books and then tap Move.**

3. **In the Collections popover shown in Figure 7-21, tap New Collection at the bottom (you may need to scroll down to see it).**

4. **On the blank line that appears, type a name.**

5. **Tap Done.**

The popover closes and you return to your Library.

Figure 7-21: You can create new groups of books in the Collections popover.

To add a book to an existing collection in the Library:

1. **Tap Select.**

2. **Tap Select All, or tap one or more books and then tap the Move button that is located in the top left of the screen (see Figure 7-22).**

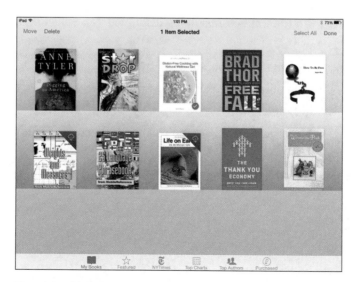

Figure 7-22: Move books into a collection.

3. **In the popover that appears, tap the collection to which you'd like to move the book.**

   The book now appears on the bookshelf in that collection.

To change which collection you're viewing, tap the button with the current collection's name to display other collections and then tap the one you want.

Deleting Books in Collections

After you download lots of books (I know one person who has 1,000), you may become organizationally challenged. iBooks lets you delete books you no longer need on your iPad to keep your bookshelf manageable. Remember that those books aren't gone; you can find and download them again anytime by using the Purchased tab at the bottom of the Store.

Here are the steps for deleting books from your iPad:

1. **When you finish a book, tap the List view button in the top-left corner of the Library.**

2. **Swipe to the left on a title in the list.**

3. **Tap Delete.**

   The book is deleted from iPad.

To delete a collection and move the books within it back into the Books library, follow these steps:

1. **With the Collections dialog displayed, tap Select and then Select All.**

2. **Tap Move.**

3. **Swipe to the left on any collection.**

   Delete buttons appear (see Figure 7-23).

4. **Tap Delete.**

   A message appears, asking you to tap Remove to remove the contents of the collection from your iPad; however, the titles aren't deleted, they're just removed from the collection. All titles within that deleted collection return to their original collections in your Library; the default one is Books.

Figure 7-23: With a quick swipe, you can access this Delete button.

Browsing the Newsstand

Newsstand is an app that focuses on subscribing to and reading magazines, newspapers, and other periodicals rather than books. Newsstand offers an interface to display the periodicals you subscribe to much like a brick-and-mortar newsstand.

Downloading periodical apps to Newsstand

When you download a free publication, you're actually downloading an app to Newsstand. You can then tap that app to buy individual issues or subscribe, as covered in the next section. To download periodical apps to Newsstand, follow these steps:

1. **Tap Newsstand on the Home screen to open Newsstand (see Figure 7-24).**

2. **Tap the Store button.**

   The Newsstand store opens, offering Featured periodicals, Top Charts, and Explore. Tap the Categories button to view categories of periodicals for your shopping pleasure. (See Figure 7-25.)

3. **Tap any of the items displayed, scroll in a category to move to other choices, or tap in the Search field at the top right and enter a search term to locate a publication you're interested in.**

   If you tap other buttons at the bottom of the screen, such as Top Charts or Purchased, you're taken to other types of content than periodicals.

Book II
Chapter 7

Using Your iPad as an E-reader

Also, if you tap Featured again after tapping one of these buttons, you're taken to other kinds of apps than periodicals. Your best bet: Stay on the Store screen that displays when you tap the Store button in Newsstand.

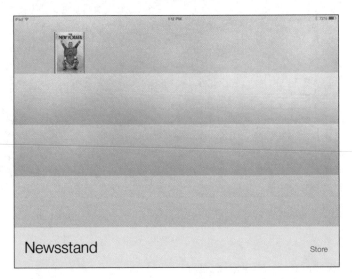

Figure 7-24: View all your subscriptions and publication issues in one place.

Figure 7-25: Browse for periodicals to your heart's content.

4. **When you find an item, tap it to view a detailed description (see Figure 7-26).**

5. **Tap the Free button and then tap Install.**

   The app downloads to Newsstand.

Figure 7-26: Get the lowdown on a particular publication by viewing details.

Buying issues

To purchase issues of periodicals within Newsstand there are variables based on the publication you're subscribing to, but here are the steps using a sample publication:

1. **Tap a periodical app in Newsstand.**

   In the example shown here, tap Latest Issue or Issues (see Figure 7-27).

2. **Tap the Price button and, in the confirmation that appears, tap Buy.**

3. **You may be asked to enter your Apple ID again and to tap Yes in one more confirmation to authorize the purchase.**

   The issue is charged to your iTunes & App Store account.

Figure 7-27: Tap Latest Issue or Issues.

Chapter 8: Playing Games

In This Chapter

✓ Appreciating iPad's gaming strengths

✓ Getting a grip on the accelerometer

✓ Finding games and accessories of all kinds

✓ Challenging friends in Game Center

iPad is, after all, a close relative of the iPhone, and no matter who tells you that he uses his iPhone to get work done, he's probably spending most of his time gaming. iPad outstrips iPhone as the ultimate portable gaming machine because of its beautiful screen (especially if you have a third-generation or later iPad with Retina display) and the ability to rotate the larger screen as you play and track your motions. You can download game apps from the App Store and play them on your device. You can also use the preinstalled Game Center app to help you find and buy games, add friends to play against, and track and share scores.

In this chapter, you discover why iPad is such a great mobile gaming device, what kinds of games are out there, how to create a Game Center account and purchase and download games, how to play games against yourself and others, and what cool accessories you must get to be a completely awesome iPad gamer.

Let the games begin!

Appreciating iPad's Gaming Strengths

The iPhone is a fun gaming device, but the screen is too small. Your computer is a good gaming device, but it may lack some of the tactile input of a touchscreen. iPad may be just right as the ultimate gaming device for many reasons, including these:

✓ **iPad's fantastic screen:** If you have an iPad Air 2 you have a few things going for you here. First, the high-resolution, 9.7" screen has a backlit LED display. As Apple describes it, it's "remarkably crisp and vivid." They're not lying. The In-Plane Switching (IPS) technology means you can hold it at almost any angle (it has a 178-degree viewing angle) and still get good color and contrast. If you own a third-generation iPad (or later), things get even better. These versions of iPad with their Retina displays give you four times as many pixels as earlier iPad models (3.1 million, to be exact). You get 2048 x 1536 resolution, greater color saturation, and a crisp image that rivals many HDTVs.

- ✔ **Faster processor:** The dual-core A8 chip in your iPad Air 2 is a super-fast processor that can run rings around your iPhone, making it a great device for gaming. The A8 chip is very speedy and drives the Retina display without sacrificing the ten-hour battery life iPads are known for. With iPad Air 2, the A8X chip offers 2.5x faster graphics than other models.

- ✔ **A built-in accelerometer and three-axis gyroscope:** Gamers will find these elements useful to shift around in a more versatile manner as they virtually move through games that involve motion. The built-in accelerometer and three-axis gyroscope let you grab your iPad and use it as a steering wheel or other game feature, so you really feel as though you're in the action. (With iPad 2, the gyroscope, accelerometer, and compass were added to help apps like Maps pinpoint your location and movements as you stroll around town.)

- ✔ **M8 coprocessor:** This feature provides the ability to sense your movements. This ability is likely to result in some interesting new gaming and exercise apps.

- ✔ **Playing games in full screen:** Rather than play on a small iPhone screen, you can play most games designed for the iPad in full-screen mode on your iPad. Having a full screen brings the gaming experience to you in a more engaging way than a small screen ever could.

- ✔ **Dragging elements around the screen:** The Multi-Touch iPad screen is responsive — and if you're about to be zapped by aliens in a fight-to-the-death computer game, that responsiveness counts.

- ✔ **The ten-hour battery life of an iPad:** This long battery life on every version of iPad means you can suck energy out of it playing games into the wee hours of the night.

- ✔ **Specialized game-playing features:** Some games are coming out with features that take advantage of iPad's capabilities. For example, Gameloft came out with a version of its N.O.V.A. game that includes a feature called *multiple-target acquisition,* which lets you target multiple bad guys in a single move to blow them out of the water with one shot. The Need for Speed racing games allow you to look in your rearview mirror to see what's coming up behind you, a feature made possible by iPad's large screen, compared to an iPhone.

- ✔ **Great sound:** The built-in stereo speakers in the iPad Air 2 and iPad mini 2 are powerful little things, but if you want things even more up-close and personal, you can plug in a headphone, some speaker systems, or a microphone using the built-in jack.

Understanding the accelerometer

The iPad has a built-in motion sensor called an *accelerometer,* as well as a three-axis gyroscope. These allow designers developing apps for iPad to have lots of fun as they use the automatically rotating screen to become part of the gaming experience. For example, they can build in a compass device that reorients itself automatically if you switch your iPad from landscape to portrait mode. Some racing games allow you to grab the iPad as if it were a steering wheel and rotate the device to simulate the driving experience.

Finding Some Very Cool Games

Now it's time to tell you about some of my favorite iPad games (the part of the book where you wonder why I get paid for what I do,'cause reviewing games is so much fun).

Looking at what's out there

First, take a look at the gaming landscape. Several types of games are available (some ported over from iPhone and some customized for iPad; price noted if not free):

- ✓ **Arcade games** include apps such as Arcade Bowling (free with in-app purchases), Pinball Arcade ($0.99), and Foosball HD ($2.99).

- ✓ **Kids' games** are sometimes educational, but almost always entertaining. These include Ace Kids Math Games (free), Addition UnderSea Adventures (free), and Monkey Word School Adventure ($1.99).

- ✓ **Card and board games,** such as Astraware Solitaire – 12 Games in 1 by Handmark, Inc. ($0.99); Mahjong Deluxe ($0.99); and Payday Roulette 2 HD ($1.99).

- ✓ **Adventure games** like Animal vs. Zombies (free), Everest: Hidden Expedition (free), AirAttack HD ($0.99), Amazon: Hidden Expedition (free with in-app purchases), and Carnivores: Dinosaur Hunter ($2,99).

- ✓ **Sports games,** such as 2XL's SnoCross ($1.99), Stick Golf HD ($2.99), and Pool Bar – Online Hustle ($2.99).

Exploring a half-dozen games

Narrowing down choices to just a few must-have games is hard because everyone likes different kinds of fun. To add to the choices, there are both iPhone- and iPad-engineered games that you can use on your iPad, and more are coming out all the time. If you have a third-generation (or later) iPad, you might want to look for games that are optimized for the new Retina display.

Still, the following list is a sampling of six recommended games for you to try that won't break the bank:

- **Scrabble for iPad ($9.99):** You remember Scrabble, that favorite old board game that can let you shine or put you to shame for your spelling and vocabulary skills? Scrabble is available on iPad, and it's hot (see Figure 8-1). Shake your iPad to shuffle tiles. Use the drag-and-drop motion to play your letters. Want to share the fun? Reach out to your Facebook friends to take the game to the multiplayer level.

- **Broken Sword – The Smoking Mirror ($0.99):** This classic adventure game lets you virtually become the main character to experience all the game has to offer. Great art and animation distinguish this game, and the iPad version (see its description in the Game Center Store and see Figure 8-2) has a handy hint system that you'll appreciate.

- **Civilization Revolution for iPad ($6.99):** If you like a world-building type of game, you'll find Civilization Revolution right up your alley. It has been fine-tuned for iPad to be even better than the iPhone version. The game also offers a feature called Scenario Creator, which lets you create your own unique challenges, essentially allowing for unlimited variety in the game.

Figure 8-1: Scrabble is awesome on the iPad.

- **Monkey Island 2 Special Edition: LeChuck's Revenge for iPad ($4.99):** A point-and-click adventure game classic on iPhone, in its iPad incarnation, Monkey Island has great graphics and sound, and an engaging story at its heart. If you like adventure games, don't miss this one.

✔ **Minecraft Pocket Edition ($6.99):** Minecraft is a wildly popular game that involves a virtual reality in which you build things with blocks (see Figure 8-3). But these aren't Tinkertoys — with Minecraft, people are building entire cities, engineering feats, and alternative realities.

✔ **t Chess Pro ($7.99):** You can play against the computer or another player. You can modify the appearance of the chess pieces. It even sports features that help chess beginners learn the game painlessly, but more advanced players will enjoy it as well.

Book II
Chapter 8

Playing Games

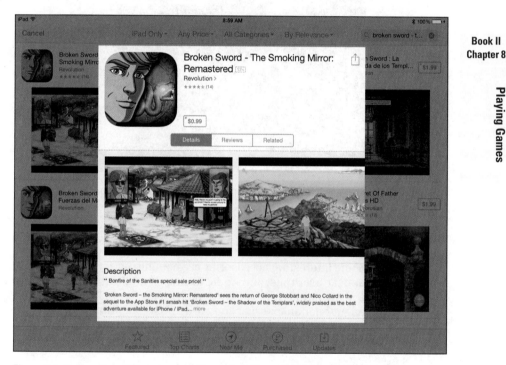

Figure 8-2: Broken Sword is a classic game updated from its iPhone version for iPad.

As well as costing money, games take up a lot of memory, so choose the games you buy wisely. If you no longer want to play a game, delete it from your iPad to save space.

Special mention: ComicBookLover (free) isn't a game, but it's a blast of an app that most gamers can appreciate. The iPad screen is perfect for those bright, crisp graphics, and iPad's navigation tools let you swipe your way through the panes in several interesting ways. This app uses CBR and CBZ files, which are available from various online sources. You can even scan your own comic books and graphic novels and use them with this app.

Figure 8-3: Minecraft is a very creative world to explore and build.

Getting Gaming Accessories

Some interesting accessories are coming out for iPad. No doubt more will appear over time, and Apple itself may add features or gaming accessories in a next-edition device. For example, for a future iPad, Apple or somebody else might offer an external control accessory so that you don't have to cover up your onscreen game to use onscreen control mechanisms, and Apple might add a feature to simulate gaming sounds.

For now, here are a couple of iPad gaming accessories that caught my attention:

- **Incipio iPad Hive Honeycomb dermaShot Silicone Case ($39.99)** is a rugged case for serious gamers. The back sports molded grips that help you keep a good hold on your iPad while playing those action-packed games.

- **JoyStick-It (around $5)** from ThinkGeek is an arcade-style stick you attach to your iPad screen. The joystick, available on Amazon.com, won't harm your screen, and you can move it around at any time. It gives you that real arcade-game feel for controlling games. It won't work with every game but does claim to work with thousands of them.

Playing through the Game Center

The Game Center is an app that comes preinstalled with iPad. If you're into gaming, you may enjoy the features it offers that allow you to challenge friends to beat your scores; buy games; and keep track of your games, friends, and achievements.

Of course, you can also download games from the App Store or play online games and play them on your iPad without having to use Game Center. What Game Center provides is a place where you can create a gaming profile, add a list of gaming friends, keep track of and share your scores and perks, and shop for games (and only games) in the App Store, along with listings of top-rated games and game categories to choose from.

Think of the Game Center as a kind of social networking site for gamers, where you can compare your scores and find players to challenge. The Achievements listing shows you your score history for all the games you play. Finally, Leaderboards allows you to compare your performance with your gaming friends.

Figure 8-4 shows you the Game Center interface with the following five choices along the bottom:

✔ **Me:** Contains your profile and summary of number of friends, games, and achievements.

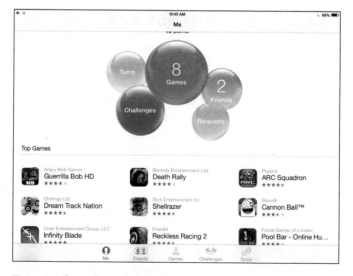

Figure 8-4: Game Center's opening screen shows an overview of your friends, games, and achievements.

✔ **Friends:** Tap to invite friends to play.

✔ **Games:** Takes you to iTunes to shop for games.

✔ **Challenges:** Friends can challenge their friends to do better than they did. Tap a friend's score in the Friends area of Game Center to challenge her.

✔ **Turns:** Shows you any requests from your friends for a game.

Opening an account in Game Center

Using the Game Center app, you can search for and buy games, add friends with whom you can play those games, and keep records of your scores for posterity. In order to do this, however, you must first open a Game Center account by following these steps:

1. **From the Home screen, tap the Game Center icon.**

   If you've never used Game Center, you're asked whether to allow *push notifications:* If you want to receive these notices alerting you that your friends want to play a game with you, tap OK. You should, however, be aware that push notifications can drain your iPad's battery more quickly.

2. **On the Game Center opening screen (see Figure 8-5), sign in.**

   If you want to use Game Center with another Apple ID, tap Create New Apple ID and follow the onscreen instructions, which ask you to enter your birth date, agree to terms, choose a security question, and so forth; or enter your current account information and tap Go.

   The screen that appears after you've signed in shows games you've downloaded, requests from other players, friends, and so on (see Figure 8-6).

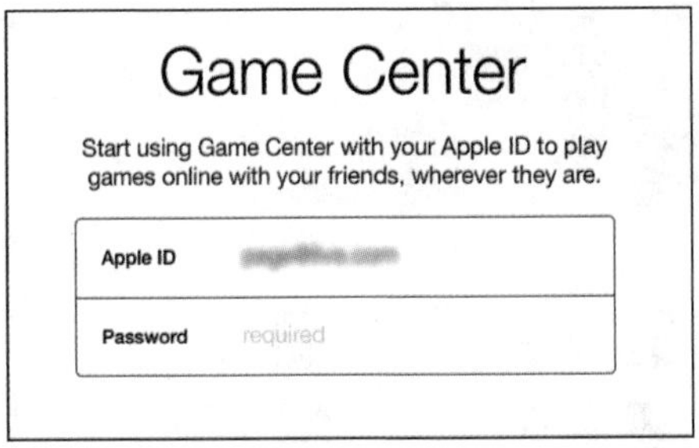

   ### Game Center

   Start using Game Center with your Apple ID to play games online with your friends, wherever they are.

   | Apple ID | |
   | Password | required |

   Figure 8-5: Sign in to Game Center here.

3. **Tap any of the floating balloons to get to these categories or tap a button along the bottom of the screen.**

When you first register for Game Center, if you use an email address other than the one associated with your Apple ID, you may have to create a new Apple ID and verify it by responding to an email message that's sent to your email address.

Figure 8-6: Tap a balloon to get to a category.

Creating a Game Center profile

When you have an account with which you can sign into Game Center, you're ready to specify some account settings. To create your Game Center profile, follow these steps:

1. **On the Home screen, tap Settings.**

2. **Tap Game Center, and in the settings that appear (see Figure 8-7), if you don't want other players to be able to invite you to play games when Game Center is open, tap the Allow Invites Off/On switch to turn off this feature.**

   If you want your friends to be able to send you requests for playing games via email, check to see whether the primary email address listed here is the one you want them to use. If the primary email address is the one you want to use, skip to Step 5.

3. **If you want to change the email address listed, tap the current Apple ID and, in the settings that appear, tap Sign Out.**

4. **On the screen that next appears, tap in the Apple ID field and enter another account.**

   Or tap Create a New Apple ID.

5. **Tap to Allow Invites or to allow Nearby Players to find you and invite you to games. (see Figure 8-7.)**

6. **If you want others to see your profile, including your real name, scroll down and tap the current profile and then tap the Public Profile On/Off switch to turn on the public profile.**

7. **Tap Done; then press the Home button when you're finished with settings and tap Game Center.**

    You return to the Game Center Home screen, already signed in to your account with information displayed about friends, games, and gaming achievements (all at zero, initially).

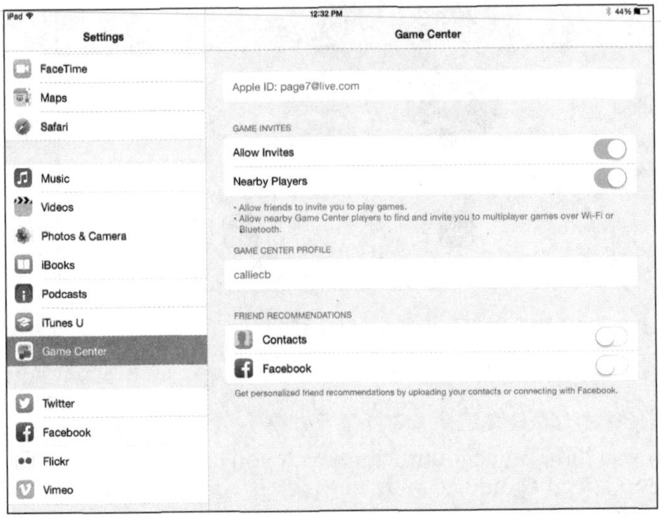

Figure 8-7: When you're playing games with others, your handle identifies you.

> **TIP**
>
> After you create an account and a profile, whenever you go to the Game Center, you log in by entering your email address and password and then tapping Sign In.

Adding friends

If you want to play Game Center games with others who have an Apple ID and an iPhone, iPod touch, Mac with Mountain Lion or later, or iPad, follow these steps to add them as friends so that you can invite them to play:

1. **From the Game Center Home screen, tap the Friends button at the bottom of the screen.**

2. **On the Friends page, tap the Add Friends button in the top (shaped like a plus sign).**

3. **Enter an email address in the To field and edit the invitation, if you like.**

4. **Tap the Send button.**

   After your friend accepts your invitation, her name is listed on the Friends screen.

Game Center includes the Friend Recommendations feature. Go to the Friends tab and then tap the A–Z button in the top-left corner. A Recommendations section appears above the list of your current friends. These are people who play the same or similar games, so if you like, try adding one or two as friends. You can go to the Points tab to view the points these folks have accumulated so that you can stay in your league.

You will probably also receive requests from friends who know you're on Game Center. When you get these email invitations, be sure that you know the person sending it before you accept it — especially if you've allowed email access in your account settings. If you don't double-check, you could be allowing a potentially abusive stranger into your gaming world.

Book II
Chapter 8

Playing Games

Purchasing and downloading games

Time to get some games to play! Remember that you can buy any game app from the App Store and simply play it by tapping to open it on your iPad. But if you want to use Game Center to buy games, here are the steps involved:

1. **Open Game Center and sign in to your account.**

2. **Tap the Games button at the bottom of the screen and, under the Recommended category, tap Show More.**

3. **In the list of games that appears, scroll through the list of featured games and tap one that appeals to you.**

4. **Tap the Price/Free App button to display details about the game.**

   Note that you can tap the Store button from here to go to the iTunes store to view more games.

   Accessing apps from the Game Center displays only game apps, as opposed to accessing apps from the App Store, which shows you all categories of apps.

5. **To buy a game, tap the button labeled with either the words Free App or the price, such as $1.99.**

6. **In the detailed app page that appears (see Figure 8-8), tap the button again and then tap the Buy or Install button.**

Figure 8-8: Tap to buy a game.

7. **Enter your Apple ID and password in the dialog that appears and then tap OK.**

   Another verification dialog appears, asking you to sign in.

8. **Follow the instructions on the next couple of screens to enter your password and verify your payment information if this is the first time you've signed in to your account from this device.**

9. **When the verification dialog appears, tap Buy or Install (for a free game).**

   The game downloads.

If you've added friends to your account (see the preceding section), you can go to the Friends page and view games that your friends have downloaded. To purchase one of these games, just tap it in your friend's list.

Playing against yourself

Many games allow you to play all on your own. Each game has different rules and goals, so you have to study a game's instructions and learn how to play it, but here's some general information about these types of games:

✔ Often a game can be played in two modes: with others or in a *solitaire* version, where you play yourself or the computer.

✔ Many games that you may be familiar with in the offline world, such as Carcassonne or Scrabble, have online versions. For these, you already know the rules of play, so you simply need to figure out the execution. For example, in the online Carcassonne game, you tap to place a tile on the board, tap the placed tile to rotate it, and tap the check mark to complete your turn and reveal another tile.

✔ All the games you play on your own record your scores in Game Center so that you can track your progress.

Challenging friends in Game Center

After you've added a friend and both of you have downloaded the same game, you can challenge her to beat your scores:

1. **Tap the Game Center app icon on the Home screen and sign in, if necessary.**

2. **Tap Me; and then tap the Games bubble.**

3. **Tap one of your scores.**

4. **In the dialog that appears, tap the Challenge bubble (see Figure 8-9).**

Figure 8-9: Keep challenging friends to widen your gaming universe.

5. **Tap a friend in the dialog that appears and then tap Next.**

6. **In the form that appears, enter a message, if you like, and then tap Send.**

   Game Center tracks your achievements, including points and perks that you've earned along the way. You can also compare your gaming achievements to those of top-ranking players across the Internet — and check your friends' scores by displaying the Friends page with the Points portion showing.

If your friends aren't available, you can play a game by tapping its title on the Games page and then tapping Play. You can then compare your scores with others around the world who have also played the game recently.

Book III

iPad on the Go

Visit www.dummies.com/extras/ipadaio for more ideas about apps that are useful to business power users.

In this book. . .

- ✔ Stay in touch with others and your home office while traveling
- ✔ Connect with clients by using video and FaceTime
- ✔ Find your way with the Maps app

Chapter 1: Configuring Your iPad to Connect Everywhere

In This Chapter

✔ **Making Wi-Fi and 3G/4G settings**

✔ **Tethering your iPad to your smartphone**

✔ **Setting up a Microsoft Exchange account**

This chapter is all about connecting, whether you're connecting to the Internet via Wi-Fi, 3G, or 4G (not available on the original iPad or iPad 2) or connecting to your company network. Apple has made an effort over the years with iPhone to support enterprises, meaning that you can use the phone to connect with your company network and vital work data. The iPad continues that tradition with support for Microsoft Exchange Server, virtual private networks (VPNs), and Lightweight Directory Access Protocol (LDAP) accounts.

Your best ally in setting up the more technical of these is your network administrator. In this chapter, I give you an overview of the capabilities of iPad to connect and some guidance in making the settings you need to make.

Making Wi-Fi and 3G/4G Settings

The way people with iPads can connect to the Internet, the grandmother of all networks, is via its Wi-Fi or 3G/4G capabilities (assuming that you have a 3G or 4G model).

The third-generation (and later) iPad and the iPad mini offer Wi-Fi only or Wi-Fi and 3G/4G, which gives you the ability to connect to a super-fast 4G LTE network; if a 4G network isn't available (and they aren't yet in many areas), your 4G iPad can still access several types of 3G networks including GSM/UMTS networks around the world.

In this section, I go into the settings you can make to manage your Wi-Fi or 3G/4G connection.

Making Wi-Fi settings

Book I, Chapter 5 gives you the information you need to connect to a Wi-Fi network, a matter of simply signing in to the network, with a password, if necessary. Now it's time to go over some of the finer points of your Wi-Fi connection.

A basic Wi-Fi setting tells iPad to automatically search for and join networks that are in range. If several networks are in range, using this setting, iPad joins the one that it used most recently.

After iPad has joined a network, a little Wi-Fi icon appears in the status bar. The number of dots indicates the strength of the signal, just as you're used to seeing on your cellphone.

To get to Wi-Fi settings, tap Settings on your Home screen and then tap Wi-Fi (see Figure 1-1).

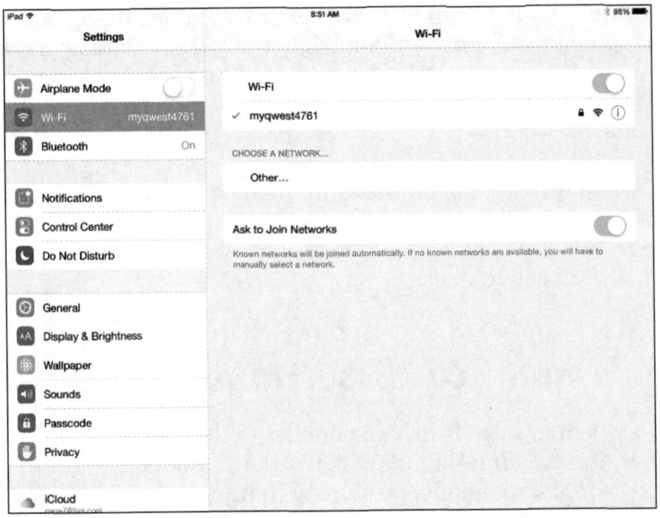

Figure 1-1: Wi-Fi settings.

Here's a rundown of the items you can work with in Settings for your Wi-Fi configuration:

- **Wi-Fi On/Off:** Simply tap this switch to On to turn on Wi-Fi. If you want it off, perhaps to avoid battery drain or because you're on an airplane and the pilot tells you to, set this to Off. (Note that iPads also have an Airplane Mode setting, which I discuss in the next section.)

- **The network you're currently connected to:** The current connection is listed. Tap it to change any settings for it or to disconnect.

✓ **Other:** If you want to join a network that doesn't appear on the list, tap Other under the Choose a Network section of these settings. In the dialog that appears, enter the network name and choose a type of security, such as WEP or WPA. When you choose a form of security and return to the dialog shown in Figure 1-2, the Password field appears. Some networks might need other information, such as a username or static IP address, to complete this dialog. Check with your administrator for any information you can't provide.

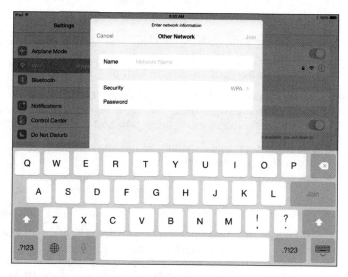

Figure 1-2: Accessing a closed network.

✓ **Ask to Join Networks:** iPad automatically connects to the previously joined network. With this setting on, an alert will appear asking if you want to join other networks that you come in range of. Tap this switch to the On position, and iPad displays all possible network connections. If a network requires a password, it sports a padlock symbol. If no known networks are available, you're asked whether you want to join unknown networks. To forget a network so that iPad doesn't join it automatically, tap the Information icon on the right of the network name and then tap Forget This Network.

To adjust settings for individual Wi-Fi networks, tap the Information icon to the right of a listed network.

You can set up Home Sharing to share music and video content from your Mac or PC with your iPad if they are on the same network and have the same Home Sharing ID as your iPad. See Book V, Chapter 1 for more about Home Sharing.

**Book III
Chapter 1**

Configuring Your
iPad to Connect
Everywhere

Making 3G/4G settings

When you own a Wi-Fi+Cellular model of iPad, in addition to modifying Wi-Fi settings as covered in the preceding section, you can make changes to your cellular data in Settings. Cellular Data settings enable you to manage data roaming and your account information (see Figure 1-3). You can use these settings to sign up for a data plan by entering your name, phone number, and credit card information; when you submit this information, your account is set up with your provider with a unique phone number associated with the account. You need this phone number to speak to customer representatives about your account.

You can find the following items under the Cellular Data category in Settings:

- **Cellular Data:** Turn 3G/4G on or off here.

- **Enable LTE:** To enable your iPad to search for and connect to LTE networks, turn on this setting. Data may load faster using LTE, but remember that downloading still takes a toll on your battery life.

- **Data Roaming:** Data Roaming is a feature of cellular networks that takes advantage of other carriers' networks, if you're out of range of your primary carrier's network. Using data roaming can result in additional charges, so you may want to turn it off when you don't need it.

- **View Account:** Tap this setting to view account information.

- **Add a SIM PIN:** You may want to protect the data on your SIM card from prying eyes. Beyond setting a password to unlock your iPad, you can assign a PIN to your SIM card here. When you've assigned a PIN, whenever you try to use a new SIM card or restart your Wi-Fi or 3G/4G iPad, you have to enter the password. Don't forget your PIN, though, or you can't unlock your SIM card.

With any Wi-Fi and 3G/4G model iPad, you also have access to the Airplane Mode setting in both the Settings and Control Center. This setting allows you to disable wireless features of your device as required by airline regulations when you're on an airline flight. With Airplane Mode turned on, you won't be able to browse, email, sync, buy stuff online, or stream videos (which you would only be able to do with a 3G/4G model a few miles up in the sky) unless the airline provides Wi-Fi. If it does, you can use the Wi-Fi only setting in the Control panel to enable this, but do turn it off before takeoff and landing. Also, the GPS locator of Maps won't work, but you can play content that you've downloaded, play games, and create documents in apps like Pages and Numbers. Just don't forget to turn off the Airplane Mode setting when you land!

Connecting with Personal Hotspot or iPhone Tethering

If you want to connect your Wi-Fi–only iPad to your smartphone to go online when out of range of a Wi-Fi network, you can tether the iPad to the phone using Verizon's, T-Mobile's, or Sprint's Personal Hotspot or AT&T's iPhone 3G/4G Tethering. *Tethering* with any of these services allows your iPad to tap into your phone's data connection to go online. You can get a connection anywhere your phone gets a connection — even if you have a Wi-Fi–only iPad model.

Tethering involves a few challenges. You don't go online instantly because you have to complete a few steps first, the connection speed might be a tad slow, and it can drain your phone battery quickly.

After you're comfortable with the trade-offs of the tethering option, you need to do two things:

1. **Add the tethering option for your carrier on the carrier's website by logging in to your account and adding the feature.**

   This can come with a cost; for example, with AT&T you might pay for tethering support (based on GB of usage) anywhere from $50 to $100 at the time of this writing.

2. **Make the setting on your iPad turn on the tethering service feature by doing the following:**

   a. *Tap the Settings icon.*

   b. *Tap Wi-Fi.*

   c. *Tap the tethering service in the Choose a Network section and make settings specific to your carrier.*

Sprint, AT&T, T-Mobile, and Verizon pricing and features for iPad Air 2/mini 3 vary. For example, Verizon offers an individual plan at $45 a month and a family plan called More Everything for up to 4 lines for $140. AT&T offers 3GB of data for $30 a month and 40GB of data for a family for $150. You need both a basic data plan and a tethering feature plan which could cost an additional $50, which can add up. Still, if you often wander into areas that have no Wi-Fi and you don't have a 3G or 4G iPad, it may — or may not — be more cost effective to use this feature.

Connecting to an Enterprise

Microsoft Exchange support opens possibilities for connecting with an enterprise network and its data remotely. If you work at a company using Microsoft Exchange and use an iPad, this is very good news.

Thanks to these enterprise features, here are some of the things you can do to connect to your organization's network and data.

Setting up a configuration profile

Microsoft Exchange is a messaging standard that allows the exchange of information between networks. With a configuration profile in place, you can set up a Microsoft Exchange account on your iPad. A *configuration profile* is a way for the network administrator at your enterprise to set up your iPad to use the systems in your company, via Microsoft Exchange or a VPN (virtual private network), which controls access to corporate email or contacts.

Your administrator should check out the Enterprise Deployment Guide and the iPad Configurator utility from Apple (www.apple.com/support/ipad/ enterprise) to set up a configuration profile. After a configuration profile is in place, it can be emailed to you or placed on a secure web page. Alternatively, your company's network administrator can install a configuration profile on your iPad for you.

When you receive a configuration profile, you can install it yourself by opening the message and tapping the file. Tap Install and enter any information that's requested, such as your password.

Setting up a Microsoft Exchange account

Many companies use Microsoft Exchange to exchange their email, contacts, and calendar information with devices. iPhone has supported Microsoft Exchange for a while now, and iPad carries on the tradition. You can use Microsoft Exchange to wirelessly sync that information to your iPad from your corporate network.

One benefit of a connection with Microsoft Exchange is that your IT administrator can wipe the data and settings off a device remotely by using a command in Exchange if it's lost or stolen, keeping those confidential business contacts private. Another option for erasing content on a lost device is to use iCloud's Find My iPad feature, covered in more detail in Book I, Chapter 9.

To set up Microsoft Exchange, follow these steps:

1. **Tap Settings.**

2. **Tap Mail, Contacts, Calendars.**

3. **Tap Add Account.**

4. **Tap Exchange.**

5. Enter your account information in the dialog shown in Figure 1-3 (email address, password, and a description) and then tap Next.

The iPad then uses Microsoft's Autodiscover feature to verify your Exchange server.

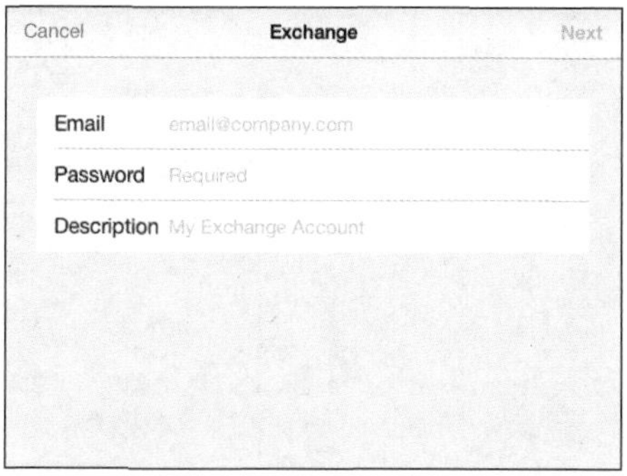

Cancel	**Exchange**	Next
Email	email@company.com	
Password	Required	
Description	My Exchange Account	

Figure 1-3: Exchange settings.

6. If your iPad can verify your information, tap Save and you're all set.

If it can't, you may have entered incorrect information. Check with your network administrator to get the info you need.

 When you're setting up a Microsoft Exchange account, you can choose which items you want to sync with, including your email, contacts, or calendar. You get choices for how existing data on your iPad is handled (merged, kept in a separate account, or overwritten).

Setting up an LDAP account

You can also set up a Lightweight Directory Access Protocol (LDAP) account. LDAP accounts allow you to search for contacts on an LDAP server, which many organizations use to store data, and access them through iPad Contacts.

Here's how to set up an LDAP account on your iPad:

1. In Settings, tap Mail, Contacts, Calendars.

2. Tap Add Account.

3. Tap Other.

4. Tap Add LDAP Account.

5. **Enter your LDAP account information (see Figure 1-4) and then tap Next to verify the account.**

6. **Tap Save.**

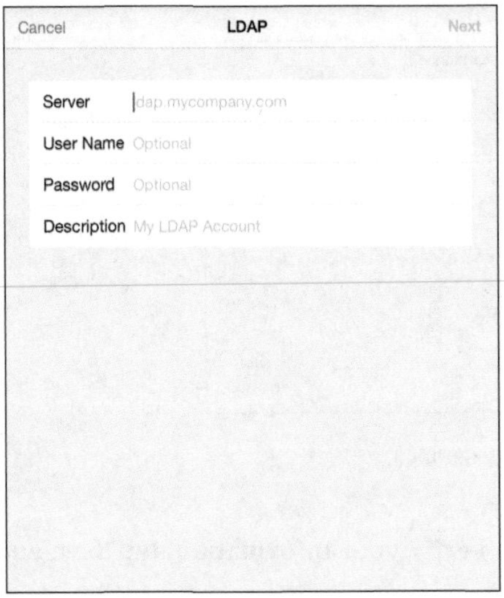

Cancel	**LDAP**	Next

Server	ldap.mycompany.com
User Name	Optional
Password	Optional
Description	My LDAP Account

Figure 1-4: The LDAP settings.

When you've set up this type of account, contacts imported from the account appear as a group in the iPad Contacts app as with any group. To see these contacts, your iPad has to be connected to the Internet because they aren't stored locally (meaning that they're stored on your company's servers). If necessary, check with your company's network administrator for information about your network and LDAP requirements.

Setting up a virtual private network

If you want to be able to connect to your organization's network, you may be able to use a virtual private network, or VPN. A VPN, which works over both Wi-Fi and 3G/4G cellular data connections, allows you to access data securely whether you're using a network outside your company — such as at home or in a café — to access the servers inside your company's network. After a VPN is set up at your company, you can use VPN settings on your iPad to connect to your company network.

You might need to ask your network administrator for information on how to make settings for accessing a VPN. If you've set up VPN on your computer, you should be able to use the same VPN settings on your iPad. You might want to let your admin know that iPad can connect to VPNs that use the L2TP, PPTP, or Cisco IPSec protocol.

To add a new VPN configuration, go to Settings and tap General⇨VPN⇨Add VPN Configuration. The settings shown in Figure 1-5 appear. Fill in the information requested and tap Save.

Figure 1-5: The Add Configuration settings.

Book III
Chapter 1

Configuring Your
iPad to Connect
Everywhere

You can have multiple VPNs set up, for example if you consult with several companies with their own VPNs. Tap the one you want to use, and then set the VPN switch to On. To switch VPNs, disconnect from one, select the new one, and then turn VPN back on. Only one VPN can be active at any time. To delete a VPN configuration, tap the blue arrow to the right of the configuration name in the General settings and then tap Delete VPN.

Have your administrator check out third-party tools that help to enable the use of the corporate network by remote iPad users. Good for Enterprise helps a user manage and update smartphone-like standards if that person's company has no single standard. Array Networks provides the iPad app Desktop Direct – My Desktops that, along with Citrix Receiver software, helps users access their desktop from afar.

Status icons

In case you're wondering what the icons in the status bar on top of the iPad screen mean relative to your connections, here's a rundown:

Icon	Meaning
✈	Airplane mode is on, and your Wi-Fi and 3G/4G connection capabilities are turned off.
3G	A 3G/4G network is available.
E	A carrier's EDGE (2G) network is available.
O	A GPRS (2G) network is available.
📶	Your iPad has a Wi-Fi Internet connection. The more bars you see, the stronger your connection.
❋	Network or data-syncing involving a third-party app is detected.
VPN	You're connected to a VPN network.

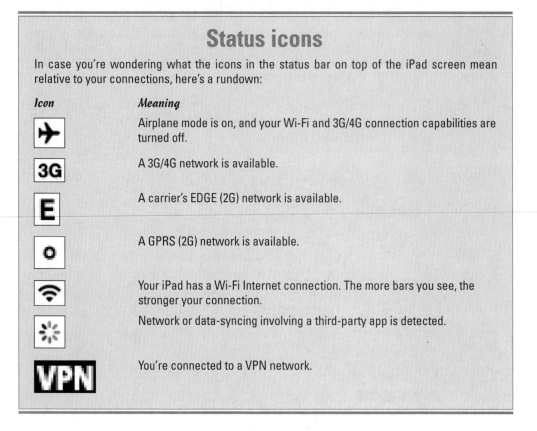

Chapter 2: Finding Your Way with Maps

In This Chapter

✔ **Going to your current location**

✔ **Knowing where you've been**

✔ **Finding directions, info, and more**

✔ **Conveying location information beyond maps**

✔ **Getting turn-by-turn navigation help**

*Y*ou may have used a maps app on a smartphone before. The big difference with the iPad is its large screen, on which you can view all the beautiful map visuals, traffic flow, and streets in standard views and even 3D as long as you have an Internet connection. You can also display a map and written directions simultaneously or have Maps speak your directions, guiding you as you drive with your 3G/4G iPad.

You will find lots of great functions in the Maps app, including getting directions with suggested alternative routes from one place to another by foot or car. You can bookmark locations to return to them again. And the Maps app makes it possible to get information about locations, such as the phone numbers and web links to businesses. You can even add a location to your Contacts list or share a location with your buddy using Mail, Message, Twitter, or Facebook.

Be prepared: This app is a fun way to find your way in the world.

Getting Where You're Going

The first duty of a map is to get you where you want to go. The Maps app can go directly to wherever you are or to any other location you wish to visit. You can also use tools that help you find different views of locales by displaying streets, terrain, or aerial views or zooming in and out for various levels of detail. In this section, you find out how to use Maps to get around.

Going to your current location

The iPad is pretty smart; it can figure out where you are at any point in time and display your current location using GPS technology (with a 3G/4G model) or a triangulation method (Wi-Fi model). You must have an Internet connection and turn Location Services on in the Privacy pane in Settings; your location can be pinpointed more exactly if you have a 3G or 4G iPad, but even Wi-Fi models do a pretty good job, and they do even better when you're surrounded by hotspots.

To display your current location in Maps, follow these steps:

1. **From the Home screen, tap the Maps icon.**

2. **Tap the Current Location icon (the arrow shown in the lower-left corner of Figure 2-1).**

   Your current location is displayed with a pin in it and a pulsating blue circle around it (see Figure 2-1). The circle indicates how accurate the location is — it could actually be anywhere within the area of the circle.

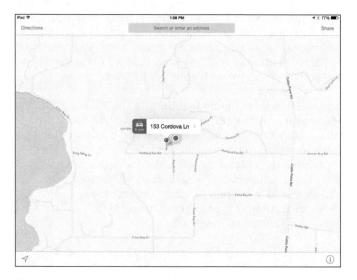

Figure 2-1: Go to your current location quickly to see where you are.

Having trouble getting Maps to work? That could be because if you turn off Location Services in Settings, Maps can't find you. Go to Settings and in the Privacy setting, make sure that Location Services is set to On for the Maps app.

3. **Double-tap the screen to zoom in on your location.**

   Additional methods of zooming in and out are covered in the "Zooming in and out" section, later in this chapter.

If you don't have a 3G/4G version of iPad, your current location is a rough estimate based on a triangulation method. Only 3G- and 4G-enabled iPads with GPS can really pinpoint your location. Still, if you type a starting location and an ending location to get directions, you can get pretty accurate results even with a Wi-Fi–only iPad.

Changing views

The Maps app offers three views: Standard, Satellite, and Hybrid. You see the Standard view by default the first time you open Maps. Here's what these views offer:

- **Standard:** Your basic street map that you might find in any road atlas
- **Satellite:** An aerial view
- **Hybrid:** A satellite view with street names included

Another cool app for those who like their maps of the topographical variety is Topo Maps for iPad from Phil Endecott ($7.99). This app taps into the United States Geological Society (USGS) and Canadian topographical maps and is great for planning that next trek into the wilderness.

Follow these steps to switch among the views in Maps:

1. **With Maps open, tap the Information button in the bottom-right corner of the screen and reveal the Maps popover, shown in Figure 2-2.**

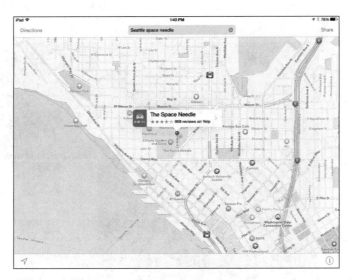

Figure 2-2: The controls for Maps are displayed when you tap the Information button.

2. **Tap the Satellite option.**

   The Satellite view, shown in Figure 2-3, appears.

Figure 2-3: Using Satellite view, you look at a location from the sky.

3. **Tap to reveal the menu again and tap Hybrid, as shown in Figure 2-4.**

   Doing this displays a Satellite view with street names superimposed.

Figure 2-4: Street names and highway numbers appear in Hybrid view.

4. **Tap the Show 3D Map button in the Maps popover.**

   A 3D effect is applied to whatever view is displayed (see Figure 2-5).

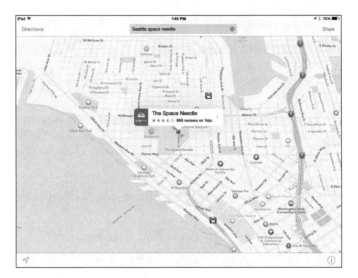

Figure 2-5: 3D seems to rotate and slant the map before your eyes.

You can drop a pin to mark a location on a map that you can return to. See the "Dropping a pin" section, later in this chapter, for more about this feature.

You can also turn on a feature that displays an overlay on the Standard map to show current traffic conditions. (The Show Traffic setting is shown earlier in Figure 2-2.) This feature works best in major metropolitan areas and displays red dashes on roads indicating accidents or road closures, and orange dashes to indicate traffic slowdowns to help you navigate your rush-hour commute or trip to the mall.

To print any displayed map to an AirPrint-compatible printer, just tap Share in the top-right corner and then tap the Print button.

Zooming in and out

If you've used an online mapping program, you know that you frequently have to move to more or less detailed views of the map to find what you're looking for: The street detail doesn't show the nearest highway, and the region level doesn't let you see that all-important next turn. You'll appreciate the feature in the Maps app that allows you to zoom in and out to see more or less detailed maps and to move around a map.

You can use the following methods on a displayed map to zoom in and out and move around a map:

- **Double-tap with a single finger** to zoom in and reveal more detail.
- **Double-tap with two fingers** to zoom out and reveal less detail.
- **Place two fingers together on the screen and move them apart** to zoom in.
- **Place two fingers apart on the screen and pinch them together** to zoom out.
- **Press your finger to the screen and drag the map in any direction** to move to an adjacent area.

It can take a few moments for the map to redraw itself when you enlarge, reduce, or move around it, so have a little patience. An area that's being redrawn will look like a blank grid but will fill in, in time. Also, if you're in Satellite or Hybrid view, zooming in may take some time; wait it out because the blurred image will resolve itself.

Going to another location

If you're at Point A and want to get to Point B — Calcutta, Des Moines, or wherever — you need to know how to find any location other than your current location using Maps. Doing this involves entering as much information as you have about the location's address in the Search field.

Try going to another location using these steps:

1. **With Maps open, tap in the Search field.**

   If you don't see the Search field in the upper-right corner, you may have to tap the Clear button.

   The keyboard opens (as shown in Figure 2-6).

2. **Type a location, using a street address with city and state, a stored contact name, or a destination, such as *Empire State Building* or *Detroit airport*.**

   Maps may make suggestions as you type if it finds any logical matches.

   Tap the Dictation key (not available on iPad 2) on the onscreen keyboard (refer to Figure 2-6) and speak a location to iPad if you prefer. Tap in the Search field and then tap the Dictation key and say the location; tap the Dictation key or in the Search field again and what you've spoken appears there.

   Double-tap the Home button and ask Siri (third-generation iPad or later) for a type of business or location by zip code. For example, if you crave something with pepperoni, say "Find pizza in 99208 zip code." The results typically display a small map that you can tap to open the Maps app to find your way there. See Book V, Chapter 6 for more about using Siri.

Figure 2-6: You can use the onscreen keyboard to enter location information.

3. Tap the Search button.

The location appears with a red pin inserted in it and a label with the location and an Information icon (shown in Figure 2-7).

Figure 2-7: The more specific the address information you enter, the more likely you are to find just the right location.

4. **Tap the Information icon to see more about the destination.**

   Note that if several locations match your search term, you may see several pins displayed in a Suggestions list.

5. **You can also tap the screen and drag in any direction to move to a nearby location.**

   See the upcoming "Dropping a pin" section to find out how to zero in on the location and get the label with links to additional information, as you see in Figure 2-7.

Add the city and state, if you know them, whenever you enter a destination. A search for *Bronx Zoo* landed me in the Woodland Park Zoo in Tacoma, Washington, because the search uses the individual words and the closest geographical location for a *Zoo* match to find results!

Remembering Where You've Been

Why reinvent the (mapping) wheel? One of the great capabilities of a mapping program is the ability to store locations you like to go to for future reference. In Maps, you can do this in a few ways. You can drop a pin on a map, which marks a beginning point for getting directions from one site to another. Or you can place a bookmark for a site you want to revisit often. You then access your bookmarks by tapping Recents in the Search field; tap Favorites to see your bookmarks.

Dropping a pin

With the iPad, pins act like the pins you might place on a paper map to note routes or favorite locations. Also, pins are markers: A green pin marks a start location; a red pin marks search results; a pin you that drop yourself appears in a lovely purple; and a blue pin (referred to as the *blue marker*) marks your iPad's current location.

Use these steps to try the pin feature of iPad:

1. **Display a map that contains a spot where you want to drop a pin to help you get directions to or from that site.**

   If necessary, you can zoom in to a more detailed map to get a better view of the location you want to pin using the techniques I cover in the earlier "Zooming in and out" section.

2. **Press and hold your finger on the screen at the location where you want to place the pin.**

   The pin appears, together with an information bar (shown in Figure 2-8).

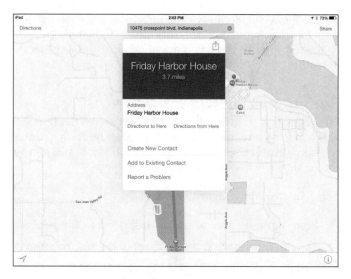

Figure 2-8: The information bar provides access to yet more Maps tools.

3. **Tap the Information bar that appears when you tap a pin to display details about the pin location (shown in Figure 2-9).**

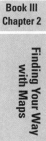

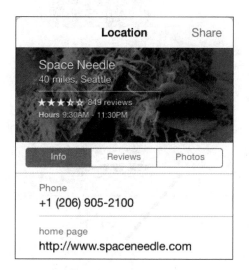

Figure 2-9: This very useful dialog gives you information and lets you share what you know.

TIP

If a site has associated reviews on Yelp, you see a More Info on Yelp button in its Information dialog. Tap this button to install the Yelp app and read the reviews. If you like the destination, add it to your contacts to find it easily in the future.

Adding and viewing a favorite

Favorites are a tried-and-true way to save a destination so that you can display a map or directions to that spot quickly. You've probably used a similar bookmark feature in a web browser. With Maps, you can save favorites and access those locations from the search field.

Here's how to add a favorite in Maps:

1. **Place a pin on a location, as described in the preceding section.**

2. **Tap the Information bar to display the Information dialog.**

3. **Tap the Share button. (See Figure 2-10.)**

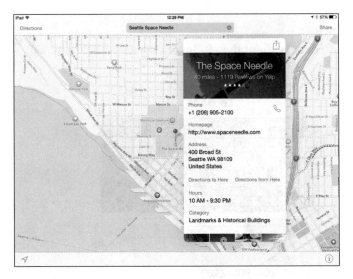

Figure 2-10: Click here to add a favorite.

4. **Tap Add to Favorites.**

   The Add to Favorites dialog and the keyboard appear (as shown in Figure 2-11). If you like, you can modify the name of the bookmark.

5. **Tap Save.**

Figure 2-11: Name the bookmark.

6. **To view your favorite bookmarks, tap the Search field at the top of the Maps screen**

   Tap Favorites, as shown in Figure 2-12.

Figure 2-12: The list of saved bookmarks.

7. **Tap a bookmark to go to the location in Maps.**

You can also view recently viewed locations even if you haven't bookmarked them. Tap Bookmark, and then, on the bottom of the Favorites dialog that appears, tap Recents. Locations you've visited recently are listed there. Tap a location to return to it.

Deleting a favorite

Eventually, a site you used to visit gets crossed off your A list. At that point, you might want to delete a bookmarked favorite, which you can easily do by following these steps:

1. **Tap the Search field, enter a location, and then tap Favorites.**

2. **Tap the Edit button.**

   A red minus icon appears to the left of your bookmarks, as shown in Figure 2-13.

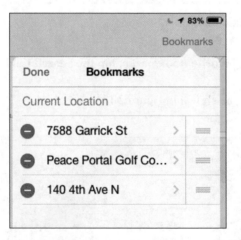

Figure 2-13: Tap a bookmark's red icon to select it for deletion.

3. **Tap a red minus icon.**

4. **Tap Delete.**

   The bookmark is removed.

To use a touchscreen shortcut after you've displayed the bookmarks in Step 1, simply swipe across a bookmark and then tap the Delete button that appears.

You can also clear all recent locations stored by Maps to give yourself a clean slate. Tap the Bookmark icon and then tap the Recents tab. Tap Clear and then confirm by tapping Clear All Recents.

Getting Directions, Information, and More

Maps can provide all kinds of information, from directions from one location to another to the street address and phone number for a particular business or landmark.

Getting directions

You can get directions by using pins that you drop on a map for the starting and ending locations, or by entering an address or name of a place, such as an airport or shopping mall. The directions are shown in a blue line leading from one place to another. You can even choose directions by car or foot. Directions also give you an idea of the miles and hours it will take you to get to your destination. (It will take you 15 hours and 43 minutes, for example, to walk from the Bronx Zoo to the Empire State Building — in case you wondered.) Here are the steps to get directions to two different locations in Maps using pins:

1. **With at least one pin on your map (at your destination) in addition to your current location, tap Directions in the top-left corner of your screen and then tap another location on the list that appears.**

   A line appears, showing the route between your current location and the closest pin. (See Figure 2-14.)

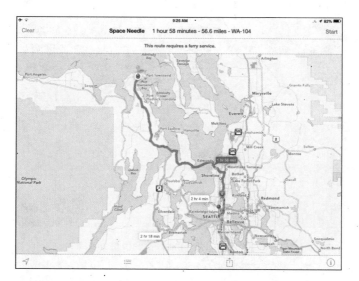

Figure 2-14: Go from pin to pin on your map to get directions.

2. **Tap the Drive or Walk tab to get the kind of directions you prefer; tap Clear to return to the Maps main screen.**

3. **You can also enter two locations in the boxes at the top of the page to get directions from one to the other.**

Here are the steps to get directions in maps by typing the addresses in the Search fields:

1. **Tap the Directions button in Maps and then tap in the field labeled Start.**

   The keyboard appears (see Figure 2-15).

2. **Enter a different starting location.**

3. **Tap in the End field and enter a destination location. Tap Route.**

   The route between the two locations displays. If you like, you can tap the Drive or Walk button to select a category of information once the route is displayed.

You can also tap the Information bar that appears when you select a pin and use the Directions to Here or Directions from Here button to generate directions.

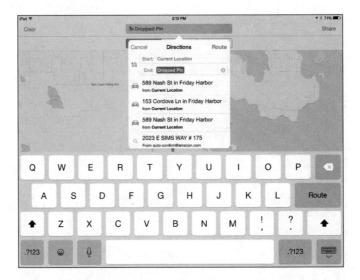

Figure 2-15: Enter addresses using the keyboard or Dictation key.

With a route displayed, an information bar appears telling you about the time it takes to travel between the two locations. If there are alternative routes, Maps notes the time it takes for any alternative routes alongside the routes on the map. Tap a route timing to make it the active route.

Getting information about a location

Previous sections of this chapter tell you how to display the Information dialog for locations in order to get directions. This section focuses on the other useful information displayed there. Using the Information button for any location, you can get the street address, phone number, and even the URL for some businesses or landmarks.

To get to the Information dialog, go to a location and tap the pin. In the information bar that appears above the pinned location, tap the arrow (shown in Figure 2-16).

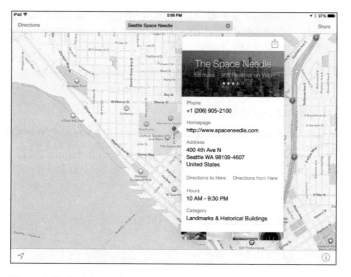

Figure 2-16: An information bar above a pinned location.

In the Information dialog, you can tap the web address listed in the Home Page field to be taken to the location's web page, if it has one associated with it.

You can also press and hold the Phone or Address field (refer to Figure 2-16) and use the Copy button to copy the phone number, for example, so that you can place it in a Notes document for future reference. When you have all the information you need, tap anywhere outside the Information dialog to close it.

Rather than copy and paste information, you can easily save all the information about a location in your Contacts address book. See the "Adding a location to a contact" section, later in this chapter, to find out how that's done.

Sending Location Info beyond Maps

When you find a location you want to come back to or tell others about, you can use features of Maps that help you out. You can save a location to the Contacts app, which also saves the address, phone number, and URL, if any. You can also share a link to locations with friends via email, Messages, AirDrop, Facebook, or Twitter. They can then access the location information by using Maps on any iOS device or Mac.

Adding a location to a contact

The beauty of this feature is that not only can you store valuable information such as phone numbers and street addresses in Contacts quickly and easily, you can also use stored contacts to quickly find locations in Maps.

Here's how this works:

1. **Tap a pin to display the information bar.**

2. **Tap the arrow on the bar.**

3. **In the Information dialog that appears, tap Create New Contact.**

   The New Contact dialog appears (as shown in Figure 2-17). Whatever information was available about the location has been entered.

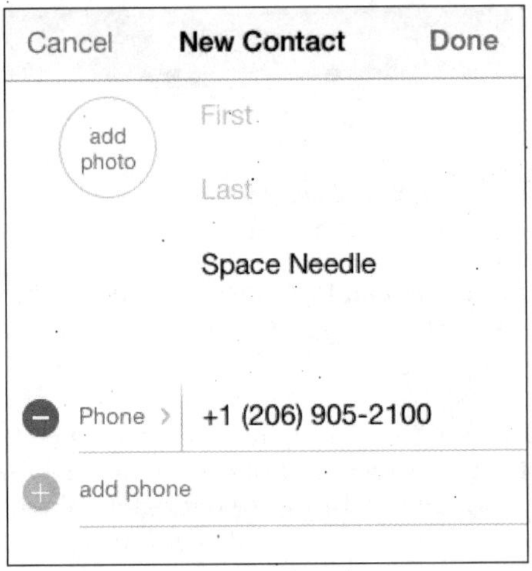

Cancel	**New Contact**	Done

add photo — First / Last

Space Needle

⊖ Phone >   +1 (206) 905-2100

⊕ add phone

Figure 2-17: Any available information can be stored to Contacts.

4. **Enter any additional information you need, such as name, phone number, or email address.**

5. Tap Done.

The information is stored in your Contacts address book.

After you store information in Contacts, you can also share it with friends from there by tapping the Share button in the address record. See Book V, Chapter 5 for more about using Contacts.

Sharing location information

Have you found a fantastic restaurant or movie theater that you absolutely have to share with a friend? From within Maps, you can use a simple procedure to email a link to your friend. When your friend is connected to the Internet and taps the link, that link opens the map to the location in Maps (a free service).

After you save a location in Contacts, take these steps to share a location:

1. Tap a pin to display the information bar.

2. Tap the Share button at the top right of the Maps screen and then tap Selected Location.

In the dialog that appears (see Figure 2-18), you can choose to share via AirDrop, text message, Facebook posting, tweet, or email.

Figure 2-18: You have a variety of ways to share locations.

3. Tap Mail to see how this option works.

4. **In the email form that appears, use the onscreen keyboard to enter a recipient's information as appropriate to the service you chose to share.**

5. **Tap Send.**

   A link to the location information in Maps is sent to your designated recipient(s).

If you tap Twitter or Facebook in Step 4, you have to have activated Twitter or Facebook and have the appropriate account set up using Settings. Tapping Message in Step 4 displays a new message form; just enter an email address or phone number in the To field, enter your text message, and then tap Send.

Use this feature to share your current location so that a friend or emergency service can find you. However, beware of sharing your current information with strangers!

Getting Turn-by-Turn Navigation Help

When you've entered directions for a route and displayed that route, you can then, with a 3G/4G iPad model, get spoken instructions that can be helpful as you're driving. Follow these steps to get spoken navigation:

1. **Tap the Start button at the bottom of the screen.**

2. **The narration begins and large text instructions are displayed, as shown in Figure 2-19.**

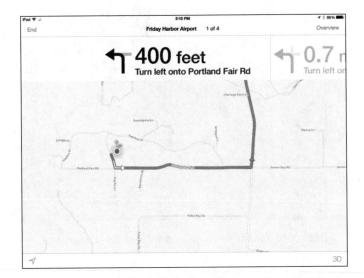

Figure 2-19: Turn-by-turn navigation may make your car's navigation system obsolete.

Continue driving according to the route until the next instruction is spoken.

3. **For an overview of your route at any time, you can tap the Overview button.**

    Tap Resume to go back to the step-by-step instructions.

To change route information from miles to kilometers, go to Settings, tap Maps, and then tap In Kilometers.

Chapter 3: Apps for Road Warriors

In This Chapter

✔ **Arranging travel**

✔ **Finding the best hotels**

✔ **Locating restaurants**

✔ **Using maps and travel guides**

✔ **Tracking your expenses**

✔ **Staying connected**

*i*Pad is practically perfect for people who travel a lot for business or pleasure. It's lightweight, slender, and stays powered up for about ten hours
at a time. Depending on the model, you can connect around the world using
3G/4G or Wi-Fi (or both) to stay in touch or browse the Internet for whatever you need. You have an onscreen keyboard, so you don't have to tote
around a physical keyboard. Robust business apps such as those in the
iWork suite let you get work done as you travel. You may never drag a laptop on a trip again!

That's why, in this chapter, the focus is on how people on
the road can use the iPad. I start by pointing out the preinstalled apps that work for travelers and then provide
some general advice and specific app suggestions for
making travel arrangements, finding great hotels and
restaurants, getting maps and travel guides, and
keeping track of what you spend as you travel. I
also provide a reminder about using Personal
Hotspot to go online using your smartphone connection, as well as about using FaceTime, a great
way to connect with others face to face.

You can use Siri with an iPad mini or third-generation
or newer iPad to ask for answers and information about
many of the things handled in the apps in this chapter, such
as the time of the next flight to Dallas or the highest-rated hotel
or restaurant in town. See Book V, Chapter 6 for more about Siri.

Starting with Built-in Apps

Before I get into the marvelous world of apps for travelers, consider the tools that come with the iPad out of the box. You can find your way around the world quite nicely with these little gems, including the following:

✔ **Maps:** This app allows you to locate worldwide locations and get detailed street maps (see Figure 3-1), show directions from one point to another, and bookmark favorite locations. You can navigate as you drive, walk around using blow-by-blow navigation, and share location information with others by email or by other means. (See Chapter 2 in this minibook for details about how to use Maps.)

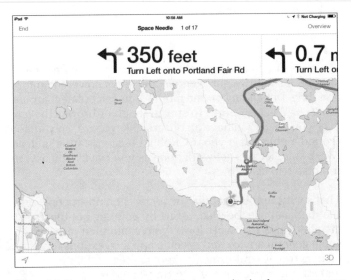

Figure 3-1: If your rental car doesn't have a navigation feature, use your iPad instead!

✔ **Contacts:** If you're going on the road to visit clients or friends and have their address information in Contacts, you can tap the address and be taken to it instantly in the Maps app. Keep phone numbers handy to get in touch when you hit town, and even use the Notes field in a Contacts entry to keep track of your business activities with that person or company. Remember that you can add fields to contact records, including job title, related people, department, and birthday using editing tools in Contacts. (See Book V, Chapter 5 for more about Contacts features.)

✔ **Safari browser:** Don't forget that if you have an Internet connection, you can use the Safari browser to get online and tap into all the travel-related information and sites on the web. Use sites such as Expedia or

Travelocity (shown in Figure 3-2) to book travel, check flight information at airline websites, go to sites such as MapQuest to get directions and maps, and so on. (For more about using Safari, go to Book I, Chapter 6.)

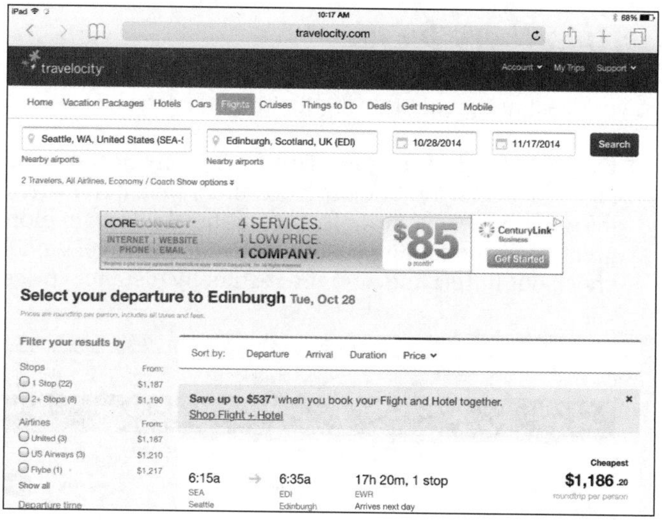

Figure 3-2: Travelocity offers price comparison services for flights, hotel, car rental, and more.

Book III
Chapter 3

Apps for Road Warriors

✔ **Mail:** This built-in email client lets you keep in touch through any accounts you set up in your iPad as long as you have an Internet connection. Find out more about setting up email accounts in Book I, Chapter 7.

✔ **Notes:** Although there isn't a travel expense tracker app in iPad, you can always use Notes or the Numbers app's Expense Report template to keep a record of what you spend or any other information about your trip that you need to recall after you get home. You can even email a note to yourself or your bookkeeper so that it's on your office computer when you get back.

Travel can get tedious with long waits in lines or terminals. Don't forget that you have a built-in music player in Music and a built-in video player in the Videos app to keep you entertained.

Making Travel Arrangements

Now I move on to apps that don't reside on your iPad when you buy it. This chapter features just a few of the available apps — more are covered at www.dummies.com/extras/ipadaio. Some are actually iPhone apps that work on the iPad (so be sure to check out the iPhone apps category), and some were built specifically for iPad.

Start at the beginning, when you're planning your trip. You need to book flights or other modes of travel and check to see that your flight is on time. You may need a rental car when you arrive and perhaps maps of public transit to help you plan your route. Examples of all these types of apps are covered in this section.

Getting there by air

This list is a mixed bag of travel-booking tools and apps that help you check on your seat assignment or flight status. Try these:

- ✒ **Expedia Hotels & Flights:** This free, nicely designed app, shown in Figure 3-3, lets you book travel online, save itineraries, and get flight information. My favorite feature is the ability to explore destinations by great deals, upcoming events, or available travel guides. You can even check out hotels and sort the results by distance, price, or rating.

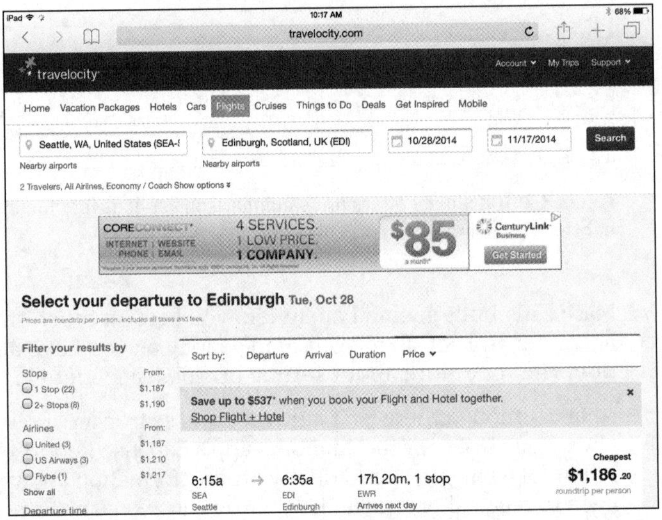

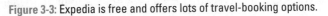

Figure 3-3: Expedia is free and offers lots of travel-booking options.

- ✒ **Seat Alerts:** You know how you always get on the plane thinking that your seat will be fine, only to find out that you're three miles from the restroom or stuck in the middle of a seven-seat row on an international flight? By using Seat Alerts, which has data from more than 60 airlines and many plane models, you get the advice you need to choose the best seat to make your travel more enjoyable. This one is free and well worth downloading in terms of in-flight comfort.

- ✒ **AirportStatus:** Get information about flight status and delays all around the United States and parts of Canada with this $0.99 app. (See Figure 3-4.) You even get information about the cause of delays, such as weather and airport closures.

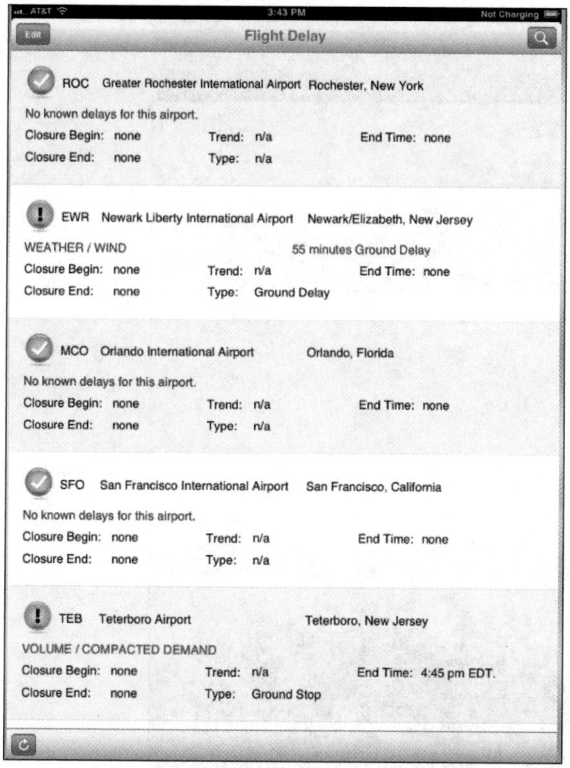

Figure 3-4: Check about delays before you leave home using AirportStatus.

Several airlines have their own mobile apps for booking or checking flight status (see Figure 3-5 for an example) and, in some cases, features for checking your standby status, checking in, and generating a boarding pass. These include

- American Airlines HD
- Alaska Airlines/Horizon Air Mobile
- British Airways
- Fly Delta for iPad
- Southwest Airlines
- United Airlines
- Virgin Atlantic Flight Tracker

**Book III
Chapter 3**

Apps for Road Warriors

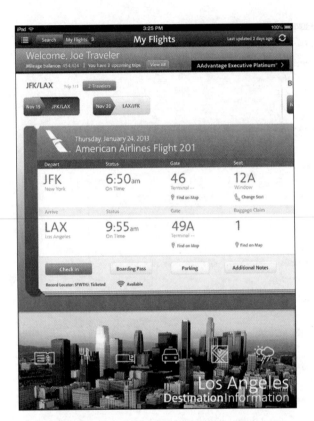

Figure 3-5: Enter information about your flight and get information back.

If you're a frequent flier, check out the Air Milage Calculator app. (Make sure to exclude the first *e* in *mileage* when searching the Apps Store for this app.) For $0.99, you can get the mileage for travel between airports worldwide with up to three legs for each trip. You can also have the app calculate bonuses based on your frequent-flier status and the class of travel.

If packing is a challenge for you and you don't have a valet to help you out (mine quit last week), try Packing Pro. Keep track of lists of what you need by trip, including your passport, clothing, and vital accessories such as an umbrella for that trip to Seattle. It costs you $2.99, but if you're organizationally challenged, it might save your neck as you prepare for business or family trips.

Renting a car

If you want to deal with your car rentals from your iPad, you'll be glad to hear that there are apps that help you do just that. Consider apps such as these that help you find the right rental deal:

✔ **ABN Car Rentals:** Helps you claim car rental discounts for Hertz cars; it even comes with a free Hertz #1 Club Gold membership. You can use this free app right at the car rental counter, typically saving about 20 percent on your car rental cost.

✔ **Airport Car Rental:** This free app lets you search for car rental agencies available at many major airports. You can enter your car rental requirements in your iPhone or iPad and let the app search for the best match at your destination airport and make real-time reservations.

You can also get individual apps for your favorite car rental companies, such as Avis Reservation App or Hertz Car Rental.

Road Trip HD is a $4.99 utility that helps you track your mileage and fuel economy, which may help you estimate your costs if your rental car doesn't include unlimited miles. It sports a nice visual graph of fuel economy, and if you use your own car on the road, the feature that lets you track mileage and fuel cost by trip can be a neat way to sum up your travel expenses every month.

Finding your way around town

Before you set off on your trip to cities such as New York, San Francisco, or Chicago, you may want to download one of these apps to get local transit system maps, schedules, and more.

Transit Maps is free and comes with one transit map, but it enables you to download transit maps as graphics files from the Internet using its own browser feature. The beauty of this app is that it helps you download large image files and view them offline, so you can check a map even if you're not able to get online.

iTransitBuddy is a series of apps costing $0.99 for various metro areas; they're designed for the iPhone but usable on the iPad. These apps have a helpful feature for looking up free transfers and schedule updates. Maps are downloaded to your device, so you don't have to have an Internet connection to use them. An iTransitBuddy app is handy for commuters as well as those who travel to metro areas on business or for pleasure.

As you're exploring a new town, make sure that you're dressed right for the weather. PocketWeather (free) lets you get weather reports on the go.

Finding Just the Right Hotels

Hotel chains have begun to jump on the app bandwagon. Some chains, such as Holiday Inn, Marriott, Hilton, and Best Western, offer apps. Some offer apps for only individual hotels within the chain. Another option for finding hotels around the country or world is to depend on hotel-booking apps for your hotel travel.

Here are a few free hotel-booking apps (be sure to check out www.dummies. com/extras/ipadaio for a few more) that can get you started on your iPad hotel search/booking experience. Most (including the Hotels.com HD app, shown in Figure 3-6) allow you to search for hotels and check ratings, price, and availability.

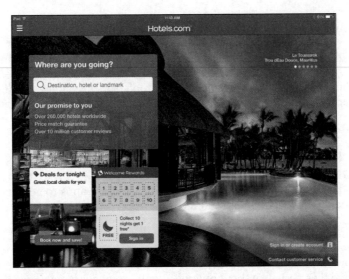

Figure 3-6: Details about hotels include a description, map, list of facilities, policies, and more.

You can also book your reservation and, in some cases, check local attractions.

- Booking.com Hotel Reservations Worldwide
- Choice Hotels
- HotelsByMe — Hotels & Hotel Room Reservations
- Hotel Tonight
- Hotwire Hotels & Cars
- Near by Me

Some general travel sites, such as Kayak and Travelocity, also have hotel searching and booking features.

Locating the Perfect Restaurant

What's a road warrior without his lunch? Hungry, that's what. So, why not use your iPad to find food? Here's a selection of some intriguing restaurant-listing apps for you to explore:

✔ **Vegetarian-Restaurants:** Do you avoid meat in your diet? If so, check out the free Vegetarian-Restaurants app (shown in Figure 3-7). Look for vegetarian restaurants worldwide as well as vegetarian recipes and information about the vegetarian lifestyle.

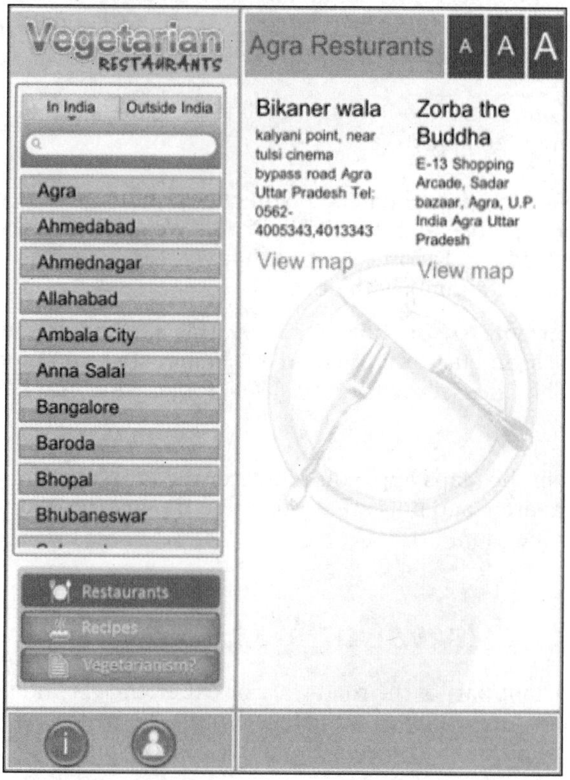

Figure 3-7: Vegetarian-Restaurants helps you locate food without meat around the world.

Book III
Chapter 3

Apps for Road
Warriors

✔ **Yelp:** This free app taps you into a huge resource of customer reviews of restaurants to help you pick the best spot for your next meal.

✔ **Michelin Travel Guide:** For anywhere from $9.99 to $18.99, you can get the latest Michelin guide by country. Michelin is kind of the gold standard in restaurant rating systems, so if you're a serious world traveler and gourmand, you can appreciate its insights into the quality of food, specialties of the house, hours, and even the name of the chef so that you can send your compliments to him or her.

- ✔ **Where to Eat? Pro:** A poor man's Michelin Guide can be found in Where to Eat? HD, a $2.99 app that has been reworked for the iPad. Search for the closest restaurants anywhere you are in the world, find the cuisine you're looking for, and customize searches.

If you want to find a restaurant with available Wi-Fi, you can find such locations using WiFi Get HD. This very handy app helps you spot hotspots even if you're not connected at the moment. This one costs $2.99. Or you can always ask Siri something like "Where can I find a good Italian restaurant?" Siri uses your location to return the information.

If you're concerned about your waistline, here are a few more free and helpful food-oriented apps:

- ✔ **Dotti's Food Score:** Can help you check out more than 600 restaurants, including those that qualify for Dotti's Weight Loss Zone ranking. Download to a Favorites list so that you can view it as you sit at a table, even in restaurants with no Wi-Fi.

- ✔ **Restaurants & Nutrition:** For $1.99, this app shows you carbohydrates, calories, and fat for more than 80 chain restaurants, such as TGI Fridays and The Cheesecake Factory. (Well, forget what I said about watching your waist!)

Note that in the Maps app, you can enter the term *restaurants* in the Search field and search, and pins are dropped on the map indicating restaurants near your location.

Using Maps and Travel Guides

One important part of the road-warrior experience is finding your way around and connecting with the local culture. For that, you can explore some mapping apps and travel guides. These will get you started:

- ✔ **Barefoot World Atlas:** With this $4.99 app, you get an interactive globe that you can browse using your finger and touchscreen. The app is optimized for third-generation (and later) iPads, so the visual experience is stunning.

- ✔ **cityscouter GmbH guides:** These handy little guides run about $3.99 per city and can be used offline. That's useful if you're on a plane, wandering around a foreign city nowhere near a hotspot, or out of range of your 3G provider's services. Find out about top attractions, take advantage of a currency converter, or find a wiki article, photos, or maps (see Figure 3-8). Many include up-to-date information about local public transportation as well.

Figure 3-8: The cityscouter.com guide to Copenhagen.

✔ **World Travel Channel:** This free app makes the programming from the Travel Channel available to help you brave bizarre foreign foods or find a hotel that's haunted.

In addition to the preceding apps, check out popular travel guides and tools such as Lonely Planet Travel Guides (as much as $14.99 each). Also, the Travel + Leisure Magazine is a free app for Newsstand, though you'll pay for each issue you buy using the app.

Tracking Your Expenses

My favorite part of any business trip is when I get that expense reimbursement check. Of course, to get that check, I have to go through my receipt collection trying to figure out what I spent where and to itemize it for my client.

To make your iPad travel experience easier, try these great apps that help you keep all your trip expenses in order:

✔ **XpenseTracker:** For $4.99, you get both an expense-tracking app and mileage log. This one comes with several PDF report templates that can come in handy.

✔ **my Travel Assistant:** With a $2.99 price tag, this app designed for the iPhone is easy to use for tracking expenses and has some very nice tools for analyzing your expenditures as well. Plus, it supports 51 languages.

✔ **MileBug:** This easy-to-use app costs $2.99 and helps you keep track of dollars spent and miles traveled.

If you frequently travel out of the country, you may want to check out www. dummies.com/extras/ipadaio for apps that help you juggle currency exchange rates.

Don't forget that when you're in the privacy of your hotel, you can use the Dictation feature on your iPad to speak your expense entries into a Numbers or other dictation-compatible app. Hands-free expense reporting!

Staying Connected

When you're on the road, staying connected with your office or family is important. That's why you should be sure to take advantage of two cool features, FaceTime and Personal Hotspot. Here's what you can do with these two:

✔ **FaceTime:** This video and audio-calling app (covered in detail in Book II, Chapter 4) allows you to take advantage of the video camera in the iPad (except for the original iPad) to call others who have the FaceTime feature on their iPad, Mac, iPhone, or iPod touch. You can use the front camera to show the person you called your own bright smile, or switch to the rear camera to let that person see what you're looking at right now. Great way to make others jealous when you snagged that sales account in Hawaii!

✔ **Personal Hotspot:** Gives you the ability to use your iPhone's 3G/4G connection (in some cases for a fee to your service provider) to take your Wi-Fi–only model iPad online when Wi-Fi is out of reach. Personal Hotspot can, in fact, perform this service for up to five Wi-Fi devices on the Verizon, Sprint, T-Mobile, and AT&T versions of iPhone. This is a very useful feature for driving road warriors who can't sit in an airport or hotel lobby to get online or make calls. (I cover Personal Hotspot in more detail in Chapter 1 of this minibook.)

Don't forget that by using the iCloud storage and sharing service, you can have all the content you buy on other Apple devices automatically synced to your iPad. If your spouse downloads some new music or a movie to her iPhone and you both use the same Apple ID, with a Family Sharing account, for example, you can access that movie on your iPad wherever you are.

Book IV

Getting Productive with iWork

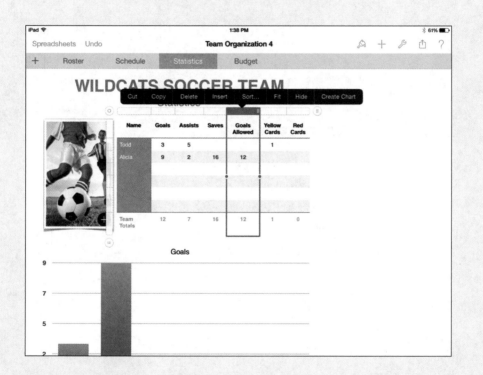

Visit www.dummies.com/extras/ipadaio for great tips for using iWork apps to get things done.

In this book. . .

- ✔ Explore the iWork for iOS apps
- ✔ Share your work on iCloud
- ✔ Create documents with Pages
- ✔ Crunch numbers with Numbers
- ✔ Create power presentations with Keynote

Chapter 1: Introducing the iWork for iOS Apps for iPad

In This Chapter

✔ Getting familiar with the iWork for iOS apps

✔ Using an iWork app with iCloud

✔ Discovering the basics of the iWork apps

✔ Improving documents by adding photos and images

✔ Managing your iWork documents

*W*ord-processing and spreadsheet applications are among the most widely used software products; presentation software is not far behind, along with programs such as graphics and database editors. Having started from scratch on the hardware side and then the operating-system side, Apple employees started dreaming about what they could do if they were to start from scratch to write modern versions of word-processing, spreadsheet, and presentation programs. They knew they'd have to follow one of their advertising campaign themes: *Think Different*.

The result was the iWork suite of applications (a collection of applications that can work together) for the Mac — Keynote, Pages, and Numbers — that were developed one by one over a period of several years.

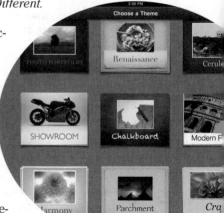

Today, iWork is a terrific suite of programs that have become a trio of dynamite apps for iPad and iPhone, and all the apps are now free when you buy a new iOS device.

In addition, Apple introduced iWork for iCloud in 2013, so you can work in very similar software interfaces online using your browser. All documents you create in these versions of iWork apps are stored both in iCloud and on your devices. (For more about iWork for iCloud, go to www.apple.com/iWork-for-iCloud).

In this chapter, the focus is on the three iWork for iOS apps, including how to use their common interface elements. You also find a summary of differences between iWork for iPad and iWork for Mac in those cases where it matters.

Presenting the iWork for iOS Apps

iWork provides applications that are office oriented — so-called productivity applications. The iWork office suite includes three apps that are similar to Microsoft Office applications (but way cooler, I think):

- **Pages:** A word-processing and page-layout application (similar to Microsoft Word)
- **Numbers:** A spreadsheet application (similar to Microsoft Excel)
- **Keynote:** A presentation application (similar to Microsoft PowerPoint)

All three apps are optimized for those iPad models with a brilliant Retina display, plus they have some new templates that you can base your presentation on.

Each program that you download from the App Store on a new iOS device is free. iCloud automatically migrates the apps and documents you create with these programs to any other Apple devices running iOS. (See Book I, Chapter 5, for more information.)

In the following sections, you take a quick look at these three iWork for iOS apps, all of which have been upgraded with the release of iOS 8.

Pages

For many people, word processing is the core of an office suite. In fact, many people don't get beyond it. Pages for Mac adds a big desktop publishing plus to word processing in that it also allows you to create page layout documents. These have the type of structure that you see in newspapers and magazines — articles don't just flow one after the other. Instead, an article on Page 1 may be continued on Page 4, and another article on the first page may be continued on Page 8. Also, objects such as photos can be anchored to associated text, or placed in specific positions on a page, and they don't move as the text around them is added or deleted.

iWork provides you with a variety of sophisticated tools to create your Pages documents. These include advanced font handling, color, tables, and charts, as well as the ability to place QuickTime movies and hypertext links in your

Pages documents. iWork applications also provide a variety of template options for your documents. Figure 1-1 shows some of the templates available with Pages for iOS.

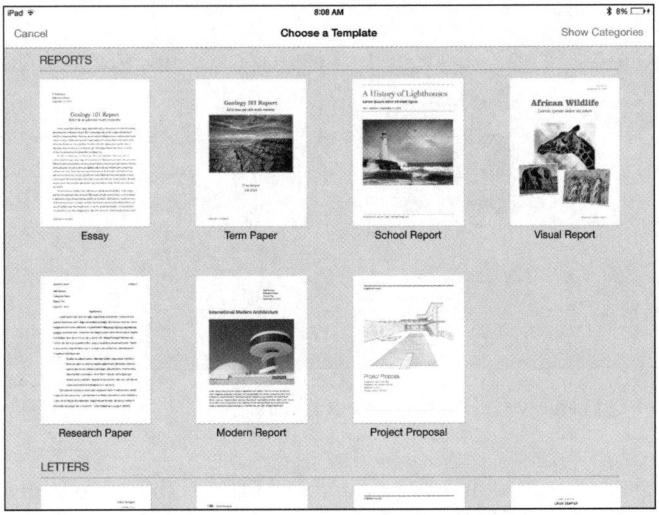

Figure 1-1: Choose a Pages template as a starting point.

For more on the Pages app, see Chapter 2 in this minibook.

Numbers

As with all spreadsheet programs, Numbers enables you to enter data in rows and columns. One of the most useful features of spreadsheets is that they perform calculations by means of formulas. For example, if you have a column listing your grocery expenditures by week, the addition of another grocery bill will cause the program to recalculate the column's total. Spreadsheets are about data (usually numbers) and fast calculation updates, but they can also help you organize data such as address lists and even generate charts to show data trends.

Spreadsheets can go beyond the common grid interface, and Numbers excels at this approach. Take a look at the Numbers document shown in Figure 1-2, which is based on the Travel Planner template.

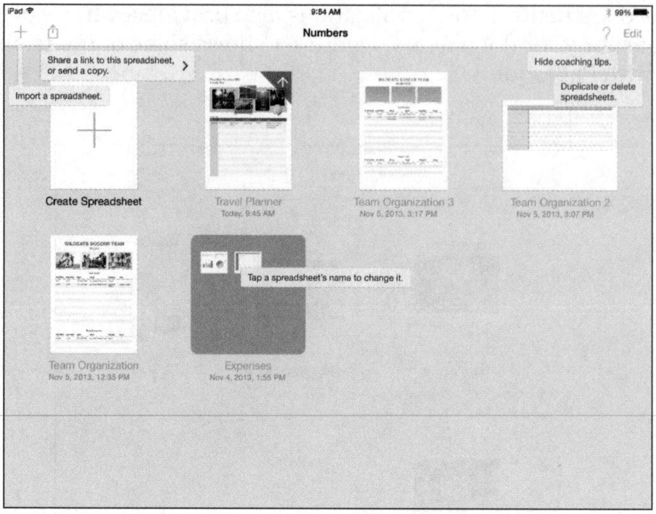

Figure 1-2: A highly visual Numbers spreadsheet.

A single document can have a number of *sheets* (like sheets in a Microsoft Excel workbook). On the iPad, sheets appear as tabs, as shown in Figure 1-2.

A Numbers sheet can contain a variety of objects such as tables and charts, but it can also contain other iWork objects, such as graphics, text boxes, movies, and audio. In Figure 1-2, the sheet is shown with a table and five pictures above it.

For more on the Numbers app, see Chapter 3 in this minibook.

Keynote

Call them lectures, classes, sermons, dog-and-pony shows, or sales pitches, but presentations are all much the same: Someone stands in front of a large or small group of people and explains, teaches, inspires, entertains, or persuades them. In some cases, a presentation can run on its own or be run by the viewer in person or online.

Today, a presentation often includes multimedia elements: slides of buildings in an architecture class; slides with music in a presentation about your community theater's latest musical production; movies of good times on the beach in a talk about Uncle Charlie's summer vacation.

Keynote was the original iWork application. Built by Apple engineers for Macworld and Worldwide Developers Conference keynote speeches delivered by Steve Jobs, Keynote has been refined over the years to become the powerful tool it is today. (See Figure 1-3.)

For more on the Keynote app, see Chapter 4 in this minibook.

Figure 1-3: Editing a Keynote presentation.

Starting Out with an iWork App

The first time you run an iWork app, you're greeted by a Welcome screen. The next time you open an app, you find yourself exactly where you were the last time you left it. Each iWork app has its own graphic. The first-time Welcome screen for Numbers is shown in Figure 1-4.

Figure 1-4: Numbers is launched for the first time on an iCloud-enabled iPad.

Tap Continue, and you're taken to a screen showing Numbers templates with callouts to some of the tools available, as shown in Figure 1-5.

Getting Familiar with the iWork Interface

You'll find that each of the iWork apps has a similar look and feel. One of the coolest advantages of iWork is that major features — not just small operations such as changing a font or selecting a color — are available using the same method in all its apps. You have only one set of features that you must understand when you're using iWork, so I give you an overview of all that common functionality here to get you started.

The iWork apps (like all apps) are updated periodically. If an update is available, you see the App Store on your iPad Home screen with a number indicating that downloads are available. Updating your iWork apps when updates are available is generally a good idea so that their interfaces remain in sync.

Recent updates have included the addition of more 3D charts in Numbers, new animations and new transitions for Keynote, new templates, the ability to share view-only docs, and the ability to search for docs by name.

Creating a new document

You create a new document in the same way for each iWork app. Follow these steps:

1. **Tap any of the iWork app icons to launch the application.**

   The Documents screen appears. This screen is titled Pages in the Pages app (see Figure 1-5), Spreadsheets in Numbers, and Presentations in Keynote.

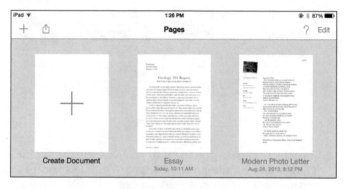

Figure 1-5: Create a new document from the Documents screen.

Note that when you first open an iWork app, you see a single document that contains basic information and instructions for that app. After that, when you create and save any documents, they will also display on the Documents screen.

If you see Documents on the button in the top-left corner while in Pages, you're not on the Documents screen; you're on the screen for working with an individual document, and tapping Documents (or Spreadsheets in Numbers or Presentations in Keynote) brings you back to the Documents screen.

2. **Tap the plus sign (+) in the square titled Create Document at the top left of the Documents screen.**

   Templates are displayed in categories. The Basic template options (see Figure 1-6) will vary depending on which app you're using. In Pages, for example, you can create a new Blank document, a Blank Landscape document, or a Note Taking document. You can also scroll down and tap

**Book IV
Chapter 1**

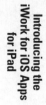

Introducing the
iWork for iOS Apps
for iPad

another document template on which to base your new document, such as Modern Report or Project Proposal.

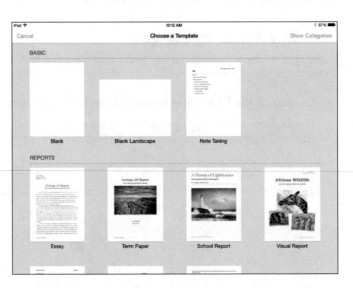

Figure 1-6: Select a template.

3. **Tap the template you want to use as a starting point, or tap Blank (Pages and Numbers) or Black or White (Keynote) to start working with a completely clean document.**

If you decide not to create a document right now, you can tap Cancel on the Templates screen and return to the Documents screen.

The templates are different for each of the iWork apps, so I discuss them in the appropriate chapters in this minibook.

Your new document opens on the screen.

Locating a document

Before long, you'll have created several documents, and chances are good that you'll want to go back and work on some of them, print them, or share them via iCloud, AirDrop, Mail, or Message. As with creating new documents, locating a document is done the same way in each of the iWork apps.

To locate a document, follow these steps:

1. **Tap any of the iWork app icons to launch the application.**

The Documents window appears. After you've created several documents, that screen looks like Figure 1-7.

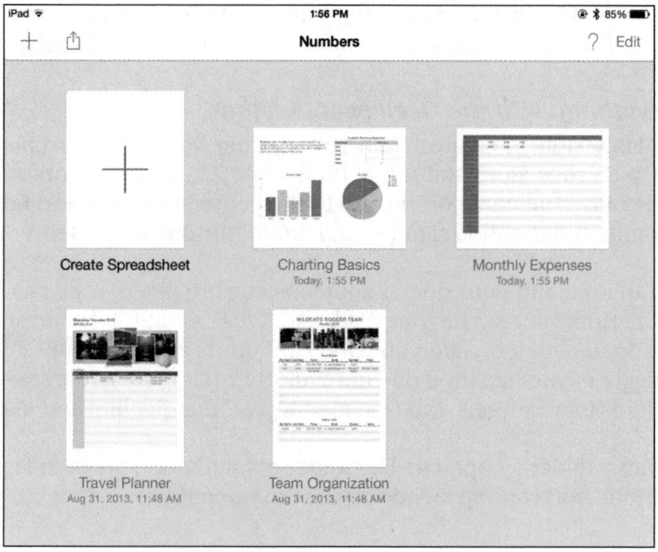

Figure 1-7: Gradually, your Documents window fills up.

2. View the documents and find the one you want to work with.

Below each document, you see its title and the date you last worked on it.

3. Tap the document you want to work with.

The document opens, and you can begin working in it.

Identifying other common iWork features

You've already seen the major iWork controls in Figures 4-2 and 4-3. In the following sections, you look at each one more closely.

Using popovers and dialogs

An important interface element in the Pages document shown in Figure 1-8 is the popover. Common to all iWork apps, the *popover* is essentially a menu. Like a menu, it goes away when you tap elsewhere. A dialog, on the other hand, offers settings and choices and you have to close it to get it off the screen.

This list describes three actions you can take with a popover:

- ✔ **Recognize the purpose of the popover.** Each popover includes an arrow that points to the object that opened it.

- ✔ **Dismiss the popover.** If you want to dismiss the popover (the equivalent of the Close or Cancel button on a dialog on your Mac or PC), tap anywhere outside the popover.

✔ **Make a selection on the popover.** When you tap a choice in a popover, it's carried out and the popover closes automatically.

Working with the Documents toolbar

Also visible in Figure 1-7 and most other figures in this chapter is the toolbar, which runs along the top of the screen. On a Documents screen, the toolbar displays the name of the app in the center, the Help and Edit buttons at the right, and the plus sign (+) and Share buttons at the left.

Tap Edit, and your document icons start to jiggle — just as the icons do on the Home screen of your iPad. (And, just as on the Home screen, tap and hold a document icon and you enter Edit mode automatically.) While the icons are jiggling, you can drag one onto another to create a folder — just as on your iPad Home screen. Tap Done to stop all that jiggling and leave Edit mode.

Tap a folder to open it. The folder expands, as shown in Figure 1-8. From there, you can tap any document to open it.

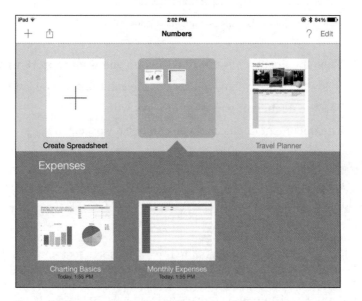

Figure 1-8: You can rename your folders at any time.

Press and hold the folder name, and the name field opens so that you can rename the folder. This press-and-hold method also works with individual document files so that you can rename them.

You can drag a document out of the folder and back to the Documents screen. When you remove the last document from a folder, the folder disappears.

When you're finished organizing and renaming your folders and documents, tap Done.

If you choose an action such as copying a document, the iWork app automatically ends the jiggle-editing without your having to tap Done.

Working with a toolbar for a single document

When you're working within a single document, you see a different toolbar, as you can see in Figure 1-9. (This is from Keynote.)

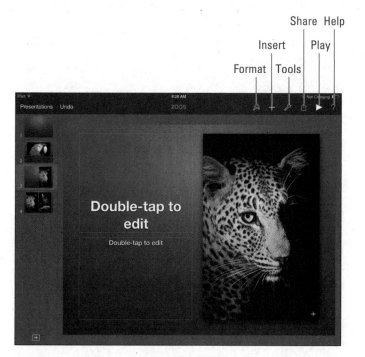

Figure 1-9: Work with a single document's toolbar in Keynote.

On the far-left side of the toolbar, the Documents button (titled Presentations in Keynote and Spreadsheets in Numbers) lets you see all your documents in Documents view. Next to Documents is the Undo button. (It's the same as the Edit⇨Undo command that you may have used in OS X for iWork and most other apps.) In the center of the window is the document's name.

At the right of the iWork toolbar is a group of buttons:

✓ **Format:** Provides information and formatting choices about the current selection in the document. From here, you may choose a style, a list

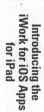

format, or a layout (alignment, columns, and line spacing) for a selected paragraph, or modify the style of an image. If nothing is selected, this button is dimmed.

✔ **Insert:** Lets you insert images from your photo albums on iPad. If you want to insert a photo into your iWork document, add it to your album by taking the photo or synchronizing it in iTunes. (I tell you more about this button in the next section.)

✔ **Tools:** The wrench-shaped button opens a popover containing tools that are based on the document as a whole rather than on the current selection within the document. Figure 1-10 shows the tools for a Pages document.

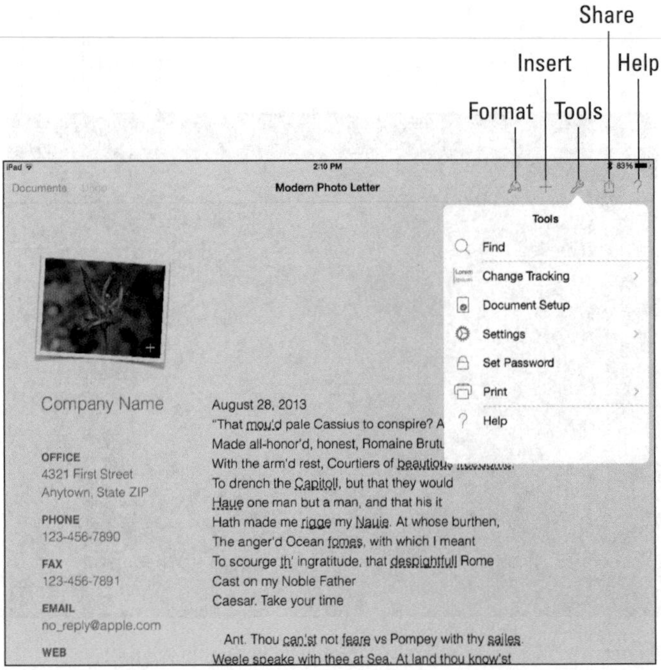

Figure 1-10: Tools for a Pages document.

✔ **Share:** Use this popover to share a link to the document via iCloud, to send a copy via Mail or Messages, or to open the document in another app (such as opening a PDF file in Adobe Reader).

✔ **Play:** In Keynote only, you tap this button to play the slideshow.

Some menus have disclosure triangles that let you drill down one more level. For example, Figure 1-11 shows the Printer Options menu. Print settings are described in Book V, Chapter 1.

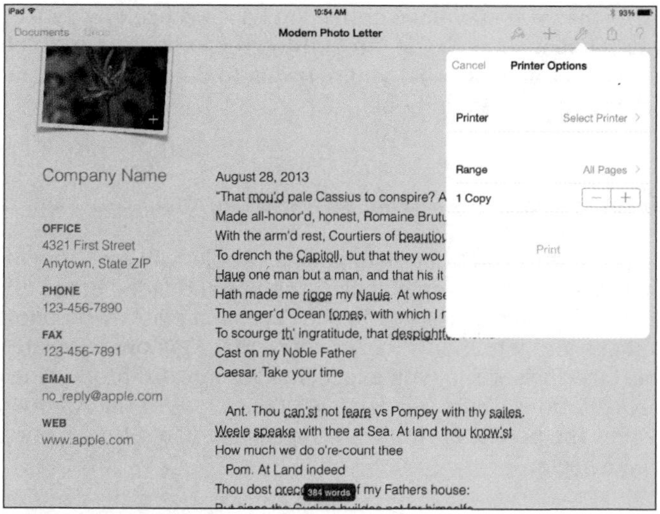

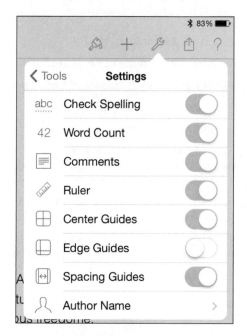

Figure 1-11: Settings for printing documents.

You can use the < button in the popover to return to the tools. The Settings submenu of the Tools menu is shown in Figure 1-12. Note that Word Count has been turned on, which causes the current word count to be displayed at the bottom of the document.

Figure 1-12: Adjusting settings.

**Book IV
Chapter 1**

Introducing the
iWork for iOS Apps
for iPad

TIP

The ruler that you may have noticed in Pages is used by its word-processing features. Similar tools at the top of the screen are used in Numbers and Keynote depending on what you're trying to do. I discuss them in the relevant chapters in this minibook.

Working with Images

One important feature that distinguishes Apple software from many other products is how easily you can use graphics and video in the documents you create. It's not unusual for you to see Pages templates with photo placeholders in them, and it certainly makes sense that Keynote templates often include photos. In today's world, you expect images in word-processing documents and presentations. But spreadsheets? Take a look at the Numbers templates to see how the people at Apple are suggesting you rethink your understanding of spreadsheets.

Photos, images, and video can be added — easily and productively — to any iWork for iPad document. You have two ways to do this:

- From the Documents window, tap the Insert button (it looks like a plus sign).
- Select a template that includes a placeholder image.

Using a template with a placeholder image requires one more step than using the Insert button. Here's how this process works:

1. **Create a document based on a template.**

   Figure 1-13 shows the Harmony template in Keynote.

2. **Tap the plus sign (+) in the bottom-left corner of the screen.**

   A pop-up displaying various types of slide styles appears.

3. **Tap a slide style that contains an image.**

   In the lower-right corner of the image placeholder that appears is an Insert button. Tapping this button allows you to access a dialog from which you can insert another image to replace the placeholder image.

4. **Tap the Insert button in the bottom-right corner of the placeholder figure to open a list of your photo albums, as shown in Figure 1-14.**

   You can browse photos on your iPad as well as albums you have created in iPhoto or other programs such as Photoshop Elements and synchronized to your iPad or from Photo Streams.

Figure 1-13: Create a document with placeholder images.

Figure 1-14: Choose a photo.

5. **Tap to select the image you want to use instead of the placeholder.**

6. **Tap and drag the handles around the edges of the image in or out (see Figure 1-15) to adjust the size of the image.**

Figure 1-15: Tap an image to reveal resizing handles.

You start with the image the same size as the frame, but if you tap and drag handles in any direction, as you see in Figure 1-16, the image is shown dimly filling more and more of the entire screen. You can use these eight handles on the frame to change its size and shape. This is a hands-on way to handle tasks such as cropping images. Rest assured that the original image file is unchanged by these steps: You're changing the image's appearance only within the document.

You can drag the image around so that the part you want is inside the frame.

Figure 1-16: Adjust the size of an image

Managing Your iWork Documents

The data for your iWork documents is stored in files on your iPad, possibly on your Mac, and also sometimes on shared WebDAV (Web-based Distributed Authoring and Versioning, used for collaboration and managing of files on the web) servers and, as you will see, on iCloud, if you choose.

You can also take advantage of the fact that iWork documents can by synced across all your devices via iCloud.

Deep down inside the iPad operating system (iOS) are files and folders, but most of the time you manipulate them through apps. When it comes to apps, the files and folders are in a special area reserved only for that app (it's called a *sandbox*).

The storage areas for files on your iPad are kept separate for each app. If you install Pages and then remove it from your iPad, your Pages documents disappear along with the Pages app. Before uninstalling any app from your iPad, make certain that you have backed up any files you've created.

Sharing documents

You've copied a file from another place onto your iPad, and now it's time to reverse the process. To share a file you've created in iWork on your iPad, follow these steps:

1. **From the Documents window, open the document you want to share.**

2. **Tap the Share button.**

   As you see in Figure 1-17, the Share popover allows you to Share a Link via iCloud (which allows others to make changes to your document); Send a Copy via AirDrop, Messages, or Mail; or open the document in another format such as PDF and share it in that format.

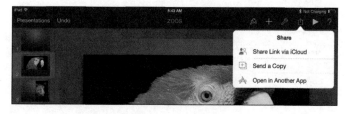

Figure 1-17: Share in a variety of ways.

Book IV
Chapter 1

Introducing the
iWork for iOS Apps
for iPad

Moving files with iTunes

You can move files to and from iTunes on your computer with a cable or with a Wi-Fi connection.

 You can also use cloud storage programs such as Dropbox to manage files, which is sometimes simpler and avoids certain constraints imposed by Apple-centric iTunes.

Moving files to your computer from your iPad

Each iWork app has its own storage area for your files. You move files from your iPad to your computer using iTunes and these steps:

1. **Connect your iPad to the computer where you want to move the files.**

   Your computer can be a Mac or PC. It must have iTunes installed. If iTunes isn't installed, see Book I, Chapter 4, and then come back here.

   You can also sync between your iPad and your computer using a Wi-Fi connection rather than a cable. On the iTunes Summary screen, select Sync with This iPad over Wi-Fi under Options. If you have that option turned off or do not want to use it, you can connect your iPad to your computer with a cable.

2. **When iTunes launches, find your iPad in the Devices section of the Source List and select it by clicking once.**

3. **Select the Apps tab from the group of tabs running across the top of the pane, as shown in Figure 1-18.**

   If you're running iTunes with the OS X Mavericks on a Mac, you won't see an Info tab to the left of the Apps tab, but you will if you're running Yosemite.

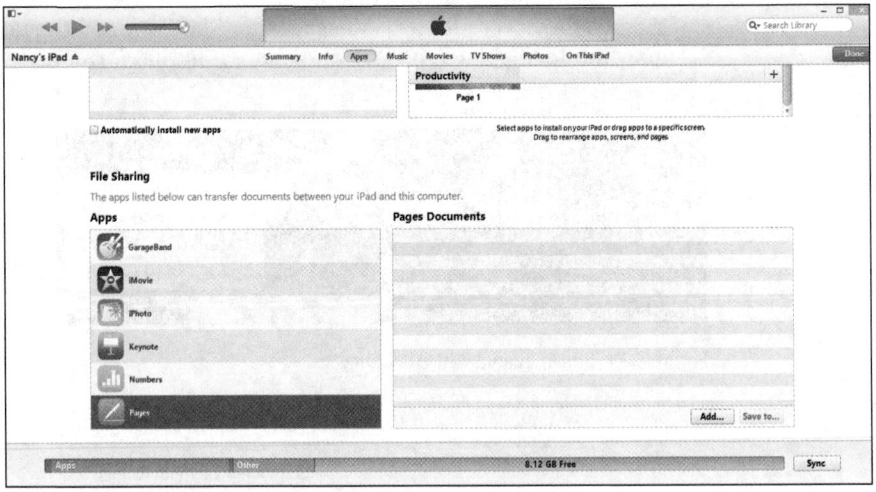

Figure 1-18: Connecting your iPad to iTunes on your Mac or PC.

4. **Scroll down to the bottom of the pane and select the iWork app you're interested in.**

   The documents on your iPad for that app are shown.

5. **Select the document you want and click Save To.**

6. **Choose the folder and the name you want to use for the saved file.**

   The file is moved to your computer.

Moving files to your iPad from your computer

The process for moving files from your computer to your iPad is similar to the process described in the preceding section. To copy files from your computer to your iPad, follow these steps:

1. **Connect your iPad to the computer from which the files are to be moved.**

   You can use a cable or a Wi-Fi connection if you have selected that option.

   You can use a Mac or PC, but you must have installed iTunes on it.

2. **Find your iPad under the Devices section of the Source List and click it.**

3. **Select the Apps tab from the group of tabs running across the top of the pane.**

4. **Scroll down to the bottom of the pane and select the iWork app you're interested in.**

   The documents on your iPad for that app are listed.

5. **Click Add in the lower-right portion of the window.**

6. **When prompted, select the file on your computer's hard drive.**

   When you select a file, it moves to the list of files in iTunes and usually moves immediately to your iPad. If it doesn't move immediately, click Sync.

In Step 5 in the preceding list, you can also simply drag the document icon from the Finder or Windows File Explorer window into the file list area.

Chapter 2: Pages Has a Way with Words

In This Chapter

- ✓ Making changes to a Pages document
- ✓ Toiling with text
- ✓ Focusing on formatting with the ruler
- ✓ Setting advanced formatting options with the Format button
- ✓ Formatting the document
- ✓ Using selection buttons

*T*his chapter delves into the *Pages* app, which is the word-processing and page-layout tool in the iWork suite of apps. Pages gives you powerful tools for creating documents of all kinds.

In this chapter, I tell you how to work with text and text boxes, format a document, and use the simple-to-use Pages interface.

To find basic instructions for managing documents and sharing them via WebDAV, iCloud, email, or iTunes, see Chapter 1 in this minibook.

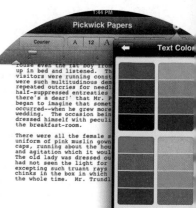

Editing a Pages Document

After you open a Pages document, you can edit it using the tools shown in Figure 2-1.

To find out how to create a new Pages document, see Chapter 1 in this minibook.

When you tap somewhere within the text, the keyboard and tools shown in Figure 2-1 appear. When you tap an image, a toolbar offering Cut, Copy, Delete, and Comment tools appears. When you leave an iWork document for another app and then return to it, remember that you return to the same location you left.

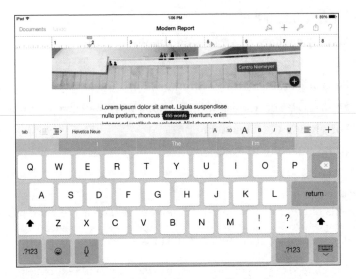

Figure 2-1: An open document with text tools displayed.

When a document is open, the Documents button is visible at the left of the toolbar, at the top of the screen; tap this button to return to the Documents window, where you can create a new document by tapping the button labeled with the plus sign (+).

When working on a multipage document, you can quickly move through the document by swiping up or down.

In Pages, you can touch and hold your finger anywhere at the right side of a page to bring up the *navigator* (shown in Figure 2-2), which shows a thumbnail of a page; you can move very quickly through the document by dragging up or down on the screen. When you're on the page you want, just lift your finger off the screen. If you don't want to leave the page you started from, swipe to the right to make the navigator disappear.

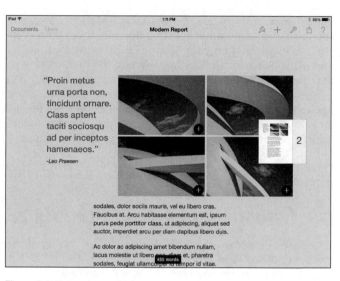

Figure 2-2: Using the navigator.

Working with Text in Pages

You can get a leg up on creating a document if you start from an iWork template (a template other than the Blank template, which is, well, blank). Even though you may see only a text placeholder in the template, the basic structure helps you get started. Templates appear when you tap the plus sign (+) on the Documents window to add a new document. Just tap a template to open it.

After you open a document, entering text is simple. You have four ways to start entering text:

- ✔ **Type text.** Tap the spot in the document where you want to enter text and start typing. You can use the onscreen keyboard or a wireless keyboard.

- ✔ **Dictate text.** Tap the Dictation key (not available on iPad 2) on the onscreen keyboard (the small microphone) and speak your text, including punctuation. Dictation also allows some simple commands such as "Next line."

- ✔ **Cut, copy, or paste text (or a combination).** Use the cut, copy, and paste tools to cut text in your Pages document and move it to another location, or to copy text in any iPad app (for example, from a website accessed by the Safari browser) and paste it into your Pages document. You get these controls by pressing and holding on text to display a set of tools.

✔ **Import text.** You can use iTunes, iCloud, Mail, or cloud storage apps such as Dropbox to move existing documents to your iPad. You can create the documents on your Mac or PC by using tools such as iWork, Microsoft Office, or Google Apps. When the document is ready, import that file saved in `.txt`, Word, or Pages formats to your iPad as described in Chapter 1 of this minibook and continue working with the document using iWork for iPad. If you work on a document using iWork for iCloud with a browser from a PC or Mac, the document will automatically be saved both in iCloud and to all your iOS devices.

After you have text in your Pages document, you can start to manage it.

Setting Basic Formatting by Using the Ruler

As is the case in most word-processing programs, a ruler at the top of a page in document editing view lets you set basic formatting. The ruler can be hidden, but tapping in the document displays it, as shown in Figure 2-3. Tapping text also displays the keyboard with formatting tools along the top. You can also tap the Format button shaped like a paintbrush at any time to display the Formats dialog.

The ruler shows you the settings for whatever is selected in the document. Tap text in the document, and the ruler is immediately enabled and reflects the settings for the selection (in this case, the margins). Tapping in the document may also bring up the onscreen keyboard and a contextual set of tool buttons, as shown in Figure 2-3. You can use them to use features such as Cut, Copy, Delete, and Paste.

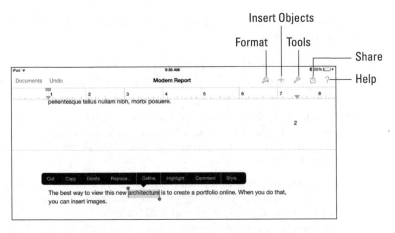

Figure 2-3: Displaying the ruler and formatting tools in Pages.

REMEMBER

Press and hold text to bring up a set of contextual buttons, a double-tap selects the word at the insertion point, and a triple-tap selects the paragraph and brings up slightly different selection buttons.

The formatting bar along the top of the onscreen keyboard provides basic formatting tools. The tools on the ruler that can be used on the selection (from left to right in Figure 2-4) are described in this list:

- **Tab:** Tap this button to set new tab stops.

- **Indent:** Tap either of the Indent buttons to indent text in one level or out one level at a time.

- **Font:** In Figure 2-4, the font is Helvetica Neue. Tap the font name to open a popover with a list of fonts to select from. Note that available fonts in Pages on iPad are fewer than in Mac or Windows programs, and you can't add fonts as you can on a computer. So if a font isn't supported on iPad, another font is substituted, which could affect layout and appearance adversely.

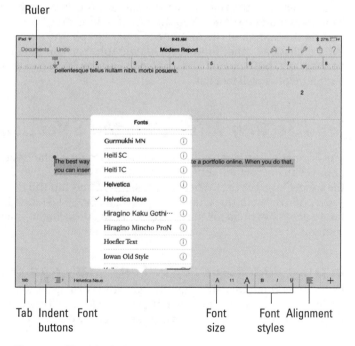

Figure 2-4: The ruler indicates settings for the current selection.

✔ **Font Size:** Tap the large *A* on the right to enlarge selected text by one point; tap the smaller *A* on the left to decrease the text size. By using the tool in the middle, you can set the font size to an exact number.

✔ **Font Styles:** You can choose bold, italic, or underlining.

✔ **Alignment:** The selected paragraph can be aligned to the left, center, or right, or justified so that both margins are straight with no ragged edges. You don't have to select the paragraph with a triple-tap for alignment to work. If you have selected a word or an insertion point, the paragraph containing either item is the selected paragraph.

✔ **Insert:** Tapping the last button on the Formatting toolbar displays a menu of insertion commands including Comment, Link, Page Break, Column Break, and Footnote. (Link appears only if text is selected; Line Break appears only if no text is selected.)

Feel free to experiment with the formatting within your Pages documents, and remember that the Undo button in the upper left is there to help you out if you change your mind about an action you've taken.

You can also use the ruler to set the margins for paragraphs. Just slide the indicators along the ruler. Note that the top indicator for the left margin reflects the margin of the first line in a paragraph; the lower indicator is the left margin of all other lines in the paragraph. You can indent the first line of a paragraph, but you can also *outdent* it (or provide a hanging first line); an outdent works well in a list.

Getting and Setting Info about the Selection

The Format button on the toolbar at the top-right of the document opens a popover that provides settings in addition to those shown on the ruler. (See the preceding section.) When you select text and tap the Format button, you see a popover with three tabs along the top: Style, List, and Layout. Select a tab to access various formatting options, as I describe in the following three sections.

Setting character style: Font, size, and color

One setting that you can adjust by using the Format button is Style. Tap the Format button, and the popover shown in Figure 2-5 opens. (The Style tab in the top-left corner of the popover is selected by default.)

The powerful Style tab of the Format popover has a wide range of functionality. The topmost section lets you set the character style for the selected text. The *character style* is simply the set of styles applied to characters. The second section of the popover lets you set the paragraph style — the style for the entire paragraph in which the selection is set.

You can't create your own paragraph styles in Pages for iOS, but you can use any you created in Pages for Mac. Pages for iOS retains styles from Pages for Mac documents internally so that they still work if you open the document back in Pages for Mac.

After selecting the characters you want to style, tap Format and then the current font setting in the popover. (It's 14-point American Typewriter in Figure 2-5.) The popover shown in Figure 2-6 opens, and you can select another font, font size, or color for the font.

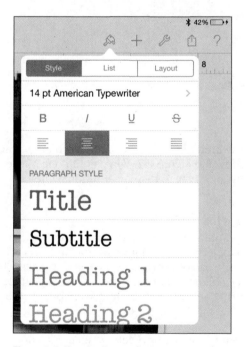

Figure 2-5: Use the Format button to set styles.

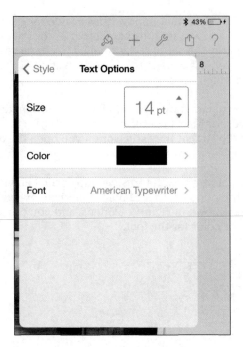

Figure 2-6: Adjust character styles.

Tap the color well (the swatch of color next to the word *Color*), and you can select a new color, as shown in Figure 2-7. You can tap one of the small circles at the bottom of this popover to display additional choices.

Creating indents and list styles

After you select a paragraph, tap the Format button and then, in the popover, tap the List tab to experiment with indentation and lists. The options shown in Figure 2-8 include arrow buttons at the top of the view that let you move the left margin in *(indent)* or out *(outdent)*. You also can choose to make automatic numbering, lettering, or bullets available by choosing a list format.

When you add an element to the list or delete an element from it, Pages automatically renumbers the list for you.

Establishing alignment, columns, and line spacing

The Layout tab in the top-right corner of the Format popover lets you set layout options, as shown in Figure 2-9. These include the options for creating columns and adjusting line spacing.

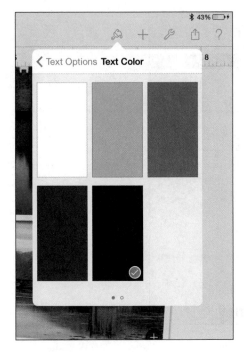

Figure 2-7: Change the font color.

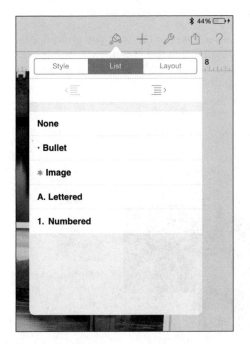

Figure 2-8: Handle indents and lists.

Figure 2-9: Adjust layout settings.

Formatting a Document

You can format the text in your document, but you should attend to one other type of formatting: formatting the document itself. It includes page headers and footers, page numbers, and backgrounds that appear on all pages. Here's how to do just that:

1. **Open a Pages document and tap Tools.**

   The Tools popover appears, as shown in Figure 2-10.

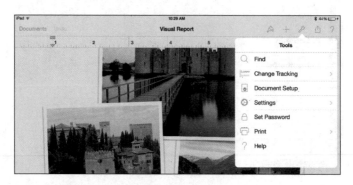

Figure 2-10: The Tools options.

2. **Tap the Document Setup option.**

   You see a blueprint-like section that's markedly different from the view you see when you edit an individual page. Note that this page will not rotate when you turn your iPad, it displays in portrait orientation only (see Figure 2-11).

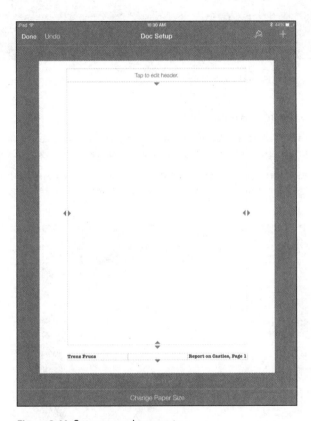

Figure 2-11: Set up your document.

3. **Tap a header or footer to customize it.**

   You can use the three footer sections to insert the author's name, a title, the version number, or the page number, for example.

4. **Type some text in the section of the header or footer that you want to customize.**

5. **To add page numbers to your document, tap in the header or footer section that you want to use for the page number; then tap the Page Numbers button in the contextual menu that appears.**

   This contextual menu is displayed only when you tap a header or footer.

   You can choose the format of the page numbers, as shown in Figure 2-12.

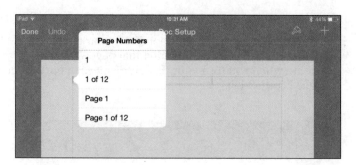

Figure 2-12: Insert page numbers.

6. **Tap the style you prefer.**

7. **Set the outer limits of the area for the page content (as well as for header and footer) by dragging the lines, as shown in Figure 2-13.**

   These settings determine the printable area of your document on the page. Margins that you set using the ruler define this area.

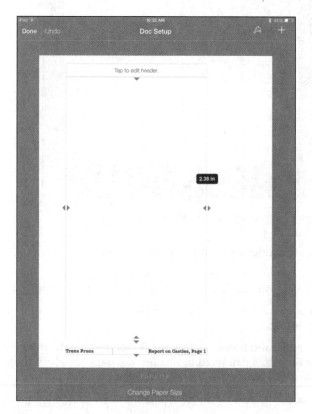

Figure 2-13: Set the print margins.

8. **Tap the Change Paper Size button on the bottom of the page and select a predefined paper size, as shown in Figure 2-14.**

   Tap US Letter to print on 8½ -x-11-inch paper or A4 to print on standard international letter paper.

Figure 2-14: Select a paper size.

9. **Tap Cancel if you decide not to change the page size and then Done to return to your document.**

   After your page is set up, you're ready to finish entering text in your document and print it when it's done.

Working with Selection Buttons

When you read this chapter from start to finish, you see various sets of selection buttons shown on the toolbar that appears whenever you press and hold in a document — and often shown with selected text. The buttons vary depending on which element is selected. Some selection buttons may look familiar to you from other apps that you may have used on the iPad and the Mac (as well as on other types of computers), including the Cut, Copy, and Paste commands.

When you select a chunk of text, you may also see these options:

- **Delete:** Delete the selected text or object.
- **Highlight:** Highlight selected text with a felt-tip marker effect.
- **Comment:** Insert a comment where you can enter a note about items in your document or comment on the work of others that you're reviewing.

Chapter 3: Counting on Numbers

In This Chapter

✏ **Getting to know Numbers**

✏ **Working with a template**

✏ **Using tabs and sheets**

✏ **Using tables, cells, and forms**

✏ **Creating new tables**

*N*umbers takes a different approach to the concept of spreadsheets. It brings to spreadsheets not only a different kind of structure but also data formats that you may never have seen. In addition to being able to use numbers and text in your spreadsheets, you can use on-off check boxes and star ratings as part of your data. Think of an inventory spreadsheet with check boxes for in-stock items and star ratings based on reviews or user feedback. What you may have thought of as just a bunch of numbers can now provide true meaning and context to users.

Numbers is a very practical addition to the other iWork apps. Tables and charts are built into both Keynote and Pages, but Numbers is the main number-crunching tool on the iPad.

In this chapter, you discover how Numbers helps organize data into manageable units. After you enter your data, you can display it in charts and graphs.

Cost Breakdown

.m	Field	Referees	Tournament Fees
$480	$180	$60	$216
$240	$90	$30	$108

$936	
2	
$468	

Paid
☑
☑

Team Costs

23%

6%

19%

51%

Introducing Numbers

When you create a Numbers document, you work with these three items:

✏ **A Numbers document:** A container for spreadsheets (sheets) and their data; similar to a Microsoft Excel workbook.

✏ **One or more sheets:** One or more spreadsheets called simply *sheets*.

✏ **Tables:** The sub-spreadsheets or tables created in other spreadsheet programs exist in Numbers as formal, structured tables rather than as a range of cells within a spreadsheet. Numbers gives them a specific name: *tables*. (And yes, a Numbers document can have no tables but must have at least one sheet.)

The simple idea of making tables into an actual part of the Numbers application rather than letting people create them any which way leads to a major change in the way you can use Numbers when compared to other spreadsheet programs. Because a table is an entity of its own and not a range of cells, you don't break the tables you've organized in a spreadsheet when you reformat another part of the spreadsheet. You can work within any table, and you can reorganize tables within a sheet, but you can't break tables by simply adding a row or column to your spreadsheet.

Figure 3-1 shows a Numbers for Mac template (Team Organization).

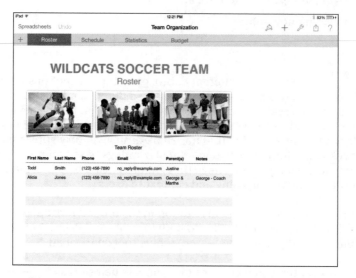

Figure 3-1: The Team Organization template in Numbers for Mac.

Figure 3-1 is a single document with four sheets visible in the tabs in the Sheets pane:

- Roster
- Schedule
- Statistics
- Budget

Some sheets contain tables or charts, and you see them listed in the Sheets pane under their corresponding documents. For example, the Roster sheet contains the Team Roster and Team Management tables (scroll down to see the Team Management table). The Budget sheet contains the Cost

Breakdown table as well as a chart (Team Costs). The idea that a single sheet can contain defined charts and tables that don't depend on ranges of cells is the biggest difference between Numbers and almost every other spreadsheet program.

As you can see in Figure 3-1, sheets can also contain images and other graphics; they aren't part of the structure of charts and tables. You simply insert these elements the same way you insert any other objects in iWork documents.

You can select individual tables. A selected table has a frame with its column and row titles as well as other controls. Note also that each table within a sheet has its own row and column numbers (you can also name them, if you want) and that each table you deal with starts with cell A1. (The first row is 1 and the first column is A.)

Various tools are available to you in the top-right corner of Numbers, as with other iWork apps. The buttons on this toolbar access settings for formatting tables; for inserting photos, charts, text, and shapes (see Figure 3-2); and for sharing documents and getting help.

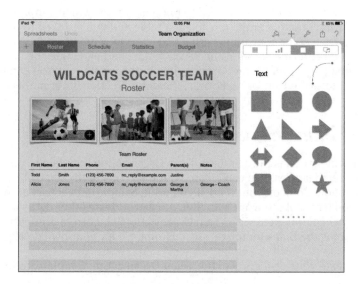

Figure 3-2: The Insert popover in Numbers.

Book IV
Chapter 3

Counting on
Numbers

Numbers lets you insert charts along with tables on your sheets, as you see in Figure 3-3. (Remember that you can also insert graphics and other objects on your sheet.)

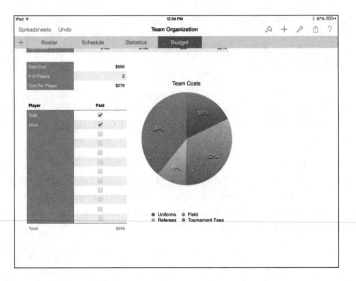

Figure 3-3: You can use charts in Numbers, too.

Numbers also includes the ability to create *forms,* which simplify data entry. When you create a form, you select a table and you're taken to a tab that displays each column heading with a text entry box next to it. You can then focus on entering data for one row at a time and eliminate the possibility of accidentally tapping and entering data in the wrong row. You can find more about forms in the "Using Forms Efficiently" section, later in this chapter.

Using the Team Organization Template

This chapter uses the Numbers Team Organization template to demonstrate Numbers features. You can create your own copy of the template so that you can follow along on your iPad, if you want. Sample data is part of the template, so you have data to work with, but you can add any other data you want. After you've experimented with Team Organization, you can pick another template, including the Blank template, and customize it for your own data.

To create your own copy of the Team Organization template, follow these steps:

1. **Launch Numbers on the iPad.**

2. **Go to the Documents window.**

   If you had a spreadsheet open when you were last using Numbers, you return to that spreadsheet. Simply tap Spreadsheets at the top left to go to the Documents window.

3. **Tap Create Spreadsheet.**

4. Scroll down and tap Team Organization.

Your new spreadsheet opens. Any changes you make are saved automatically.

Working with Tabs and Sheets

Every tab displays a sheet, which can have one or more tables or charts (or both) on it as well as graphics and text frames. Tabs help you organize the contents of your Numbers documents. In this section, I tell you what you need to know about setting up tabs in a document.

Adding a new tab

As with all iWork apps, starting a new Numbers document involves choosing a template. Each template has its own predefined tabs. The Blank template has only one tab (cleverly titled Sheet 1). You can add more tabs by using the plus sign (+) tab on the left end of the tabs (see Figure 3-4).

Tap here to add a new tab.

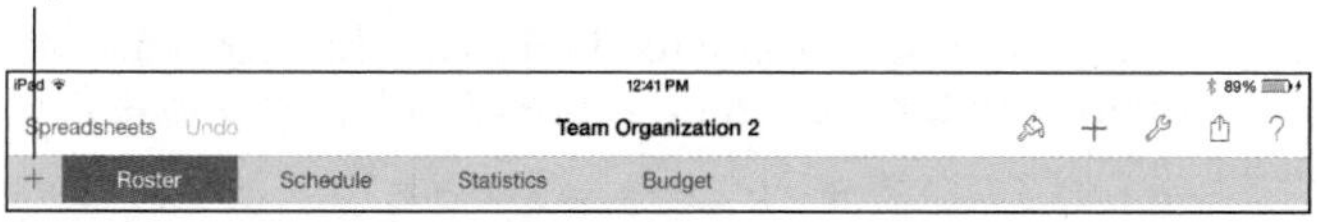

Figure 3-4: The plus sign (+) tab always appears to the left.

Tap the plus sign (+) tab, and Numbers asks whether you want to add a new sheet or a new form. Tap New Sheet, and Numbers creates a new tab that contains one table (see Figure 3-5). The sheet is labeled Sheet 1. See the section "Changing a tab's name," later in this chapter, for how to rename the tab. (If you're interested in forms, I tell you about that topic later in this chapter, in the "Using Forms Efficiently" section.)

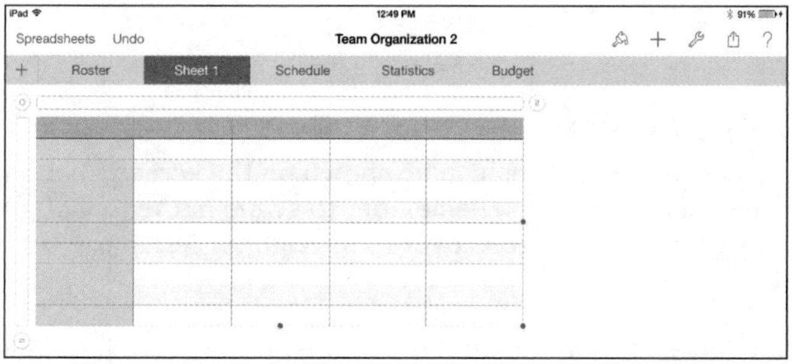

Figure 3-5: Add a new sheet.

Deleting or duplicating a tab

If you add a tab by mistake, you can remove it. Also, if you want to reuse a tab as the basis for a new tab, Numbers allows you to duplicate it. To perform either of these actions, tap and hold the tab you want to delete or duplicate, and a contextual menu appears below it (see Figure 3-6). All you have to do now is tap the option (Duplicate or Delete) for the action you want to take.

Figure 3-6: Duplicate or delete a tab.

Remember that a double-tap opens the tab so that you can edit its name. A single tap opens the tab's content. A press-and-hold opens a contextual menu, if available.

Rearranging tabs

If you don't like the order of your tabs, drag a tab to the right or left in the row of tabs to the desired new position, and then release your finger when the tab is in the position you want (see Figure 3-7).

Figure 3-7: Rearrange tabs.

Navigating tabs

If you have more tabs than can be shown on the screen, just swipe right or left to slide along the tabs. Remember to swipe in the row of tabs. Swiping the body of the sheet scrolls over to the right or left of the content on that sheet.

If you're holding your iPad in portrait orientation, turn it to landscape orientation to show more tabs on the screen.

Changing a tab's name

Double-tapping text anywhere in Numbers allows you to edit the text. The same statement applies to tabs, too. Double-tap the name of a tab to begin editing it (see Figure 3-8). The onscreen keyboard appears, and you can delete the current name and enter a new one.

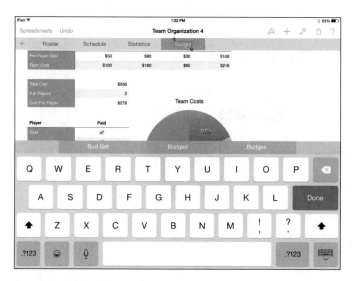

Figure 3-8: Edit a tab's name.

Using Tables

Tables are at the heart of Numbers — they're where you enter your data. This section shows you how to work with a table as a whole; the later section "Working with Cells" shows you how to work with individual cells within a table.

Selecting a table

To be able to work on a table, you need to select it. If the table isn't visible in the current tab, just tap the tab it's in first. To select a table in Numbers, tap it.

If you need to find an entry within a table, it's easy to do. Tap the Tools button (the wrench icon near the top-right corner) to open the Tools popover. Tap Find and enter a word or phrase; then tap Search on the keyboard to search the entire Numbers document for a match in that table.

When a table is selected, its appearance changes (see Figure 3-9). A selected table is framed with gray bars above (the column frame) and to its left (the row frame). To the left of the column frame, a button with concentric circles lets you move the table. To the right of the column frame, as well as beneath the row frame, are buttons, each with four small squares (looking a bit like table cells). These Cells buttons let you add rows, columns, or cells and manipulate the cells in the table. (See the later section "Working with Cells.")

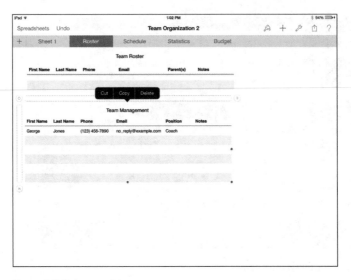

Figure 3-9: Select a table.

Select a table by tapping it once. Note that the location of your tap is important:

- ✔ **If you tap in a cell, the table and that cell are selected.**

- ✔ **If you tap inside the table bounds but outside the cells, the table itself is selected.** For example, if you tap the table's title or the blank space to the left or right of the title, the table itself is selected. (Refer to Figure 3-9.)

Moving a table

You can move a table around on its sheet. Select the table and tap the round button to the left of the column frame. Then drag the table where you want it. (See Figure 3-10). Numbers shows you the absolute coordinates of the location you're dragging to. Light-colored lines called *guides* help you align the table to other objects on the sheet. These lines appear and disappear as the table is aligned with the edges or centers of other objects.

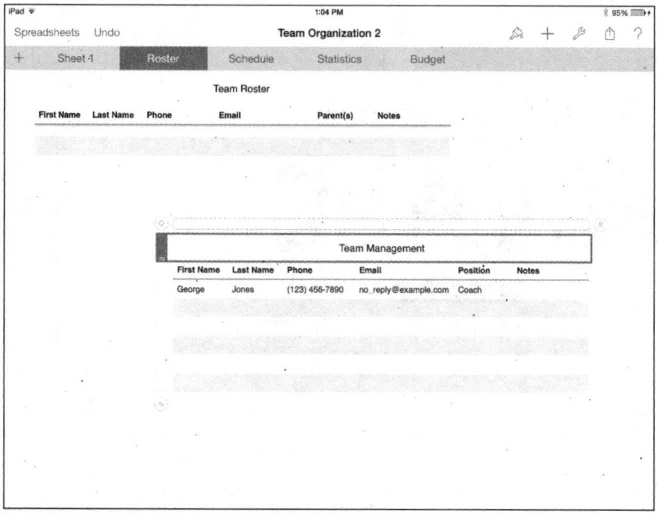

Figure 3-10: Relocate the table.

TIP

You can select several objects at the same time. Tap and hold the first object to select it, and then, while still holding down your finger, tap with another finger the other objects you want to add to the selection. After that, they move or resize together. (You may need to use two hands for this task.)

Cutting and pasting a table

You can select a table and then drag it around on a sheet by using the round button at the top left of the column frame; you can resize the table as described in the "Resizing a table" section, later in this chapter. But what if you want to place the table on a different sheet? To copy (or cut) and paste a table onto a different sheet, follow these steps:

1. **Select the table by tapping the round button at the top left.**

   The Cut, Copy, and Delete tools appear, as shown in Figure 3-11.

2. **Tap Cut from the selection buttons that appear.**

3. **Tap the tab of the sheet you want to add the table to.**

4. **Tap in the sheet (but not in an existing table).**

   This step brings up new selection buttons.

5. **Tap Paste.**

6. **Move and resize the table as you want.**

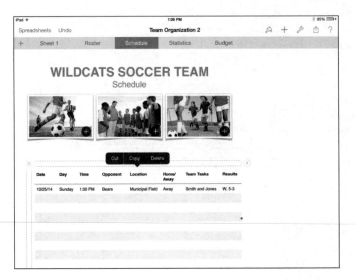

Figure 3-11: Select an entire table.

Adjusting columns or rows

If you've ever used a spreadsheet program, you know that data you enter doesn't always fit into the default column and row sizes. In Numbers, you can select the columns or rows you want to work on and then rearrange or resize them.

Especially with spreadsheets that have lots of rows and columns, resizing can be easier when using a stylus.

Selecting a row or column

Tap in the row frame to select the corresponding row, as shown in Figure 3-12.

Figure 3-12: Select a row.

Tap in the column frame to select the corresponding column.

After you select a row or column, you can adjust the selection by dragging the handles (the round buttons) at the top and bottom for rows and at the left and right for columns, as shown in Figure 3-13.

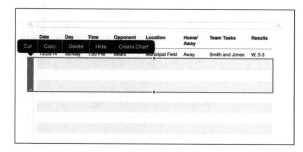

Figure 3-13: Adjust a selection.

The selection buttons Cut, Copy/Paste, Delete, Hide, and Create Chart appear above a selected row, whereas Cut, Copy, Delete, Fill, or Comment appear above a selected cell. Figure 3-14 shows several cells selected within a column.

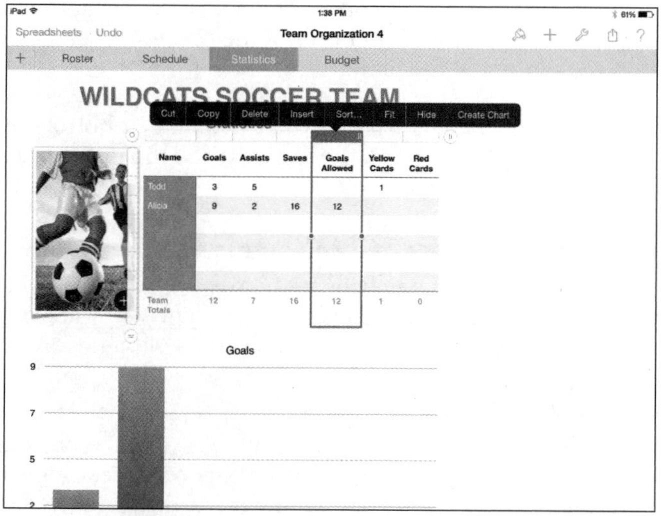

Figure 3-14: Select a few cells in a column.

The selection button you tap affects the selected column or cell.

For example, use the Merge selection button to merge selected cells in a column (or row).

Resizing a row or column

The two vertical lines (known as the Cells button) in the top-right corner of the column frame (refer to Figure 3-14) and the two horizontal lines in the bottom-left corner of the row frame (refer to Figure 3-12) let you resize the selected columns or rows. You always resize a column to its right and a row to its bottom, whether you're making it larger or smaller. The contents are automatically adjusted, and the adjoining rows or columns are moved aside.

Moving a row or column

Sometimes, you want to rearrange the rows or columns in a sheet. With one or more rows or columns selected, press and drag it (or them) to a new position. All selected rows or columns move as a unit, and the other rows or columns move aside.

Resizing a table

You can resize a table in two ways: add or remove rows or columns to or from the table, or leave the number of rows and columns the same and change the overall size of the table. You may even want to do both.

Adding or removing rows and columns at the right or bottom

Tap the Cells button in the top-right corner of the column frame to add a new column at the right of the table. To add a new row at the bottom, tap the Cells button in the bottom-left corner of the row frame, and a new row is added to the bottom of the table.

To remove a blank column or row at the right side or bottom of a table, drag the appropriate Cells button to the left or to the top of the frame — the extra rows or columns disappear.

Adding or removing rows and columns inside the table

Select the row or column below or to the right of the new row or column. From the selection buttons, tap Insert to add a new row above the selected row or a new column to the left of the selected column.

Changing a table's size

Select the table so that the handles (small blue dots) are visible at the right side and bottom. These handles work like any other resizing handles in Numbers: Simply drag them horizontally or vertically to change the table's size. The content of the table automatically resizes to fit the new table size. The numbers of rows and columns remain unchanged, but their sizes may be adjusted.

You can select the table by tapping the round button at the top-left of the table. (Refer to Figure 3-11.)

Read more about formatting tables in the "Working with New Tables" section, later in this chapter.

Working with Cells

Double-tap a cell if you want to add or edit data. A blue outline appears around the cell, and the keyboard appears so that you can begin entering data.

Single-tap if you want to select a cell. The cell is outlined, and the table-selection elements (the column and row frames, the Cells button, the round button to the left of the column frame, and the button to the right of the column frame as well as the button beneath the row frame) appear.

A double-tap makes the cell available for editing. Figure 3-15 shows how, after a double-tap in a cell, the keyboard appears.

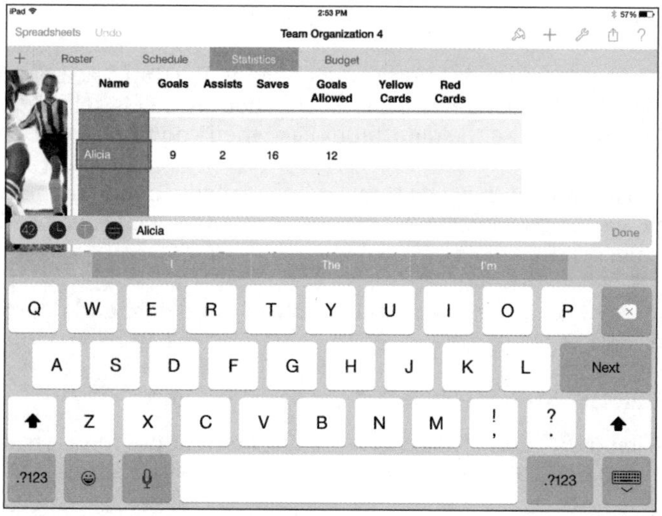

Figure 3-15: Start to edit a cell's data.

After you set up your spreadsheet, most of your work consists of entering and editing data of all types. That's what you find out about in the next section.

Entering and editing data

The keyboard for entering data into a Numbers cell is a powerful and flexible tool — it's four keyboards in one. Above the keyboard, the Formula bar lets you quickly and easily enter formulas. (Refer to Figure 3-15.) On the left of the Formula bar are four buttons that let you switch from one keyboard to another. You can choose these keyboards, starting from the left:

- **Numeric (42 icon):** Lets you use the numeric keyboard.

- **Date and Time (clock icon):** Lets you enter dates and times.

- **Text (T icon):** Displays the standard text keyboard.

- **Formulas (= icon):** Opens the formula-editing keyboard.

Whichever keyboard you're using, you see the characters you're typing in the Formula bar above the keyboard. To the right of the oblong area is a button labeled Done (or a check mark, depending on which keyboard you're using) that moves your typing into the selected cell and then hides the keyboard.

The Dictation feature on iPad works in Numbers and the other iWork apps. Tap the Dictation key on the onscreen keyboard and speak your text; tap the key again to insert the text in your document.

You can bring up the keyboard when you double-tap a cell or another text field (such as a tab name). That means that the cell is selected and the keyboard knows where the data should go when you tap OK or Done.

Note that many of these features are unavailable on a Bluetooth keyboard, which may or may not have a number pad and special symbols used in entering formulas.

To the right of the keyboard in the numeric and date-and-time keyboards are three large keys:

- **Delete:** This is the standard keyboard Delete key.

- **Next (adjacent):** The Next key with the right-pointing arrow inserts the typed data into the selected cell and moves to the next cell to the right.

- **Next (next line):** The Next key with the hooked arrow pointing left and up inserts the typed data and moves to the next line and to the leftmost cell in the section of cells you're entering. For example, if you start in the third column of the fourth row, the Next (next line) key moves you to the third column of the fifth row, not the first column.

Entering numeric data

The numeric keyboard (accessed by tapping the 42 button) has a typical numeric keypad along with four large buttons on the left (see Figure 3-16).

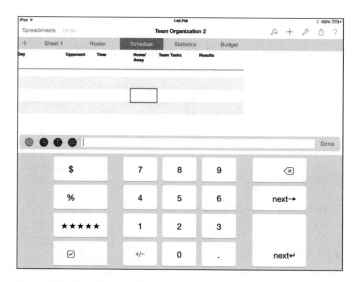

Figure 3-16: Use these tools to input numeric data.

These four buttons let you choose the formatting for the cell you're editing. If you need a symbol (such as stars for ratings or a currency symbol), it's added before or after the numeric value as is appropriate. Your formatting options, from top to bottom, are described in this list:

- **Currency:** This option adds the appropriate currency symbol, such as $, £, or €.

- **Percentage:** The percent symbol follows the value.

- **Stars (rating):** This option lets you display a number from 1 to 45 as a star rating. Numbers greater than 5 display with five stars. To change the number of stars, type a new number or tap the star display in the cell or in the display above the keyboard. You can use stars in a spreadsheet and then sort the column of stars so that the ratings are ordered from highest to lowest, or vice versa.

- **Check box:** A check box is either selected or not. Check boxes are selected and deselected by a user or as the result of a calculation.

Customizing check boxes

A check box can indicate, for example, that an item is in stock or out of stock (yes/no or true/false). However, you can also use it to represent numeric data. Computers and programs often represent nonzero and zero values as yes/no or true/false values. That's one way you can use check boxes to track inventory. If you show the number of in-stock items in a cell, you can use a check box to indicate that none is in stock (a deselected check box) or that items are in stock (a selected check box). Numbers handles the conversion for you.

Here's how check box customization can work:

1. **Double-tap a cell to start editing it; tap the 42 icon and then tap the Checkbox button when the keyboard opens.**

   You see a check box in the selected cell; in the area above the keyboard, you see the word *false,* as shown in Figure 3-17. The green outline distinguishes the word *false* from text you type in. It has the value *false* because, before you type anything, its numeric value is zero.

42 ✦ ✦ ✦ ☑ false	Done

   Figure 3-17: A check box starts as off and false.

2. **Type a nonzero value.**

   This value can represent the number of items in stock, for example.

3. **Tap the Checkbox button again.**

   You see that the value you typed changes to *true* (see Figure 3-18) and that the check box is selected in the table.

   Because the formatting is separate from the data value, you can sometimes display the in-stock inventory count as a number and sometimes as the check box. Customers are likely to care only about the check box, but the inventory manager cares about the number.

42 ✦ ✦ ✦ ☑ true	Done

   Figure 3-18: A nonzero value is on and true.

Everything in Numbers is linked, so you don't have to worry about a sequence for doing most things. If you've followed these steps, you've seen how to enter a number and have it control a check box, but that's only one of at least three ways of working with a check box.

With a cell selected and the Checkbox formatting button selected, you see the true/false value above the keyboard and the check box itself in the table cell. Tap the check box in the table cell: The true/false value is reversed, as is the state of the check box itself.

Likewise, if you tap the word *true* or *false* in the display above the keyboard, the check box flips its value and true/false reverses.

When you tap a formatting button, it turns blue and formats the number in the selected cell (or cells). You can tap another formatting button to switch to another format (from stars to a percentage, for example). Tapping a highlighted formatting button turns it off without selecting another.

Entering date/time data

Tap the clock button above the keyboard to enter date/time or duration data, as shown in Figure 3-19. The Date & Time button lets you specify a particular moment, and the Duration button lets you specify (or calculate) a length of time.

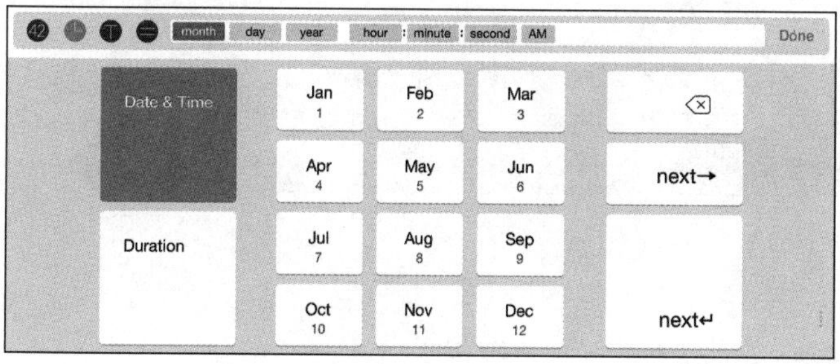

Figure 3-19: Enter date and time, or duration, data.

Above the keyboard, the units of a date or duration display. To enter or edit a date or time (or both), tap Month in the Formula bar and use the keypad to select the month. (The keys have both the month name abbreviations and the month numbers on them.) Similarly, tap any other time increment and enter a value. As you do so, the display changes to show the value. (Tapping AM or PM toggles the value — you don't need to type anything.)

Entering text data

When you tap the T button to enter text, the standard QWERTY keyboard appears, as shown in Figure 3-20.

As with most onscreen keyboards, you can switch among letters, numbers, and special characters. (If you need a refresher on how to do it, see Book I, Chapter 2.) Everything you type or dictate is inserted into the selected cell until you tap the Done button, which is at the right of the display above the keyboard. If you enter a Return character, it's part of the text in the cell. The cell automatically expands vertically to accommodate the text you type, and you can resize the column so that the cell is the appropriate size. Remember, these specialized features are not available on Bluetooth keyboards, so it's often preferable to use the onscreen keyboard when using Numbers.

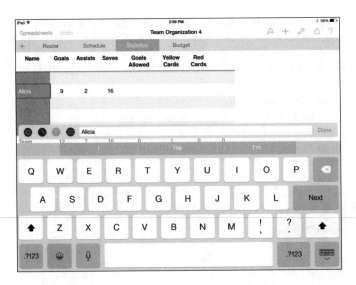

Figure 3-20: Enter text.

Entering formulas

Tapping the equal sign (=) button lets you enter a formula, which automatically computes values based on the data you type. The result of the formula can display in a cell in any of the usual formats, and that value can be used in a chart.

When you're entering a formula, the four buttons controlling the date-and-time, text, and numeric keyboards disappear. In their place, a button with three dots appears. Tapping this button returns you to the display that gives you access to the other three keyboards. This setup is just a matter of Numbers saving space onscreen.

Formulas are accompanied by good news and bad news. The good news is that you don't have to type many common formulas: Almost all spreadsheets have the same built-in list of formulas. The bad news is that the list of formulas is quite long.

Formulas can consist of numbers, text, dates, durations, and true/false values. They can also include the results of formulas and the values of individual cells.

The example in this section, which presents the basics of creating a simple formula in Numbers, adds a number to the value of an existing cell and then displays the result in the cell that contains the formula. In this example, I use the Team Organization template that you see in the figures throughout this chapter.

The formula adds 2½ hours to the starting time of a game and displays the estimated completion time in a new column. Follow these steps:

1. **Rename the Time column in the Schedule tab to** Start.

2. **Add a column to its right and name it** End.

3. **Select the cell in which you want to insert the formula by double-tapping it.**

   I selected the End column cell next to Start, as you can see in Figure 3-21.

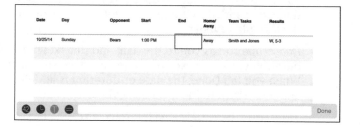

Figure 3-21: Select the cell that will contain the formula.

4. **Tap the equal sign (=) button at the top-left side of the keyboard.**

   The keyboard changes to the formula keyboard, as shown in Figure 3-22.

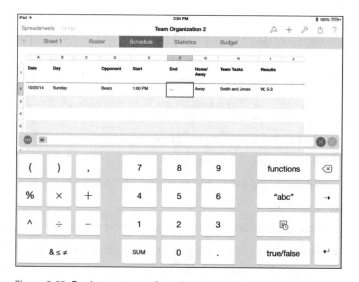

Figure 3-22: Begin to create a formula.

The table's column and row frames now contain row and column identifiers. The columns are labeled A, B, C, and so on; the rows are labeled 1, 2, 3, and so on. Every cell can be identified by its coordinates (such as A1 for the top-left cell).

Also note that at the right of the keyboard is a different set of buttons than on the text, date, and number keyboards. On the right side of the keypad, you'll find four buttons that represent the following:

- *Functions:* Brings up a list of functions for use in formulas. (Refer to Step 3.)

- *abc:* Displays the text keyboard. You can type text and tap Done, and the text is added to the formula you're constructing. You return to the formula keyboard.

- *Date/Time:* Takes you to the date-and-time keyboard. The date or duration you enter uses the same interface shown in Figure 3-19. When you tap Done, the date or duration is added to the formula, and you return to the formula keyboard.

- *True/False:* Uses the same interface as check boxes; the result is added to the formula you're constructing, and you return to the formula keyboard.

5. **Add the game starting time to the formula.**

   Just tap the cell containing the game start time. The formula reflects the name of the table and the referenced cell. In this case, that reference is

   C2

   This references column C, row 2 in the Game Schedule table. You don't have to type a thing — just tap, and the correct cell is referenced.

   You now need the formula to add 2½ hours to the starting time.

6. **Tap + from the operators on the left side of the keyboard.**

7. **Tap the Date/Time button on the right side of the keyboard and then tap the Duration button at the left.**

8. **On the Formula bar, tap Hours and enter** 2.

9. **Tap Minutes and enter** 30.

   Figure 3-23 shows what the screen looks like now.

10. **Tap Done.**

    You're done entering the duration. You return to the formula keyboard.

11. **Finish the formula by tapping the button with a check mark on it.**

    Figure 3-24 shows the formula as it is now. Note that rather than seeing the Done button, as with other keyboards, you see a button with a check mark and a button with an X at the right. The X cancels the formula, and the check mark completes it. If you want to modify the formula with the keys (including Delete) on the keyboard, feel free.

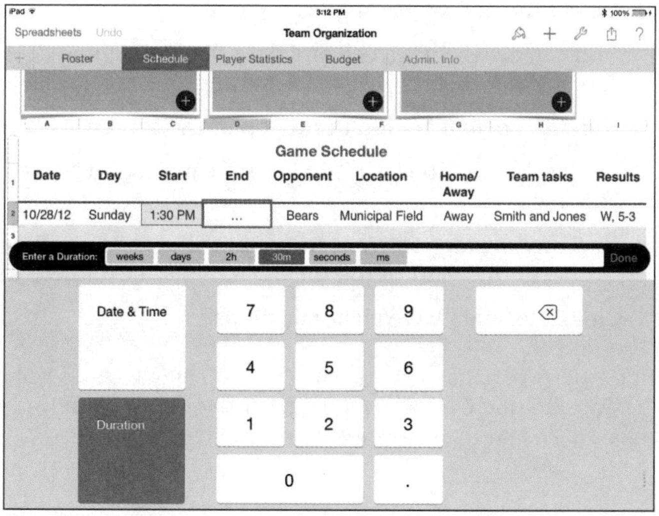

Figure 3-23: Enter the formula.

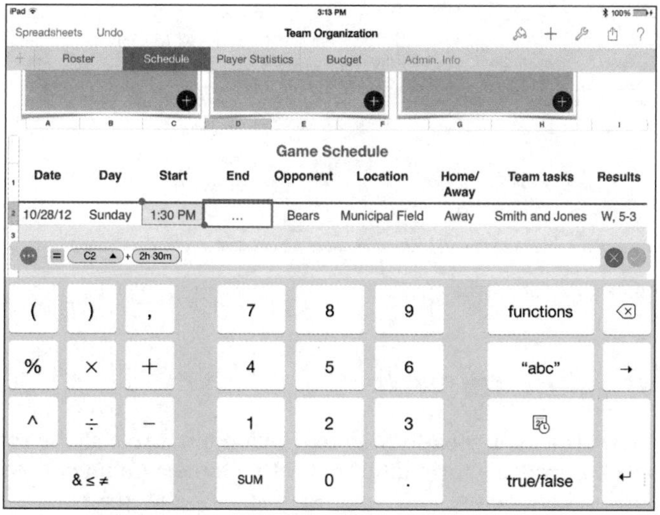

Figure 3-24: Tap the check mark to accept the formula.

Changing a cell's content formatting

Your end time may include the date, which is probably not what you want. Here's how to change the formatting of a cell's contents:

1. **Select the cell by making a single tap.**

   You can also select a cell and drag the highlighted selection to include more than one cell. Your reformatting affects all selected cells.

2. **Tap the Format button at the top of the screen.**

3. **In the Format popover, tap the Information button to the right of Date & Time.**

4. **Tap the format you want to use in the selected cell or cells, or tap the arrow at the right of the format name to customize the format.**

   Not all formats have customizations.

To properly format the end time cell, you may want to remove the date. In the Date & Time Options popover, set the date option for None, as shown in Figure 3-25, and the time option for the hour.

Figure 3-25: Format the result.

Using Forms Efficiently

A *form* is a user-friendly way to provide input to a single row of a spreadsheet. Because a form interacts with a table, you must create a table in your spreadsheet before you can create an associated form.

To create a form, tap the plus sign (+) tab on the left end of the row of tabs. You're asked whether you want to create a new sheet or a form. (Refer to Figure 3-25.) Tap New Form, and you see a screen similar to the one shown in Figure 3-26, which uses the Team Organization template for the example.

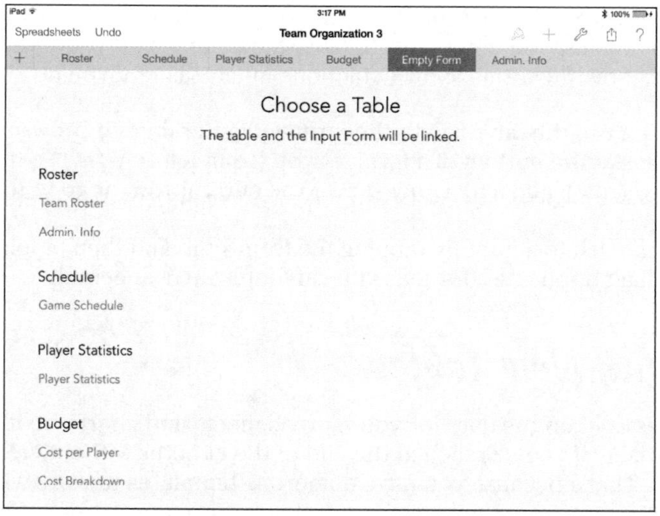

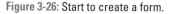

Figure 3-26: Start to create a form.

You see a list of all the sheets and all the tables on them. Choose the one that the form will be used with. In this case, I'm using my Team Management table.

Every form is associated with only one table, and every table can be associated with only one form (though it doesn't have to be associated with any forms).

The form is then created automatically, as shown in Figure 3-27.

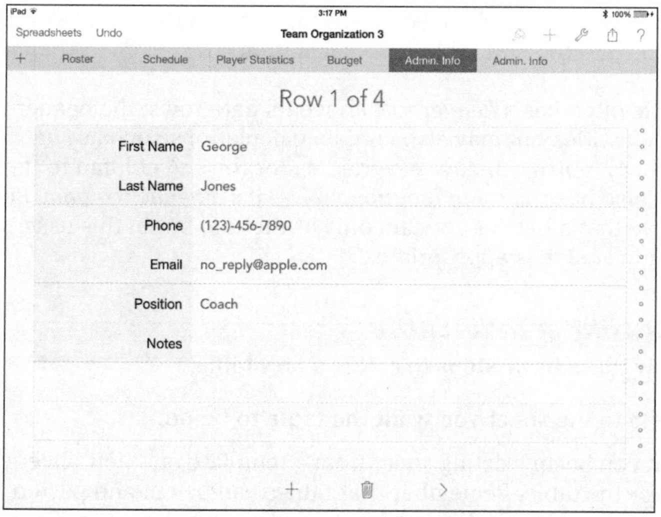

Figure 3-27: Use a form to browse, enter, and delete data.

The labels for the rows on the form are drawn from the labels of the columns on the tables. You don't have to label the columns on your tables, but it makes creating forms and calculations much easier if you do.

You can use the tab to go to the form and enter data or browse it. The four buttons at the bottom of a form let you (from left to right) go to the previous record (row), add a new row, delete the current row, or go to the next row.

You can delete a form by tapping the form's tab and then tapping Delete, but you can't duplicate a form as you can duplicate a sheet tab.

Working with New Tables

Tables contain the data for your spreadsheets and charts, so it may be a bit surprising if you've reached the end of the chapter without creating a single table. That's because you have numerous templates to work with. You don't have to start from the beginning; instead, you can start from further along in the development process.

Tables can be relatively small and focused. You can use formulas to link them, and that's a much better strategy than putting every single piece of data into an enormous spreadsheet.

Tables aren't simply repositories of data; they also drive charts. When you're organizing data in a table, you may want to consider how to transform it to create the kind of charts you want.

As you're planning the structure of your tables and sheets, pay attention to the moments when you realize that you have to add more data to a table. Ask whether you truly need more data in that table or need a table that can be linked to the first table by a calculation.

A table often has a *header row* above its data rows; the header row usually contains titles but may also contain calculations such as sums or averages. Numbers tables can have several header rows. A column to the left of the table also has the same functionality — it's a *header column*. People often believe that a header appears only at the top, but in this usage, it appears on whichever side is appropriate.

Creating a new table

Follow these basic steps to create a new table:

1. **Go to the sheet you want the table to be on.**

   It can be an existing sheet from a template or a new sheet you create just for the table. Remember that tables can be cut and pasted, so you have a second (and third and fourth and so on) chance to determine the sheet for your table.

2. **Tap the Insert Objects button (the + button) in the toolbar at the top of the window.**

   The Insert Objects popover opens.

3. **Tap the Tables tab.**

4. **Swipe from one page to another to find the table layout you like.**

   Though you can change any element in the table layout, start with one close to what you want to end up with.

   There are five pages of templates — each of the five pages has the same layouts but with different color schemes. This list describes them from the upper-left corner, as shown in Figure 3-28:

   • *Header row and a header column at the left:* This is one of the most common table layouts.

   • *Header row at the top:* This one works well for a list such as students in a class.

   • *No header row or header column:* Before choosing this blank spreadsheet, reconsider. Headers and titles for the tables make your spreadsheet more usable. You can add (or delete) them later and change them, but take a few moments to identify the table along with its rows and columns as soon as you create it.

   • *Header and footer rows and a label column:* This one works well for titles at the top and left and for sums or other calculations at the bottom.

   • *Check boxes in the left column:* This option makes a great list of things to do.

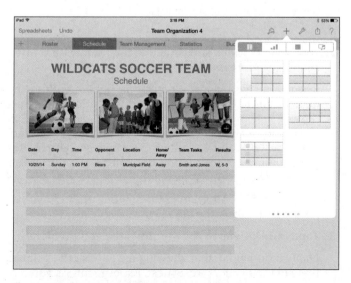

Figure 3-28: Create a new table.

5. **Tap the table layout you like.**

   It's placed on the sheet you have open.

Changing a table's look

Whether you recently created a new table or created it long ago, you might want to change its appearance. Here's how:

1. **Select the table you want to format (to select the table, tap inside the table bounds but outside the cells) and tap the Format button in the toolbar.**

   The Format popover opens, as shown in Figure 3-29. You can change the basic color scheme and layout by tapping the design you want to use.

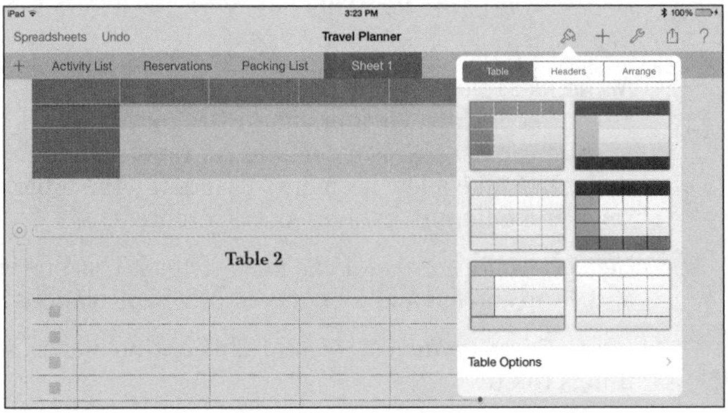

Figure 3-29: Use Format to reformat a table.

2. **Tap Table Options and fine-tune the table with a title, outline, and shading for alternating rows (see Figure 3-30).**

   Every table has a name. (It starts as Table #, with the next sequence number for all your tables.) The Table option simply controls whether the title is shown. Change the name to something meaningful that you can use in referencing it in formulas. Likewise, each table is a certain size. The Table Outline option determines whether a thin line is applied as the table's border. In the Alternating Rows option, every other row is shaded with a contrasting color.

   For large tables, alternating the shading of the rows can make it easier for users to follow the data.

3. **Tap Grid Options to show or hide the cell dividers.**

   Many people think that showing the lines in the main table and hiding them in the headers looks best. Experiment. As you tap to turn options on or off, the display changes so that you can see the effect.

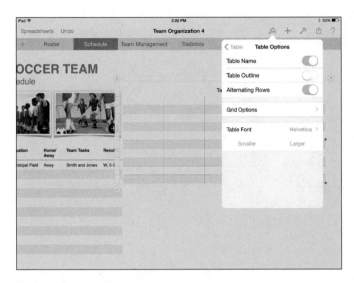

Figure 3-30: Set table options.

4. **Tap Table Options to return to that popover and then tap Table Font or the Smaller or Larger text size buttons to format the text in the table.**

5. **Tap Table in the popover and then tap the Headers tab to modify headers for rows and columns.**

   You can set the number of header rows or columns. (You have either zero footer rows or one footer row.) These elements are created using the existing color scheme.

   Freezing rows and columns keeps the header rows and columns on each page. As you scroll the data, the data itself moves, but the headers never scroll out of sight. This option is often the best one unless the table's content is self-explanatory.

6. **When you're finished, tap anywhere outside the popover to close it.**

Chapter 4: Presenting Keynote

In This Chapter

✏ **Considering important issues before you create a presentation**

✏ **Working with Keynote**

✏ **Animating a presentation with transitions and builds**

✏ **Preparing to present**

✏ **Playing a presentation**

Keynote, the first component created for iWork, was originally written for Steve Jobs to use in presentations at conferences and trade shows, including Apple's Worldwide Developers Conference and IDG Worldwide's Macworld conferences. After these "trials by fire," Keynote was joined by Pages to become the first two components of iWork.

Presentation software is a different type of product in comparison to the other two iWork applications. It typically consists of content presented by a speaker (whether in person or in absentia) to an audience.

With Keynote you have a few presentation possibilities. Small-group or one-on-one presentations using iPads are made possible because you can easily present short but impressive presentations almost anywhere. In addition, you can connect the iPad to a projector or TV via a VGA adapter or HDMI adapter, and present to larger groups from a smaller machine. On iPad, you can also use the video-mirroring feature AirPlay and Apple TV to put your iPad display on your TV screen. If you choose to display a presentation to a single person or small group on the iPad itself and you have a third-generation (or later) iPad, you'll find the Retina display a dazzling way to wow your audience.

In this chapter, you find out how to prepare and stage a presentation using Keynote. After adding text to slides and using animated transitions, you'll soon have a sophisticated and useful presentation.

Concepts to Consider before You Create a Presentation

A presentation is meant to be viewed. A person (usually you, but sometimes the viewer) controls the pace of the presentation. Follow these tips when building a presentation:

- **Weigh small-group versus large-group presentations.** You have options on iPad in addition to the traditional model of presenting to a group. This model offers an opportunity for one-on-one presentations that you can give in almost any setting, such as a sales call in a client's office. If you're working on a small-group or one-on-one presentation, the text and graphics don't have to reach across a ballroom to the viewer's eye, so size elements on the slide accordingly.

- **Make use of existing content.** Keynote for iOS helps you easily transfer presentations between your iPad and your Mac via iTunes. It also syncs its content via iCloud. Sometimes, that's the right thing to do. You can reuse the slides and rearrange them (possibly splitting a large presentation into many). Restructuring and rearranging an existing Keynote presentation that's going to be presented to a small group rather than to a larger audience can be a good idea.

- **Consider your canvas.** When working on a presentation, you're using a small canvas. A slide has much less space to hold information than does a piece of paper (or a spreadsheet page). No matter how large your audience, never overcrowd your slides.

- **Avoid too much variety.** Using too many graphical object styles (such as illustrations, photos, and line drawings) or too many font styles (such as bold and underline) can make for a choppy-looking presentation. Luckily, Keynote themes help you provide a cohesive and clean look for your presentation. Even though you may make small changes to text and add graphics, try to maintain an overall look and feel.

- **Add movement to slides.** You have options for movement (see the "Using Transitions and Builds" section, later in this chapter) that you don't have with printed documents. You can add effects to transition from one slide to another. Experiment with the Keynote transitions and use them to help people understand your progress in the presentation. For example, you can use a transition to introduce a new topic.

Getting Started with Keynote on iPad

You get started with the Keynote app the same way you do with Numbers or Pages: Create a new document or open an existing one. The basic windows are the same, but Keynote has some minor differences. This section is your guide.

Navigating the Keynote screen

When you open (or create) a Keynote document (which is always presented in landscape orientation), the basic Keynote screen appears, as shown in Figure 4-1. The name of the document is centered on the toolbar at the top. At the left, the Presentations button returns you to the Documents window, where thumbnail images represent the first page of each of your saved files.

Figure 4-1: The basic Keynote screen.

On the right side of the toolbar (refer to Figure 4-1) are the usual buttons. The buttons, from left to right, are described in this list:

- **Format:** As always, this button lets you modify the selected object or objects. Your choices depend on which type of object is selected. (If nothing on the slide is selected, the button is grayed out.)

- **Insert Objects:** Lets you insert media such as photos, tables, charts, and shapes, as shown in Figure 4-2.

Figure 4-2: Insert objects into slides.

✔ **Tools:** Shows you the popover you see in Figure 4-3. You can use various tools to add transitions and builds, find text in the presentation, work with Presenter Notes and presentation tools, work with Keynote's internal settings, set a password to protect the Keynote document, print, or go to Help for assistance using the application.

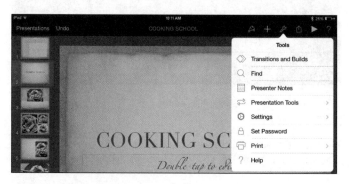

Figure 4-3: Use the Keynote tools.

✔ **Share:** Share by using iCloud; sending a copy via AirDrop, Message, or Mail; or opening the presentation in another app in a format such as PDF or PowerPoint.

✔ **Play:** Use this button to play your presentation on your iPad screen; if you have an external display adapter or Apple TV enabled in the Control Center, the slides appear on the display while the iPad screen shows the controls.

Tap Settings on the Tools menu to access the following tools (see Figure 4-4):

✔ **Check Spelling:** Turn on this option to have Keynote alert you to spelling issues as you type.

✔ **Slide Numbers:** This option lets you turn slide numbers on and off. Just as with pages of a Pages document, you should let the app handle the numbering so that the slide (or page) numbers are correct even if you move elements around, delete slides, or add slides.

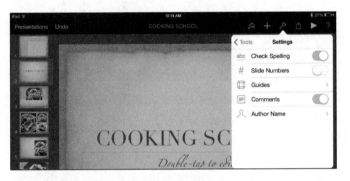

Figure 4-4: Use the advanced tools in Keynote.

✔ **Guides:** The Guides option on the Advanced menu makes a setting available to display guidelines that appear as you move an object toward the center of the slide or other objects, at the edges of the slide, or in 10-percent increments horizontally and vertically along the slide. You can choose which style of guide you want to appear.

✔ **Comments:** Tap this selection to turn Comments off or on. When you turn them on, small yellow sticky notes appear in a presentation wherever there's a comment.

✔ **Author Name:** Tap this option to enter a name for Keynote to use in any comments you insert (see Figure 4-5).

One difference between Keynote and the other iWork apps is that it always appears in landscape (horizontal) orientation; as you rotate the iPad, the image doesn't rotate because the slides are all designed to be shown horizontally. It isn't a Keynote limitation as much as a nod to the realities of projectors and other displays.

**Book IV
Chapter 4**

Presenting Keynote

Figure 4-5: Provide an author name for your presentation and comments.

On the left side of the screen, in the navigator, are thumbnail views of the slides in your presentation. To go to any slide in your presentation, just tap its thumbnail.

Creating your first Keynote slide and adding text

The templates in all iWork apps provide you with useful starting points. In Keynote, you're almost certain to find prebuilt slides you can use, and then it's only a matter of organizing your own data. To create a presentation, follow these steps:

1. **Tap Keynote on the Home screen.**

2. **On the Documents window, tap the plus sign (+) to create your new presentation from a template or from another presentation, as described in Chapter 1 of this minibook.**

3. **Tap the Standard or Wide tab, depending on the appropriate scale of slides for your presentation, and then tap a theme to use it on your new presentation.**

   A new presentation based on that theme opens.

4. **Double-tap a text placeholder on the slide to edit it.**

   The text placeholder opens for editing and the onscreen keyboard appears.

5. **Enter any text you want and then tap the slide itself or the Hide Keyboard key in the bottom-right corner of the onscreen keyboard to close the keyboard when you're done.**

Formatting text

With Keynote — perhaps more than with the other iWork apps — it's more fill-in-the-blanks than fuss around with formatting. You can get right to work. The font is determined by the theme you choose, but you can modify its size and add effects such as bold and italic. Here's how:

1. **Double-tap text to select the type you want to change.**

2. **Tap the Format button, and from the various tabs of the Format popover, choose a text style option (Title or Subtitle, for example), and tap any of the formatting choices (Bold, Italic, Underline, or Strikethrough) to apply them to the selected text.**

3. **Tap anywhere else on the screen to hide the Format popover.**

Adding a new slide

To add a new slide, tap the plus sign (+) in the lower-left corner (see Figure 4-6) and choose the style of slide from the gallery that appears. Want to add a bulleted list? Just choose a slide style with a bulleted list already on it.

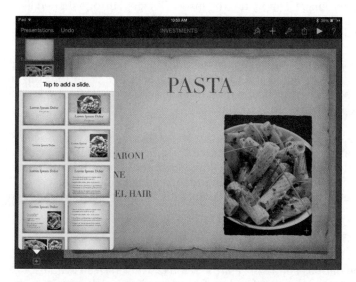

Book IV
Chapter 4

Presenting Keynote

Figure 4-6: Add a new slide.

You can choose the layout for the slide you're adding from the thumbnails shown in the popover. As Figure 4-7 demonstrates, the layouts for new slides vary from template to template.

Figure 4-7: Slides vary by template.

Adding media

Themes provide image placeholders for some slides. To change a place-holder image, simply tap the Insert Objects button (shaped like a plus sign) in the lower-right corner of the current image. A popover opens, showing the various albums in the Photos app. Locate an item and tap to insert it.

If you want to add an image outside a placeholder, make sure that no place-holder is selected and then tap the Insert Objects button. Tap any of the four tabs: Tables, Charts, Shapes, or Media. Choose the item you want to insert, and it appears on your slide.

You can now tap and move the object around with your finger. Keynote pro-vides the coordinates for precise positioning and also provides you with guidelines as you align the object with the center of the screen or the edge of another object via rulers on the top and left side of the screen. To resize an object, drag a corner handle until it's the size you want and then let it go.

Managing slides

Tap a slide in the navigator to select it. Tap the slide again to bring up the selec-tion buttons shown in Figure 4-8. You can now take an action; for example, tap Delete, and the slide is gone. (Remember, if you make a mistake, just tap Undo at the top left of the screen.) The Transition button brings up a selection of transition effects to apply (see the next section for more about this).

Figure 4-8: Delete a slide.

You can also use the contextual menu's selection buttons to cut, copy, and paste slides. After you have cut or copied a slide (tap it twice and then tap Cut or Copy), tap the slide after which you want it to appear, and then tap Paste. (You always paste the contents of the Clipboard after the slide you select.)

Another option appears in the selection buttons: Skip. It collapses the selected slide in the navigator into a thin line. When you play the presentation, the slide is skipped over. The thin line in the navigator is big enough for you to tap it to bring up its selection buttons: Tap the Don't Skip button to bring the slide back to full size and include it in the presentation.

Select the slide from the navigator. If you tap the slide itself, the selection buttons act on the selected object within the slide.

Using Transitions and Builds

You can enliven a presentation and make it a better communication tool by using Keynote animations to animate the transition as you move from one slide to another. You can also use animations to build a slide. *Building* refers to the process of applying an animation effect that controls how each bullet or another object within a single slide appears onscreen. The process of creating transitions and builds is much the same, and I cover them in this section.

A little animation is a good thing. Feel free to try all the options, but then decide which one — or maybe two — you want for your presentation. Too many animations are distracting and compete with the content you're presenting, unintentionally becoming the focus for the audience.

Working with transitions

Tap a slide and then tap Transition from the toolbar that appears (refer to Figure 4-8). Tap a transition effect, such as Clothesline. Tap the Options tab to make transition settings. To preview the transition, tap Play.

Transitions can work on slides as a whole or work on parts of slides; when they work on parts of slides, they're often called *builds*. Note that a transition consists of two parts:

- ✓ **Effects:** These are the visual effects that are displayed.

- ✓ **Options:** Options include the direction in which the animation moves as well as whether it starts in response to a tap or when a previous transition is finished. Options also include the duration of the transition or the amount of delay before it starts.

Though a transition may appear to happen *between* two slides, it happens *after* you tap a slide to go to the next one. The transition is attached to the first slide in the sequence of two adjacent slides.

Here's how to build a transition:

1. **In the navigator on the left side of the screen, press and hold the slide for which you want to build a transition and tap Transition in the tools that appear.**

   The list of transition effects appears in a popover, as shown in Figure 4-9. A number of transition effects are available; swipe up and down to see them all. (The list of transitions is controlled by the Effects button at the bottom-left corner of the popover.)

2. **When you find a transition effect that interests you, tap the name and then tap Play to select it and see a preview.**

3. **Tap the Options button in the bottom-right corner of the popover (see Figure 4-9) to set the effect options, as shown in Figure 4-10.**

4. **Set the duration and when the effect should start.**

   If you want the effect to start after a delay of a certain duration, use the Delay setting.

Figure 4-9: Choose an effect.

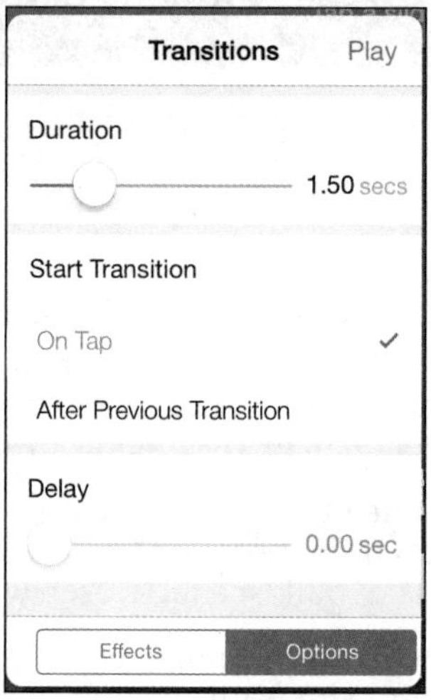

Figure 4-10: Set the duration and start.

5. Continue to change the effects and options until you're satisfied.

Options vary depending on the effect you've selected. You'll probably want to try the combinations by tapping the Play button in the upper-right side of the popover several times.

6. Tap Done in the upper-right corner of the screen to apply the transition and return to the navigator.

After you apply a transition effect to a slide, the Transitions button appears next to the slide whenever you select that slide in the navigator (see Figure 4-11). You can tap the Transition option to open the Transitions popover to edit the effect.

Figure 4-11: The effect is indicated on the slide in the navigator.

Working with builds

Builds are much like transitions except, rather than occurring between slides, they work when elements within a single slide are displayed and control how those elements appear on the slide. For example, you might build a bulleted list displaying one bullet at a time. Here's how to set a build:

1. **In the display portion of the screen, tap the object you want to build.**

   Each object can have two sets of builds: effects used when the object appears and an effect when it disappears.

2. **Tap to choose the type of build you want to apply — either a build-in or a build-out, as shown in Figure 4-12.**

3. **Select the build effect you want to use, as shown in Figure 4-13.**

   As with slide-to-slide transitions, as soon as you select an effect, tap the Play button and the effect previews for you.

4. **Tap the Options button at the bottom of the popover to set options, as shown in Figure 4-14.**

   You can begin the build when you tap or after the previous object appears. You can also set a delay in seconds before the next step in the build begins. Note that a number in a yellow circle is created on the object you're applying the build to; you can tap the number later to go back and change the effect or options.

Figure 4-12: Set builds for an object.

Figure 4-13: Select the build effect.

5. **Tap the Delivery button at the bottom of the popover to select whether the build happens all at one time or with the addition of each component.**

    Depending on what the selected object is, this step can build each item in a bulleted list separately or each wedge in a pie chart in sequence. (Delivery options are not available if they don't apply.)

Figure 4-14: Choose an option.

Managing multiple builds on a single slide

As you create builds, each one is numbered. The numbers appear in small, yellow circles as soon as you have chosen an effect. You can manage the sequence of these builds. To do so, follow these steps:

1. **Select the appropriate slide, tap the Tools button, and then tap Transitions and Builds.**

    You see the yellow circles around the numbers of the builds on that slide (see Figure 4-15).

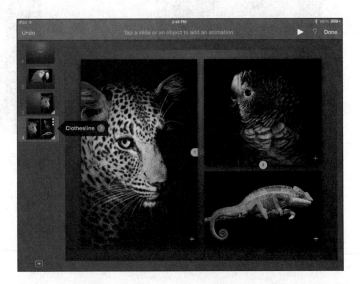

Figure 4-15: Numbers in yellow represent builds on an object on the slide.

2. **Tap any build to edit it using the techniques you used to create the build.**

   See the previous section.

   The yellow circle for a build is shown in Figure 4-16. You can see two transitions for the selected object. In this case, transition 2 is the build-in, and transition 1 is the build-out. (That happens to be the order they were created in, but they don't have to be in that order.) Thus, you can separately tap either transition number to change its settings or even delete it if you've gone transition-crazy.

Figure 4-16: Edit an existing build.

3. **To reorder the builds, tap a build number and then tap the Order button in the bottom-right corner of the popover (see Figure 4-17).**

   Drag builds to arrange them in the order you want them executed (see Figure 4-17). The numbers automatically change. Keynote picks up identifying text, such as the title, so that you can keep them straight.

4. **Tap the Play button in the top-right corner of the popover to test the builds.**

5. **When you're satisfied, tap Done.**

Figure 4-17: Set the build order.

Preparing to Present

After you've dotted every *i* and crossed every *t* in your presentation, added all the great ideas you've been storing in your brain, and tweaked the animations, your presentation is done. However, you still have to prepare to present your presentation.

Using a projector

The cable known as the Lightning to VGA Adapter ($49 from the Apple Store) connects your iPad to any VGA device, such as a projector. With it, you can use Keynote to give your presentation. There's also a $39 version for older iPad Dock connectors.

The Digital AV Adapter cable accessory is available for $49 for the Lightning version and $39 for the Dock version. You can use it to connect to devices such as HDTVs and many projectors that have HDMI connectors.

When you connect a projector (or any other type of display) to your iPad with the HDMI or VGA adapter, the Keynote app can sense that it has a second display. It uses this display when you start a slideshow in the Keynote app. (See the "Playing Your Presentation" section, later in this chapter.) While it's sending the presentation to the external display, it lets you control it from your iPad. Figure 4-18 shows what you see on the iPad as it plays a presentation on an external display.

Figure 4-18: Control a presentation on an external display.

The slides appear on the external display, but you can control the presentation using your iPad. On the left side of the screen, a navigator shows thumbnail images of your slides. Being able to see the next slide helps you transition to it elegantly without shuffling papers and distracting your audience and yourself. You can tap the arrows in the center of the iPad screen to move forward and backward among slides.

You can also mirror or stream what's on your iPad screen using an Apple TV connected to your HDTV's HDMI port.

Mirroring shows what's on your screen, such as a Keynote slide. You can zoom in and out and rotate your screen on your iPad, and that's what you'll see mirrored on your TV. As you move through your Keynote presentation on your iPad, the presentation on the TV changes right along with it.

Using nanopresentations

iPad is a game-changer in many ways. Its size (and therefore its portability) and its remarkably clear screen (especially on third-generation or later iPads with Retina display) are only two of its features that open great new opportunities. Keynote for iOS can help you take advantage of *nanopresentations* (presentations you make one-on-one or to a small group of people).

Whether you're used to presentations as a presenter or an audience member, you'll probably be pleasantly surprised at how well presentations to small groups can work. Perhaps the most interesting difference is the

**Book IV
Chapter 4**

Presenting Keynote

simplest one: Because the speaker can sit down and join the audience around a table, in a circle, or in a group of chairs, the speaker/audience or teacher/student paradigm of many presentations is immediately broken — and this can be a breath of fresh air. It certainly seems to make discussions and audience questions livelier.

For presentations to large (or even medium-size) groups, your iPad and a projector work well. But for a smaller group, a projector is often a bit of over-kill. You can use your iPad for a presentation to a few people seated around a table or — to be more iPad-like — seated or standing anywhere they want.

Think about the possibilities. If you're selling something that's not easy to carry around, a photo album on your iPad is a helpful way to show prospective customers what you're talking about. But a Keynote presentation — even a handful of slides shown one-on-one — can be much more effective and impressive than a photo album or brochure.

Great presentation pointers

Here are a few presentation pointers:

- **Avoid the dark.** If you're using a projector, use the least possible amount of room-darkening for your presentation. Make certain you can see your audience.

- **Use question-and-answer sections.** Use frequent, short Q&A sections in your presentations to involve your audience as much as possible.

- **Use a road map.** Let people know where they're going in your presentation and where they are at any moment. When you're reading a book, the heft of the unread pages gives you an idea of how far you've come. With a presentation, one slide after another can come out of the dark with no clue to how each one fits into the presentation.

- **Use big font sizes.** Have you ever looked closely at the presentations given by the late Steve Jobs and others at Apple? Consider using 60 points for the font size.

Whether you're creating your Keynote presentation on a Mac or an iPad or using iWork for iCloud with your browser, you're probably close to the screen. Your audience will be far away (even if you're just sitting across a table from them). In addition, you may have become accustomed to using font sizes that print well. Those font sizes are smaller than sizes that appear well on a screen. Go big.

- **Buy a dock or cover for your iPad that acts as a stand.** Several iPad cover options let you prop up your iPad display so that somebody sitting across from you can get a good view of its screen. Check out the Apple iPad accessories section in the online store, or search for *iPad covers* at a search engine and find one that appeals to you.

- **Check out the physical setup.** Leave time to check out your equipment and space before the presentation to make sure everything works properly.

Are you canvassing door to door for a politician or a cause? Again, a Keynote presentation of perhaps half a dozen slides can present the issue with pictures, text, and diagrams. You can even hand a printed version of the presentation out for people to ponder after you've gone. You can fill in the gaps and answer questions, but it's certainly more effective than knocking on a door and asking whether you can come in and set up a computer and a projector.

 One great advantage of nanopresentations is that instead of talking to a large group that's sitting in the dark, you're presenting to a few people sitting around a table or on a sofa with you. People generally don't have enough time to doze off or become distracted.

Playing Your Presentation

After you prepare all the elements in your presentation, little remains to do when you want to play it. Tap the Play button at the right side of the toolbar to begin playing. The transitions and builds happen automatically.

Tap to advance to the next slide. If you're using an external monitor, tap the Next and Previous buttons. (Refer to Figure 4-18.)

If your presentation contains hyperlinks, simply tap to open them in Safari on iPad. (Keynote automatically detects hyperlinks by the presence of an Internet schema, such as `http://`.)

The Keynote app has a built-in laser pointer, so to speak: Tap and hold the iPad screen, and a red pointer appears on the display along with a set of pointers that use other colors. (If you're using an external display or projector, it appears on that display as well.) You can then emphasize parts of the slide to the audience. One advantage of this method is that you can continue to face your audience while pointing out details on the slides. The alternative is to walk over to the slide, turn your back on the audience, and point — not an outstanding idea. (Audience members sometimes sneak out the moment you turn your back.)

Book V
Using iPad to Get Organized

In this book. . .

- ✔ Jot down quick messages with the Notes app
- ✔ Sync files to your computer
- ✔ Store and print documents online
- ✔ Keep your schedule with Calendar and Reminders
- ✔ Manage people through the Contacts app
- ✔ Talk to Siri

Chapter 1: Managing Files and Printing

In This Chapter

✔ Understanding how iPad stores files

✔ Sharing files by emailing, AirDrop, or through the cloud

✔ Setting up Home Sharing

✔ Printing wirelessly from iPad

*O*kay, I'm going to be very upfront about this: Apple has not used a traditional paradigm for moving files to and from your iPad or managing files on the device. In essence, this is partially a chapter about the following:

✔ What iPad does differently from how traditional file management is handled by OS interfaces such as OS X's Finder or Windows Explorer (Windows 7 and earlier) or File Explorer (Windows 8 and later). (For brevity, I just refer to this feature using the Windows 8 nomenclature, File Explorer, in the rest of this chapter.)

✔ How you can get things in and out of the device without a USB port or DVD drive.

One exciting way to back up content is *iCloud,* which allows you to store content online, and I discuss that in this chapter as well as in Book I, Chapter 5. In addition, you can share content with somebody in close proximity by using the AirDrop technology.

The other topic in this chapter is printing, and there are two options here: Use iPad's native printing capability with a compatible wireless printer or use a third-party printing app.

Finding Your Files

iPad stores files locally by app, or if you use iCloud, iPad automatically stores and shares files among iOS devices and with your Mac or PC. Here's how this works.

How iPad stores files

Though there's no Mac Finder or Windows File Explorer on iPad where you can view all your stored files in one place, apps on iPad do store files. Open the Photos app, for example, and you see lots of photos, each one contained in a separate file. The Music app contains audio files, Videos contains movie files, iBooks contains e-book files, and if you own Pages, it contains word-processing documents (as shown in Figure 1-1), and so on.

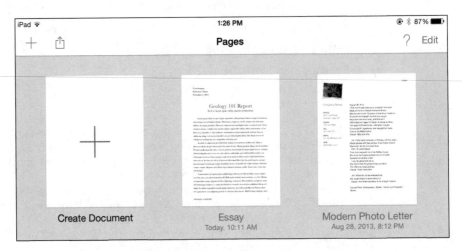

Figure 1-1: Documents stored by Pages.

Though there's no Windows File Explorer feature on iPad, when you connect iPad to a PC, you can use the Windows File Explorer feature on your computer to view the files stored on your iPad.

How did those files get there? You may have created them in an app on your iPad; you may have downloaded them from the Internet, as with music or video purchases from iTunes; or you may have synced them from your computer or had them pushed to all your iOS devices from iCloud, as with music files or photos. Perhaps you grabbed a document from a website or from an online storage service such as Dropbox.

Depending on the app you open, you may see a Documents button to display thumbnails of documents (refer to Figure 1-1); libraries of photos, as in Photos; albums of music or individual song files, as in Music (see Figure 1-2); or bookshelves or lists of e-books, as in iBooks. Each app offers a slightly different way to find whatever you've created on, downloaded to, or synced to your iPad.

Figure 1-2: Music shows you files by album, song, composer, artist, and more.

See Book II, Chapter 1, for information about buying and downloading content, and see Book I, Chapter 5, for information about syncing to your computer and buying apps. Book IV, Chapter 1, gives some details about moving files around for use with iWork products.

Going with iCloud

iCloud isn't so much a place as it is a storage service. If you choose to back up or share files by using iCloud, you can't go to a website and organize those files. Rather, they're automatically backed up from your devices, and new files created or downloaded to one device are automatically pushed to your other devices. In essence, this process is invisible to you. You still access these files by opening the associated app.

Note that iCloud Drive, which released just as this book was going to press, will eventually replace simple iCloud storage. iCloud Drive includes storage, calendar and contact syncing capabilities, email, location services, and app sharing.

Sharing Files

As mentioned in the previous section, iPad doesn't let you get at files the way your computer does with a series of folders and files. You open files in individual apps, such as Photos and Videos. You can't save files to a storage medium, such as a flash drive that you can remove and place in another computing device. Therefore, managing and sharing your files with other devices or other people works a bit differently on your iPad.

You have a few options for getting files out of your iPad:

- ✔ Sync them via iCloud, which automatically pushes them to other iOS devices.

- ✔ Email them.

- ✔ Sync via iTunes with a computer to share things like calendar events, contact records, music, or photos, which is covered in Book I, Chapter 5.

- ✔ Share them over a network.

- ✔ Share them with somebody in close proximity using AirDrop.

Also consider using wireless devices from manufacturers such as Kingston or Maxell for external storage.

Relying on good old email

You can use tools in individual applications to email files to yourself or others. Emailing files to yourself can be useful if you've worked on a document on your iPad and then want to get a copy of it on your computer. You can't exactly save a copy because (remember) no removable storage medium exists on your iPad, so you email the file and open and save the email attachment to your computer hard drive or other storage.

Here's an example of emailing from an app; in this case, Photos:

1. **Open Photos and locate a picture you want to email.**

2. **Tap the picture to open it and then tap the Share button to display the Sharing popover shown in Figure 1-3.**

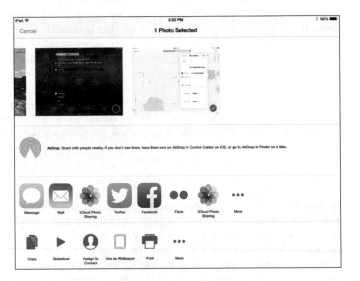

Figure 1-3: View the several options for sharing.

3. **Tap Mail.**

The email form shown in Figure 1-4 appears.

Cancel	Alpacas	Send
To:		
Cc/Bcc, From: pubstudio@icloud.com		Images: 1.6 MB
Subject: **Alpacas**		

Figure 1-4: The email form and onscreen keyboard appear together.

4. **Fill out the email form and tap Send to get the email on its way to yourself or somebody else.**

Getting up close with AirDrop

To use the AirDrop feature, you need to be near another AirDrop–enabled device (I'm talking within a few feet). Then, as in the previous email example, you can use the Share popover from within an app. (Refer to Figure 1-3.) Tap AirDrop in that popover, and any eligible devices in your vicinity appear. Tap the device you want to share with, and the content appears on the other device when the recipient accepts it.

That's it!

Going through the cloud

In addition to iCloud, there are other cloud-based options for sharing files. Apps such as Dropbox and FileFly, and Easy Wi-Fi Sharing and Viewing (a wireless file-sharing app) allow you to upload files to an online site and, using an app you download to your iPad, access and view those files. Some of these options provide more flexibility for managing your files than iCloud does.

Take a look at how this works with Dropbox, which is a good, free, file-sharing app that provides one of the easiest ways to get any and all files to and from your iPad to any and all other computers and devices.

Dropbox is a cloud-based service that allows you to store your files on its servers and access them on any device that's connected to the Internet. (Figure 1-5 shows you what the Dropbox interface looks like if you surf there using Safari.) It directly supports (in the form of dedicated software) OS X, Windows, Linux, Android, BlackBerry, and of course, iOS.

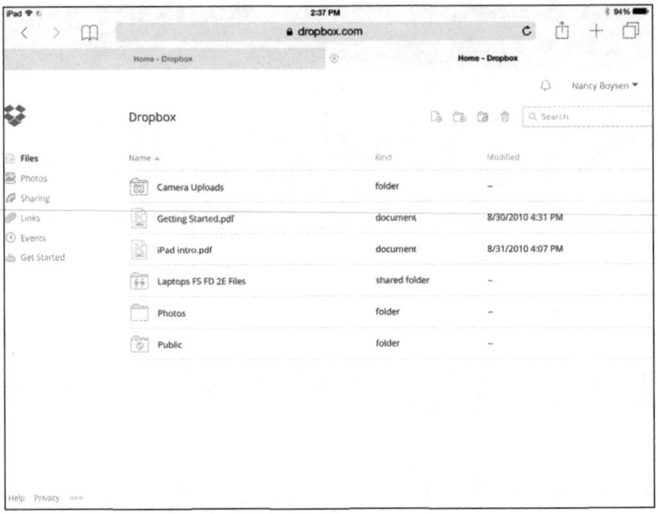

Figure 1-5: Accessing Dropbox through Safari.

When you're on a computer, Dropbox works like any other folder on your hard drive. When you open it with your browser, you have instant access to all your files. When you drop something into your folder, it's copied to the company's servers, and then pushed out to anywhere you've set up with your Dropbox account, including your iPad or others you're sharing folders with.

After you download the Dropbox app, you can open a file on iPad and print or view it, but not edit it, unless you choose the option of opening the document with an app you have on your iPad that would be a logical fit. Figure 1-6 shows the iCloud app for iPad with shared photos from iPad's Photos app available; this feature is offered to you the first time you log in to Dropbox from the Dropbox app on your iPad.

TIP

Dropbox folders can be selectively shared with other Dropbox users, making it a great tool for any sort of collaborative project.

Figure 1-6: Share your photos via Dropbox.

Setting Up Home Sharing

With Home Sharing, you can stream content from any Mac or PC to your iPad directly. You simply set up Home Sharing on your iPad, turn on the feature in iTunes on your computer, and you're good to go.

Here are the steps for setting up Home Sharing when you're connected to a Wi-Fi network:

1. **On your computer, open iTunes.**

2. **Click the File menu and choose Turn On Home Sharing.**

   The Home Sharing dialog appears.

3. **Enter your Apple ID and password and then click Create Home Share.**

   A message appears, telling you to use the same account you just signed in to on devices you want to share with.

4. **Click Done.**

5. **On your iPad, tap Settings and then tap Music.**

6. **In the Home Sharing section, shown in Figure 1-7, enter your Apple ID for the same account you used in iTunes on your computer and, beneath the ID, enter a password.**

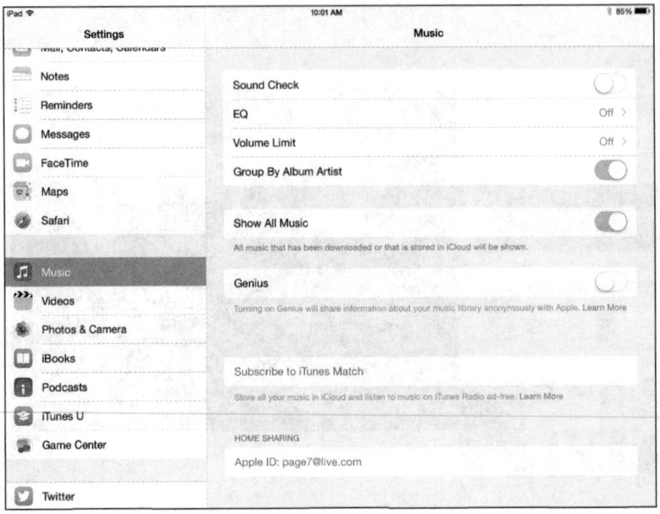

Figure 1-7: The Home Sharing settings for Music.

7. **Tap the Home button and then tap Music.**

   Music opens.

8. **Tap Songs and then tap a shared song to download it from the cloud.**

   To view shared videos, follow the same procedure for Videos settings and the Videos app.

Printing from iPad

If you need to print from your iPad, you can use its built-in wireless printing capability or a third-party app, which is likely to give you a few more printing controls.

Native printing capability is part of iPad's bag of tricks. This capability requires a wireless-enabled printer that supports the AirPrint protocol. All the major printer manufacturers offer AirPrint–compatible printers, including HP, Epson, Canon, Brother, and Lexmark, so check to see whether your model has such support.

The only control you have over your printing is to set the number of copies to be printed; with some printers, you can also specify a page range and double-sided printing. You can also use an app such as Printopia or AirPrint Activator 2 on your computer to print through that computer from iPad to shared and networked printers, whether wireless or wired.

You can print photos, notes, email messages, web pages, and documents from iWork apps such as Pages. Tap the Share button (available in most apps) to display a popover including the Print command. When you tap that command, you see the Printer Options dialog. Follow these steps to print:

1. **In the Printer Options dialog, shown in Figure 1-8 (the screen you see if you haven't yet used this feature with your printer), tap Select Printer.**

   iPad searches for any available wireless printers.

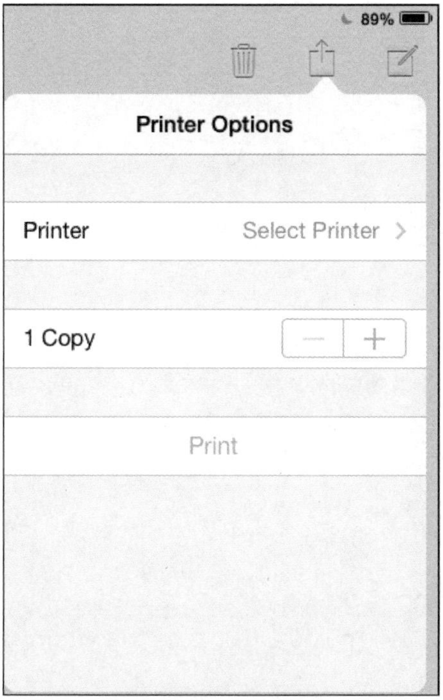

Figure 1-8: Choose your printer and the number of copies and print away!

2. **Tap your printer to select it.**

3. **Tap Printer Options to return to the Printer Options dialog and tap the + or – button in the Copies field to adjust the number of copies.**

4. **Tap Print.**

   Your document or photo prints.

When you have print jobs going to your printer, you can access a Print Summary popover that shows the name of the document that's printing, the printer it's printing to, the number of copies, when the print job started, and its status (for example, Printing 1 of 3). You access this summary by double-tapping the Home button to open the App Switcher. There, scroll to the left in the list of apps to locate the Print Center app. Tap it, and the summary displays.

Chapter 2: Making Notes

In This Chapter

> ✔ **Opening a blank note and entering text**
>
> ✔ **Creating a new note**
>
> ✔ **Finding, sharing, and deleting a note**
>
> ✔ **Displaying the Notes List**
>
> ✔ **Printing a note**

*N*otes is a preinstalled app that you can use to do everything from jotting down notes at meetings to maintaining to-do lists. It isn't a robust word processor like Apple Pages or Microsoft Word by any means, but for taking notes on the fly or dictating a poem using the Dictation feature (not available on the original iPad or iPad 2) while you sit and sip a cup of tea on your deck, it's a useful option.

In this chapter, you discover how to enter and edit text in Notes and manage notes by navigating among them, searching for content, sharing, deleting, and printing them.

Making Notes

Notes are pretty simple to create — kind of like grabbing a sticky notepad, jotting down your thoughts, pulling off the note and sticking it somewhere, and starting to write the next one. You can even use Siri to create a note and the Dictation feature to speak your note contents. You can use the included editing tools to select, cut, copy, and paste. Notes are saved for you in a list of notes so that you can easily find the one you need (covered in the "Finding Notes" section, later in this chapter), and they can be synced across iOS devices and your Mac.

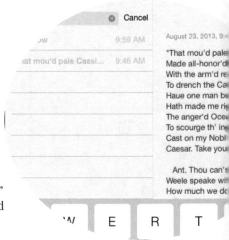

Opening a blank note and entering text

If you have no stored notes, Notes opens with a new, blank note displayed. (If you have used Notes before, it opens to the last note you worked on. If that's the case, tap the New Note button in the top-right corner to create a new, blank note.)

Here are the steps to get going with Notes:

1. **Tap the Notes app icon on the Home screen.**

   Depending on how you have your iPad oriented, you see the screen shown in Figure 2-1 (portrait) or Figure 2-2 (landscape).

2. **Tap the blank page.**

   The onscreen keyboard, shown in Figure 2-3, appears.

3. **Tap keys on the keyboard to enter text.**

   If you're using a third-generation (or later) iPad or an iPad mini, tap the Dictation key — see Figure 2-3 — and speak your text using iPad's speech recognition feature).

   For more about Dictation, see Book I, Chapter 3.

Figure 2-1: This clean page format avoids clutter.

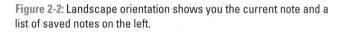

Figure 2-2: Landscape orientation shows you the current note and a list of saved notes on the left.

Figure 2-3: Use the onscreen keyboard or your Keyboard Dock or Bluetooth keyboard, if you have one.

Here are some tips for working with the virtual keyboard:

- **Enter numbers or symbols.** Tap the keys labeled .?123 on either side of the keyboard. The numeric keyboard, shown in Figure 2-4, appears. When you want to return to the regular keyboard, tap either of the keys labeled ABC.

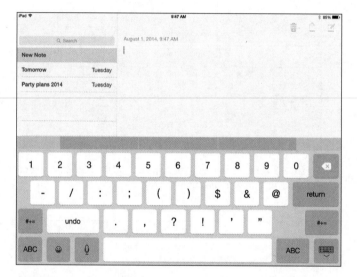

Figure 2-4: Use this alternative keyboard for numbers and many common symbols.

- **Capitalize a letter.** Tap the Shift key and then tap the letter.

  If you turn on the Enable Caps Lock feature in Settings, you can also turn on Caps Lock by double-tapping the Shift key; tap the Shift key once to turn off the feature.

- **Start a new paragraph or the next item in a list.** Tap the Return key.

- **Edit text.** Tap to the right of the text you want to edit and tap the Delete key to delete text to the left of the cursor or enter new text.

- **Change the default font.** Go to the Notes Settings.

Tap either of the keys labeled #+= to access more symbols, such as the percentage sign, the euro symbol, and additional bracket styles. Tapping and holding some of these keys displays alternative characters. This also works on some keys on the alphabetic and numeric keyboards. (For example, tapping and holding N gives you foreign language options such as the Spanish *ñ*, and pressing and holding the exclamation key on the numeric keyboard offers the upside-down exclamation point used in some languages.)

No need to save a note — it's automatically kept until you delete it.

Creating a new note

If you have stored notes, when you open Notes, the most recently used note displays. If you then want to create a new note, it's a simple procedure. To create a new note, tap the New Note button (the one that looks like a page with a pen on it) in the top-right corner. The current note is saved and a new, blank note appears (refer to Figures 2-1 and 2-2). Enter and edit text as described in the preceding section.

If your iPad is in portrait orientation and you want to display the list of saved notes beside the current note, tap the Notes button to view a list of notes.

Using copy and paste

Let's face it, most of us don't nail what we write on our first draft. That's why, after you enter content into a note, you may want to modify it. The Notes app includes essential editing tools you're familiar with from using word processors: Select, Copy, and Paste. You can use these to duplicate content or to cut and paste it from one part of a note to another.

To use the Copy and Paste tools, follow these steps:

1. **With a note displayed, press and hold your finger on a word.**

   The selection tools, shown in Figure 2-5, appears.

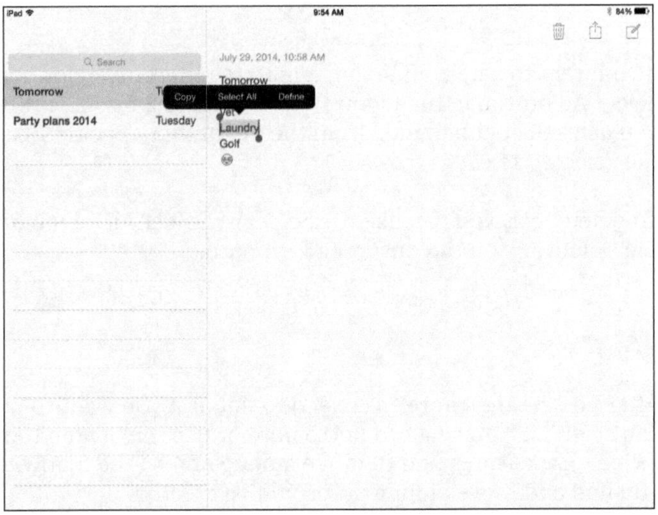

Figure 2-5: This menu provides selection and pasting tools.

2. **Tap the Copy button.**

3. **Press and hold your finger in the document where you want to place the copied text.**

4. **On the menu that appears (see Figure 2-6), tap the Paste button.**

   The copied text appears.

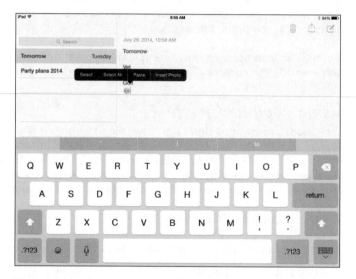

Figure 2-6: Use the press-and-hold method again to display the editing menu.

If you want to select all text in a note to either delete or copy it, tap the Select All button in the menu (refer to Figure 2-5). All text is selected, and you can select commands from the menu that appears to cut, copy, or paste the selected text.

To delete text, you can use the Select or Select All command and then press the Delete key on the onscreen keyboard.

Finding Notes

After you create a note, you need to find it if you want to view or edit it. You can scan the Notes List to find a note or use the Search tool. You can also swipe on the Notes pad to move among notes. The following sections help you find and move among notes you've created.

Displaying the Notes List

The Notes List contains all your notes listed chronologically by the last date/ time you modified the note. This list isn't available in portrait orientation, but it's the list you need in order to see the notes you have stored. If you're using landscape orientation, a list of notes appears by default on the left side of the screen.

If you're using portrait orientation, you can display this list in portrait orientation by tapping the Notes button in the top-left corner of the screen; the Notes List appears, as shown in Figure 2-7. Tap any note in the list to display it.

The Notes List is also the Accounts List if you've enabled notes syncing in iCloud or other sharing sites in Settings.

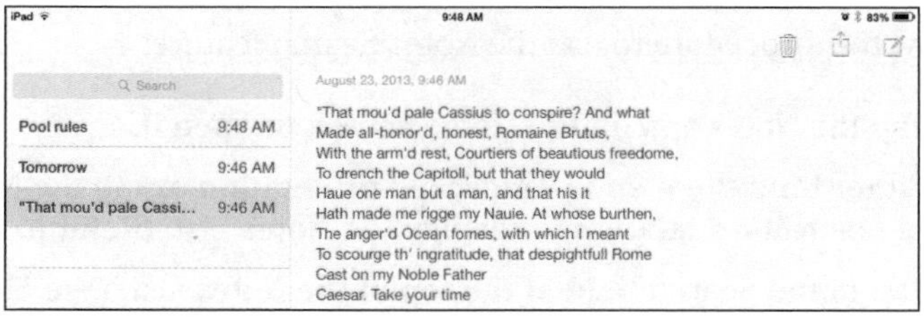

Figure 2-7: Tap the Notes button to display a list of saved notes.

Moving among notes

If you want to look for a note based on how long ago you created it, you should know that notes are stored with the most recently created or modified notes at the top of the Notes List. Older notes fall toward the bottom of the list. The date and/or time you last modified a note also appears in the Notes List to help you out.

It's easy to move among notes you've created:

1. **Tap the Notes app on the Home screen to open it.**

2. **With the Notes List displayed, tap a note to open it.**

   You can display the Notes List by either turning iPad to landscape orientation or tapping the Notes button in portrait orientation; see the preceding section for more on viewing the Notes List.

Notes isn't a file-management pro; it allows you to enter multiple notes with the same title, which can cause confusion. Be advised, and name your notes uniquely!

Remember that Notes names your note using the first line of text. If you want to rename a note, first display the note, tap at the end of the first line of text, and then tap the Delete key on your onscreen keyboard to delete the old title. Enter a new title; it's reflected as the name of your note in the Notes List.

Searching Notes

If you're not sure which note contains that very important item, you can search to locate a note that contains certain text. The Search feature lists only notes that contain your search criteria; however, it highlights only the first instance of the word or words that you enter within a note.

The Spotlight Search feature in iPad also locates notes that match any search term you enter there, along with many other types of content. See Book I, Chapter 2, for more about the Search feature.

Follow this procedure to use the Notes Search feature:

1. **Tap the Notes app on the Home screen to open it.**

2. **Either hold the iPad in landscape orientation or tap the Notes button in portrait orientation to display the Notes List. (Refer to Figure 2-7.)**

3. **Tap in the Search field at the top of the Notes List. (See Figure 2-8.)**

   The onscreen keyboard appears.

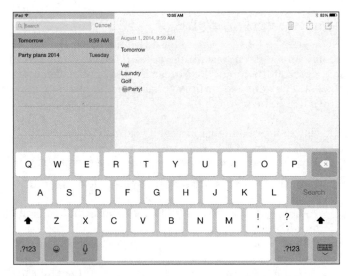

Figure 2-8: Enter search terms using the onscreen keyboard or Keyboard Dock.

4. **Begin to enter the search term.**

   All notes that contain matching words appear on the list, as shown in Figure 2-9.

Figure 2-9: The Search feature narrows the results by words that match your entry.

5. **Tap a note to display it and then locate the instance of the matching word, which is highlighted with a yellow background. Tap the item again to highlight subsequent occurrences of the search term.**

Sharing a Note

Today, it's all about sharing content. If you want to share what you wrote with a friend or colleague, or even access your note on your main computer to move it over into a word-processing program and flesh it out, you can easily share the contents of a note by following these steps:

1. **With a note displayed, tap the Share button on the top of the screen.**

2. **In the pop-up menu that appears, tap Mail.**

   You can also share using AirDrop by tapping that button and then tapping on the nearby device you want to send the note to at this point.

3. **In the email form that appears (see Figure 2-10), type one or more email addresses in the appropriate fields.**

   At least one email address must appear in the To, Cc, or Bcc field.

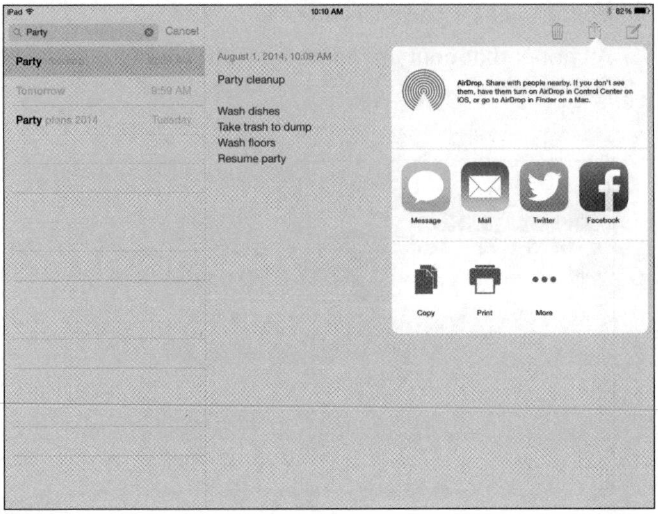

Figure 2-10: Enter addressees; use Bcc if you don't want that recipient to be visible to others.

4. **If you need to make changes to the subject or message, tap in either area and make the changes by using either the onscreen keyboard or the Dictation key (on a third-generation or later iPad) to speak your changes.**

5. **Tap the Send button.**

   Your email is sent.

If you want to print a note in Step 2, tap Print rather than Mail. Complete the Printer Options dialog by designating an AirPrint–enabled wireless printer (or a shared printer on a network that you can access using AirPrint) and indicating how many copies to print; then tap Print.

To cancel an email message and return to Notes without sending it, tap the Cancel button in the email form and then tap Delete Draft on the menu that appears. To leave a message but save a draft so that you can finish and send it later, tap Cancel and then tap Save Draft. The next time you tap the Mail button with the same note displayed in Notes, your draft appears.

Deleting Notes

Over time, notes can accumulate, making it harder to find the note you need in the long list that displays. There's no sense in letting your Notes List get cluttered or leaving old content around to confuse you. When you're done with a note, delete it. Follow these steps:

1. **Tap the Notes app on the Home screen to open it.**

2. **With the iPad in landscape orientation, tap a note in the Notes List to open it.**

3. **Tap the Trash Can icon at the top of the screen, as shown in Figure 2-11.**

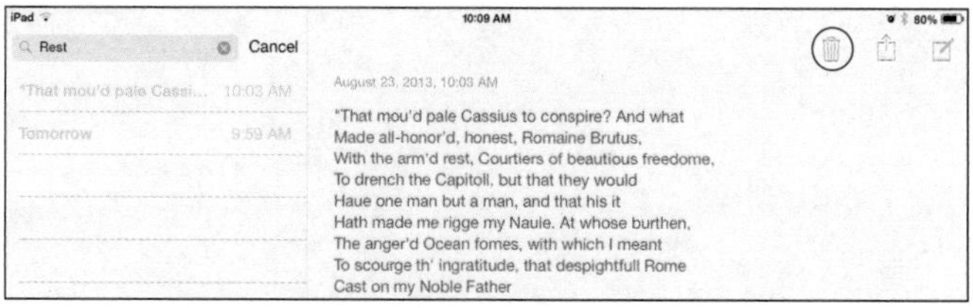

Figure 2-11: With a note displayed, tap the Trash Can button to delete it.

4. **Tap the Delete Note button that appears. (See Figure 2-12.)**

The note is deleted.

Figure 2-12: Go ahead; delete whatever you
don't need with a tap of this button.

Notes is a nice little app, but it's limited. It offers very few formatting tools and only one font for your text. You can't paste pictures into it. (Actually, you can, but what appears is the filename, not the image.) So if you've made some notes and want to graduate to building a more robust document in a word processor, you have a couple of options. One way is to use the Pages word-processor application for iPad, which comes with newer iPads, and copy your note (using the Copy and Paste feature discussed earlier in this chapter). Alternatively, you can send the note to yourself in an email. Open the email and copy and paste the text into a full-fledged word processor, and you're good to go.

If you want to move beyond Notes and use a note-taking app that lets you write with a stylus, check out PaperDesk for iPad ($3.99) or Penultimate (free) in the App Store. Both make drawing and writing handwritten notes easy and fun. Pogo Sketch and Pogo Stylus are two good stylus tools to check out (at www.tenonedesign.com).

Chapter 3: Keeping On Schedule with the Calendar and Clock Apps

In This Chapter

✓ Viewing your calendar

✓ Adding and repeating calendar events

✓ Working with, searching, and sharing calendars

✓ Deleting events

✓ Using the Clock app

Most people have busy lives full of activities that aren't always easy to keep straight. You may need a way to keep on top of all those work-related and personal activities and appointments. The Calendar app on the iPad is a simple, elegant, electronic daybook that helps you do just that.

In addition to being able to enter events and view them by the day, week, month, or year, you can set up Calendar to provide alerts to remind you of your obligations, and you can search for events by keyword. You can also set up repeating events, such as the weekly staff meeting, a regular social get-together, or monthly flea treatments for your cat. By taking advantage of the new Family Sharing feature in iOS 8, you can create a family calendar that everybody in your family can add events to.

Another useful preinstalled app is Clock. Though simple to use, Clock helps you view the time in multiple locations, set alarms, and use a timer and stopwatch.

In this chapter, I show you how to master simple procedures for getting around in your calendar, creating a family calendar, entering and editing events, setting up alerts, and searching. You also discover the simple ins and outs of using Clock.

Taking a Look at Your Calendar

You've probably used calendar apps in a slew of settings — in your email client, on your cellphone, and even in robust contact-management programs. The Calendar app on iPad is more robust than some and less robust than others, but it's quite a nicely designed and simple-to-use program that saves you the cost of buying one more app, plus it syncs with your computer and iCloud, Google, Exchange, or Office 365 calendar. Calendar offers several ways to view your schedule, so the first step in mastering Calendar is to understand how to navigate those various views.

You get started by tapping the Calendar app icon on the Home screen to open it. Depending on what you last had open, you may see today's calendar or the weekly, monthly, or yearly calendar or an open event.

Next, tap one of the top buttons described here to change the view:

✔ **Today:** This view, shown in landscape orientation with Search open in Figure 3-1, displays your daily appointments and a small monthly calendar on the left page, along with an hourly breakdown of the day on the right page. In portrait orientation, the two pages are narrower. Tap an event on this list to view more details.

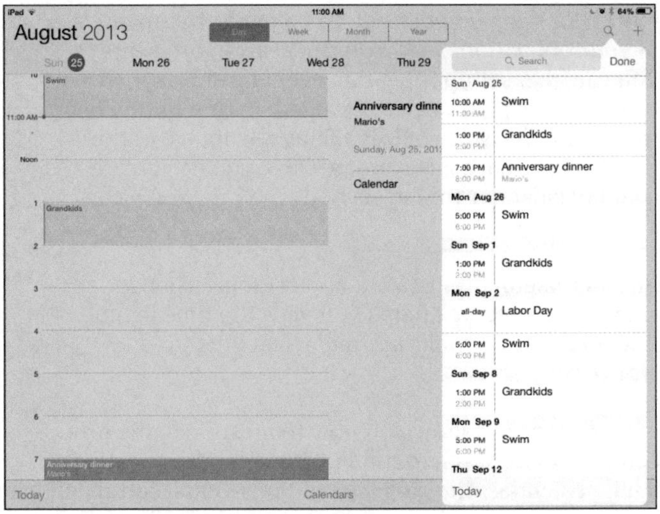

Figure 3-1: Calendar in landscape orientation.

✔ **Week:** Use Week view to see all your events for the current week, as shown in Figure 3-2. In this view, appointments appear in their scheduled time slots on the grid.

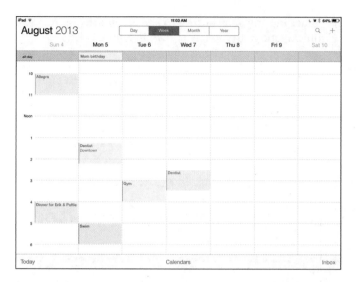

**Book V
Chapter 3**

Keeping On
Schedule with the
Calendar and
Clock Apps

Figure 3-2: Tap another week in the row beneath the weekly calendar to jump there.

✔ **Month:** See one month at a time and switch among months in Month view (see Figure 3-3). You see the name and timing of each event. In this view, days that have scheduled events display the color of the calendar associated with the event.

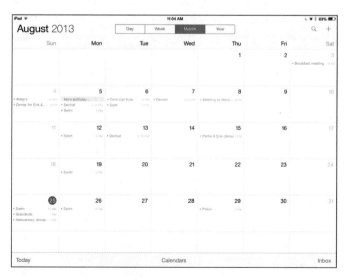

Figure 3-3: Tap a month name along the bottom of the screen to jump to another month.

✔ **Year:** Tap the Year button to see all months in the year so that you can quickly move to one, as shown in Figure 3-4.

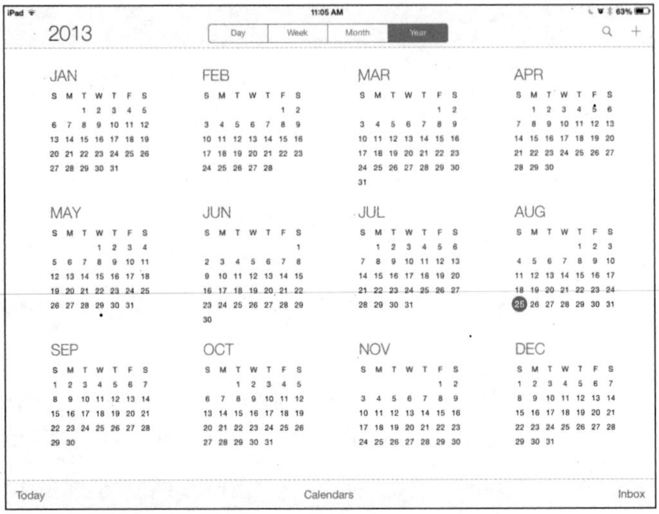

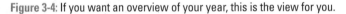

Figure 3-4: If you want an overview of your year, this is the view for you.

✔ **List:** Tap the Search button to see the List view, which displays your daily calendar with a list of all commitments for the month in a list to the right side of the page, as shown in Figure 3-5.

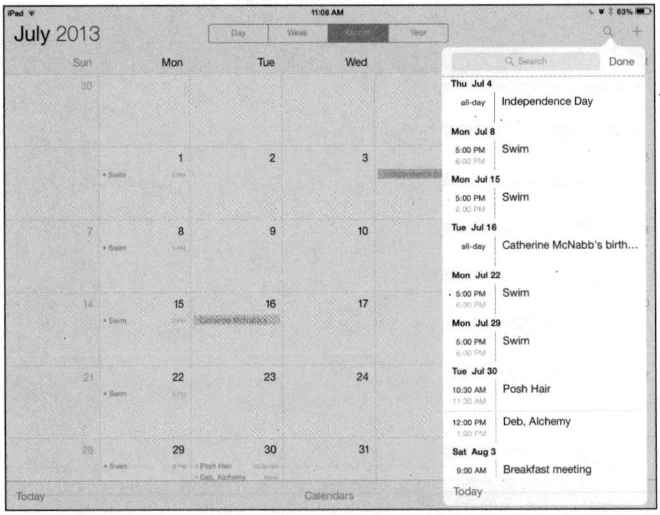

Figure 3-5: List view shows today and all the days containing events in the month ahead.

**Book V
Chapter 3**

Keeping On
Schedule with the
Calendar and
Clock Apps

To move from one day, week, month, or year to another, use your finger to scroll up or down the list.

To jump back to today, tap the Today button in the bottom-left corner of Calendar. And now you know the basics about views in Calendar!

The portrait and landscape orientations of your iPad with the Calendar app give you a slightly different display. Play around with turning your iPad in different directions to see which one you prefer to work in.

Note that you can tap text that mentions a reservation or phone number in an email to add an event to Calendar.

If you're looking for a more robust scheduling app, consider buying Pocket Informant HD for $12.99. This app is easy to use and has helpful scheduling tools for your tasks. You can also sync information that you save in the app by using Google Calendar. Also, if you want to use a calendar program for business, check out Shifty ($13.99), a work-shift management app that has tools that can be quite useful to managers and supervisors.

Adding Calendar Events

Events in your life might range from business meetings to karaoke dates, but whatever the nature of your appointments, Calendar can help you keep them all straight. You can enter single events or repeating events and include alerts to remind you that they're coming up.

Adding one event at a time

If you've used other calendar programs, you know that adding events is usually a simple procedure. You can easily add events to iPad's Calendar app, but if you haven't used a touchscreen computer or smartphone, it's worth a walk-through.

Follow these steps to add an event to your calendar:

1. **With Calendar open in any view, tap the Add button to add an event.**

   The New Event dialog, shown in Figure 3-6, appears.

2. **Enter a title for the event and, if you want, a location.**

3. **Tap the All-day button for an all-day event, or tap the Starts or Ends field.**

   The tools for setting a date and time, as shown in Figure 3-7, displays.

Figure 3-6: Add your event details in this dialog.

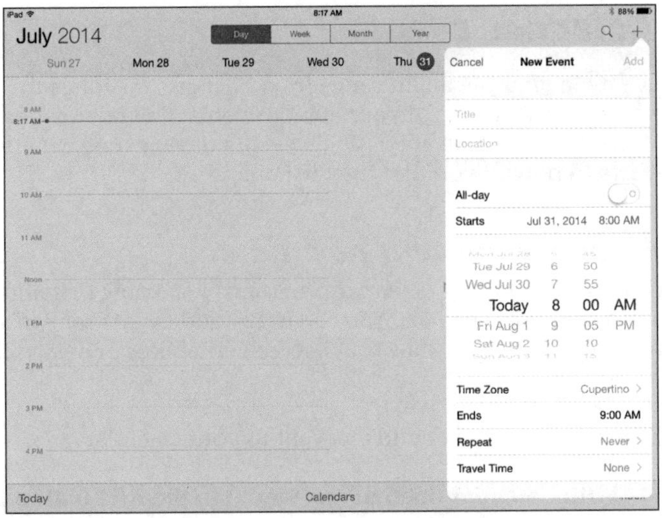

Figure 3-7: Use this cool slot machine–like interface to set up event timing details.

4. **Place your finger on the date, hour, minute, or AM/PM column, and swipe your finger to scroll up or down.**

5. **(Optional) To add notes, use your finger to scroll down in the New Event dialog; then tap in the Notes field.**

6. **After all items are set correctly, tap Add.**

Book V
Chapter 3

Keeping On
Schedule with the
Calendar and
Clock Apps

Note that you can edit any event at any time by simply tapping it in any view of your calendar. The Edit dialog appears, offering the same settings as the Add Event dialog. (Refer to Figure 3-6.) Just tap the Done button in this dialog to save your changes or Cancel to return to your calendar without saving any changes.

Adding events with Siri

Siri, the personal assistant feature, offers a hands-free way to schedule events. There are several ways to schedule an event with Siri because the feature is pretty flexible. For example, you can say, "Create event," and then Siri asks you first for a date and then for a time. Or you can say, "I have a meeting with John on April 1st," and Siri might respond by saying, "I don't find a meeting with John on April 1st; shall I create it?" Then you can say, "Yes" to have Siri create it, asking you for more details like the time and place.

Follow these steps to have Siri schedule an event for you:

1. **Press and hold the Home button.**

2. **Say a command such as "Create meeting October 3rd at 2:30 p.m."**

3. **When Siri asks you whether you are ready to schedule the event, say "Yes."**

You can also use Siri to delete events, change details about an event, or remind you about an event. Siri recognizes holidays so that you can say, "Schedule a family dinner on Christmas," and Siri will know what you mean. Play around with Siri; it's a lot of fun!

Creating repeating events

Many events in your life probably happen regularly: that Tuesday evening book club, the monthly sales meeting, or your company's yearly audit, for example. You can use the Repeating Events feature of the Calendar app to set repeating events.

Follow these steps to create a repeating event:

1. **With any view displayed in the Calendar app, tap the Add button to add an event.**

    The Add Event dialog (refer to Figure 3-6) appears.

2. **Enter a title and location for the event and set the start and end dates and times (see the preceding section).**

3. **Scroll down the page if necessary and tap the Repeat field.**

    The Repeat dialog, shown in Figure 3-8, appears.

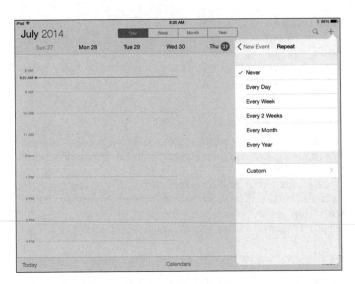

Figure 3-8: You have to use preset intervals, but you can choose from among several.

4. **Tap a preset time interval: Every Day, Week, 2 Weeks, Month, or Year.**

   If you want, you can tap Custom and enter a Frequency and Day. For example, you can create an event to happen monthly, but only every three months, or daily every three days.

5. **Tap New Event to close the Repeat dialog, and then tap Add.**

   You return to the Calendar.

 If you have an iCloud, Exchange, or Gmail account, your iPad recognizes and supports all calendars you've compiled there as well as those you've synced and the iPad calendar. Be sure to set the Calendar switch to on in the Settings app's Mail, Contacts, Calendars pane for any accounts that you want Calendar to access.

Adding alerts

Once upon a time, helpful assistants placed printed paper schedules of the day's activities in front of their bosses to remind them of scheduled commitments. Today, I'm not sure anybody but the highest-paid CEOs get this type of service. Instead, most people set up alerts in calendar programs to remind them where to be, and when.

Luckily, in the iPad Calendar app, you can easily set up alerts by following these steps:

1. **Tap the Settings icon on the Home screen and then tap Sounds.**

Book V
Chapter 3

Keeping On
Schedule with the
Calendar and
Clock Apps

2. **Scroll down and tap Calendar Alerts and then tap any alert tone, which causes iPad to play the tone for you.**

3. **After you choose a tone, tap Sounds to return to the Sounds settings.**

4. **Press the Home button and then tap Calendar.**

5. **Create an event in your calendar or open an existing one for editing (see the preceding sections).**

6. **In the Add Event dialog or Edit dialog for an existing event (refer to Figure 3-6), tap the Alert field.**

   The New Alert dialog appears, as shown in Figure 3-9. Note that if you want two alerts — say, one per day before and one hour before — you can repeat this procedure using Second Alert instead. The Second Alert field appears directly below the Alert field in the Add Event dialog after you set an alert.

7. **Tap any preset interval, from 5 Minutes Before to 2 Days Before or at the time of an event.**

8. **Tap New Event or Edit Event to return to the New Event or Edit Event dialog.**

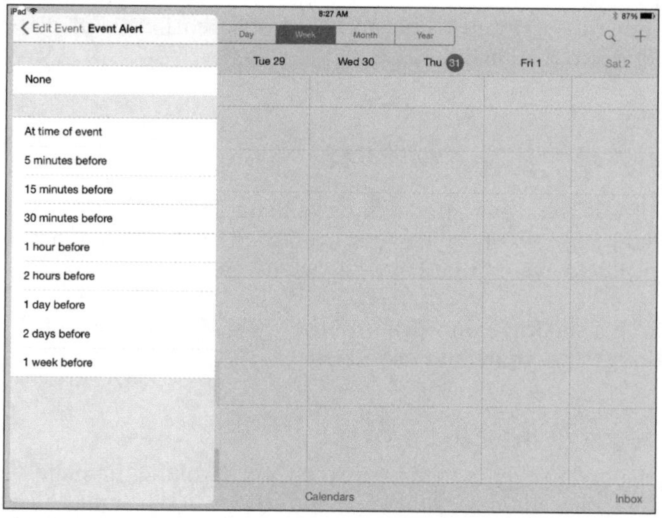

Figure 3-9: Use these preset intervals to set up alerts.

9. **Tap Add (for a new event) or Done (if you're done editing an existing event) to save the alert.**

10. **Tap the Day button to display the date of your event in Day view and then tap the event.**

Note that the alert and time frame are listed under the event in that view, as shown in Figure 3-10.

Swim	Edit
Monday, Jul 8, 2013	5 PM to 6 PM
Calendar	• Home >
Alert	1 hour before >

Today   Calendars

Figure 3-10: An alert is noted along with the appointment in your calendar.

If you're on the road and change time zones, iPad may not recognize the local time, which can cause your alerts to become useless. To avoid this problem, you can adjust the time of your iPad manually by using the Date & Time feature in the General category in Settings.

To view any invitation or event that you accepted, which placed an event on your calendar, tap Inbox, and a list of invitations is displayed. Tap Done to return to the calendar.

Working with Your Events

After you have entered some events in Calendar, you can use features to search for events, sync your events with other calendars on other devices, or delete events that have been canceled.

In this section, you work with the various events on your calendar to keep things up-to-date and organized.

Searching calendars

Displaying events by day or week and scrolling the pages is one way to look for appointments, but if you need to view a particular event and can't remember its time frame, you can use the Calendar Search feature to find it.

Don't forget that you can also search for events in your calendar by speaking a command to Siri or searching with the Spotlight Search feature.

Follow these steps to search for events in Calendar:

1. **With Calendar open in any view, tap the Search field (refer to Figure 3-5) in the top-right corner.**

The onscreen keyboard appears.

**Book V
Chapter 3**

Keeping On
Schedule with the
Calendar and
Clock Apps

2. **Tap in the Search field and type a word or words to search by and then tap the Search key on the onscreen keyboard.**

   As you type, the Results dialog appears, as shown in Figure 3-11.

   Tap any result to display it in the view you were in when you started the search.

   The event details are displayed.

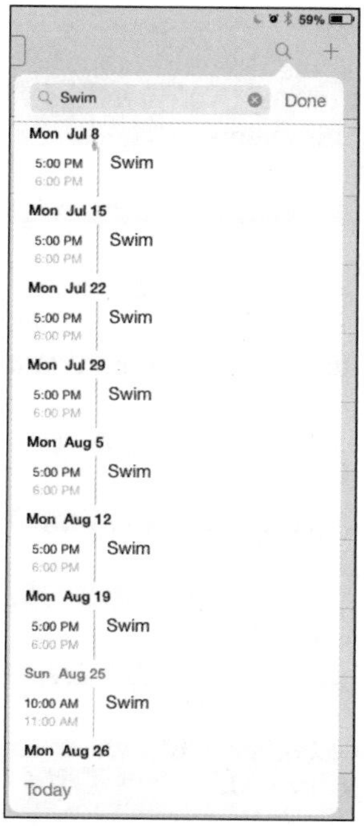

Figure 3-11: Every instance of an event that includes your search term displays.

Working with multiple calendars

You can choose a calendar — for example, Business, Personal, Parties, Classes, and Volunteering — for every event. If you're synchronizing your calendars with your Mac or PC or by using iCloud, Google Calendar, Microsoft Exchange, or AOL, each source can have its own calendar. You can also sync a local calendar on your Mac or Windows PC via iTunes. On your iPad, tap Calendars at the bottom of the screen in the Calendar app. Every calendar is listed with a dot of a different color.

You can choose calendars on this list to display the events from several calendars at one time, including calendars you sync with from your PC or Mac, only your PC calendar, only your Mac calendar, cloud-based calendars, or only your iPad calendar. With the Calendar app open, tap the Calendars button, and in the Calendars dialog, tap to select or deselect the calendars you want to display: All from My *<Account>*, Birthday Calendar, My Calendar, or US Holidays. If you have synced to calendars from other sources, you can choose them by tapping them to select or deselect them; for example, tap All iCloud to show all your iCloud-synced calendars. Tap Done, and your chosen calendar displays. When you add a new event, use the Calendar field to choose the calendar you want to add the event to.

If you've created lots of events, you might want to tap Hide All Calendars in the Calendar app, and then tap the one or two calendars you need to see now so that you can quickly find their events.

Syncing Calendars

If you use a calendar available from an online service, such as Yahoo! or Google, you can sync to that calendar to read events that are saved in it on your iPad. To sync a calendar, follow these steps:

1. **Tap the Settings icon on the Home screen.**

2. **Tap the Mail, Contacts, Calendars option on the left.**

3. **Tap Add Account.**

   The Add Account options, shown in Figure 3-12, appear.

4. **Tap an email choice, such as Outlook, Gmail, or Yahoo!**

5. **In the settings that appear (see Figure 3-13), enter your name, email address, and email account password.**

6. **Tap Next.**

   iPad verifies your address.

7. **On the following screen, tap the On/Off switch for the Calendars field.**

8. **Your iPad retrieves data from your calendar at the interval you have specified, so to review these settings, tap the Back button in the top-left corner of the pane, and then tap the Fetch New Data option in the Mail, Contacts, Calendars pane.**

9. **In the Fetch New Data pane that appears (see Figure 3-14), be sure that the Push option's On/Off switch is set to on (green) and then choose the frequency option you prefer your iPad to use for querying the server for new data: every 15 or 30 minutes, hourly, or manually.**

   More frequent pushing of data can use battery power and incur data charges on a 3G/4G connection.

Book V
Chapter 3

Keeping On
Schedule with the
Calendar and
Clock Apps

Figure 3-12: Choose accounts with calendars to copy to iPad.

Figure 3-13: Enter your calendar account information.

If you store your contacts' birthdays in the Contacts app, the Calendar app displays each one when the day arrives so that you don't forget to pass on your congratulations!

You can also have calendar events automatically shared with your iPad if you use a service such as iCloud. The service can sync calendars from multiple email accounts with your iPad calendar. Keep in mind that if you choose to have data automatically shared with your iPad, your battery may drain faster.

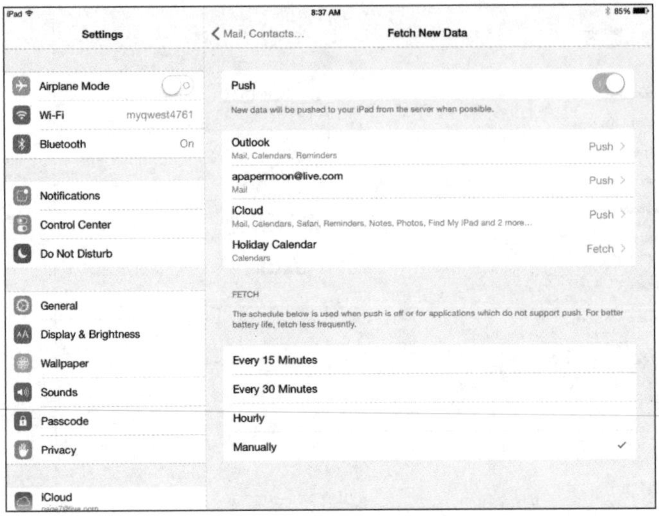

Figure 3-14: Choose how often you want data pushed to your iPad.

If you set up the new Family Sharing feature (see Book I, Chapter 5 for how to do this), you create a family calendar that you can use to share family events with up to five other people. After you set up Family Sharing, you have to make sure that the Calendar sharing feature is on.

After setting up Family Sharing, to set up a family calendar, follow these steps:

1. **Tap Settings.**

2. **Tap iCloud and check that Family Sharing is set up on the second line of the settings on this pane (see Figure 3-15) (it will say Family rather than Set Up Family Sharing if it has been set up). If it's not set up, go to Book I, Chapter 5 for step-by-step instructions for setting it up.**

3. **Tap the On/Off switch for Calendars to turn it on if it's not already on.**

4. **Tap the Home button and then tap Calendars; next, tap the Calendars button at the bottom of the screen, and in the popover that opens, scroll down and make sure that Family is selected. Tap Done.**

5. **Now when you create a new event in the New Event dialog, tap Calendar and choose Family or Show All Calendars.**

   In the details of events is a notation that an event is from the family calendar.

**Book V
Chapter 3**

Keeping On
Schedule with the
Calendar and
Clock Apps

Figure 3-15: Start by turning Family Sharing on in the Settings app.

Deleting Events

Face it: Things change. When that scheduled luncheon or meeting is canceled, you may want to delete the appointment in Calendar. Here's how:

1. **With Calendar open, tap an event.**

   The event details are displayed.

2. **Tap the Edit button.**

3. **In the Edit Event dialog, scroll to the bottom and then tap the Delete Event button, shown in Figure 3-16.**

   Confirming options appear, including a Delete Event button.

   If this is a repeating event, you can delete either this instance of the event or this and all future instances of the event. (See Figure 3-17.)

4. **Tap the button of the option you prefer.**

   The event is deleted, and you return to Calendar view.

If an event is moved but not canceled, you don't have to delete the existing one and create a new one; simply edit the existing event to change the date and time in the Edit Event dialog.

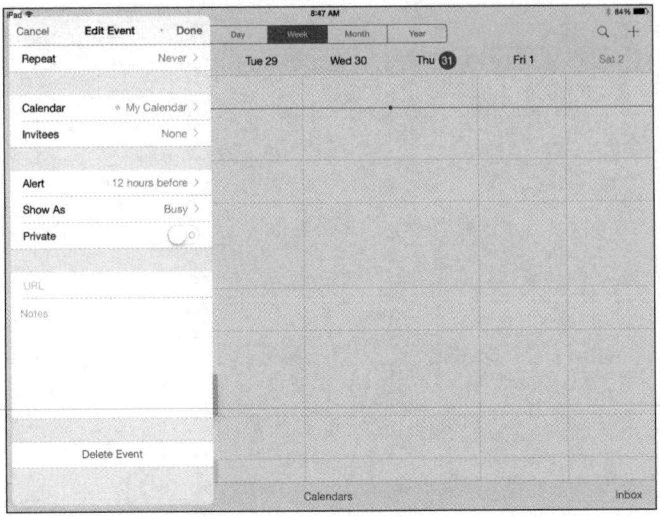

Figure 3-16: Get rid of an event you no longer need by tapping Delete Event.

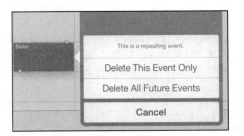

Figure 3-17: Choose whether to delete one instance or all instances of a repeating event.

Using Clock

The Clock app comes preinstalled on your iPad. Using Clock, you can view the time anywhere in the world, set up alarms for certain times, and even use the timer and stopwatch features of Clock to keep track of the timing of events.

Displaying Clock

Tap the Clock app to open it. In World Clock view, preset location clocks are displayed along the top, and the location of these clocks on the world map are displayed below along with the current temperature in that location. To see more views in Clock, follow these steps:

**Book V
Chapter 3**

**Keeping On
Schedule with the
Calendar and
Clock Apps**

1. **Tap a clock along the top of the screen to display it full screen. (See Figure 3-18.)**

   The temperature for the location is displayed to the right of the clock and the date and location are displayed on the left.

Figure 3-18: Clock lets you enlarge the display.

2. **Tap World Clock to return to the World Clock screen.**

   If the World Clock button isn't visible, tap the screen once and it appears.

Cities that are in time zones currently in nighttime are displayed in black. Clocks for cities that are currently in daytime are displayed in white.

Adding or deleting a clock

You can add a clock for many locations around the world (but not everywhere). You can also get rid of a clock when you no longer need it (especially useful for those who travel to different time zones frequently).

To add a clock, follow these steps:

1. **With Clock displayed, tap Add on the clock on the far right.**

2. **Tap a city on the list, or tap a letter on the right side to display locations that begin with that letter.**

   The clock appears in the last slot on the right, and the location is displayed on the world map.

To delete a clock, follow these steps:

1. **To remove a location, tap the Edit button in the upper-left corner of the World Clock screen.**

2. **Tap the minus symbol next to a location (see Figure 3-19) and then tap Delete.**

Figure 3-19: Delete a city when you no longer need to know its time.

Setting an alarm

Want to make sure that you're on time for that big meeting or date? Use the Alarm feature in the Clock app and make sure that you have your iPad near at hand.

Follow these steps to set an alarm:

1. **With the Clock app displayed, tap the Alarm tab.**

2. **Tap the Add button.**

3. **In the Add Alarm dialog, shown in Figure 3-20, take any of the following actions, tapping Back after you make each setting to return to the Add Alarm dialog:**

   • Tap *Repeat* if you want the alarm to repeat at a regular interval such as every Monday or every Sunday.

   • Tap *Sound* to choose the tone the alarm will play.

   • Tap the On/Off switch for *Snooze* if you want to use the Snooze feature.

   • Tap *Label* if you want to give the alarm a name such as "Take Pill" or "Call Mom."

**Book V
Chapter 3**

Keeping On
Schedule with the
Calendar and
Clock Apps

Figure 3-20: Alarms keep you from missing important events.

4. **Place your finger on the three sliders at the top of the dialog, scroll to set the time you want the alarm to occur, and tap Save.**

    The alarm appears on the calendar on the Alarm tab.

    To delete an alarm, tap the Alarm tab and tap Edit. All alarms appear. Tap the red circle with a minus in it, and then tap the Delete button.

Using Stopwatch and Timer

Sometimes life seems like a countdown or a ticking clock counting up the minutes you've spent on a certain activity. You can use the Stopwatch tab of the Clock app to time the length of an activity such as a walk. Use the Timer feature to do a countdown to a specific time such as the moment when your chocolate chip cookies are done baking.

These two work very similarly: Tap the Stopwatch or Timer tab and tap the Start button. When you set the Timer, iPad uses a sound to notify you when time's up. When you start the Stopwatch, you have to tap the Stop button when the activity is done (see Figure 3-21).

Figure 3-21: Time your next walk to work using the Stopwatch feature.

Note that you can use the Lap feature with Stopwatch to time a quick series of events within a larger event, such as timing each of ten laps in a swimming race and getting a total time at the end of the race. Just tap the lap button while recording time to tally one lap and move on to the next. Tap Stop when all laps are complete.

Chapter 4: Working with Reminders and Notifications

In This Chapter

✓ Adding a new task in Reminders

✓ Editing a task

✓ Scheduling and displaying reminders

✓ Making a new list

✓ Syncing with other devices and calendars

✓ Completing or deleting a reminder

✓ Managing notifications from Notification Center

✓ Using Do Not Disturb

The Reminders app and the Notification Center feature warm the hearts of iPad owners who need help remembering the details of their lives.

Reminders is a kind of to-do list that lets you create tasks and set reminders so that you don't forget important commitments. Notifications let you review all elements that you should be aware of in one place, such as new mail messages, text messages, calendar appointments, reminders, and alerts.

If you occasionally need to escape all your obligations, try the Do Not Disturb feature. Turn this feature on and you won't be bothered with alerts till you turn it off again.

In this chapter, I tell you how to set up and view tasks in Reminders, and I explain how Notification Center can centralize all your alerts.

Reminders
Badges, Alerts

Calendar
Badges, Alerts

Photos
Badges, Sounds, Banners

Game Center
Badges, Sounds, Banners

Mail

FaceTime
Badges, Alerts

Astronomy
Badges, Banners

Dropbox
Badges

Creating a Task in Reminders

Reminders help you stay on schedule, avoid embarrassing missed appointments, and stay on top of your hundreds of errands each and every day. Creating a task in Reminders is pretty darn simple.

Note that when you first begin to use Reminders, you'll have only the Reminders list to add tasks to. However, you can create your own categories of reminder lists; see the "Creating a List" section, later in this chapter, to find out how to do this.

To create a reminder, follow these steps:

1. **Tap Reminders on the Home screen.**

2. **On the screen that appears (see Figure 4-1), tap a blank slot in any category in the displayed list to add a task.**

   The onscreen keyboard appears.

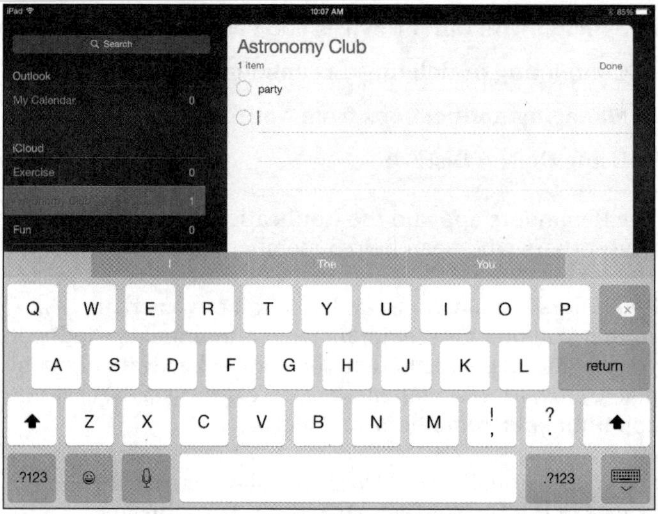

Figure 4-1: Add a reminder task.

3. **Enter a task name or description using the onscreen keyboard and tap the Done button.**

   The new task is added to the Reminders list.

You can create reminders using Siri. Just press and hold the Home button till Siri asks what you need to do, and then say something like "Create a reminder to call Mom this Thursday at noon." Siri displays the reminder and asks you to confirm that you want to create it. Just say, "Yes," and it's done.

See the next task to discover how to add more specifics about an event for which you've created a reminder.

Editing Task Details

What's a task without the details? For example, try to remember the task Pick Up Grammy Award without having a few notes to specify when and where and what you should wear. Reminder tasks help get you where you need to be when you need to be there.

To edit a task and add details, follow these steps:

1. **Tap a task and then tap the Details button (it looks like a small *i*) that appears to the right of it to open the Details dialog (see Figure 4-2).**

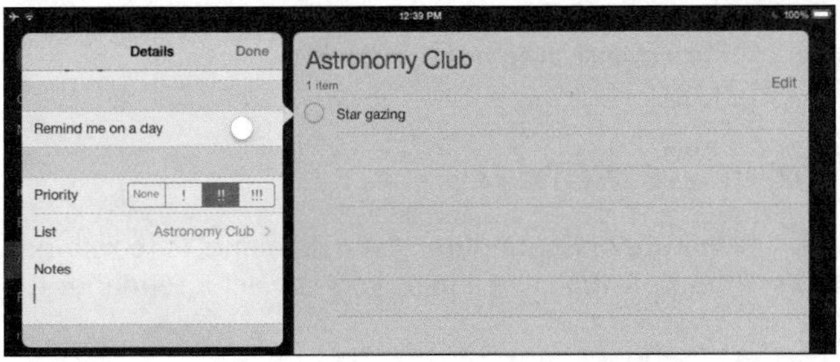

Figure 4-2: Add the information you need about a particular event in this dialog.

2. **Tap a Priority.**

   Choose None, Low, Medium, or High from the choices that appear.

   The Notes priority settings display the associated number of exclamation marks on a task in a list to remind you of its importance.

3. **Tap List and then, from the options that display (see Figure 4-3), select a list to put your task on.**

4. **Tap Details to return to the dialog and then tap Notes.**

5. **Using the onscreen keyboard, enter a note about the task.**

6. **Tap Done when you're finished entering details.**

Figure 4-3: Your event can be viewed in the Reminders app.

Scheduling a Reminder

A major feature of Reminders, given its name, is to remind you of upcoming tasks. After you've saved a task, you can set a reminder for it.

To set a reminder, follow these steps:

1. **Tap a task and then tap the Details button that appears to the right of the task.**

2. **In the dialog that appears, tap Remind Me on a Day to turn the feature on.**

3. **Tap the Alarm field for the On a Day field to turn it on.**

   A list of dates and times appears.

4. **Tap the date that appears below this setting to display the date and time, as shown in Figure 4-4.**

5. **Tap and swipe the Day, Hour, and Minute fields to scroll to the date and time for the reminder.**

6. **Tap the Done button.**

   The settings for the reminder are saved.

If you want a task to repeat with associated reminders, tap the Repeat field, and from the Details dialog that appears, tap Every Day, Week, 2 Weeks, Month, or Year (for annual meetings or fun-filled holiday get-togethers with the gang). Tap Done to save the setting. To stop the task from repeating, tap the End Repeat field, tap End Repeat Date, and select a date from the scrolling calendar.

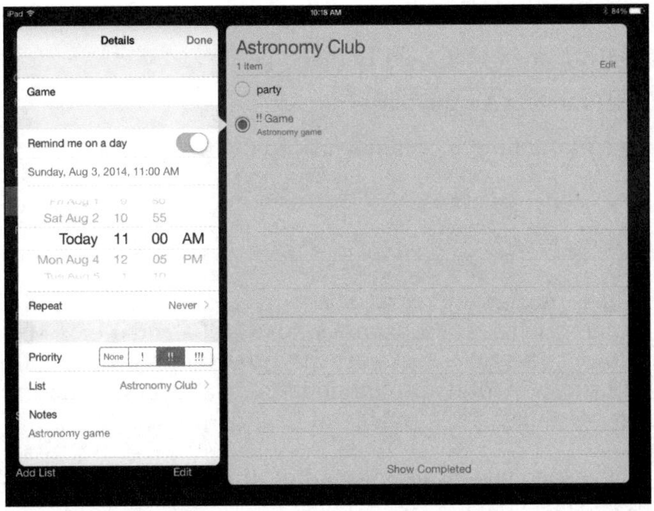

Figure 4-4: Scroll to set the date and the time of your event.

You can scroll the monthly calendar display to show months in the past or future by tapping the forward or backward arrows, and tap any date to show its tasks in the daily list on the right.

Creating a List

You can create your own lists of tasks to help you organize different parts of your life. To do so, follow these steps:

1. **Tap Reminders on the Home screen.**

   Reminders opens.

2. **Tap Add List to display the New List form, shown in Figure 4-5.**

Figure 4-5: Lists might include reminders for personal or work-related events.

3. **Enter a name for the list and tap a color.**

   The list name will appear in that color in List view.

4. **Tap Done to save the list.**

5. **Tap a blank line to create a task in the list.**

Syncing with Other Devices and Calendars

You can determine which tasks are synced to your device from other devices or calendars such as Outlook in Windows or Calendar on a Mac. To make all the settings in this task work correctly, first set up your default calendar and then set up your iCloud account under Accounts in the Mail, Contacts, Calendars settings.

After you've made these settings, follow these steps to sync with other devices and calendars:

1. **Tap Settings on the Home screen.**

2. **Tap iCloud.**

3. **Make sure that in the pane on the right, both Calendars and Reminders are set to On. (See Figure 4-6.)**

4. **Tap Mail, Contacts, Calendars and scroll down to the Calendars category of settings.**

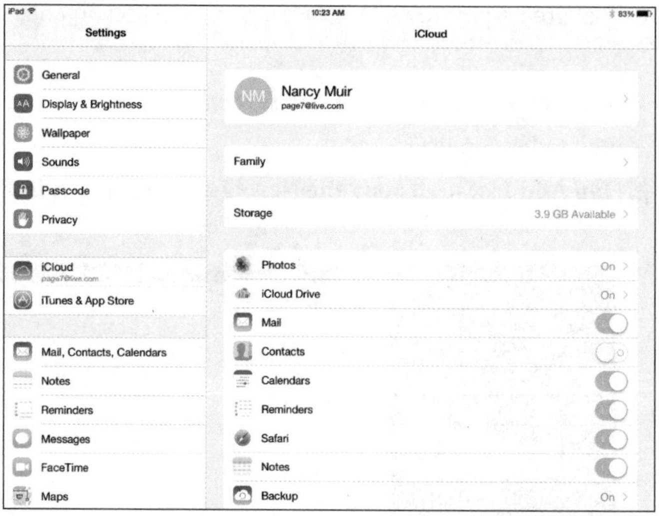

Figure 4-6: Make settings to control what information is shared with your iPad via iCloud.

5. **Tap Sync and then choose how far back to sync reminders (see Figure 4-7).**

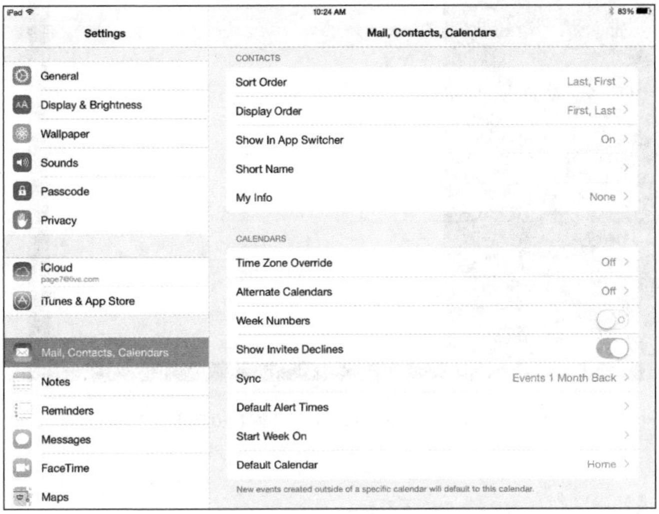

Figure 4-7: If you don't need all reminders, sync to a specific period.

Deleting a Reminder

Are you making progress in checking tasks off your list? You may want to delete a task so that you don't continue to get notifications about it or to give yourself a feeling of accomplishment. Here's how:

1. **With Reminders open and a list of tasks displayed, tap the circular check box to the left of a task or tasks.**

2. **Tap Edit and then tap the red circle to the left of each item you want to delete (see Figure 4-8).**

   The task is deleted.

3. **Tap Done to return to List view.**

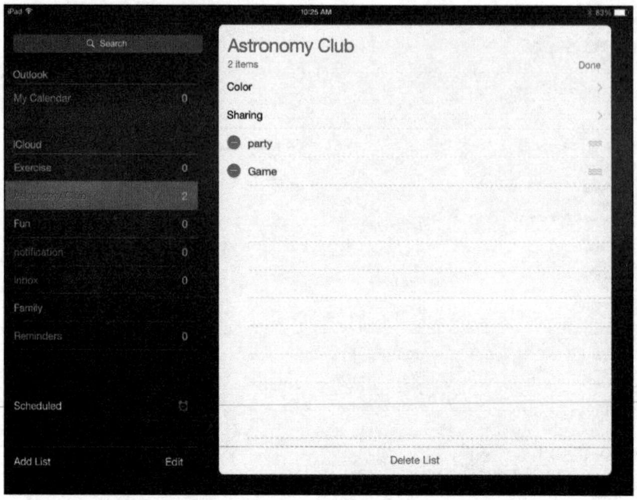

Figure 4-8: Choose as many tasks as you like to delete.

Setting Notification Types

Notification Center is a list of various alerts, appointments, and useful information such as stock quotes and weather that you can display by swiping down from the top of any iPad screen. Notifications is on by default, but you can change certain settings to control which types of notifications are displayed.

Follow these steps to set notification types:

1. **Tap Settings.**

2. **Tap Notifications.**

   In the settings that appear (see Figure 4-9), you see a list of items that you can set to be included in Notification Center. For example, Messages and Reminders might be included, but alerts in game apps might not.

3. **Tap any item, such as Reminders.**

   Notifications settings appear for that app, as shown in Figure 4-10.

4. **Tap the Show in Notification Center On/Off switch to include or exclude that item from Notification Center.**

5. **Choose how to be notified:**

   - *Alert Style:* No alert or banner appears.

   - *Banners:* A banner appears and then disappears automatically.

   - *Alerts:* You have to take an action to dismiss the alert when it appears.

   - *Badge App Icon:* Places a red circle and a number on icons on your Home screens to represent alerts associated with those apps.

- *View in Lock Screen:* Turn on this setting if you want to be able to view alerts when the Lock Screen is displayed.

6. **When you've finished making settings for an individual app, tap the Notifications button to return to the Notifications settings or tap the Home button.**

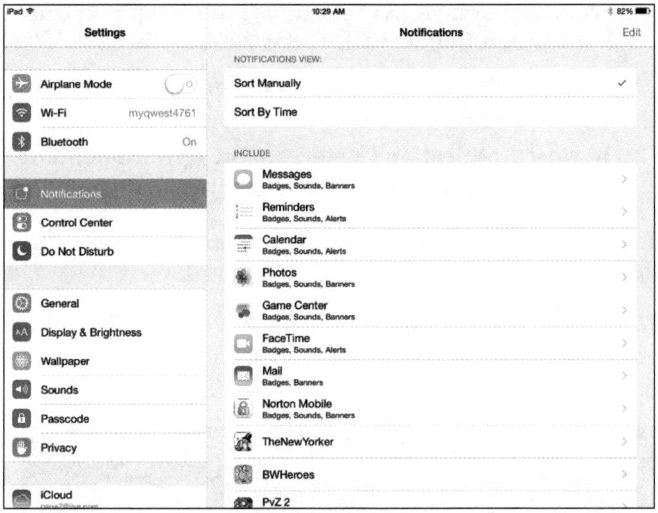

Figure 4-9: Choose your Notification Center options here.

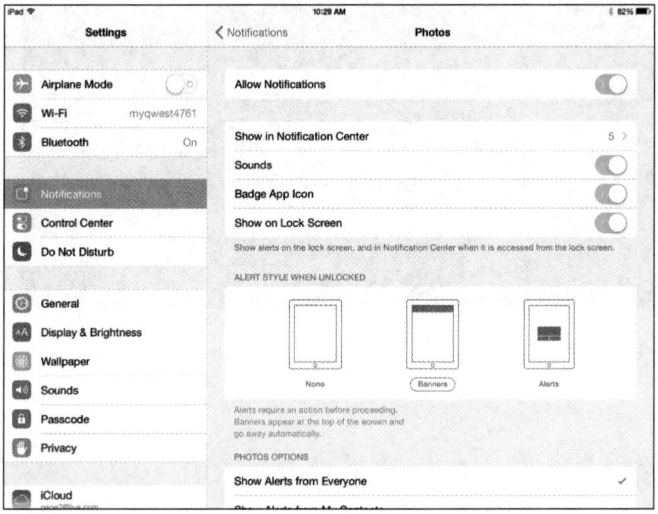

Figure 4-10: Control each item you want to include in Notification Center in this pane.

Viewing Notification Center

After you specify which alerts and reminders should appear in Notification Center, you can review them regularly to keep yourself on track.

To view notifications, follow these steps:

1. **From any screen, tap the status bar on top and drag down to open Notification Center with Today's items displayed. (See Figure 4-11.)**

   Note that items are divided into lists by type, such as Reminders, Calendar items, and Mail.

2. **To close Notification Center, tap the upward-pointing arrow in the bottom-center of Notification Center and drag up, toward the status bar.**

To determine which alerts and reminders display in Notification Center, see the preceding task.

You can also view Notification Center from the Lock screen. Just swipe down from the top of the screen to reveal it, and swipe up to hide it again.

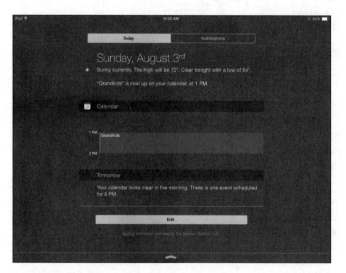

Figure 4-11: Notification Center is a convenient one-stop location for all your commitments and reminders.

Checking Out Today and Notifications Tabs

There are two tabs in Notification Center (refer to Figure 4-11): Today and Notifications. Each view gives you a unique perspective on the tasks on your plate. To look at the information on each of these tabs, follow these steps:

1. **Swipe down from the top of the screen to display Notification Center.**

2. **Tap Today (see Figure 4-12) to show all reminders and other items you've selected to display in Notification Center (see the earlier section, "Setting Notification Types") that occur today.**

   Note that you can also swipe to the right to move to the next tab.

3. **Tap the Notifications tab to see items for today and tomorrow plus missed and other future items.**

Figure 4-12: The Today and Notifications views give you a clearer perspective on your commitments.

Going to an App from Notification Center

To jump easily from Notification Center to any app that causes an alert or reminder to be displayed, follow these steps:

1. **Swipe down from the top of the screen.**

   Notification Center displays.

2. **Tap any item in a category, such as Reminders or Stocks.**

   The item opens in its originating app.

   If you've tapped an email message, you can reply to the message by using the procedures described in Book I, Chapter 7.

Get Some Rest with Do Not Disturb

Do Not Disturb is a simple but useful setting you can use to stop any alerts and FaceTime calls from making a sound or being displayed. You can make settings to allow calls from certain people to get through or to allow several repeat calls from the same person in a short time period to come through. (Apple has assumed in designing this app that such repeat calls may signal an emergency situation or urgent need to get through to you.)

To set up Do Not Disturb, follow these steps:

1. **Tap Settings.**

2. **Tap Do Not Disturb to turn the feature on.**

3. **Tap the Manual On/Off switch to turn the feature on.**

4. **In the other settings shown in Figure 4-13, do any of the following:**

   - *Tap Scheduled* to allow alerts during a specified time period to be displayed.

   - *Tap Allow Calls From* and then, from the next screen, select Everyone, No One, Favorites, or All Contacts.

   - *Tap Repeated Calls* to allow a second call from the same person in a three-minute time period to come through.

5. **Tap the Home button to return to the Home screen.**

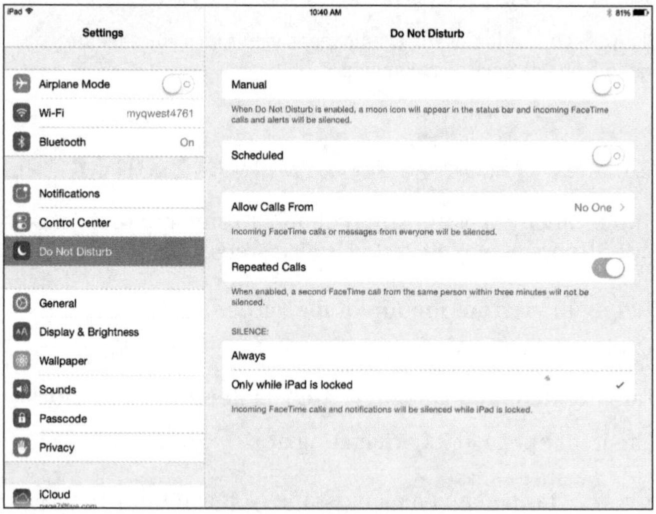

Figure 4-13: Manage how Do Not Disturb operates from here.

Chapter 5: Managing Contacts

In This Chapter

- Adding contacts
- Syncing contacts with iCloud
- Adding social media info
- Specifying related people
- Adding a ringtone and photo to a contact
- Sharing contacts
- Using Maps to view a contact's location
- Deleting a contact

*C*ontacts is the iPad equivalent of the address book on your cellphone. In fact, if you own an iPhone, it's similar to your Contacts app. The Contacts app on iPad is simple to set up and use, and it has some powerful little features beyond simply storing names, addresses, and phone numbers.

For example, you can pinpoint a contact's address in the iPad Maps application. You can use your contacts to quickly address emails, messages, and tweets. If you store a contact record that includes a website, you can use a link in Contacts to view that website instantly. And, of course, you can easily search for a contact by a variety of criteria, including people related to you by family ties or mutual friends, or by groups you create.

In this chapter, you discover the various features of Contacts, including how to save yourself time by syncing your email contacts lists to your iPad instantly.

Populating Your Contacts with Information

The Contacts app's sole purpose is to store contact information and make it available to you, but first you have to make that information available to the Contacts app. You can do it by manually adding records one at a time, by syncing via iTunes, syncing contacts with other accounts such as your Gmail or Yahoo! email, or pushing your contacts to other devices via iCloud to transfer your contacts instantly.

If you have access to or can set up a lightweight directory server (LDIF or LDAP), you can import the contacts stored in such a directory. You can do this by choosing Settings⇨Mail, Contacts, Calendars and then tapping Add Account. Choose Other and then, under Contacts, tap Add LDAP Account.

Adding contacts

You can, of course, enter your contacts the old-fashioned way, by typing their names, addresses, phone numbers, and other information in a contact form.

Follow these steps to create a new contact record:

1. **Tap the Contacts app icon on the Home screen to open the application.**

    If you haven't yet entered a contact, you see a blank address book with the Add (plus) icon at the top of the Contacts List, as shown in Figure 5-1.

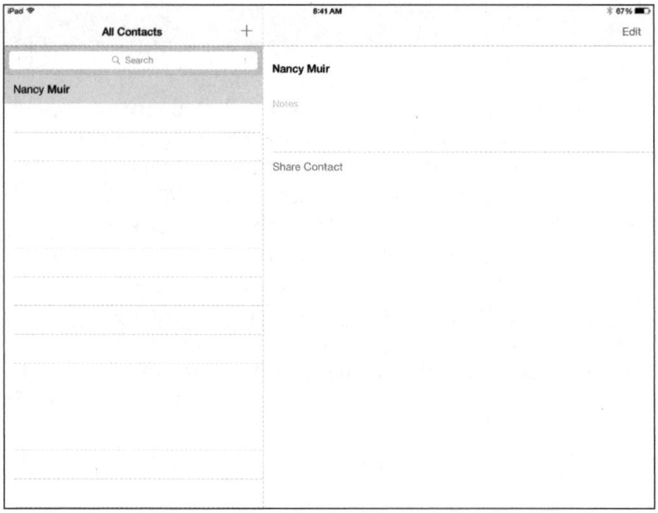

iPad ᶜ		8:41 AM		⚡ 67% ■▯
	All Contacts ╋			Edit
	Q Search		Nancy Muir	
	Nancy Muir		Notes	
			Share Contact	

Figure 5-1: Tap to add a new contact.

2. **Tap the Add button (the + button).**

    A blank Info page opens, and the onscreen keyboard displays, as you can see in Figure 5-2.

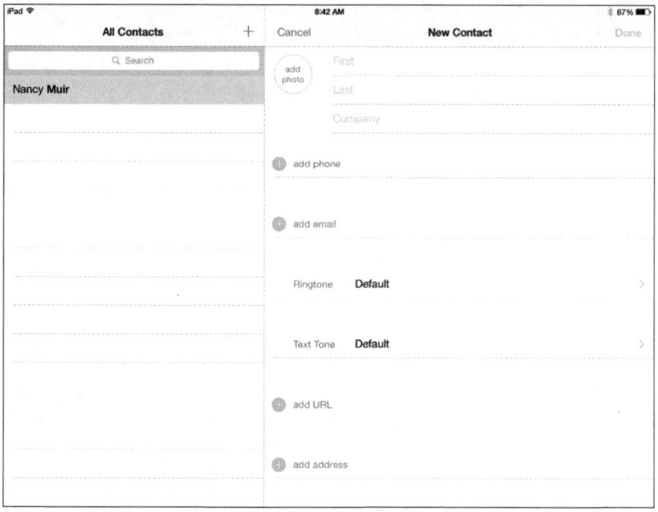

Figure 5-2: Enter as much information about your contact as you want.

3. **Enter some contact information.**

   Enter a first name in the First field, for example. To create a contact, only a first name, last name, or company name is required.

   To scroll down the contact page and see more fields, swipe upward on the page.

   If you're entering a phone number that requires a pause, such as when you access an outside line from your workplace, insert a comma into the number at the spot where the pause must occur. This comma produces a one-second pause. You can also enter a period (.) in the number to pause until you tap Dial to continue. If you sync this contact information to your phone via iTunes, it's then set up to dial correctly.

4. **(Optional) To add information such as a mailing or street address, tap the related Add field, which opens additional entry fields.**

5. **(Optional) To add another information field such as Nickname or Job Title, tap Add Field toward the bottom of the pane. In the Add Field dialog that appears (see Figure 5-3), choose a field to add.**

   You may have to swipe your finger upward to view all available fields.

   If your contact's name is difficult for you to pronounce, add the Phonetic First Name (or Phonetic Last Name) field to that person's record.

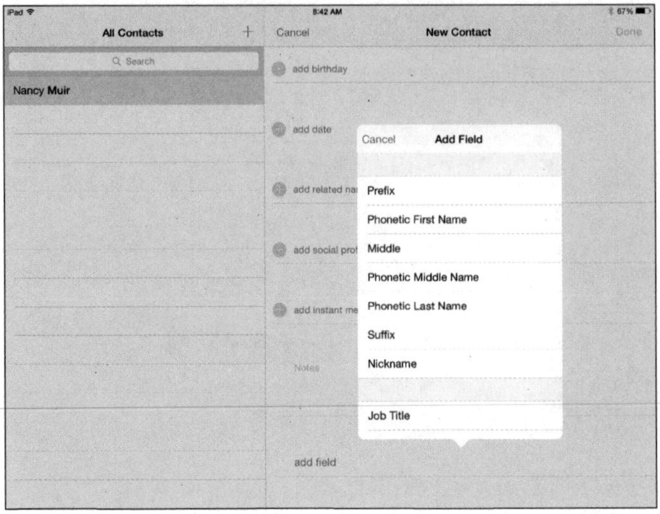

Figure 5-3: Round out a contact's information by adding information fields.

6. **Tap the Done button when you finish making entries.**

   The new contact appears in your address book. Figure 5-4 shows an address book with several entries added.

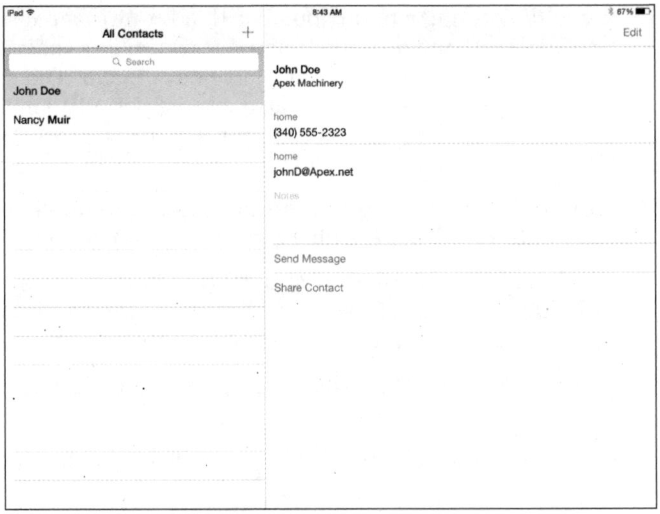

Figure 5-4: A list of contacts, arranged alphabetically.

If you've set up a *Lightweight Directory Access Protocol* (LDAP) account on iPad to connect with your organization's directory service, you may be able to access its directories via Contacts. See Book III, Chapter 1, for more about setting up an LDAP account.

If you want to add multiple email addresses to a contact so that you can easily send email to all of that contact's email addresses, enter a work email address in the steps above, and another Add Email field titled Other opens. Tap the pop-up and enter an appropriate title; then enter another email address there. Another Other field opens, and so on. Simply enter all email addresses you want included for that contact and then tap Done.

A new feature in iOS 8 allows you to create a new contact from contents of an email such as an email signature. If that information isn't already in your Contacts app, a banner appears at the top of the message offering you the option of adding the person to Contacts.

Syncing contacts with iCloud

You can use your iCloud account to sync contacts from your iPad to iCloud to back them up. These also become available to your iCloud email account, if you set one up. Note that these steps can also be used for Google and Exchange accounts through the Mail, Contacts, Calendars section of Settings.

Follow these steps to sync your contacts:

1. **Tap Settings on the Home screen and then tap iCloud.**

2. **In the iCloud settings shown in Figure 5-5, tap Contacts to sync contacts.**

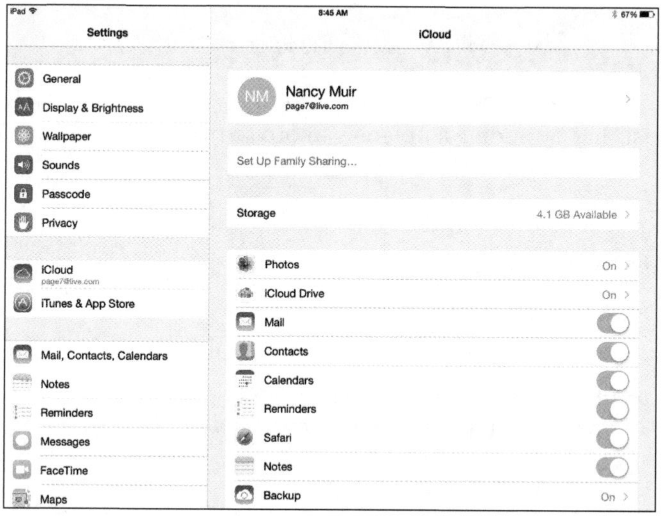

Figure 5-5: Choose what to sync through iCloud here.

3. **Tap Merge (see Figure 5-6) to merge your iPad Contacts contents with iCloud.**

Figure 5-6: Merge your iPad Contacts contents with iCloud.

If you don't use a server-based syncing method with accounts such as iCloud, Google, or Exchange, you can use iTunes to automatically sync contacts among all your Apple devices and even a Windows PC. See Book I, Chapter 5, for more about making iTunes settings to specify how your contacts are synced in iTunes.

You can use the iTunes Wi-Fi sync feature in the General pane in Settings to sync with iTunes wirelessly from a computer connected to the same Wi-Fi network.

Assigning a Photo to a Contact

It's always helpful to associate a face with a name. In Contacts, you can do just that by adding a person's photo to his contact record. You can add photos from various sources, such as

- The Photos app's albums
- Digital cameras
- Email attachments
- iPad's camera
- Photo collections stored on your computer or in iCloud (see Book II, Chapter 6, for more about working with the Photos app)

Follow these steps to add a stored photo to a contact record:

1. **With Contacts open, tap the contact to whose record you want to add a photo.**

2. **Tap the Edit button.**

3. **On the Info page that appears, tap Add Photo.**

4. **Tap Choose Photo from the popover (see Figure 5-7).**

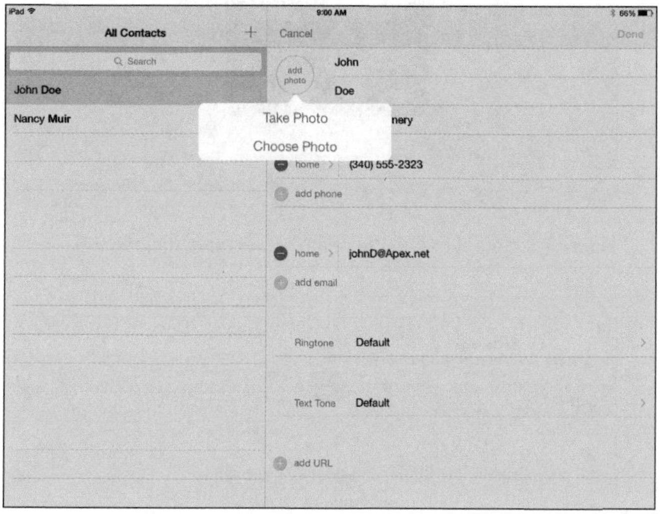

Figure 5-7: Choose the location of the photo you want to include.

5. **In the Photo Albums popover that appears, tap Camera Roll or My Photo Stream, Photo Library, or any photo album you might have created yourself, depending on where the photo is stored.**

   You can also choose Take Photo to take that contact's photo on the spot.

6. **In the photo album that appears, tap a photo to select it.**

   The dialog shown in Figure 5-8 appears. If you want to modify the photo, move the image around in the frame with your finger, or shrink or expand it by pinching your fingers inward or outward, respectively.

7. **Tap the Use button to use the photo for this contact.**

   The photo appears on the contact's Info page, as shown in Figure 5-9.

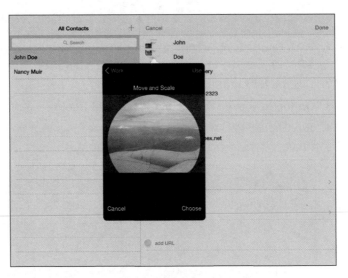

Figure 5-8: Select or edit the photo you want to include.

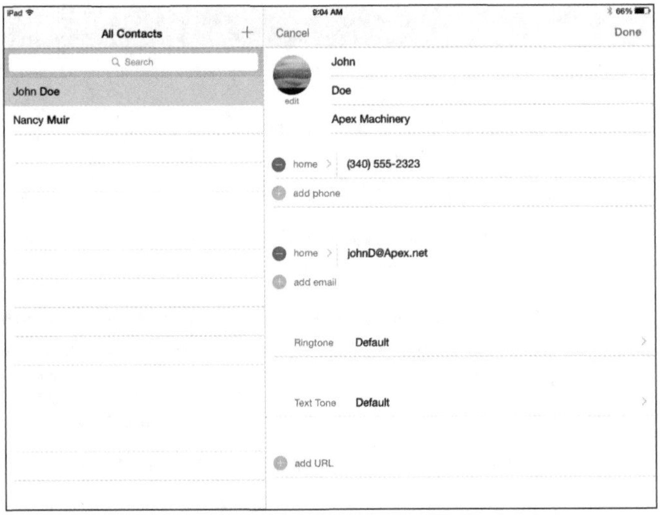

Figure 5-9: A photo displayed with a contact in iPad.

8. Tap Done to save changes to the contact.

To edit a photo you've added to a contact record, simply display the contact information and tap Edit. Tap Edit under the photo and then choose Edit Photo from the menu that appears, and then, in the dialog that appears (refer to Figure 5-8), use the described gestures for moving and scaling the image with your fingers. Tap Use when you're done to save the changed figure.

If you want a more powerful contact-management app, check out Contacts Journal – iPad Edition. It syncs with your Contacts app content and can also sync with a computer contact-management program such as Outlook. The most helpful aspect of Contacts Journal for road warriors is that it maintains a record of whom you've visited and when you've emailed those people.

Book V
Chapter 5

Managing Contacts

Adding Twitter or Facebook Information

You can add Twitter and Facebook information to a contact so that you can quickly *tweet* (send a short message) to contacts using Twitter or post a message to your contact's Facebook account.

To specify Facebook or Twitter account information for a contact, first be sure that you've activated and set up a User Name and Password for your Facebook and/or Twitter accounts under Settings. Then follow these steps:

1. **With Contacts open, tap a contact.**

2. **Tap the Edit button.**

3. **Scroll down and tap Social Profile.**

4. **In the list that appears (see Figure 5-10), enter a Twitter label.**

   If you want to create a different social networking field, tap Add Social Profile. A Facebook field appears. You can also tap again to get a Flickr account, and then a LinkedIn account, and so on.

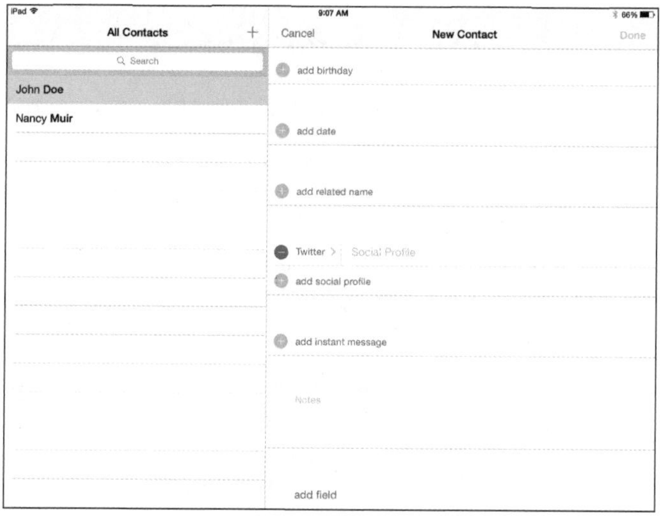

Figure 5-10: Choose Twitter to begin composing a tweet.

5. **Tap Done.**

   The information is saved.

   The account now displays whenever you select the contact, as shown in Figure 5-11. You can send a tweet, a Facebook post, or other message by simply tapping the username for a service and choosing the appropriate command (such as Tweet).

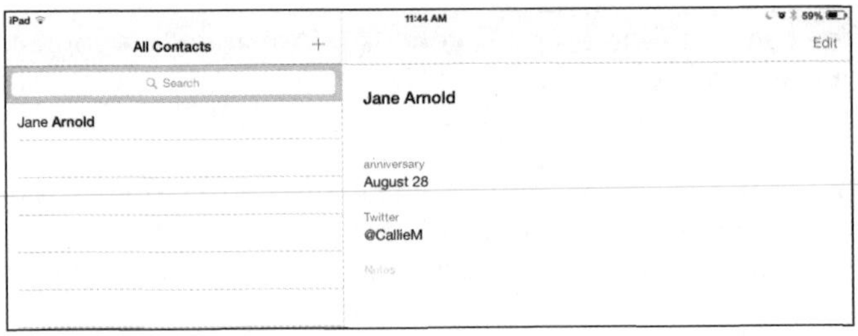

iPad	11:44 AM	59%
All Contacts +		Edit
Q Search	**Jane Arnold**	
Jane Arnold		
	anniversary	
	August 28	
	Twitter	
	@CallieM	
	Notes	

Figure 5-11: Your contact is now associated with the appropriate social network.

 If you prefer to add Facebook information instead of Twitter, tap Add Social Profile just under the Twitter field in Step 5 and enter the contact's Facebook information. (You can also click the Add Social Profile link again and choose Flickr, LinkedIn, Myspace, Sina Welbo, or Add Custom Service in the fields that appear.)

Designating Related People

You can quickly designate a relation — such as your mother, assistant, friend, or manager — in a contact record if the person is saved to Contacts. To add a relationship to a contact, follow these steps:

1. **Tap a contact and then tap Edit.**

2. **Scroll down the record and tap Add Related Name.**

   A new field, labeled Mother, appears (see Figure 5-12). You can tap a field name such as Mother, and a list of other possible relationships appears.

3. **Enter the contact name for the contact's relationship or tap the Information icon to the right of the field.**

   A list of your contacts appears, from which you can choose the person.

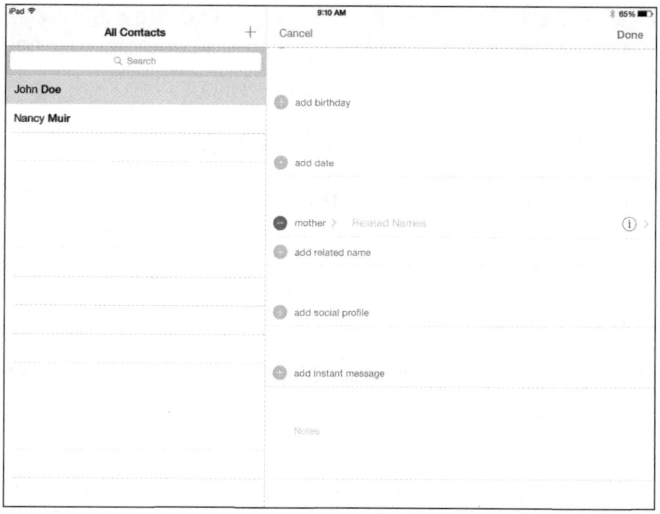

Figure 5-12: This field defaults to Mother, of course.

4. Tap Add Related Name again.

A new blank field for Father appears (see Figure 5-13). Tap the Information button and select the relationship you want.

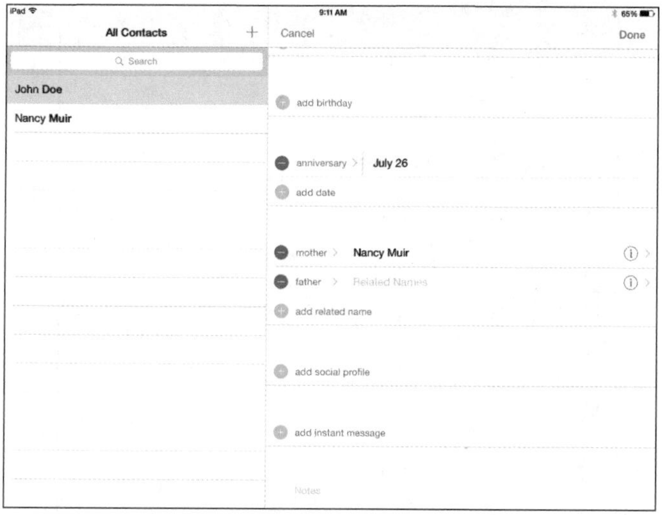

Figure 5-13: You can make someone a friend, an assistant, and a spouse, if you want!

TIP

After you add a relation to a contact record, whenever you select the person on the Contacts main screen, all related people for that contact are listed.

Setting Ringtones and Text Tones

If you want to hear a unique tone whenever you receive a FaceTime call or a text from a particular contact, you can set up this feature in Contacts. For example, if you want to be sure that you know instantly when your spouse, a sick friend, or your boss is calling, set a unique tone for that person by following these steps:

1. **Tap to add a new contact or select a contact from the list of contacts, and tap Edit.**

2. **Tap the Ringtone field.**

   If you want to assign Text Tones, make that choice in this step. A list of tones appears (see Figure 5-14). You can also tap Buy More Tones at the top of this list to buy additional ringtones from Apple or a variety of third-party sites, or even create your own.

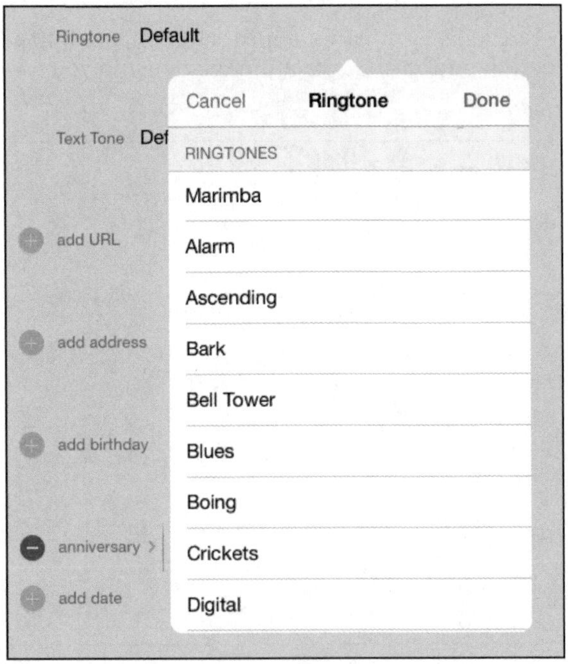

Ringtone	Default

Cancel **Ringtone** Done

Text Tone Def RINGTONES

Marimba

add URL Alarm

Ascending

add address Bark

Bell Tower

add birthday Blues

Boing

anniversary > Crickets

add date Digital

Figure 5-14: Choose from these available ringtones.

3. **Tap a tone to preview it.**

4. **When you hear a tone you like, tap Done.**

5. **Tap Done again to close the contact form.**

If your Apple devices are synced via iCloud, setting a unique ringtone for an iPad contact also sets it for your iPhone, iPod touch, and Mac for FaceTime, and Messages. See Book I, Chapter 5, for more about iCloud.

You can set a custom tone for FaceTime calls and text messages through Settings⇨Sounds. You can also create your own custom ring/text tones in GarageBand on a Mac or iOS device, with any of several ringtone-maker apps, or by using the contents of your iTunes Library on either a Mac or PC.

Finding Contacts

You can use the Spotlight Search feature to find a contact in the Contacts app by looking for that person's first or last name or a company name. This feature on the iPad is much like every search feature you've ever used. It's somewhat simple in comparison to others because you can search only for names and because no advanced search techniques are available.

You can also use Siri or the Spotlight Search feature to locate contacts that match specified search criteria. Swipe down from near the top of any Home screen to display the Spotlight screen.

Follow these steps to search for a contact:

1. **With Contacts open, tap in the Search field at the top of the left page (see Figure 5-15).**

   The onscreen keyboard opens.

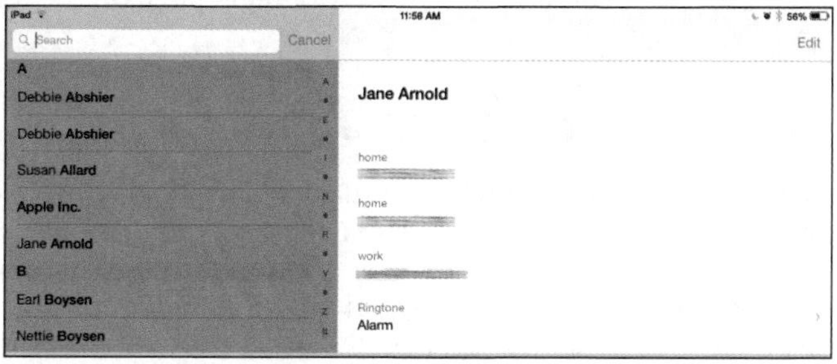

Figure 5-15: Easily search for contacts.

2. **Type the first letter of either the first or last name, or the company name.**

   All matching results appear, as shown in Figure 5-16. In the example, typing **J** displays Jane Arnold and Ted And Joan Stier in the results, which both have *J* as the first letter in either their first or last names.

3. **Tap a contact's name in the results to display that person's information on the page on the right (see Figure 5-16).**

iPad 🛜	
🔍 J ❌	Cancel
Jane **Arnold**	›
Ted And Joan **Stier**	›

Figure 5-16: Search results narrow as you type.

You can search by phone number, website, or address in Contacts as well as by name.

If you've entered many contacts, you can use the alphabetical listing that appears along the right side of Contacts to locate a contact: Tap and drag to scroll the list of contacts on the All Contacts page on the left.

Using Contacts beyond the Contacts App

Contacts isn't simply a static database of names and addresses. After you've entered contact information into the app, you can use the information to reach out to people in several useful ways. You can jump to a contact's website to see what she, or her company, is up to online; use a contact's email information to quickly send an email message; share the contact information with somebody else; or find the physical address of the contact by using the iPad Maps app.

Visiting a contact's website

Everybody (well, almost everybody) now has a website, so whether your contact is a person or an international conglomerate, you're likely to find an associated website that you might want to access now and then. You can access it from your iPad by using the Contacts app.

If you entered information in the Home Page field of a contact record, the text you entered automatically becomes a link to that person's website. With Contacts open, tap a contact to display the person's contact information on the page at the right and then tap the link in the Home Page field, as shown in Figure 5-17.

iPad	12:04 PM	55%
Q 555 Cancel		Edit
Jane Arnold >	home	
Hank Greene >	home	
Laren Mitchell >	work	
	Ringtone Alarm	
	home page http://ipadmadeclear.com	
	anniversary August 28	
	mother Jane Arnold	
	Twitter @CallieM	
	Notes	
	Share Contact	

Figure 5-17: Tap to go to a web page related to a contact.

The Safari browser opens with the web page displayed.

You aren't returned directly to Contacts after you follow a link to a website. You have to tap the Home button and then tap the Contacts app icon again to reenter the application. Or you can use the multitasking feature to get back to Contacts by double-tapping the Home button and choosing Contacts from the icons that appear along the bottom of the screen. However, if you have the Multitasking Gestures setting turned on in the General pane of Settings, you can do the four-finger swipe to the left to return to the app you just left and keep swiping to go to the apps on the multitasking bar in sequence.

Addressing emails using contacts

If you've entered an email address for a contact, the address automatically converts to a link in the record that allows you to open an email form and send a message. This shortcut is handy for getting in touch. Note that the steps outlined here also work for creating Messages or placing Facetime calls.

First, be sure that you've entered an email address in the contact's record and then follow these steps:

1. **Tap the Contacts app icon on the Home screen to open Contacts.**

2. **Tap a contact's name to display her contact information on the page on the right, and then tap the email address link labeled Work, as in the example shown in Figure 5-18.**

   Note that people you've contacted recently are displayed along the top of the multitasking screen, which you get to by double-pressing the Home button. When you tap a recent contact, any available methods of connecting with her in her record, including Messages or Facetime, are listed; just tap a button to make the connection.

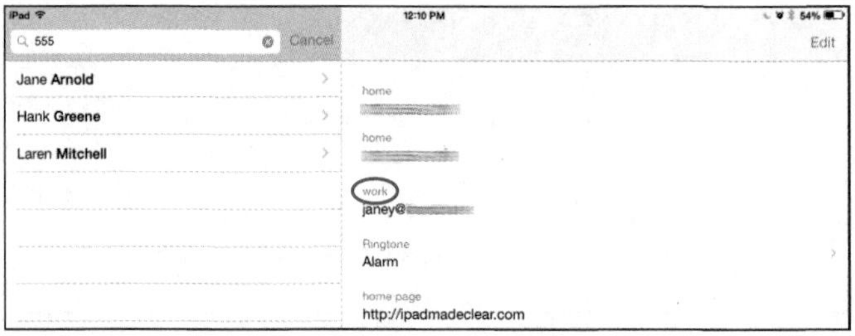

Figure 5-18: Tap to open a new email message.

The New Message form appears with the contact's email address already entered, as shown in Figure 5-19. The title bar of this form initially reads *New Message* but changes to the specific title as you type on the Subject line.

3. **Tap in a field and use the onscreen keyboard to enter a subject and a message.**

4. **Tap the Send button.**

   The message is sent.

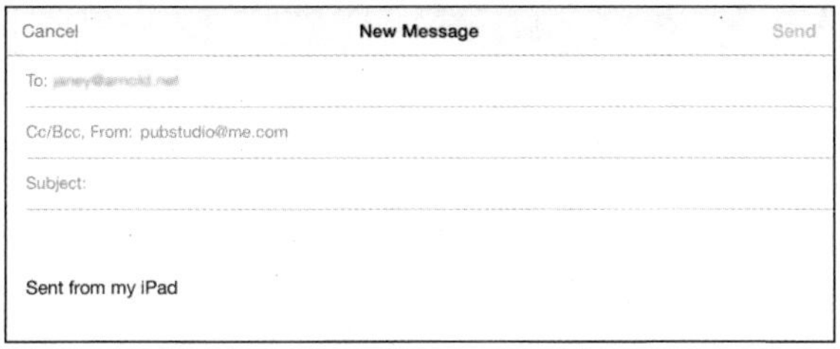

Cancel	New Message	Send
To: janey@aarnold.net		
Cc/Bcc, From: pubstudio@me.com		
Subject:		
Sent from my iPad		

Figure 5-19: A new email message form.

Sharing contacts

After you've entered contact information, you can share it with others in an email message. Sharing is especially handy when you store locations in Contacts, such as your favorite restaurant or movie theater.

Here's how to share your contacts' information:

1. **With Contacts open, tap a contact name to display its information.**

2. **On the information page, tap the Share Contact button.**

   If you want, you can select AirDrop, and then tap the name of a device near to you to send the contact information wirelessly to that device.

3. **In the popover that appears, shown in Figure 5-20, tap Mail or Message.**

   The New Message form appears. Both the email and message form let you enter a message and include the contact information as an attachment to be sent to the recipient. Figure 5-21 shows the email form.

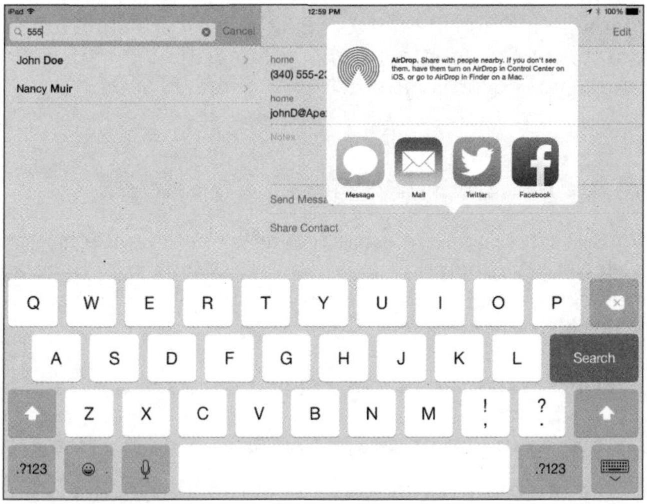

Figure 5-20: Easily share contact information with others.

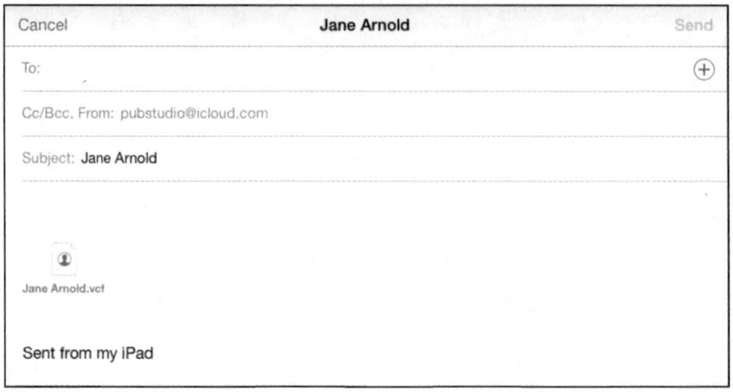

Cancel	Jane Arnold	Send
To:		⊕
Cc/Bcc, From: pubstudio@icloud.com		
Subject: Jane Arnold		

Jane Arnold.vcf

Sent from my iPad

Figure 5-21: Fill out the email form to share your contact.

4. **On the email New Message form, use the onscreen keyboard to enter the recipient's email address.**

   Note: If the person's information is saved in Contacts, you just have to type his or her name here.

5. **Enter information in the Subject field.**

6. **If you like, enter a message.**

7. **Tap the Send button.**

   The message goes to your recipient with the contact information attached as a .vcf file (in the *vCard* format, commonly used to transmit contact information).

Someone who receives a vCard containing contact information simply clicks the attached file to open it. At that point, the recipient can perform various actions (depending on the recipient's email or contact-management program) to save the content. Other iPhone, iPod touch, or iPad users can easily import .vcf records into their own Contacts apps.

Viewing a Contact's Location in Maps

If you've entered a person's street address in Contacts, you have a shortcut for viewing that person's location in the Maps app. Once again, this is useful for places you need to visit for the first time, such as several clients' offices on that next business trip.

Follow these steps to pinpoint your contacts in the iPad Maps app:

1. **To open the Contacts app, tap its icon on the Home screen.**

2. **Tap the contact you want to view to display her information.**

3. **Tap the address.**

   Maps opens and displays a map of the address, as shown in Figure 5-22.

You can use information stored in Contacts to access more than your friends' addresses. You can also save information about your favorite restaurant or movie theater, or any other location, and then use Contacts to jump to the associated website in the Safari browser or to the address in Maps.

After you jump to a contact's location in Maps, you may want to use the features of Maps to display different views, determine the condition of traffic on that route, or calculate the route between two locations. For more about using the Maps application, see Book III, Chapter 2.

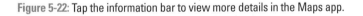

Figure 5-22: Tap the information bar to view more details in the Maps app.

Deleting Contacts

Remember that iPad's storage capacity is limited compared to your typical computer. Though a contact record is tiny compared to a TV show, there's no sense keeping lots of old records around when you no longer need them. When you need to remove a name or two from your Contacts, doing so is easy.

Follow these steps to delete contacts on your iPad:

1. **With Contacts open, tap the contact you want to delete.**

2. **On the information pane on the right, tap the Edit button.**

3. **Drag your finger upward to scroll down (if necessary) and then tap Delete Contact at the bottom, as shown in Figure 5-23.**

   A confirmation alert appears.

4. **Tap Delete Contact to confirm the deletion.**

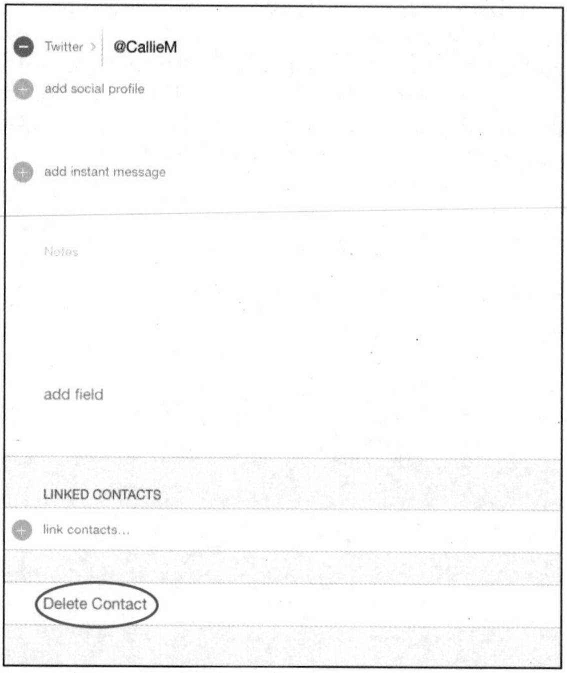

Figure 5-23: Tap Delete Contact to get rid of an unwanted contact.

Chapter 6: Talking to Your iPad with Siri

In This Chapter

✔ Activating Siri and understanding all that Siri can do

✔ Calling people and creating reminders and alerts

✔ Adding tasks to your Calendar

✔ Playing music, getting directions, and asking for facts

✔ Using Siri to search the web or send email, tweets, or messages

✔ Getting helpful Siri tips

*O*ne of the coolest features of iPad is Siri, a personal assistant feature that responds to spoken commands using a third-generation (or later) iPad and iPad mini. With Siri, you can ask for nearby restaurants, and a list appears. You can open apps with a voice command and with iOS 8, for the first time, Siri can open the App Store. You can dictate your email messages rather than type them. Calling your mother is as simple as saying, "Call Mom." Want to know the capital of Rhode Island? Just ask. Siri checks several online sources to answer questions ranging from the result of a mathematical calculation to the size of Jupiter. You can also have Siri perform tasks such as returning calls and controlling iTunes Radio. Finally, you can even play music, and with iOS 8 comes integration with Shazam, a music identifier service that can identify tagged songs for you.

Some things you can ask m

Call home

Call my brother at work

Launch Photos

What's Emily's address?

Will it be hot today?

Activating Siri

When you first go through the process of setting up your iPad or iPad mini, making settings for your location, using iCloud, and so on, at one point, you see the screen shown in Figure 6-1. To activate Siri, just tap Use Siri and then tap Next. When you first set up your iPad, it reminds you about using Siri by displaying a message.

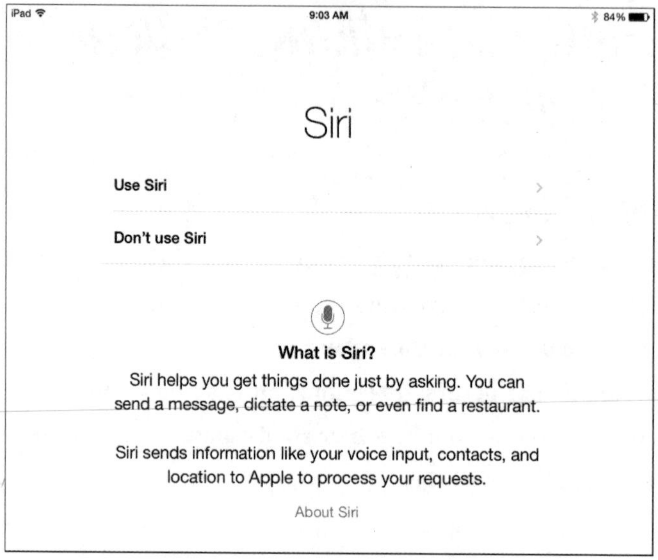

Figure 6-1: Activate Siri now or later, but definitely give it a try!

If you didn't activate Siri during the registration process, you can use Settings to turn Siri on by following these steps:

1. **Tap Settings on the Home screen.**

2. **Tap General and then tap Siri (see Figure 6-2)**

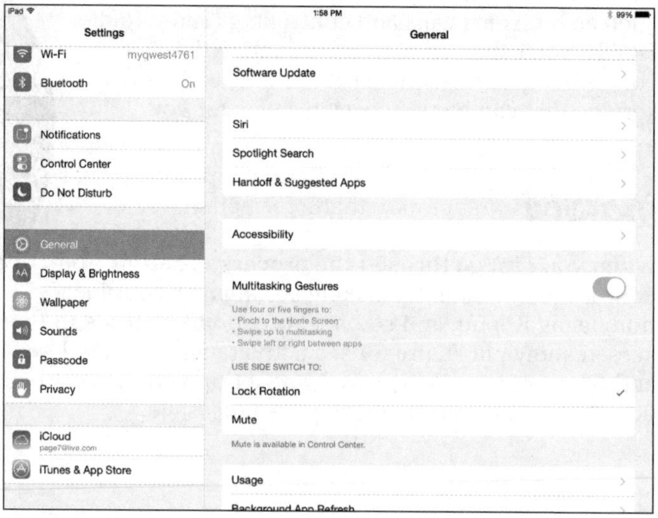

Figure 6-2: Siri offers a few simple settings.

3. **In the dialog in Figure 6-3, tap the On/Off switch to turn Siri on.**

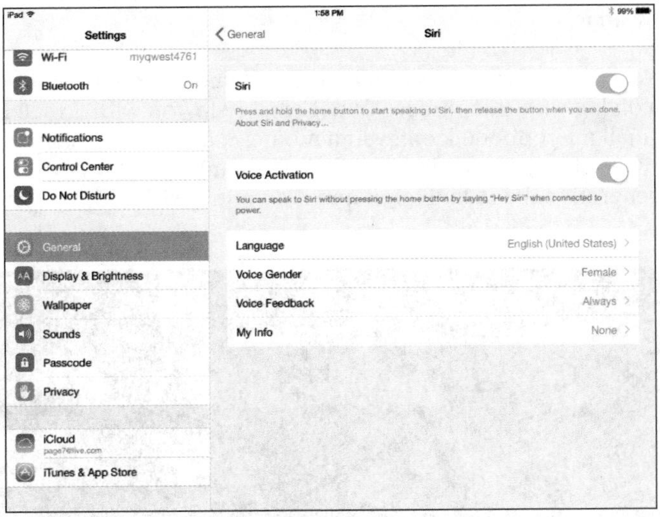
iPad
1:58 PM
99%
Settings
General
Siri
Wi-Fi
myqwest4761
Bluetooth
On
Notifications
Control Center
Do Not Disturb
General
Display & Brightness
Wallpaper
Sounds
Passcode
Privacy
iCloud
iTunes & App Store
Siri
Press and hold the home button to start speaking to Siri, then release the button when you are done.
About Siri and Privacy...
Voice Activation
You can speak to Siri without pressing the home button by saying "Hey Siri" when connected to power.
Language
English (United States)
Voice Gender
Female
Voice Feedback
Always
My Info
None

Figure 6-3: Get Siri going here.

4. **If you wish to change the language Siri uses, tap Language and choose a different language in the list that appears.**
5. **To change the gender of Siri's voice from female to male, tap Voice Gender and then tap Male.**
6. **If you want to be able to activate Siri hands free when your iPhone is plugged in to power by saying "Hey, Siri," set Voice Activation to On.**
7. **Tap My Info and select your own contact information in the Contacts list that appears.**

   Siri now knows your name, phone number, website, contacts who are related to you and their relationship, and so on, so it can respond to requests that require that information.

WARNING!

You can make a setting that allows Siri to be used when the Lock screen is displayed, but Siri can then bypass any passcode you've required. If somebody else gets his hands on your iPad and you have this set to On, it could compromise your data security. To change this setting under General settings, tap Passcode Lock. When the lock is set to on, you can use the Siri field to turn access via Siri on or off.

Siri is available on the iPad only when you have Internet access, and cellular data charges could apply when Siri checks online sources if you're using a 3G/4G iPad model. In addition, Apple warns that available features may vary by area.

Now, to use Siri, press and hold the Home button until Siri opens, displaying a dialog with the phrase, "What can I help you with?" (see Figure 6-4) and a small microphone icon; wait a moment, and Siri begins to show you the types of commands it can follow. Remember that this works with only third-generation iPads and later, and iPad minis with iOS 6 or later installed.

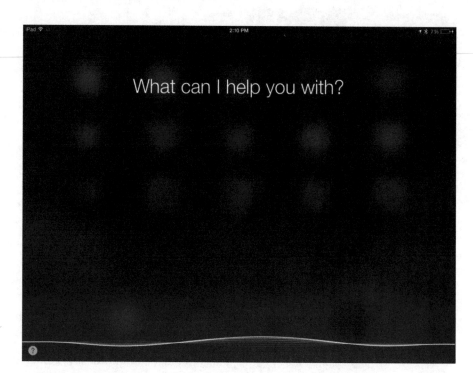

What can I help you with?

Figure 6-4: Siri awaits your command.

Understanding All That Siri Can Do

Siri allows you to interact with many apps on your iPad by voice. You can pose questions or ask to do something, such as make a FaceTime call or add an appointment to your calendar. Siri can also search the Internet or use an informational database called WolframAlpha to provide information on just about any topic. You don't have to be in an app to make a request involving another app.

Siri also checks with Wikipedia, Bing, and Twitter to get you the information you ask for. In addition, you can use Siri to tell iPad to play your voicemail, open and search the App Store, or control iTunes Radio playback.

Siri is the technology behind the iPad's Dictation feature. When you have the onscreen keyboard open, note that it contains the Dictation key, which you can tap to begin to dictate and tap to end dictation. This works in any app that uses the onscreen keyboard.

You don't need to use any preset structure for the questions you pose to Siri; you can phrase things in several ways. For example, you might say, "Where am I?" to see a map of your current location, or you could say, "What is my current location?" or "What address is this?" and get the same results. Also, Siri gets better at responding to your requests the more you use it, as it learns more about you from your browsing habits and requests.

When you ask a question about, say, setting up an appointment, Siri responds to you both verbally and with text information, in a form as with email (see Figure 6-5) or in a graphic display for some items such as maps. When a result appears, you can tap it to make a choice or open a related app.

Figure 6-5: If you ask to send an email, Siri provides the email form.

With iOS 8, you can activate Siri hands-free. With your iPhone plugged into a wall outlet, car power port, or computer's USB port, just say "Hey, Siri" and Siri opens up ready for a command. In addition, with voice recognition, Siri displays in text what it's hearing as you speak, so you can verify that it has understood you instantly. This streaming feature makes the whole process of interacting with Siri faster.

With iOS 8, Siri now supports 22 languages, so you can finally show off those language lessons you took in high school.

Siri works with FaceTime, the App Store, Music, Messages, Reminders, Calendar, Maps, Mail, Clock, Contacts, Notes, and Safari. In the following tasks, I provide a quick guide to some of the most useful ways you can use Siri.

Staying in Touch and Staying on Schedule with Siri

When you're on the run, Siri can be a wonderful ally. You can ask Siri to make calls for you, set up reminders and alerts, and even add appointments to your calendar, all by speaking your requests.

Calling contacts via FaceTime

First, make sure that the people you want to call are entered in your Contacts app and include their phone numbers in their records. If you want to call somebody by stating your relationship to her, such as "Call sister," be sure to enter that relationship in the related field in her contact record and make sure that the settings for Siri (refer to Figure 6-2) include your contact name in the My Info field. (See Chapter 5 in this minibook for more about creating contact records.)

1. **Press and hold the Home button until Siri appears.**

2. **Speak a command such as "Make a FaceTime call to Earl" or "FaceTime Mom."**

   If two contacts exist who might match a spoken name, Siri responds with a list of possible matches (see Figure 6-6).

Which 'Earl'?	3:56 PM
Earl Boysen	
Earl	
Other...	

Figure 6-6: If two similar contacts exist, Siri asks you to choose.

3. **Tap one of the contacts in the list or state the correct contact's name to proceed.**

   Siri places the call.

4. **To end the call before it completes, tap the Home button and then tap End.**

To cancel any spoken request, you have four options: You can say "Cancel," tap the Microphone button on the Siri screen, tap the Home button, or tap anywhere on the screen outside the Siri panel.

Creating reminders and alerts

You can also use Siri with the Reminders app. For example, you might want to set a reminder to meet a friend for lunch next Tuesday. Rather than opening the Reminder app and adding a new reminder and settings for it, you can tell Siri to do it for you.

To create a reminder using Siri, follow these steps:

1. **Press and hold the Home key and then speak a command, such as "Remind me to call Dad on Thursday at 10 a.m." or "Wake me up tomorrow at 7 a.m."**

   A preview of the reminder is displayed (see Figure 6-7), and Siri asks you whether it should create the reminder.

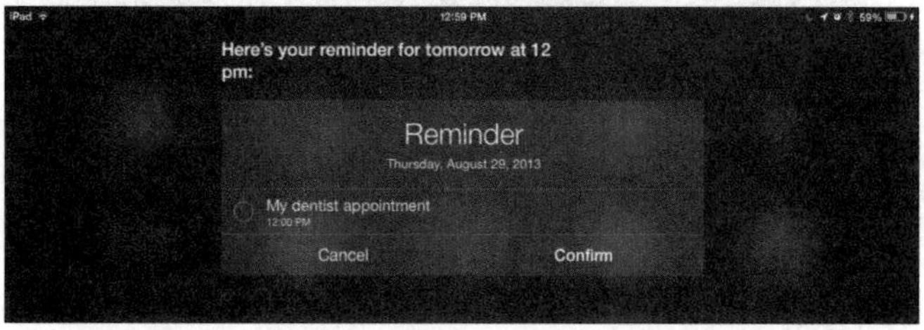

Figure 6-7: Siri presents the reminder as it understood it for you to confirm.

2. **If Siri asks you to confirm, tap or say Confirm to create the reminder or alert.**

3. **If you want a reminder ahead of the event you created, activate Siri and speak a command, such as "Remind me tonight about the play on Thursday at 8 p.m."**

   A second reminder is created, which you can confirm or cancel if you change your mind.

Adding tasks to your Calendar

If you live by your Calendar appointments, you'll be happy to hear that Siri can also set up events on your Calendar for you. Siri not only records the event on your Calendar, but it also alerts you if a conflict exists.

Follow these steps to set up an event using Siri:

1. **Press and hold the Home button and then speak a phrase, such as "Set up meeting at 10 a.m. on October 12th."**

   A sample calendar entry appears, and Siri asks whether you want to confirm it.

2. **If a conflict exists with the appointment, Siri tells you that you already have an appointment at that time (see Figure 6-8) and asks whether you still want to set up the new appointment.**

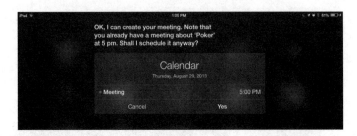

Figure 6-8: Double-booked? Siri lets you know.

3. **Say Yes or Cancel or tap the Yes or Cancel button.**

Playing Music

How often do you find that you don't have the time or free hands to unlock the iPad screen, open Music, search for music, and tap to play it? Well, you'll find worse problems in the world, but if this is one that nags at you, just press and hold the Home button and tell Siri to play your favorite tune. You can use Siri to play a song from the Music app or play a station on iTunes Radio.

To play music using Siri, follow these steps:

1. **Press and hold the Home button until Siri appears.**

2. **To play music, speak a command, such as "Play music" or "Play 'As Time Goes By'" to play a specific song or album.**

3. **When the music is playing, use commands such as "Pause music," "Next track," or "Stop music" to control playback.**

One of the beauties of Siri is that you don't have to follow a specific command format as you do with some other voice-command apps. You could say, "Play the next track" or "Next track" or "Jump to the next track on this album," and Siri gets your meaning.

Letting Siri Put You in the Know

You're late for an appointment and need help. You can call on Siri. From getting you directions to your next appointment to calling up your customer's website to check her product catalog or check facts on the price of the client's stock today, Siri can find it all.

Getting directions

You can use the Maps app and Siri to find your current location, find nearby businesses such as restaurants or a bank, or get a map of a location. Be sure to turn on Location Services to allow Siri to know your current location. (Go to Settings and tap Privacy⇨Location Services to make sure that the Location Services setting and Siri are turned on, both are in the same dialog.)

Here are some of the commands you can try to get directions or a list of nearby businesses:

✔ **"Where am I?"**

Displays a map of your current location. If you have a Wi-Fi–only iPad, this location may be approximate.

✔ **"Where is Apache Junction, Arizona?"**

Displays a map of that city.

✔ **"Find restaurants."**

Displays a list of restaurants near your current location, as shown in Figure 6-9; tap one to display a map of its location.

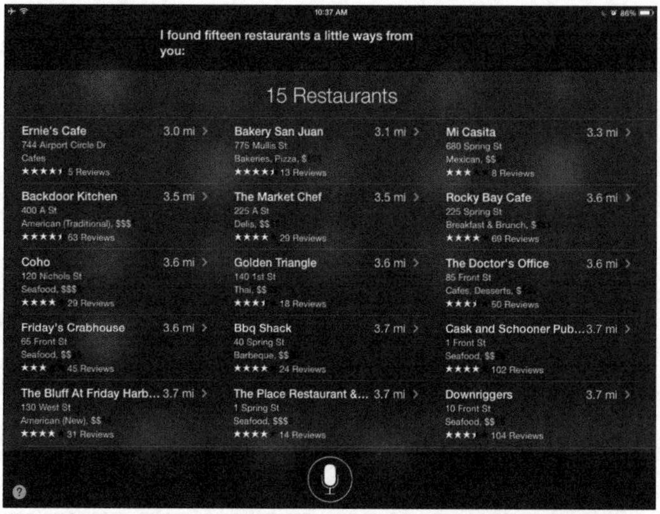

Figure 6-9: If you're hungry, Siri could be your new best friend.

✔ **"Find Bank of America."**

Displays a map with the location of that business (or in some cases, several nearby locations, such as a bank branch and all ATMs) indicated.

When a location is displayed in a map, tap the Information button on the location's label to view its address, phone number, and website address, if available.

Note that all your requests to Siri are routed through Apple servers. If you are, say, a spy and you don't want your movements and activities stored on somebody else's server, avoid using Siri for directions or reminders! But if you're a law-abiding citizen, don't worry about this.

Asking for the facts

WolframAlpha is a self-professed online computational knowledge engine. That means it's more than a search engine because it provides specific information about a search term rather than multiple search results. If you want facts without having to send time browsing websites to find those facts, you'll find that Wolfram Alpha is a very good resource.

Siri uses WolframAlpha and sources such as Wikipedia and Bing to look up facts in response to questions such as "What is the capital of Kansas?"; "What is the square root of 2003?"; or "How large is Mars?" Just press and hold the Home button and ask your question; Siri consults its resources and returns a set of relevant facts.

You can also get information about many facts, such as the current weather, stock prices, or the time. Just say a phrase like one of these to get what you need:

✓ **"What is the weather?"**

This shows the weather report for your current location. If you want weather in another location, just specify the location in your question.

✓ **"What is the price of Apple stock?"**

Siri tells you the current price of the stock or the price of the stock when the stock market last closed. (Let's hope you own some.)

✓ **"What time is it?"**

Siri tells you the time in your time zone and displays a clock (see Figure 6-10).

Figure 6-10: Stay on schedule with Siri's help.

Note that Siri can understand many languages and therefore works in many countries. If you love to travel, Siri could help make your next trip much easier.

Searching the web

Siri can use various resources to respond to specific requests such as "Who is the Queen of England?" For more general requests, however, Siri searches the web.

For example, if you speak a phrase, such as "Find a website about birds" or "Find information about the World Series," Siri can respond in a couple of ways. The app can simply display a list of search results using the default search engine specified in your settings for Safari, or suggest, "If you like, I can search the web for such-and-such." In the first instance, just tap a result to go to that website. In the second instance, you can confirm that you want to search the web or cancel.

Sending Email, Tweets, or Messages

You can create an email, a tweet, or an instant message using Siri and existing contacts. For example, if you say, "Email Jack Wilkes," a form opens already addressed to that contact. Siri asks you the subject and what to say in the message; speak your message and then say "Send" to speed your message on its way.

Siri also works with the Messages app. Tap Siri and say, "Message Sarah." Siri creates a message and asks what you want to say. Say, "Tell Sarah I'll call soon," and Siri creates a message for you to approve and send.

It's hard to stump Siri. For example, at this point in time, Siri can't tweet unless you download and set up the Twitter app. But if you try to speak a tweet, Siri gives you a link to tap to install the app! After you install these apps, you can say things to Siri such as "Post Tweet" or "Post to Facebook," and Siri asks what you want to say, lets you review it, and posts it. Siri can also connect you with Flickr and Vimeo when you have those apps installed.

Getting Helpful Tips

I know you're going to have a wonderful time learning the ins and outs of Siri, but before I close this chapter, here are some tips to get you going:

   ✔ **If Siri doesn't understand you:** When you speak a command and Siri displays what it thought you said but misses the mark, you have a few options. To correct a request you've made, you can tap Tap to Edit under the command Siri heard and edit the question by typing, or you can tap the Microphone key on the onscreen keyboard and dictate the correct information. If a word is underlined in blue, it's a possible error. Tap the word and then tap an alternative that Siri suggests. You can also simply speak to Siri and say something like, "I meant Sri Lanka" or "No, send it to Sally." If even corrections aren't working, you may need to restart your iPad to reset the software.

- **Headsets and earphones:** If you're using iPhone EarPods or a Bluetooth headset to activate Siri, instead of pressing the Home button, press and hold the center button (the little button on the headset that starts and stops a call).

- **Using Find My Friends:** You can download a free app from the App Store called Find My Friends that allows you to ask Siri to locate your friends geographically, if they are carrying a device with GPS turned on and location tracking allowed.

- **Getting help with Siri:** To get help with Siri features, just press and hold the Home button and ask Siri, "What can you do?"

- **Joking around:** If you need a good laugh, ask Siri to tell you a joke. It has quite the sense of humor . . .

Index

M

M8 Motion Coprocessor, 8, 274
Mac Rumors, 162
MacMall, 14
Mail app
  adding accounts, 117–120
  attachments, adding, 124
  attachments, opening, 121
  business travel uses, 321
  formatting text, 128–129
  IMAP accounts, 120–121
  iOS 8 features, 9
  junk mail, 134
  LDAP accounts, 295–296
  marking messages unread, 130–131
  messages, composing, 126–127, 486–487
  messages, creating contact from, 475
  messages, creating events from, 131–132
  messages, deleting, 133–134
  messages, flagging, 130–131
  messages, forwarding, 124–126
  messages, opening, 121, 123
  messages, printing, 132
  messages, replying to, 124–126
  messages, sending using Siri, 127, 501
  Microsoft Exchange accounts, 294–295
  moving messages to folders, 134–135
  notifications, general discussion, 122
  notifications, upon reply to message, 131
  overview, 63–64, 121
  POP3 accounts, 120–121
  Quote Level feature, 128
  searching in, 35–37, 129–130
  settings for, 150
  sharing contacts using, 487–488
  sharing files using, 420–421
  sharing highlighted text from e-book
    using, 263
  sharing location information from map
    using, 315–316
  sharing notes using, 435–436
  sharing videos using, 204–205
  signatures, 126

  system sounds, 148
  Trash folder, 134
  turning off downloading, 121
  viewing inboxes, 123
  VIP List feature, 135–137
maintenance
  battery life and, 156–157
  cases/covers, 154–155
  cleaning screen, 153–154
maps
  adding location to contact, 314–315
  business travel uses, 320
  current location, 300
  directions on, 311–312
  dropping pins on, 306–307
  favorites, 308–310
  gestures for, 300, 304
  getting directions using Siri, 499–500
  location information, 313, 315–316
  overview, 68
  printing, 303
  recent locations, 310
  searching for location, 304–306
  searching using Siri, 499
  sending via iMessage service, 230–231
  traffic on, 303
  turn-by-turn navigation, 316–317
  viewing contact location on, 488–489
  views for, 301–303
  Yelp reviews on, 308
  zooming in, 303–304
margins, in Pages documents, 356, 364
Match service, iTunes, 81, 82, 185
memory
  purchasing iPad, 11–12
  updating iOS and, 37
merging contacts, 476
Messages app
  clearing conversation, 231–232
  group messaging, 232
  iOS 8 features, 9
  overview, 64
  sending audio messages, 229
  sending map of current location, 230–231

S